KILVERT'S DIARY
THE REV. FRANCIS KILVERT

William Plomer, C.B.E., D.Litt, F.R.S.L., the novelist, poet and biographer, was President of the Kilvert Society, which was formed in 1948 to foster an interest in the Rev. Francis Kilvert, his work, his diary, and the countryside he loved. William Plomer himself won the Queen's Gold Medal for Poetry in 1963 and died in 1973.

KILVERT'S DIARY

1870-1879

Selections from
the Diary of
**THE REV.
FRANCIS KILVERT**

*

Chosen, edited
and introduced by
William Plomer

Penguin Books

Penguin Books Ltd, Harmondsworth, Middlesex, England
Viking Penguin Inc., 40 West 23rd Street, New York, New York 10010, U.S.A.
Penguin Books Australia Ltd, Ringwood, Victoria, Australia
Penguin Books Canada Limited, 2801 John Street, Markham, Ontario, Canada L3R 1B4
Penguin Books (N.Z.) Ltd, 182–190 Wairau Road, Auckland 10, New Zealand

—

Selections from the Diary of the Rev. Francis Kilvert
FIRST PUBLISHED IN THREE VOLUMES
Volume I: 1870–1871, in 1938
Volume II: 1871–1874, in 1939
Volume III: 1874–1879, in 1940

THIS ONE-VOLUME
SELECTION FIRST PUBLISHED BY
JONATHAN CAPE 1944

—

Published in Penguin Books 1977
Reprinted 1977, 1978, 1980, 1982
Reissued in the Penguin Country Library 1984
Reprinted 1986

—

Made and printed in Great Britain by
Richard Clay (The Chaucer Press) Ltd,
Bungay, Suffolk
Set in Linotype Juliana

INTRODUCTION

Since its first appearance in three volumes (1938–40) Kilvert's
Diary has become established as a minor classic. Its recognized
place among the very best of English diaries has been gained by
special qualities. It is the work of a man with a watchful eye and
a clear style: Kilvert has the uncommon gift of making one see
vividly what he describes. His detailed picture of life in the
English countryside in mid-Victorian times is unmatched, and
every sentence he writes helps to build up a self-portrait so
personal and intimate that one gets to know him like a friend.

Kilvert reveals himself as an essentially modest, innocent, truth-
ful and unworldly young man, sociable, and with a strong love of
life and of landscape, with a sense of drama and a good vein of
humour. His life was strongly affected by two things – his sus-
ceptibility to the beauty of young women and girls, and his lack
of money and of what used to be called prospects. As a faithful
country clergyman, he moved with equal ease among people of
both the landowning and labouring classes, and by both was
welcomed equally. His good nature and good manners, his vitality,
his love of children, and his practical sympathy with the unfortunate, won him much affection. If he did not question the values
of his own class, he was never indifferent to sufferings which they
permitted, and did what he could, with his evidently magnetic
presence and voice, to lessen those sufferings. He knew that not
far from the convivial and copious dinners and picnics, the lively
croquet and archery parties, could be found loneliness, squalor,
and hunger, and sometimes murders and suicides.

Robert Francis Kilvert (1840–72) was one of the six children of
the Reverend Robert Kilvert, rector of Hardenhuish and later of
the neighbouring parish of Langley Burrell, in Wiltshire, and of
his wife, Thermuthis Coleman. He was educated privately, went
up to Oxford, was ordained, and for a time acted as curate to his
father.

Then for seven years (1865–72) he served as curate to the Reverend Richard Lister Venables, vicar of Clyro in Radnorshire. This was in most ways the happiest time of his life. The charming and lifelike account he has left of the places and people he knew has caused the still beautiful region centred upon Clyro to be known as the Kilvert Country and to become a place of literary pilgrimage.

There is another Kilvert Country – his native district round Chippenham in Wiltshire. He returned there in 1872 for another spell of four years as curate to his father. In 1876 he was presented to the remote living of St Harmon, in north Radnorshire, and in the following year to that of Bredwardine, on the Wye in Herefordshire, not far from his beloved Clyro.

In August 1879 he married Elizabeth Anne (1846–1911), daughter of John Rowland, of Holly Bank, Wootton, near Woodstock. Only a month after the wedding he died suddenly of peritonitis and was buried at Bredwardine. There was no child of the marriage, and Mrs Kilvert did not marry again.

She inherited the Diary and is said to have destroyed two large sections of it for personal reasons: one section is thought to have recorded Kilvert's courtship of her. What was left was contained in twenty-two notebooks. Only three of these now survive, the rest having been destroyed by an elderly niece of Kilvert's who had inherited them from her brother.

A few notes on some of the persons mentioned in the Diary may be helpful. Francis ('Frank') Kilvert had one brother, Edward Newton, referred to as 'Teddy' or 'Perch'. His four sisters were Thermuthis ('Thersie'), who married the Reverend W. R. Smith of Monnington-on-Wye; Emily ('Emmie'), who married Samuel Wyndowe and went to India; Frances ('Fanny') who became a Clewer Sister; and Sarah Dorothea Anne ('Dora'), who married James Pitcairn.

Henry Dew (1819–1901) was rector of Whitney-on-Wye from 1843 until his death. He married Mary Monkhouse (1821–1900), who was closely related to Wordsworth's wife. His sister, Louisa, married William Latham Bevan (1821–1908), archdeacon of Brecon and vicar of Hay: they lived at Hay Castle, where Kilvert was a frequent visitor. Daisy (or Fanny) Thomas of Llanthomas died unmarried.   W.P.

6

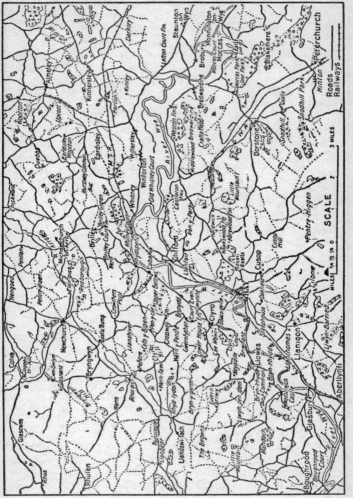

CLYRO AND DISTRICT

SCALE

MILES 1½ 1 ½ 0   1   2   3 MILES

Roads
Railways

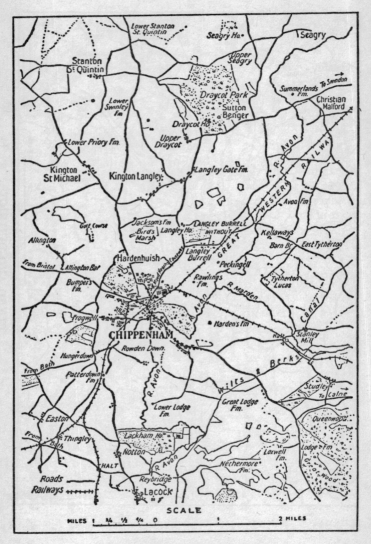

CHIPPENHAM AND DISTRICT

1870

Tuesday, 8 February

From Wye Cliff to Pont Faen. Miss Child in great force. She showed me her clever drawings of horses and told me the adventures of the brown wood owl 'Ruth' which she took home from here last year. She wanted to call the owl 'Eve' but Mrs Bridge said it should be called 'Ruth'. She and her sister stranded in London at night went to London Bridge hotel (having missed the last train) with little money and no luggage except the owl in a basket. The owl hooted all night in spite of their putting it up the chimney, before the looking glass, under the bedclothes, and in a circle of lighted candles which they hoped it would mistake for the sun. The owl went on hooting, upset the basket, got out and flew about the room. The chambermaid almost frightened to death dared not come inside the door. Miss Child asked the waiter to get some mice for 'Ruth' but none could be got.

Wednesday, 9 February

A very cold night and a slight shower of snow fell early this morning. Then it froze all day. The mountains all white. Went up the Cwm to White Ash. Old Sarah Probert groaning and rolling about in bed. Read to her Mark vi and made sure she knew the Lord's Prayer by heart, making her repeat it. Hannah Jones smoking a short black pipe by the fire, and her daughter, a young mother with dark eyes and her hair hanging loose, nursing her baby and displaying her charms liberally.

Went with the Venables to dine at Whitney Court, driving in the mail phaeton and sitting behind with Charlie. Bitterly cold with a keen E. wind but we were well wrapped up and the hood kept the wind off us going. Miss Jane from the Rectory at dinner. Lent Miss Dew Robertson's Lectures on *Corinthians*. The Squire and his mother made the rest of the party. A grand night with stars glittering frosty keen and we came home at a rattling pace.

9

Friday, 11 February

Last night broke the key of my musical box whilst winding the box up. Went down at midnight and tried to turn the broken key barrel with the tongs – unsuccessfully, and the teeth of the comb stuck in the midst of a tune hitched on the spikes all night. Very bad for the box, so I got up early and directly after breakfast ran over to Hay across the fields in a keen white bright frost. Bevan the watchmaker wound up the box, set it right and mended the key. Bought 4 valentines at Herthen's after searching through a tumbled heap for a long time and ordered some cheese at Hadley's. Coming back the hills were lovely. The morning spread upon the mountains, beautiful Clyro rising from the valley and stretching away northward dotted with white houses and shining with gleams of green on hills and dingle sides, a tender blue haze over the village and woods in the valley and Clyro Court a dim grey.

Baskerville in his brougham with the old bay cob came to the door at 6.3. Very cold drive. Mrs Bevan, Mary, and the Crichtons arrived before us all in Mrs Allen's yellow chariot. The Welfield (Edward) Thomases staying in the house. Mr and Capt. Thomas from Llanthomas. Mrs and Miss Thomas of Llwyn Madoc staying in the house. They came in last and went into dinner immediately. Miss Thomas looking very pretty and nice in blue silk high dress, sat opposite me at dinner and afterwards when we came into the drawing-room she came up and shook hands cordially and kindly, talked to me till Baskerville's carriage was announced. It was a very happy evening.

Septuagesima Sunday, St Valentine's Eve

Preached at Clyro in the morning (Matthew xiv, 30). Very few people in Church, the weather fearful, violent deadly E. wind and the hardest frost we have had yet. Went to Bettws in the afternoon wrapped in two waistcoats, two coats, a muffler and a mackintosh, and was not at all too warm. Heard the Chapel bell pealing strongly for the second time since I have been here and when I got to the Chapel my beard moustaches and whiskers were so stiff with ice that I could hardly open my mouth and my beard was frozen on to my mackintosh. There was a large christening party from Llwyn Gwilym. The baby was baptized in ice which was broken and swimming about in the Font.

Monday, St Valentine's Day
A pretty flower Valentine from Incognito. Walked to Hay with Mr V. We went to Williams the drapers' and looked at blankets, sheets and coverlets, as we propose to spend some of the surplus Communion Alms in bedding for the poor people who want it much this vigorous weather. Called at the castle.

Tuesday, 15 February
Visited Edward Evans in the village. He was ill with cold from this vicious poisonous E. wind, and sitting before the fire. Finding they have no blankets but only sheets and a coverlet I gave him an order on Williams for a pair of blankets and I hope his wife will fetch them this afternoon. Coming back called on the Lewises at the Bronith and the old Peninsular veteran. The red round moon hanging over Clifford Hill. Owls hooting in the dusk across the dingles and from the height of Cefn Cethin. Volunteer band in Hay playing across the valley, a review in preparation for a Volunteer Concert to-night.

Wednesday, 16 February
At Burnt House James Phillips at home, a long legged Radnorshire man who said he had never been drunk. Told me how Mr Ffoulkes had dived to the bottom of Craig-pwll-du and very nearly getting entangled in roots and weeds at the bottom, had declared he would not take England to do it again. Fine mild afternoon and a strange blue light upon woods and dingles.

Thursday, 17 February
Edward Evans better and very thankful for wine and a pair of blankets. Visited Sackville Thomas, Jinny very funny and in good spirits. Polly saying hymns very fast. Sackville sitting hat on by a scorching fire and the venomous east wind blowing full in at the open door. Jinny says 'unhackle' for undress and 'to squeeze your ears against your head and say nothing' means to be discreetly silent and cautiously reticent. Market people passing by open door with shawls and handkerchiefs tied over hats and bonnets. Next to Mrs Bowen's Bird's Nest. Then to Lower Cwmbythog. Grand

11

handsome Mrs Evans nursing her baby in the dark ruinous old hovel, a brave patient woman and practically religious. Gave Mrs Evans an order for 2 pairs of sheets. Slithering down the steep rocky lane full of a torrent of ice. How this poisonous E. wind strains and weakens the eyes.

Sexagesima Sunday, 20 February

Drunk too much port after dinner at Cae Mawr last night and a splitting headache all today in revenge. Eyes better but not much. Everything in a daze and dazzle and I could hardly see to read. Got through the services somehow, but in the afternoon came to a deadlock in the middle of the 1st Lesson. A blessed change in the weather. Wind westerly and no longer deadly poison.

Monday, 21 February

My carpet bag went up to Llysdinam in the Whitechapel, Brewer driving. Mr V. and he drove down and picked it up. Mr V. went to a magistrates' meeting in Hay where the Glasbury policeman was tried for stealing 2 German silver spoons worth 9d a piece. I joined him at Hay (having walked over) at 1.15 and we went up to Llysdinam together by that train.

Tuesday, 22 February

Reading *Quarterly Review*. Mrs V. went out for a drive, on the Rhayader road, the carriage and cushions thoroughly aired and warmed with hot water bottles and warming pans.

After luncheon went for a walk with Mr V. to the top of Drum du. When we got to the cairn Plynlimmon was quite visible, but only the ghost of Cader Idris to be seen. We went away disappointed but had not gone far before the clouds suddenly lifted and a sun burst lit up grandly the great snowslopes of round-backed Plynlimmon and the vast snowy precipices of the giant Cader Idris near 50 miles away. We hurried back to the cairn and had a glorious view to N. and W. of the Fans of Brecon and Carmarthen. Mr V. fell heavily on his back head over heels among the stones of the cairn, his foot having slipped, but he saved his opera glasses.

Reading the Mordaunt Warwickshire Scandal Case. Horrible disclosures of the depravity of the best London society.

[This remarkably squalid case came in for much public notice. Sir Charles Mordaunt of Walton Hall in Warwickshire petitioned for a divorce from his wife on the grounds of her adultery with several persons, two of whom were named as co-respondents. The question of Lady Mordaunt's sanity was much discussed, and among other points that emerged in the evidence were that on a visit to the Crystal Palace she had sat down on a gravel-walk, and that another time she had stuck a branch of a fir-tree in her boots. She had more than once received the Prince of Wales as a caller in her husband's absence, and the petitioner said in evidence that he had warned her against continuing that acquaintance, and that he had had his reasons for doing so. The Prince appeared as a witness, and his letters to Lady Mordaunt were made public. They were trivial and discreet, and their nearest approach to intimacy was an acknowledgement of a present of some 'very pretty muffetees'. He seems to have sent her a valentine, and she had one of his handkerchiefs. *The Times* thought he had been 'too careless of his reputation' and said he had 'learnt by a painful experience how watchfully he must walk whose life is the property and the study of the world'. On the 26 February the same paper said 'we have had more than a week's surfeit of details not easily characterized in decent language', and 'we might have been spared the publicity of details leading to no result save that of injury to public morality'.]

Writing a sermon for Ash Wednesday. Dined with Mrs V. who drove down with Brewer from Llysdinam in the yellow Perthcart with the grey mare this afternoon. A lovely evening and the Black Mountain lighted up grandly, all the furrows and water courses clear and brilliant. People coming home from market, birds singing, buds bursting, and the spring air full of beauty, life and hope. Farm labourers threshing with the machines at Llowes Court. Ash and beech and elms being felled in Clyro Court lands, and going away in timber carriages. Alders being cut down on the left bank of Wye. A market woman's chestnut horse restive in the road and market folk on foot winding their way home through fields by Wyeside.

A lovely warm morning so I set off to walk over the hills to Colva, taking my luncheon in my pocket, half a dozen biscuits, two apples and a small flask of wine. Took also a pocket book and opera glasses. Went on up the Green Lane. Very hot walking. At the Green Lane Cottage found Mrs Jones and a daughter at home sewing. Price Price sitting half hidden in the chimney corner but alas there was no Abiasula as the last time I was there. Price Price something like his sister Abiasula. A sturdy boy, with a round rosy good-humoured face and big black eyes, volunteered to guide me to Colva Church. So he came out of his chimney corner in the ingle nook and we started at once, accompanied by a grey and black sheepdog puppy. We were out on the open mountain at once. There was the brown withered heather, the elastic turf, the long green ride stretching over the hill like a green ribbon between the dark heather. There was the free fresh fragrant air of the hills, but, oh, for the gipsy lassie with her wild dark eyes under her black hood. As we went down the Fuallt a grouse cock uttered his squirling crow and flew over the crest of the hill. I never heard a grouse crow before. 'What's that bird crying?' I said to the boy. 'A grouse', he said, adding, 'There he goes over the bank. They be real thick hereabout.'

Tried to get across the swift Arrow (swollen by the junction of the Glasnant just above) by climbing along a rail but we failed 2nd had to go up a meadow till we got above the meeting of the waters, when we crossed the Glasnant on a hurdle laid flat over the stream and then we jumped the Arrow. Up the steep breast of the Reallt to Dol Reallt and along the road to the Wern and Bryntwyn from whence a field path leads to Colva Church. Here Price Price left me after showing me across one field. I asked him to have some bread and cheese and beer at the Sun Inn, Colva, but he would not and could scarcely be prevailed on to take sixpence. Tried the echo in the field against the belfry and west end of the poor humble dear little white-washed church sequestered among its large ancient yews. The echo was very clear, sharp and perfect. Richard Meredith told me of this echo. Mrs Phillips, the landlady of the Sun, was much frightened when I asked for her husband, uneasy and nervous lest I should have come to apprehend him for having been in a row or doing something wrong. But when I said I wanted the words of an old song, she was greatly relieved and said at once, 'Oh I know who you are. You are the gentleman from Clyro.' I laughed and she began to smile. Mrs Phillips took me into the parlour where I sat down, tore a leaf out of my pocket book and wrote with my address a request that Phillips would send me by post 1. the song about our Saviour, 2. the song about Lazarus, 3. the song about King James and the Tinker. Mrs Phillips brought me a pint of excellent light bright beer, some hard sweet home-baked bread, and some hard cheese, carrying the bread and cheese in her arms as she ran in with it, as I was in a hurry to push on.

Reached Clyro just in time to dress for dinner at Cae Mawr. But as I was going out I was sent for to baptize Mrs Jones the jockey's baby opposite and I was only too thankful that it was so near and that I had not to right about face and march back up to the top of Clyro Hill again. The child was said to suffer from convulsions, so I baptized it, but it was probably quite well. The name selected was as far as I could make out Mahalah which Mrs Jones declared to be the name of one of Cain's wives, on the authority of a book she had read called the Life of Abel. She called her elder girl Thirza, which she says was the name of Cain's other wife. Not a happy allusion.

March Eve, Monday
In Chain Alley, Hay, at Prissy Prosser's door, saw Marianne Price grown tall and slight, her dark large eyes as beautiful soft and pure as ever.

Home after midnight in wind and rain, cheered by the solitary light in Hay looking towards the Moors. Wind rustling through trees at Peter's pool, branches creaking loud.

Shrove Tuesday, St David's Day, Leek Day, March Day
Reading Edmund Jones' curious book which I brought from Hard-wick Vicarage last night, an account of Aberystruth Parish, Mon-mouthshire. A ludicrous naive simplicity about his reflections and conclusions. He thinks Providence took particular pains in making his parish which he thinks one of the most wonderful in the world. Writing a sermon for Ash Wednesday.

Ash Wednesday, 2 March

Received by post through Kington from the clerk and publican of Colva two old songs, imperfect but very curious and of some merit. One about our Saviour has the true ballad swing, the other about Dives and Lazarus. The clerk had forgotten the song about King James and the Tinker but said 'he would try to think of him'.

Thursday, 3 March

Luncheon at 12, walked to Hay in rain and went to the Castle. The 4 girls singing *Pilgrims of the Night* round the organ in the hall, Mary playing. Mary was very kind and lent me the best volume of Mrs Barrett Browning's Poems. I read aloud to them my Colva Ballads which interested them much. Bought 2 copies of *Alone in London* and took one down to Prissy Prosser's for Marianne Price. The child was out, her grandmother sent for her and she came running out of breath and radiant with delight. Her lovely dark eyes lighted up at the thought of a new book and looked shyly up to thank me from under her long silky lashes.

Friday, 4 March

A wild stormy night. The Dulas, Clyro, roaring red, and the Wye surging broad yellow and stormy. Heaven pity the *Pilgrims of the Night* who had no shelter. Pussy had a new brass comb in her clustering light curly hair and her blue bright eyes looked up very archly. The Dingle Flower of fair Llandovery goes back to her home among the sweet Carmarthenshire hills tomorrow. I took her *Alone in London* as a Sunday School prize and wrote her name in it. Her delight was unbounded and she evidently felt much more than she said, for she was very shy and the English did not come readily.

Called at Cae Mawr. The Morrells told me that Mrs and the Miss Baskervilles have returned suddenly from St Leonards on Sea, having been routed horse and foot with great slaughter and loss by bugs or fleas. They intended to stay at St Leonards a month or more longer.

Saturday, 5 March

Very cold last night, and sharp frost and the day brilliant and the air exquisitely clear though the wind was East. The view from the banks lovely, the river winding down from Glasbury like a silver serpent, flowing beneath at the foot of the poplars. Hay in the distance bright in brilliant sunshine. Every watercourse clear upon the mountains in the searching light. As the sun went down a pink and then a deep purple glow bathed the mountains and Cusop Hill and a keen frost set in. The rich pink and deep purple light very unusually splendid.

1 Sunday in Lent, 6 March
After evening church, visited the Pughs and found Mary at home. She gave me a more extraordinary account than any that I have yet heard about the falling of the gable at Clyro Court, the house-keeper's marvellous descent through the floor into the kitchen from her bedroom, during the great storm on the morning of January 8th, 1870.

Tuesday, 8 March
Yesterday there was an inquest at the Blue Boar, Hay, on the body of the barmaid of the Blue Boar who a day or two ago went out at night on an hour's leave, but went up the Wye to Glasbury and threw herself into the river. She was taken out at Llan Hennw. She was enceinte. Met the Morrell children returning from a walk with the first white violets and primroses.

Thursday, 10 March
A heavenly day, lovely and warm, real spring. People busy in their gardens planting and sowing. Everyone rejoicing in the unclouded splendid weather, and congratulating each other on it in their greetings on the road. The roads lively with market women riding to the Hay. A woman on a cream coloured horse with black mane and tail riding past the school and alternately in sunshine and the shadow of the Castle clump over the hill.

John Watkins in the Cwm no better, staggering round and round his house whirling his head round about like a mad man or a Polar bear, unable to sit down, he says, so kneeling on the floor sometimes to rest himself. He gets no rest in bed or at night, dreads the coming on of darkness and is haunted by evil thoughts and dreams. He seems to be suffering from despondency and remorse, and is plainly in a most miserable pitiable state of mind and body.

Wednesday, 16 March

I ate so much hare that I could hardly walk and saw stars, but at 4 went up the hill by the Bron, Penllan and Little Wern y Pentre. Round the corner of the Vicar's Hill to Little Twyn y Grain, passing by the Great Twyns which I am happy to see is falling into ruin, the window frames falling in. How well I remember and how short a time ago it seems though nearly five years. I never pass the house without thinking of that afternoon when after neglecting Margaret Thomas' dying son for a long time I went to call and was inexpressibly shocked to find that he had died only ten minutes before . . .

Faint sunshine on Bryngwyn Hill and a cold cheery gleam of water from the great peat bog below on the edge of which stands the grey cluster of buildings and the tall dark yew of Llanshifr. I went down there and waded across the yard to the house through a sea of mud and water. The kitchen was very dark, the bank rising steep in front of the window. Mrs Morgan gave me some tea and cake. On the settle sat a man perfectly still, silent and in such a dark corner that I could not see his face. Morgan showed me the remains of the moat, where the Scotch pedlar was hidden after being murdered for the sake of his pack while lodging in the house and where his skeleton was found when the moat was cleared out. The moat that is left is a broad deep formidable ditch and rather a long pond at one end of the house and full of water. Llanshifr a fearfully wet swampy place, almost under water and I should think very unhealthy. One of the twin yews was lately blown down and cut up into gate posts which will last twice as long as oak. The wood was so hard that Morgan said it turned many of the axes as if they were made of lead. I wonder in which of these yews Gore hid the penknife before his death which made him restless as hidden iron is said to do, and caused his spirit to come back rummaging about the house and premises and frightening people out of their wits. It was getting dusk as I left Llanshifr and after I had plunged about for some time in the swampy Wern up to my ancles in water I lost my bearings and missed the way, so that I might have been belated but that I heard the welcome clank of plough chains as the team came down home and Joe the Llanshifr ploughman directed me up to the Holly House. Struck over the top of the

18

Vicar's Hill and as I passed Cross Ffordd the frogs were croaking, snoring and bubbling in the pool under the full moon.

Tuesday, 22 March
Called at John Watkins in the Cwm. He was just in the same abject wretched pitiable state, shaking from head to foot fancying himself unable to sit down or keep still, remorse gnawing at his mind. Neighbours say he is 'roguish' and shams, probably it is the cunning of insanity. Went on to White Ash and directly old Sarah Probert heard me come in she began to groan and roll about in the bed. I told Sarah to cheer up but she rolled and groaned all the more and said I was a 'rum' un' and a 'Job's comfort'.

The Clyro women stride about the village like storks. The industrious blacksmith chinks away at his forge night and morning late and early, and the maidens and mothers go up and down the water steps with their pitchers continually. Heavy loads of timber, large long trees on the timber carriages grinding through Clyro village every evening from Cross Ffordd and Cabalva.

Wednesday, 23 March
Looked in upon the old soldier and stayed there reading and chatting to him an hour and a half. Talking of wolves he said he remembered when the English army was in Spain at Correa, every night soon after sunset he used to see the wolves come down to drink at the river. Then they would walk up the hill again into the coverts and vineyards, sometimes there were 4 or 5 of them at once. They were like mastiffs and as big. The soldiers used to scare them by snapping the locks of their flint muskets and making a flash in the pan.

Saturday, 26 March
A delicious day upon Clyro Hill. It was sunny and warm under the sheltering bank and woods of Wern Vawr and pleasant walking along the low road leading to the old farm house with its large projecting and high-gabled porch. There was a stir about the house and yard. They had killed a fat stall-fed heifer yesterday and a party of people much interested in the matter, among them old Jones and his wife, were busy cutting up the carcase in the barn. A man went to and fro from the barn to the house with huge joints

of beef having first weighed them on the great steelyard which hangs at the barn door. In the house Mrs Jones of New Building an old daughter of the house was engaged in the great kitchen taking up the joints from the table where the man laid them and carrying them into an inner room or larder to put them in salt. By the fire sat a young woman who hid her face and did not look up. She had a baby lying across her lap.

I decided to explore the lane running parallel with the brook towards Painscastle and discover the old Rhos Goch Mill. There was a good deal of water and suddenly I came upon the mill pond and the picturesque old mill with an overshot wheel. I crossed one of the streams on a larch felled across the water for a bridge and came back round the front of the cosy old picturesque ivy-grown mill house with its tall chimney completely covered with ivy. A handsome young man with a fine open face, fresh complexion and dressed as a miller was having a romp with a little girl before the door. He said his name was Powell, his father was dead and he carried on the business and with the most perfect politeness and well bred courtesy asked me to come in and sit down. So this is the place that I have heard old Hannah Whitney talk of so often, the place where the old miller sleeping in the mill trough used to see the fairies dancing of nights upon the mill floor.

At Rhos Goch Lane House no one was at home so I stuck an ivy leaf into the latch hole.

Round the corner of the Vicar's Hill to Cefn y Blaen where I found Davies, the new tenant of the Pentre. While talking to Davies outside I heard old William Pritchard within coughing violently. I went in and sat some time talking to him and his niece Mrs Evans. He remembers the old house of Cefn y Blaen and the large famous room which he says was 20 *yards* long and was used for holding a Court of Justice in for the country round in the time of Charles II. I asked him if he had ever heard any talk of Charles II ever having been about in this country. 'Oh yes,' he said, 'I have a jug that the King once drunk out of at Blaen cerdi. He had breakfast that day in Brecon, dined at Gwernyfed and slept at Harpton, passing through Newchurch. His army was with him and riding two and two in the narrow lanes the line reached from Pen Vaen in Newchurch, through the village up to Blaen cerdi.

At Blaen cerdi all the farm people, boys and girls ran out to see the King pass. The King was afoot. He stopped opposite the house and asked my ancestress Mary Bayliss to give him something to drink. She went to the house and fetched him milk and water in this jug which has been handed down with the tradition in my family. I have always heard that this Mary Bayliss was an extraordinarily fine beautiful woman. I never learnt that the King gave her anything in return for the draught. Before this jug came into my possession it was broken by some water being left to freeze in it, but it can easily be cemented, being in two large pieces, the bottom having been broken off. David Jones the auctioneer in Hay offered me a great deal of money for the jug.

'Charles II was in hiding for some time in this country and went about in disguise as a lady's servant. Once when he was in the pantry with the butler of the house where they were staying he asked the butler if he would give him a glass of wine. The butler said in a meaning way, "You are able to command what wine you like".'

Monday, 28 March
Williams says the petty chief great landlords were called 'Normandy Kings'. One of them lived at Cefn y Blaen, one at Llanshifr, another at Great Gwernfydden. The one who lived at Painscastle was a giant. This giant carried off to Painscastle 'screaming and noising' Miss Phillips of the Screen Farm near Erwood whom he found disporting herself with her lover Arthur on or at Bychllyn Pool. Arthur sent for help to Old Radnor Castle and Cefn y Blaen. At Cefn y Blaen there were then 40 men each 7 feet high. The giant on the other hand sent for succour to Court Evan Gwynne where there was an 'army', also to Hay Castle and Lord Clifford of Clifford Castle. While these hostile forces were converging upon Painscastle, a woman in the castle favoured the girl's escape and dressed her in man's clothes to this end. Arthur, watching for her outside and not knowing of the disguise, seeing what he thought was a man and one of his enemies coming out of the castle shot his lover dead with an arrow. Arthur then furious stormed the castle with a battle axe: took it and killed the giant. Next day the opposing parties arrived at the Rhos Goch, there was a fearful battle

near Rhyd Llyden and the Painscastle party was defeated with great slaughter by the forces from Old Radnor and Cefn y Blaen.

Tuesday, 29 March

Turned aside into the meadow to look at the great stone of Cross Ffordd. It is a long time since I stood beside it, and I had forgotten that the stone was so large. I suppose no one will ever know now what the grey silent mysterious witness means, or why it was set there. Perhaps it could tell some strange wild tales and many generations have flowed and ebbed round it. There is something very solemn about these great solitary stones which stand about the country, monuments of some one or something, but the memory has perished and the history is forgotten.

Home at 6, dressed for dinner. At 6.30 Charles with the mail phaeton and the two mares, grey and bay, dashed up to the door in grand style. I was ready and away we went to the Vicarage to pick up the Vicar who took the reins. At Peter's Pool we overtook and passed at a dashing pace the Clyro Court brougham with one horse wherein were the Squire and Mr Frank Guise the recorder of Hereford bound like ourselves for dinner at Oakfield. It was refreshing to see the Vicar's stylish equipage driven by himself with two servants behind, dashing past the small humble turn-out of the Squire, rather reversing the usual order of things.

Thursday, April Eve

Read to old Price the keeper and then walked to Hay across the fields.

In Hadley's shop I met Dewing who told me of a most extraordinary misfortune that befell Pope the curate of Cusop yesterday at the Whitney Confirmation. He had one candidate Miss Stokes a farmer's daughter and they went together by train. Pope went in a cutaway coat very short, with his dog, and took no gown. The train was very late. He came very late into church and sat down on a bench with the girl cheek by jowl. When it came to his turn to present his candidate he was told by the Rector (Henry Dew) or someone in authority to explain why he came so late. The Bishop of Hereford (Atlay) has a new fashion of confirming only two persons at a time, kneeling at the rails. The Bishop had marked two young people come in very late and when they came

22

up to the rails he thought from Pope's youthful appearance and from his having no gown that he was a young farmer candidate and brother of the girl. He spoke to them severely and told them to come on and kneel down for they were extremely late. Pope tried to explain that he was a clergyman and that the girl was his candidate but the Bishop was overbearing and imperious and either did not hear or did not attend, seeming to think he was dealing with a refractory ill-conditioned youth. 'I know, I know,' he said. 'Come at once, kneel down, kneel down.' Poor Pope resisted a long time and had a long battle with the Bishop, but at last unhappily he was overborne in the struggle, lost his head, gave way, knelt down and was *confirmed* there and then, and no one seems to have interfered to save him, though Mr Palmer of Eardisley and others were sitting close by and the whole Church was in a titter. It is a most unfortunate thing and will never be forgotten and it will be unhappily a joke against Pope all his life. The Bishop was told of his mistake afterwards and apologized to Pope, though rather shortly and cavalierly. He said, what was quite true, that Pope ought to have come in his gown. But there was a little fault on all sides for if the Bishop had been a little less hasty, rough and overbearing in his manner things might have been explained, and the bystanding clergy were certainly very much to blame for not stepping forward and preventing such a farce. I fear poor Pope will be very much vexed, hurt and dispirited about it.

Tuesday, 5 April
The day broke cloudless after a sharp frost. Up early and went to Cae Mawr to breakfast, at 8 o'clock. Drove to Hay in Morrell's carriage. We drove on to Llanigon, the air fresh, cold driving. Alighted at Llanigon village and sent the carriage back. Walked up by the Church and took the field path to the Cilonw Farm.

Down the pretty steep winding lane we went skirting the Honddu. Across the valley at the mouth of a great dreadful dingle stood the ruins of the house which was swept away while the people were dancing, by an avalanche of snow or a torrent of snow water let loose by a sudden thaw. A young man who was coming up from Llanthony to join the party was saved by his greyhound unaccountably hanging behind, whining and running back so as to entice his master home again. I had not seen Capel y Ffin for 4 years but I remembered the place perfectly, the old chapel short stout and boxy with its little bell turret (the whole building reminded one of an owl), the quiet peaceful chapel yard shaded by the seven great solemn yews, the chapel house, a farm house over the way, and the Great Honddu brook crossing the road and crossed in turn by the stone foot bridge. Before the chapel house door by the brookside a buxom comely wholesome girl with fair hair, rosy face, blue eyes, and fair clear skin stood washing at a tub in the sunshine, up to the elbows of her round white lusty arms in soapsuds. We asked her how far it was to the place where the monks were building their monastery. 'Oh,' she said, smiling kindly and stopping her washing for a moment to direct us. 'Oh, none just. Please to go over the brook and up the lane.' Two tramps were lounging against the bridge lighting their pipes and said to each other when we had passed, 'They are only going to see the monks'.

A few minutes walk up a lane now dry but which is probably a watercourse in winter, and looking through the hedge we exclaimed, 'There they are'. Two black figures were working in a sloping patch of ground laid out as a garden, one digging and the other wheeling earth to him in a barrow. They were dressed in long black habits girt round the waist with scourge cords knotted at the ends and dangling almost to the ground. The black hoods or cowls were drawn over their heads leaving their faces bare, and their naked feet were thrust into sandals with which they went slip slop along as with slippers down at heel. Father Philip was digging. Brother Serene or Cyrene was wheeling earth to him from a heap thrown out of the excavation dug for the foundations of the monastery. He seemed very much oppressed by his heavy black dress, for the sun was hot and he stopped when he had wheeled his empty barrow back to the heap and stood to rest and wipe his streaming brow. They both seemed studiously unconscious of our presence, but I saw Brother Serene glancing furtively at us from under his cowl when he thought he was under cover of the heap of earth. We at first thought of speaking to them but decided not to afterwards, fearing they might think our trespassing an intrusion on their privacy, uncourteous and rude. We spoke to the

24

masons of whom there were two working at the foundations. They spoke with great respect and some awe of the monks and did not seem the least inclined to laugh at them. They answered all our questions too very civilly. We saw the foundation stone which Father Ignatius[1] came down to lay three weeks ago. Then he returned to London and at present there are only these two monks in residence. They have one servant a young man who was also wheeling earth. They lodge at a farm house close by and live a good deal on milk. They allow no woman to come near them and do their own washing. Probably however there is little of that to do. They may wear linen but they don't show any and perhaps they did not take off their habits when at work because they had nothing under. They looked very much like old women at work in the garden. It does seem very odd at this age of the world in the latter part of the 19th century to see monks gravely wearing such dresses and at work in them in broad day. One could not help thinking how much more sensible and really religious was the dress and occupation of the masons and of the hearty healthy girl washing at the Chapel House, living naturally in the world and taking their share of its work, cares and pleasures, than the morbid unnatural life of these monks going back into the errors of the dark ages and shutting themselves up from the world to pray for the world. 'Laborare est Orare.' The masons had raised the foundation walls to the level of the ground and believed the house would be built by the end of May, which I doubt. The monks as usual had chosen a pretty and pleasant place on a fine slope at the foot of the mountain where there was good soil and plenty of good water, a trout stream and sand for mortar. The house which seemed from the ground plan, as far as we could make it out, to be a long shallow building will look S.E. down the valley towards Llanthony Abbey. The monks have bought 32 acres. It is said they have collected £50,000 which may probably be divided by 10. Very few people came to the ceremony of laying the foundation stone.

We crossed a field and the fold of a farm house, scrambled down

1. For an account of the peculiar career and 'extravagance of conduct' of 'Father Ignatius' (the Rev. J. L. Lyne, 1837–1908) and of his effort to revive monasticism in England the reader is referred to the *Dictionary of National Biography*.

a narrow stony lane and struck the main road again. About a mile above Llanthony we descried the Abbey ruins, the dim grey pile of building in the vale below standing by the little river side among its brilliant green meadow. What was our horror on entering the enclosure to see two tourists with staves and shoulder belts all complete postured among the ruins in an attitude of admiration, one of them of course discoursing learnedly to his gaping companion and pointing out objects of interest with his stick. If there is one thing more hateful than another it is being told what to admire and having objects pointed out to one with a stick. Of all noxious animals too the most noxious is a tourist. And of all tourists the most vulgar, illbred, offensive and loathsome is the British tourist.

Morrell and I arrived at Clyro 7.50 and dined together comfortably at Cae Mawr sitting up talking afterwards till half past twelve. We were rather tired with our 25 miles walk, but not extraordinarily so.

Wednesday, 6 April

I hear with great satisfaction that Henry Warnell the gipsy of Hearts Ease, Clyro Hill, got six weeks hard labour without the option of paying a fine for assaulting Price of the Swan without the slightest provocation and kicking him in the bad place so violently and viciously that though Price sprung quickly back just in time to save himself a stout pair of corduroy trousers was rent.

Thursday, 7 April

I had the satisfaction of managing to walk from Hay to Clyro by the fields without meeting a single person, always a great triumph to me and a subject for warm self congratulation for I have a peculiar dislike to meeting people, and a peculiar liking for a deserted road. When I looked out between 11 and 12 before going to bed I saw one of the magnificent sights of the world, the crescent moon setting.

> When down the stormy crescent goes
>   A light before me swims,
> Between dark stems the forest glows,
>   I hear a noise of hymns.

Friday, 8 April

In the green lane between York and Cefn y Fedwas I came upon
Smith of Wernwg hedging. He told me that a child had arrived at
Pen-y-worlodd and wanted to know if something cannot be done
to separate Stephen Davies and Myra Rees. I said there was no law
to prevent people living in concubinage. People are very indignant
about this affair and think it a great scandal to the parish, and
rightly so. But what is to be done? The man's family are mad with
him especially Mrs Smith of New Barn, but no one has any influence over him. He is infatuated with the girl, whose tongue is
so desperate and unscrupulous that everyone is afraid of her.
Esther Gore openly accuses her of being 'a liar, a thief, a whore,
and a *murderer*' and offers to swear and prove that Myra has made
away with one infant, if not with more.

Saturday, 9 April

Mr Brierley the curate of Presteign and Chaplain to the High
Sheriff made two unfortunate mistakes. In going to Church he sat
down *beside* the Judge with his hat *on*, and came to dinner with
the Judge without his robes. Consulted Mr V. about Stephen
Davies and Myra Rees but he does not see what can be done.

From Cwmbythog I crossed the dingle and the brook and the
little meadow and so up the path by the quarries along the hillside
to John Morgan's the old soldier's. He and Mary his wife were
cosily at tea. Talking of the Peninsular War he said he well remembered being in a reserve line at Vittoria when a soldier sitting close
to him on the edge of a bank had his head carried off by a cannon
ball which struck him in front on the throat. The head rolled
along the ground, and when it ceased rolling John Morgan and the
other soldiers saw it moving and 'playing' on the ground with a
twitching of the features for five minutes after. They thought it so
extraordinary that the subject was often talked over round the
camp fires as an unprecedented marvel. There was one Lieutenant
Bowen an Irishman who joined the regiment between the battles
of Vittoria and the Pyrenees. He was very vicious to the men and
much hated. Just before the battle of the Pyrenees (which John
Morgan calls the Battle of the Pioneers) this Lieutenant Bowen
became very mild and humble to the men fearing he should be shot

27

on purpose by his own soldiers in the battle from revenge. He was not shot.

Monday, 11 April
Hay Fair and a large one. The roads thronged with men and droves of red white-faced cattle hustling and pattering to the Fair, an unusual number of men returning drunk.

Tuesday, 12 April
Last night the Swan was very quiet, marvellously quiet and peaceful. No noise, rowing or fighting whatever and no men as there sometimes are lying by the roadside all night drunk, cursing, muttering, maundering and vomiting.

Good Friday, 15 April
Took cross buns to Hannah Whitney, Sarah Williams, Margaret Griffiths, Catherine Ferris, Mary Jones, five widows.

Saturday, Easter Eve, 16 April
I awoke at 4.30 and there was a glorious sight in the sky, one of the grand spectacles of the Universe. There was not a cloud in the deep wonderful blue of the heavens. Along the Eastern horizon there was a clear deep intense glow neither scarlet nor crimson but a mixture of both. This red glow was very narrow, almost like a riband and it suddenly shaded off into the deep blue. Opposite in the west the full moon shining in all its brilliance was setting upon the hill beyond the church steeple. Thus the glow in the east bathed the church in a warm rich tinted light, while the moon from the west was casting strong shadows. The moon dropped quickly down behind the hill bright to the last, till only her rim could be seen sparkling among the tops of the orchards on the hill. The sun rose quickly and his rays struck red upon the white walls of Penllan, but not so brilliantly as in the winter sunrisings. I got up soon after 5 and set to work on my Easter sermon getting two hours for writing before breakfast.

At 11 I went to the school. Next I went to Cae Mawr. Mrs Morrell had been very busy all the morning preparing decorations for the Font, a round dish full of flowers in water and just big enough to fit into the Font and upon this large dish a pot filled and covered with flowers all wild, primroses, violets, wood anemones, wood sorrel, periwinkles, oxlips and the first blue bells, rising in a gentle pyramid, ferns and larch sprays drooping over the brim, a wreath of simple ivy to go round the stem of the Font, and a bed of moss to encircle the foot of the Font in a narrow band pointed at the corners and angles of the stone with knots of primroses. At 2 o'clock Hetty Gore of the Holly House came down from Cefn y Blaen and upset all my arrangements for the afternoon saying that old William Pritchard there was very ill not likely to live and wishes to see me this afternoon that I might read to him and give him the Sacrament. Hetty Gore thought he might not last many days. So I was obliged to go to the Vicarage explain and give up my drive. Found the schoolmaster and a friend staying with him just going out to get moss and carrying the East window-sill board from the Church to the school to prepare it for tomorrow with the text 'Christ is Risen' written in primroses upon moss. Shall I ever forget that journey up the hill to Cefn y Blaen in this burning Easter Eve, under the cloudless blue, the scorching sun and over the country covered with a hot dim haze? I climbed up the Bron panting in the sultry afternoon heat. Went up the fields from Court Evan Gwynne to Little Wern y Pentre and envied the sheep that were being washed in the brook below, between the field and the lane, by Price of Great Wern y Pentre and his excited boys. The peewits were sweeping rolling and tumbling in the hot blue air about the Tall Trees with a strange deep mysterious hustling and quavering sound from their great wings.

Pritchard was not nearly so ill as I had been led to expect. In fact he would not allow he was seriously ill and said he only had asthma. Indeed he almost said that he had sent for me merely because he liked to receive the Sacrament at Easter and could not go to his own Church (Colva). If I had known this I am not sure that I should have taken the trouble to come up in such a hurry to-day and deny myself my drive. But it seems that he had a very bad fit of coughing this morning when Hetty Gore was here and frightened her by almost choking. Mrs Evans of Cefn y Blaen was very anxious that Pritchard, who is her uncle and is staying with her, should make his will as he had told her he meant to leave her all his property, and a former will is still in being leaving his property to someone else. She took me aside before we went upstairs and with a low mysterious voice and foolish conscious face asked me to urge him to make his will in her favour. I told her that I would not interfere with family matters or influence him to dispose of his property to her advantage exclusively, and that I could only advise her uncle in a general way and as a matter of common prudence, for a sick and elderly man, to settle his affairs as he thought right without delay. Which I accordingly did. Coming back it was cooler for the fierceness of the sun was tempered and I met a refreshing cool breeze.

When I started for Cefn y Blaen only two or three people were in the churchyard with flowers. But now the customary beautiful Easter Eve Idyll had fairly begun and people kept arriving from all parts with flowers to dress the graves. Children were coming from the town and from neighbouring villages with baskets of flowers and knives to cut holes in the turf. The roads were lively with people coming and going and the churchyard a busy scene with women and children and a few men moving about among the tombstones and kneeling down beside the green mounds flowering the graves. An evil woman from Hay was dressing a grave. (Jane Phillips). I found Annie Dyke standing among the graves with her basket of flowers. A pretty picture she would have made as she stood there with her pure fair sweet grave face and clustering brown curls shaded by her straw hat and her flower basket hanging on her arm. It is her birthday to-day. I always tell her she and the cuckoos came together. So I went home and got a little birthday present I had been keeping for her, which I bought in the Crystal Palace in January, a small ivory brooch, with the carved figure of a stag. I took the little box which held it out into the churchyard and gave it to her as she was standing watching while the wife of one of her father's workmen, the shepherd, flowered the grave that she came to dress, for her.

More and more people kept coming into the churchyard as they finished their day's work. The sun went down in glory behind the dingle, but still the work of love went on through the twilight and into the dusk until the moon rose full and splendid. The figures continued to move about among the graves and to bend over the green mounds in the calm clear moonlight and warm air of the balmy evening.

At 8 o'clock there was a gathering of the Choir in the Church to practise the two anthems for to-morrow. The moonlight came streaming in broadly through the chancel windows. When the choir had gone and the lights were out and the church quiet again, as I walked down the Churchyard alone the decked graves had a strange effect in the moonlight and looked as if the people had laid down to sleep for the night out of doors, ready dressed to rise early on Easter morning. I lingered in the verandah before going to bed. The air was as soft and warm as a summer night, and the broad moonlight made the quiet village almost as light as day. Everyone seemed to have gone to rest and there was not a sound except the clink and trickle of the brook.

Easter Day, 17 April

The happiest, brightest, most beautiful Easter I have ever spent. I woke early and looked out. As I had hoped the day was cloudless, a glorious morning. My first thought was 'Christ is Risen'. It is not well to lie in bed on Easter morning, indeed it is thought very unlucky. I got up between five and six and was out soon after six. There had been a frost and the air was rimy with a heavy thick white dew on hedge, bank and turf, but the morning was not cold. There was a heavy white dew with a touch of hoar frost on the meadows, and as I leaned over the wicket gate by the mill pond looking to see if there were any primroses in the banks but not liking to venture into the dripping grass suddenly I heard the cuckoo for the first time this year. He was near Peter's Pool and he called three times quickly one after another. It is very well to hear the cuckoo for the first time on Easter Sunday morning. I loitered up the lane again gathering primroses.

The village lay quiet and peaceful in the morning sunshine, but by the time I came back from primrosing there was some little stir and people were beginning to open their doors and look out into the fresh fragrant splendid morning.

There was a very large congregation at morning church, the largest I have seen for some time, attracted by Easter and the splendour of the day, for they have here an immense reverence for Easter Sunday. The anthem went very well and Mr Baskerville complimented Mr Evans after church about it, saying that it was sung in good tune and time and had been a great treat. There were more communicants than usual: 29. This is the fifth time I have received the Sacrament within four days. After morning service I took Mr V. round the churchyard and showed him the crosses on his mother's, wife's, and brother's graves. He was quite taken by surprise and very much gratified. I am glad to see that our primrose crosses seem to be having some effect for I think I notice this Easter some attempt to copy them and an advance towards the form of the cross in some of the decorations of the graves. I wish we could get the people to adopt some little design in the disposition of the flowers upon the graves instead of sticking sprigs into the turf aimlessly anywhere, anyhow and with no meaning at all. But one does not like to interfere too much with their artless, natural way of showing their respect and love for the dead. I am thankful to find this beautiful custom on the increase, and observed more and more every year. Some years ago it was on the decline and nearly discontinued. On Easter Day all the young people come out in something new and bright like butterflies. It is almost part of their religion to wear something new on this day. It was an old saying that if you don't wear something new on Easter Day, the crows will spoil everything you have on.

Between the services a great many people were in the churchyard looking at the graves. I went to Bettws Chapel in the afternoon. It was burning hot and as I climbed the hill the perspiration rolled off my forehead from under my hat and fell in drops on the dusty road. Lucretia Wall was in chapel looking pale and pretty after her illness. Coming down the hill it was delightful, cool and pleasant. The sweet suspicion of spring strengthens, deepens, and grows more sweet every day. Mrs Pring gave us lamb and asparagus at dinner.

Easter Tuesday, 19 April
Set off with Spencer and Leonard Cowper at 2 o'clock for Mouse Castle. By the fields to Hay, then to Llydiart-y-Wain. It is years since I have seen this house and I had quite forgotten how prettily it is situated. At least it looked very pretty today bosomed among its white blossoming fruit trees, the grey fruitful homestead with its two large gleaming ponds. Thence up a steep meadow to the

left and by some quarries, over a stile in a wire fence and up a lovely winding path through the woods spangled with primroses and starred with wood anemones among trees and bushes thickening green. It was very hot in the shelter of the woods as we climbed up. The winding path led us round to the back of the hill till at last we emerged into a bold green brow in the middle of which stood a square steep rampart of grey crumbling sandstone rock with a flat top covered with grass bushes and trees, a sort of small wood. This rampart seemed about 15 feet high. The top of the hill round the base of the rampart undulated in uneven swells and knolls with little hillocks covered with short downy grass. One of the knolls overlooking the wooded side of the hill towards Hay was occupied by a wild group. A stout elderly man in a velveteen jacket with a walking stick sat or lay upon the dry turf. Beside him sat one or two young girls, while two or three more girls and boys climbed up and down an accessible point in the rampart like young wild goats, swarmed up into the hazel trees on the top of the rock and sat in the forks and swung. I could not make the party out at all. They were not poor and they certainly were not rich. They did not look like farmers, cottagers or artizans. They were perfectly nondescript, seemed to have come from nowhere and to be going nowhere, but just to have fallen from the sky upon Mouse Castle, and to be just amusing themselves. The girls about 12 and 14 years old climbed up the steep rocks before and just above us quite regardless of the shortness of their petticoats and the elevating and inflating powers of the wind. We climbed up too and found no castle or ruin of one. Nothing but hazels and bushes. A boy was seated in the fork of one hazel and a girl swinging in the wind in another. We soon came down again covered with dust and went to repose upon an inviting knoll green sunny and dry, from which two girls jumped up and ran away with needless haste. The man lay down in the grass on his face and apparently went to sleep. The girls called him 'Father'. They were full of fun and larks as wild as hawks, and presently began a great romp on the grass which ended in their rolling and tumbling head over heels and throwing water over each other and pouring some cautiously on their father's head. Then they scattered primroses over him. Next the four girls danced away down the path to a spring in the wood with a pitcher to draw more water, leaving a little girl and little boy with their father. We heard the girls shrieking with laughter and screaming with fun down below at the spring in the wood as they romped and, no doubt, threw water over each other and pushed each other into the spring. Presently they re-appeared on the top with the pitcher, laughing and struggling, and again the romp began. They ran after each other flinging water in showers, throwing each other down and rolling over on the grass. Seeing us amused and laughing they became still more wild and excited. They were fine good looking spirited girls all of them. But there were one or two quite pretty and one in a red frock was the wildest and most reckless of the troop. In the romp her dress was torn open all down her back, but whilst one of her sisters was trying to fasten it for her she burst away and tore it all open again showing vast spaces of white, skin as well as linen. Meanwhile the water that had been ostensibly fetched up from the spring to drink had all been thrown wantonly away, some carefully poured over their father, the rest wildly dashed at each other, up the clothes, over the head down the neck and back, anywhere except down their own throats. Someone pretended to be thirsty and to lament that all the water was gone so the whole bevy trooped merrily off down to the spring again. I could not help envying the father his children especially his troop of lithe, lissome, high-spirited, romping girls with their young supple limbs, their white round arms, white shoulders and brows, their rosy flushed cheeks, their dark and fair curls tangled, tossed and blown back by the wind, their bright wild saucy eyes, their red sweet full lips and white laughing teeth, their motions as quick, graceful and active as young antelopes or as fawns, and their clear sweet merry laughing voices, ringing through the woods. Meanwhile the father began to roll down the hillockside to amuse his younger children who remained with him, laughing heartily. And from the spring below rose the same screaming and laughing as before. Then we heard the voices gradually coming near the top of the hill ascending through the wood, till the wild troop of girls appeared once more and the fun began again. Next the father went to hide himself in the wood for the girls to find him and play hide and seek. And in the midst of their game we were obliged to come away and leave them for it was nearly 4.30. So we ran down the winding path, past the spring through the primrose and anemone starred woods to the meadow, quarry, farm and road. I cannot think who the wild party were. They were like no one whom I ever saw before. They seemed as if they were the *genii loci* and always lived there. At all events I shall always connect them with Mouse Castle. And if I should ever visit the place again I shall certainly expect to find them there in full romp.

The air blew sweet from the mountains and tempered the heat of the sun. All round the brow of the hill the sloping woods budded into leaf, the birds sang in the thickets and the afternoon sun shone golden on the grassy knolls.

Tuesday, 26 April

John Morgan was tottering about his garden with crutches, gathering stones off the beds and hoeing the earth between the potato rows. I took the hoe from the old soldier and hoed three rows for him, finishing the patch. Then we went indoors and sat down by the fire.

The whole country is now lighted up by the snowy pear blossoms among their delicate light-green leaves. The pear trees stand like lights about the gardens and orchards and in the fields. The magnificent great old pear tree opposite the Vicarage is in bloom.

Wednesday, 27 April

At noon got out my old Swiss haversack, crammed night necessaries into it, made a brown paper parcel of my dress coat, and strapping all together started after luncheon for Whitney Rectory, walking with my pack slung over my shoulders by the fields to Hay to catch the 1.50 train.

At Whitney I walked down to the Rectory by the private path through the shrubbery. I went up the meadow to the Stow and found that Dewing had just gone out. However he had seen me coming and had left a message with the servant to ask me to wait and he would be in in a few minutes. I waited in the drawing room. The last time I was in that room was when Mr Venables and I rode to call upon the Dewings just after their marriage. And now she is dead. How well I remember the bride cake and wine on the table and she sitting in the window looking so well, so radiant and happy.

The lilies of the valley that were planted by Miss Dew close by the front door in the little flower border to welcome the young bride on the first coming home, after her marriage on the 14 May, are now just coming up. So early dead, not 23, and to the poor bereaved husband after the short gleam of happiness all seems like a dream. Her pretty portrait still on the dining room mantelpiece. In the dining room on the bookshelves stood two cases of stuffed birds, one case of gulls and petrels, all the sea-birds from Plymouth. The other was a case of country birds, a cuckoo, jay, yappingale, starling, blackbird and thrush, all nicely set up by her brother Mr Hinckstone. After waiting and waiting I went out into the garden and strolled about the sunny lawn where a slight shower from a black cloud had beaded the grass with bright drops. Presently I saw Miss Dew in her black dress coming slowly up the green meadow. I thought of William Wordsworth the poet who often used to come and stay at this house with blind Mr Monkhouse who had nearly all his poems off by heart. Miss Dew came in by the wicket gate leading from the garden into the meadow and stayed some time telling me about Mr Dewing.

Thursday, 28 April
Only Mr Venables was at dinner at Cae Mawr. Champagne at dinner and some splendid mutton and I was very hungry. Last night one of Cheese's clerks came to lodge here. I met him at the gate this evening and liked his looks, but when I came in after dinner I found the house poisoned with tobacco smoke.

May Eve, Saturday
Mr Venables started in the Hay omnibus from Clyro Vicarage for London for his two months' absence at 10.15.

This evening being May Eve I ought to have put some birch and wittan (mountain ash) over the door to keep out the 'old witch'. But I was too lazy to go out and get it. Let us hope the old witch will not come in during the night. The young witches are welcome.

Monday, 2 May

A bright cold morning, & while the sun was yet low the shadow of one of the five poplars fell across part of the spire of another, deepening & richening the green.

Tuesday, 3 May

Started at noon to walk to Newchurch. Went by Whitty's mill. Stopped on the steep hill above the mill to enjoy the sight of the peaceful little hamlet, and the chink of the forge at Pentwyn sounded sweet, clear and busy across the dingle. I turned up by the old deserted kiln house, empty now, silent, desolate, with its high steep brown tiled roof and white dirty walls. This old field path is quite new to me. I have never travelled it before. Just above the kiln I saw and gathered the first red campion. Luxuriantly large cowslips grew on the bank and marsh buttercups in the ditch. It is a strange country between the kiln and Whitehall. Thes trees look wild and weird and a yew was stifling an oak. The meadow below Whitehall looked sad and strange and wild, grown with bramble bushes, thorns, fern and gorse. Poor Whitehall, sad, silent and lonely, with its great black yew in the hedge of the tangled waste grass-grown garden and its cold chimney still ivy-clustered. I walked round and looked in at the broken unframed windows and pushed open a door which swung slowly and wearily together again. On another door at the house end were carved two figures of ploughs. A dry old mixen withered before and close to the front entrance. Here were held the Quarterly Dances. What fun. What merry makings, the young people coming in couples and parties from the country round to dance in the long room. What laughing, flirting, joking and kissing behind the door or in the dark garden amongst the young folks, while the elders sat round the room with pipe and mug of beer or cider from the 'Black Ox' of Coldbrook hard by. Now how is all changed, song and dance still, mirth fled away. Only the weird sighing through the broken roof and crazy doors, the quick feet, busy hands, saucy eyes, strong limbs all mouldered into dust, the laughing voices silent. There was a deathlike stillness about the place, except that I fancied once I heard a small voice singing and a bee was humming among the ivy green, the only bit of life about the place. From the old long low brown cottage of Whitehall with its broken roof with a chimney at each gable end I went up the lane to Pant-y-ci speculating upon the probable site of the Coldbrook and the Black Ox which was the house of call on Clyro Hill for the drovers of the great herds of black cattle from Shire Carmarthen and Cardigan on their way down into England. I thought I saw the place where the house probably stood. No one was at home at Pant-y-ci so I stuck a cowslip in the latch hole by way of leaving a card and went on to Crowther's Pool.

By Tyn-y-cwm Meadows to Newchurch village and in turning in at the old Vicarage garden door I heard the hum of the little school. The door under the latticed porch was open and as I went in a pretty dark girl was coming out of an inner door, but seeing me she retreated hastily and I heard an excited buzzing of voices within the schoolroom and eager whispers among the children: 'Here's Mr Kilvert – It's Mr Kilvert.' Not finding the good parson in his study I went into the schoolroom and fluttered the dove cot not a little. The curate and his eldest daughter were away and pretty Emmeline in a russet brown stuff dress and her long fair curls was keeping school bravely with an austere look in her severe beautiful face, and hearing little Polly Greenway read. Janet and Matilda dressed just alike in black silk skirts, scarlet bodices and white pinafores, and with blue ribbons in their glossy bonny dark brown curls, were sitting on a form at a long desk with the other children working at sums. Janet was doing simple division and said she had done five sums, whereupon I kissed her and she was nothing loth. Moreover I offered to give her a kiss for every sum, at which she laughed. As I stood by the window making notes of things in general in my pocket book Janet kept on interrupting her work to glance round at me shyly but saucily with her mischievous beautiful grey eyes. Shall I confess that I travelled ten miles today over the hills for a kiss, to kiss that child's sweet face. Ten miles for a kiss.

I do think the way the Vaughan girls wear their short curling hair is the most natural and prettiest in the world. Oh if fashionable young ladies could but see and perceive and understand and know what utterly ludicrous guys they made of themselves, with the towers and spires and horns and clubs that they build and torture their hair up into ! But slaves to fashion must its gods adore.

Wednesday, 4 May

I rose early, wrote, and loitered down the sunny lane before breakfast. A lovely morning and I heard the first turtle dove trilling. I was standing on the bridge plank over the waste water looking at the black and white ducks and a fine drake preening themselves and splashing about in the mill pond when Price of the Swan came down the lane. We were standing talking where the waste water crosses the road and Price said, suddenly pointing, 'Look there'. There was a small animal running about the stones by the brook side in the sun – whirling round in circles and behaving very strangely. Price pronounced it to be a small kind of weasel catching flies. I said I thought it was a mouse, and it proved to be a shrew. Price called it 'a hardy straw'. It was whirling and whisking round swiftly among the stones in little circles, sometimes almost on its side, showing its white belly, tumbling about, darting to and fro rapidly, and conducting itself in the most earnest but ludicrous manner. It was so absorbed in catching flies or whatever it was about that it did not see us or care about us though we threw stones at it, and allowed us to come quite near and turn it over with a stick and push it into the water. It squeaked but did not run away and I took it up. It clung on to Price's stick, dropped on to the ground, and then vanished into a hole in the bank.

I lent Hannah a book and brought away a fern green from off the great flat porch stone over the door of the Oaks. They are good for making ointment. The brook and Painscastle mill pond glancing like silver. A beautiful sunny afternoon and the cuckoo calling everywhere. Met Mrs Cooper in the churchyard and she told me Cooper is very ill with stoppage.

Friday, 6 May

I set off for Newchurch again, my second visit there this week.

When I got out on to the open of the Little Mountain the lapwings were wheeling about the hill by scores, hurtling and rustling with their wings, squirling and wailing, tumbling and lurching on every side, very much disturbed, anxious and jealous about their nests. As I entered the fold of Gilfach y rheol, Janet issued from the house door and rushed across the yard and turning the corner of the wain-house I found the two younger ladies assisting at the castration of the lambs, catching and holding the poor little beasts and standing by whilst the operation was performed, seeming to enjoy the spectacle. It was the first time I had seen clergyman's daughters helping to castrate lambs or witnessing that operation and it rather gave me a turn of disgust at first. But I made allowance for them and considered in how rough a way the poor children have been brought up, so that they thought no harm of it, and I forgave them. I am glad however that Emmeline was not present, and Sarah was of course out of the way. Matilda was struggling in a pen with a large stout white lamb, and when she had mastered him and got him well between her legs and knees I ventured to ask where her father was. She signified by a nod and a word that he was advancing behind me, and turning I saw him crossing the yard with his usual outstretched hand and cordial welcome. I don't think the elder members of the family quite expected that the young ladies would be caught by a morning caller castrating lambs, and probably they would have selected some other occupation for them had they foreseen the coming of a guest. However they carried it off uncommonly well.

Monday, 9 May
Now the various tints of green mount one over another up the hanging woods of Penllan above the dingle. Over the level line of brilliant larch green rises the warmer golden green brown of the oaks. But the most brilliant green of all is the young green of the beeches. The brilliance of the beeches is almost beyond belief. The turtles were trilling softly and deeply in the dingles as I went up the steep orchard. The grass was jewelled with cowslips and orchises. The dingle was lighted here and there with wild cherry, bird cherry, the Welsh name of which being interpreted is 'the tree on which the devil hung his mother'. The mountains burned blue in the hot afternoon and the air felt quite sultry as I climbed the hill.

Saturday, 14 May
Over the great old fashioned house door of Court Evan Gwynne hung the sprigs of birch and wittan, the only remnants of the old

custom I have noticed this May. The sprays had been hanging since May Eve and were rather withered.

Sunday, 15 May
Spoke to Wall about the desirability of trying to get James Allen to dislodge his immoral tenants at Cwmpelved Green.

Monday, 16 May
Morrell drove down and picked me and my luggage up at 7.30 and drove me to the station. The morning was most lovely, a perfect day for travelling, and it was a luxury simply to sit still and be carried through the exquisite scenery of Herefordshire and Gloucestershire.

Got to Chippenham shortly before 2 p.m. I walked up by Cocklebury, the lane and fields deliciously shady green and quiet. My Father came across the Common to the black gate waiting for me by that way, then came over the field to meet me.

The orchard and garden apple trees are in full bloom and the pink stage of the blossom having passed, the trees seem loaded as if with snow, a sea, a mass of blossom. The copper beech is in its early purple splendour and the great laburnum near it just about to burst into blossom. The broom that I transplanted has grown much and is in fine bloom now. The whole place is looking almost more lovely than ever I saw it, and the grass of the lawn so smooth and brilliantly green.

Wednesday, 18 May
Went down to the Bath Flower Show in Sydney College Gardens. Found the first train going down was an Excursion train and took a ticket for it. The carriage was nearly full. In the Box tunnel as there was no lamp, the people began to strike foul brimstone matches and hand them to each other all down the carriage. All the time we were in the tunnel these lighted matches were travelling from hand to hand in the darkness. Each match lasted the length of the carriage and the red ember was thrown out of the opposite window, by which time another lighted match was seen travelling down the carriage. The carriage was chock full of brimstone fumes, the windows both nearly shut, and by the time we got out of the tunnel I was almost suffocated. Then a gentleman

tore a lady's pocket handkerchief in two, seized one fragment, blew his nose with it, and put the rag in his pocket. She then seized his hat from his head, while another lady said that the dogs of Wootton Bassett were much more sociable than the people.

Thursday, 19 May
All the afternoon I had a bad face ache and could enjoy nothing. I tried laudanum and port wine, but nothing did any good.

Sunday, 22 May
Day after day this glorious cloudless weather goes on. We all went to Church this morning except Dora, walking together as one great family through the may, between the hawthorn hedges and trees laden with sweet snowy blossom. The Bowling green, Becks and the Barrow meadow are sheets of gold buttercups, seas of gold stretching away under the elms. In Becks there are scarlet may trees and the deep blue sky over all.

Tuesday, 24 May
Chippenham bells pealing and firing all day for the Queen's birth-day. Perch fished while I lay on the sloping grass bank and read the Spanish Student. The river was very low and the roach and dace have not yet come up. The air was full of 'green drake' or may fly just up and all swarming over the river, and the little bleak leaping at them every moment.

Holy Thursday, 26 May
The bells ringing for the Ascension. Went to Church with my Father through the sunny golden fields variegated with clover and daisies and ground ivy. The Church bell tolling for service through the elms. A small congregation, but many bees buzzing about the Church windows as if a swarm were flying. My Father says this has happened on several Ascension days and once the Church-warden John Bryant came after a swarm of his to the Church on Ascension day, clinking a frying pan and shovel. My Father told him that the bees showed the people the way to Church.

Every morning Summerflower brings splendid watercresses from Kellaways Mill. Last Tuesday morning I was out early before breakfast, walking along the Common on Maud Heath between the may hedges. Just as I heard the breakfast bell ring across the

Common from the Rectory and turned in at the black gate a man crossed the stile carrying a basket. He said his name was Summerflower, that he had fasted since yesterday morning and that he could buy no breakfast before he had got watercresses to sell.

Friday, 27 May
After dinner at 3, drove to Monkton with Fanny to a croquet & archery party.

Saturday, 28 May
From Langley to Clyro by early express.

Charles while driving me over told me of the charge brought against Brewer by Janet, late kitchenmaid at Clyro Vicarage, accusing him of being the father of her child. Janet wrote to him at Clyro, making the charge, as soon as the child was born, and poor Mrs Brewer opened the letter, read it, and sent it on to her husband. I am told she is nearly heartbroken. Poor child. Charles fears the charge is too well founded. I was thunderstruck. I always thought so well of Brewer and believed him to be such a very different man.

Monday, 30 May
Mrs Smith of New Barn paid me an interminable visitation and hindered me a long while to no purpose, wanting me to write to Mr Weere and ask him to let them have Pen-y-wyrlod, if her brother Stephen Davies has to leave. Mr Weere paid his tenant and farm an unexpected visit and finding him living in open concubinage with Myra Rees gave him notice. I told Mrs Smith that Mr Weere is a perfect stranger to me and that I could not interfere with what is not my business.

Tuesday, June Eve
Hamar of Boatside has had the measles heavily. I met him in the road one day and he said 'I suppose I have had the measles,' as if he did not know that he had. It is the curious aggravating Herefordshire use of the word 'suppose'.

June Day, Wednesday
Going out to the School at 10 found Mary Brooks, the Vicarage housemaid, at the door just going to ring. She had run down

breathless with an open letter just received in her hand to announce that Mrs Venables was confined of a nice little girl at 1.5 a.m. yesterday. Three cheers. The news flew through the village like wild fire. Charlie Powell, Richard Brooks and John Harris rushed to the Church and the bells were soon in full peal.

Hannah Whitney standing at her door knitting heard the bells ringing and asked 'What has God sent her?' The bells ringing at intervals all day. Mrs Price of the Swan sent the ringers a gallon of beer. I sent them another gallon, and went to the belfry to see them ringing. I went to bed early and saw a broad strong light striking through my N.W. bedroom window on the wall opposite. I found afterwards it was a tar barrel bonfire which Cooper and Evans the schoolmaster were making upon the Bron in honour of Miss Venables.

Thursday, 2 June
To Llanthomas at 4.30. Crichton and W. Thomas just going out trout fishing. They brought home a nice basket of fish. The ladies with Henry Thomas had gone up the bank sketching.

Heard that Kingcraft won the Derby yesterday instead of the favourite Macgregor who was thought safe to win.

The Llanthomas carriage took the Crichtons home and I went with them as far as Wye Cliff gate, Henry Thomas lending me a capital bearskin sort of coat to drive in. As we drove home the night was still and warm, the landrails were craking in the grass and the crescent moon was setting bright and clear. As I walked down the Long Mills hill the brick-kiln glowed bright and red through the dusk.

Friday, 3 June
Went to see John Morgan and found the old soldier sitting out in his garden, so I brought a chair out of the house and sat with him reading and talking to him. The beans were deliciously sweet-scented and a white flower something like Whitsuntide stock. At the Lower House the orchard boughs were so thick and close that the sun could not penetrate them, and the sunlight only got into the orchard at a gap in the west side through which it came streaming in low in a long bright streak along the brilliant green

rich velvety-looking grass like sunshine through a painted Cathedral window.

Sitting room windows open till very late. A group of people talking and laughing loud in the Swan porch and on the steps in the dusk. I was delighted to hear Teddy Evans proposing to some other children to play the old game of 'Fox a Dandley'. Then they chose 'dens' and began running about catching each other and I thought I heard the 'Cats of Kinlay' mewing. Perhaps that is part of the game. I had no idea the old game was still played by the present generation of children. Teddy Evans was singing

> My Mother said that I never should
> Play with the gipsies in the wood &c.

Whitsun Day, 5 June

Very hot in morning Church, and an enormous bumble bee crawled over the white cloth and everything else during the Holy Communion. A number of white dresses and light colours in Church in honour of Whitsuntide. After afternoon Church walked across the fields to Hay. Went to the Castle and found them all at tea. Went with them to Church and preached for Bevan. Rather disconcerted at seeing Mrs Crichton in Mr Allen's seat just below, for she had heard the same sermon at Clyro in the morning.

A letter from Mr Venables confirming the Brewer scandal. I had been hoping almost against hope that it might not be true. It is a sad scandal for the Vicarage. He says he has never had such a scandal in his house before. Mrs Venables does not know of it yet. They were obliged to keep it secret from her lest it might do her harm and shock her so as to hasten matters. She is getting on very well. Dr Farre allows her chicken and claret and talks of moving her to a sofa about next Wednesday. Mr V. very kindly puts the Vicarage at the disposal of my people from June 20 to July 1.

Whitsun Monday, 6 June

Called at Clyro Court. Mrs Baskerville said she had heard that a lady had been carried out of Hay Church fainting under the influence of a sermon from Mr Welby. The story is probably untrue.

Whitsun Tuesday, 7 June

Up early and writing in my bedroom before breakfast. The swallows kept on dashing in at the open window and rustling round the room. The road sides are now deep in the dry withered wych blossom blowing and rustling about lightly and falling from the Churchyard wyches. Thunder muttering again this morning, but still a cloudless sky, a wind from the E. and hot sun, everything parching and burning up. When are we to have rain? At the school Gipsy Lizzie looking arch and mischievous with her dark large beautiful eyes, and a dazzling smile showed her little white teeth, as she tossed her dark curls back.

The village was very quiet in the still burning heat and there was scarcely a sound. At 2.30 went up to Mrs Corfield's in the Cwm. Mrs Corfield lying in bed very weak and sweating heavily under two blankets and a coverlet. I advised that one blanket should be removed. Holes in the roof open to the sky ventilated the bedroom, but no window would open and the bedroom was very hot.

Climbed up the Holme. Meredith's sister in the yard feeding her fowls. Walked round the garden and then went indoors. She said she could not bear to come to Clyro Church because her sister who committed suicide from New Barn by drowning herself in the Wye below Boatside is buried opposite the Church door. And this is the birth place of Sarah Smith. Sarah of the Cwm. To me there seems to be a halo of glory round this place. Yet in what poor mean dwellings these wild rich natures, these mountain beauties, are born and reared.

Wednesday, 8 June

As I was writing a sermon (with open windows to the laburnum and horsechestnuts) on Barnabas, the son of consolation, a note was brought to me from David Vaughan and his son William was waiting outside. So I had him in and gave him some beer. He was rather shy and constrained and sat for a long time quite still with the tumbler of beer in his hand and looking at nothing. I could not conceive why he did not drink the beer. Then I thought he was ill. At last he faced round on his chair half wheel, and pronounced solemnly and formally, 'My best respects to you, Sir'.

After having delivered himself of this respectful sentiment he imbibed some beer. It was a bit of perfect good breeding. I suppose he had been during the long pause while he sat so still cogitating what would be the proper thing to say or perhaps trying to prepare a set speech for so distinguished an occasion.

Thursday, 9 June

In the night there came a cooler wind and fair showers out of the west. The falling white blossoms of the clematis drift in at the open window on the fresh morning breeze. In the garden there are red roses, and blue hills beyond. Last night the moon was shining in at my west window through the lacing boughs of the mountain ash – the moonbeams fell across the bed and I saw 'the gusty shadow sway' on the white bed curtain. Called at Cae Mawr at 3.30 and found Mr and Mrs Morrell playing croquet with his sister and Miss Morrell of Moulsford who are staying in the house, having returned with him on Tuesday. Joined them and we had two merry games. The two eldest Miss Baskervilles came in by the wicket gate while we were playing and we had tea on the lawn. I staid to dinner. After dinner we had archery.

Friday, 10 June

Woke in the night and saw the moon through the mountain ash setting red over the Old Forest. Colder and cloudy, but yet no wind and all things drier and drier. Gusty N.W. wind and a perpetual and maddening banging of doors.

Thursday, 16 June

The old soldier showed my brother his Peninsula medal with the Vittoria, Pyrenees and Toulouse clasps, and after some talk about the army and the Peninsula we left. It was fearfully sultry as we walked home and at 9 p.m. a thunderstorm came. It seemed as if three or four thunderstorms were rolling and working round far off. The lightning was exceedingly fine. Broad flares and flames of rose colour, violet, and brilliant yellow. Heavy rain came on and lasted for an hour. The air was much cooled and everything refreshed.

Friday, 17 June
Perch went groping about in the brook and brought in a small crayfish which crawled about the table, horns, tail and claws like a fresh-water clean brown lobster. I did not know there were any crayfish in the brook.

We went to a croquet party at Clyro Court, calling at Cae Mawr by the way. The party divided between croquet and archery.

Saturday, 18 June
It was very hot walking, a sultry heat. At Hay Castle I found a number of young ladies playing croquet with Pope, Margaret Oswald, Jenny Dew, Lucy Allen, Charlotte and Edith Thomas. At lawn tea Charlotte Thomas emptied her cup of tea into her lap and then in getting up shot part of the contents of her lap out on to Mrs Allen's dress.

Tuesday, 21 June
Today we went for a picnic to Snodhill Castle in the Golden Valley. A great break very roomy and comfortable came round with a pair of brown horses and we all got in. Mrs Oswald, Captain and Mrs Bridge, Perch, Jim Brown, Arthur Oswald and myself. The sun glared fiercely as we started, but driving made life tolerable and some heavy clouds came rolling up which made us fear a thunderstorm. The Haigh Allens drove up, then the Harry Dews, and the party was complete. So the company and provisions were packed into the four carriages and the procession set out through the narrow lanes. The girls ran out into the porches of the quaint picturesque old-fashioned farm houses of the Golden Valley to see the string of horses and carriages and the gay dresses of the ladies, an unwonted sight to the dwellers in the Golden Valley. At the foot of the Castle Hill we got out and every one carried something up the steep slippery brown bare grass slopes.

The first thing of course was to scale the Castle mound and climb up the ruins of the Keep as far as might be. It was fearfully slippery and the ladies gallantly sprawled and struggled up and slithered down again. Then a fire was to be lighted to boil potatoes which had been brought with us. Rival attempts were made to light fires, Bridge choosing a hole in the ruins and Powell preferring a hollow in the ground. Powell, however, wisely possessed himself of the pot and potatoes so that though the other fire was lighted first it was of no use and the divided party reunited and concentrated their minds and energies upon the fire in the hollow. Three sticks were propped together, meeting in a point, gipsy fashion, and from them was hung the pot, full of new young potatoes just covered with water. Wood was picked up off the ground and torn out of a dry hedge and a fierce fire was soon roaring under the pot making the trees and banks opposite quiver and swim in the intense heat. The flames soon burnt through one of the supports and when the fire was at the fiercest down came the three sticks and the pot upside down hissing into the midst of the flames. The pot lid flew off, out rushed the water and potatoes and a cloud of steam arose from the fire. Arthur Oswald gallantly rescued the pot with a pot hook in spite of the intense heat which was very difficult to endure. There were loud cries and everyone was giving unheeded advice at once. At length the pot was settled upright on the embers, more water having been poured in, and another armful of dry wood heaped upon it, so that the pot was in the midst of a glowing fire. Twenty minutes passed, during which the gentlemen stood round the fire staring at the pot, while the ladies got flowery wreaths and green and wild roses to adorn the dishes and table cloth spread under an oak tree and covered with provisions. Then the pot hook was adjusted, the pot heaved and swung off the fire, a fork plunged into the potatoes and they were triumphantly pronounced to be done to a turn. Then there was a dispute how they should be treated. 'Pour away the water', said one. 'Let the water stay in the pot', said another. 'Steam the potatoes', 'Poor them out on the ground', 'Hand them round in the pot', 'Put them on a plate', 'Fish them out with a fork'. They were, however, poured out on the ground and then the pot fell upon them, crushing some and blackening others. Eventually the potatoes were handed round the table cloth, every one being most assiduous and urgent in recommending and passing them to his neighbour. There was plenty of meat and drink, the usual things, cold chicken, ham and tongue, pies of different sorts, salads, jam and gooseberry tarts, bread and cheese. Splendid strawberries from Clifford Priory brought by the Haigh Allens. Cup of various kinds went round, claret and hock, champagne, cider and sherry, and people sprawled about in all attitudes and made a great noise – Henry Dew was the life of the party and kept the table in a roar. After luncheon the gentlemen entrenched themselves upon a fragment of the Castle wall to smoke and talk local news and politics and the ladies wandered away by themselves. At last we all met upon the mound where Mary Bevan and someone else had been trying to sketch the Keep, and sat in a great circle whilst the remains of the cup, wine, and soda water were handed round. Then we broke up, the roll of the carriages was heard coming through the lanes below and everyone seized upon something to carry down the steep slippery grass slopes.

At the Rectory we strolled about the garden. Dinner was announced, quite unnecessarily as far as I was concerned, for I wanted nothing. The room too was steaming hot. After dinner the carpet was taken up in the drawing-room and there was a dance on the slippery dark oak floor which was sadly scratched and scored by the nailed boots of the gentlemen and some of the ladies. Tom Powell slipped and fell. Tom Brown, dancing a waltz with his nephew Arthur Oswald, came down with a crash that shook the house and was immediately seized head and heels by Henry Dew and Mr Allen and carried about the room. We danced the Lancers, and finished with Jim Rufen but it was almost too hot. Then the carriages were ordered and we came away.

The drive home in the cool of the evening was almost the pleasantest part of the day. The light was so strong that we could hardly believe it was ten o'clock. The longest day, and the strong light glow in the North showed that the Midsummer sun was only just travelling along below the horizon, ready to show again in five hours. Passing by Hawkswood and the ghost-haunted pond we told ghost stories until Mrs Oswald was almost frightened out of the carriage.

Wednesday, 22 June

It was settled some time ago that my father and Perch should go a-fishing to Llangorse Lake and stay a night there. Today was fixed on for the expedition. At dinner time my Father kindly asked me to be one of the party. My Father went down to the Lake while J. and I proceeded to Stephen Pritchard's house to see if we could get beds and a boat. Pritchard was out fishing on the Lake but his housekeeper told us we could have supper and three beds, and the boatman Evans went down with us to the landing stage. Stephen Pritchard's house stands upon the common very near the Lake, almost hidden in a bosoming bower of trees. On the square hedge-guarded lawn in front of the cottage a picnic party from Brecon, a number of girls in light dresses and young men, were seated on green benches round a green table covered with a white cloth in a shady corner having tea or dinner.

Evans the Monmouthshire boatman rowed us past the island to the edge of a field of perch weed, but the weather was too dry and hot for fishing, the fish were sulky or sick, and all we caught was five little perch. To me, however, the fishing was of very little consequence. I had not expected to catch anything and was not disappointed. The beauty of the evening and the Lake was extraordinary, and in the west the Fan stood grand and blue and peaked like a volcano. The feathery perch weeds waved like forests under water, the cuckoo was calling about the hills and around the lake, though he has done singing at Clyro and is gone, or at least is silent. From the lake shores came musical cattle calls, faint shouts, the barking of dogs and the melodious sounds of evening. The boatman told us that within the last ten years the American weed had crept into the dyke and was spreading fast all over it and doing much mischief. There used to be a great quantity of grebe, he said, but they had been slaughtered without mercy. Tern came here in numbers and last Christmas a bittern was shot on the common near Pritchard's house.

The picnic party now came from the house to the landing stage and we saw them embark and push off. The boatman said the men were dissenting ministers and he laughed at them, calling them 'duck merchants'. I asked what he meant and he said it was a regular local name for these persons – because they were fond of ducks. They had a boat load of ducks on board now at any rate and they seemed to be having good fun for we heard the girls screaming and laughing across the water. Then they began to sing a rather pretty air. Another boat passed us with some students of Trevecca College rowing towards land. Meantime from the picnic party in the other boat came distant sounds of loud screaming and laughter as if a great romp were going on and as if the girls were being kissed and tickled.

Friday, Midsummer Day
Up at 6.30 and to breakfast at Cae Mawr soon after 7.30. Perch ready for a walk to Llanthony.

[Here follows an account of the walk.]

When we entered the Abbey precincts the courtyard was swarming with people. Some were walking about, some sitting down under the penthouse on either side of the Abbey Tavern door, some standing in knots and groups talking. The kitchen too was buzzing and swarming like a hive. Beauchamp came forward and met us and we were shown into the upper long room. Here the servant girl Sarah told us that it was Mr Arnold Savage Landor's rent day. Mrs Beauchamp came in and said she was afraid she could not cook anything for us as there was so much cooking going on in the kitchen for the tenants' dinners. However, she promised some bread, butter, cheese and beer and boiled eggs. While these things were being got ready we amused ourselves by looking out of the window at the people in the green courtyard below. A tent or rather an awning had been reared against the wall of the Lady Chapel. The wind flapped the canvas sides and strained at the ropes. The cloth was spread on the table. No viands had yet appeared but a savoury reek pervaded the place and the tantalized tenants walked about lashing their tails, growling and snuffing up the scent of food hungrily like Welsh wolves.

For our part we consumed 18 eggs amongst us and a proportionate amount of bread, cheese, butter and beer.

Wednesday, 29 June
Going to the school I met two strange looking people, a young man and a girl. He was dressed entirely in white flannel edged with black and wore a straw hat. He looked like a sailor. They hesitated a moment at the Churchyard gate, then turned in and walked across the Churchyard and I saw them no more.

Saturday, 2 July
My Father left us for Langley. At the station sitting in the waiting shed was a man dressed in a slop with his head entirely covered

with a black shawl except a patch of white handkerchief over the face. The shawl was arranged like an animal's snout. Not a feature was visible. He looked strange, horrible, unearthly, half like a masked burglar and half like a snouted beast. The station people knew nothing of him except that he came down the road from Clifford. I suppose he had met with some fearful accident which had disfigured his face.

There seemed to be a good deal of disputing and quarrelling through the village about yesterday's sale and the things bought. A quarrel arose at the New Inn and Henry Warnell the gipsy came cursing, shouting and blaspheming down the road into the village mad with rage because someone had accused him of something and threatened 'to send him back to Hereford where he was before', the sting of the remark lying in this fact that the gipsy had just come out of Hereford jail where he has been undergoing sentence for assaulting and kicking William Price the innkeeper. The whole village was in an uproar, some taking one part and some another, and it was long before the storm died away and the gipsy's wrath was appeased and his sense of honour satisfied.

Monday, 4 July
Since the inspection [1] the classes and standards at the school have been arranged and Gipsy Lizzie has been put into my reading class. How is the indescribable beauty of that most lovely face to be described – the dark soft curls parting back from the pure white transparent brow, the exquisite little mouth and pearly tiny teeth, the pure straight delicate features, the long dark fringes and white eyelids that droop over and curtain her eyes, when they are cast down or bent upon her book, and seem to rest upon the soft clear cheek, and when the eyes are raised, that clear unfathomable blue depth of wide wonder and enquiry and unsullied and unsuspecting innocence. Oh, child, child, if you did but know your own power. Oh, Gipsy, if you only grow up as good as you are fair. Oh, that you might grow up good. May all God's angels guard you, sweet. The Lord bless thee and keep thee. The Lord make His Face to shine upon thee and be gracious unto thee. The Lord lift up His countenance upon thee peace, both now and *evermore*. Amen.

---

1. This took place on 1 July.

Mr Venables offered us the dog cart this afternoon, and we drove with the new bay horse from Tattersalls' to call at Wye Cliff. Then we drove to the castle where we found Mrs and Miss Allen and Mrs Bevan lying ill upon a sofa. It seems the young gentleman in flannels and the young lady whom I saw walking through Clyro village last Wednesday are young Lyne and his sister. They are staying at the Swan at Hay with their Father and Mother. Their brother Ignatius[1] is soon expected down to look after his monastery in the Black Mountain. They seem to be very odd people. The two young people came to Clyro Church on Sunday afternoon and when my Mother went up to the Church door she had to run the gauntlet between them as they sat on tombstones opposite each other kicking their heels. They were at a croquet party at Hay Castle last week and young Lyne made himself very ridiculous taking off his hat when women spoke to him, and he persecuted poor little Fanny Thomas almost to the verge of distraction, taking off his hat to her whenever she made a stroke. After they came out of Clyro Church on Sunday afternoon young Lyne grinned in a boy's face and said, alluding to Mr Venables, who had performed the Service, 'What a very nice clergyman you have here'. In the evening of the same day the whole family were at Hay Church. When Church was over rain was falling and a number of people blocked the porch. The Lynes were all standing together one behind another. Crichton whispered in Mary Bevan's ear, 'Did you ever read a book called *Line upon Line*?'

Wednesday, 6 July
At 3 o'clock went to Wye Cliff by the meadows. The targets were pitched in the long green narrow meadow which runs down to the river and the summer houses, one of the prettiest archery grounds I ever saw, the high woods above and the river below. It was a pretty sight to see the group of ladies with their fresh light dresses moving up and down the long green meadow between the targets, and the arrows flitting and glancing white to and fro against the bank of dark green trees. At 6 tea, coffee, cider cup, &c. was laid

1. See footnote on p. 25.

54

out in the summer house and when 3 dozen arrows had been shot we left off shooting and went to tea and I made up the score. All through the hot burning afternoon how pleasant sounded the cool rush and roar of the Wye over its rapids & rocks at the end of the meadow.

Thursday, 7 July
At 5.30 started to walk to Clifford Priory to dinner, going to Hay across the fields. I arrived before any of the other guests and in the dark cool drawing room I found Mr Allen, his brother Major Allen, and Major Allen's two bewitching pretty little girls, Geraldine and Edith. Fair Helen of Troy prettier than ever followed with her sister from Hardwick Vicarage, Henry Dew and Emily, Pope and Mr Allen, Llanthomas, Mary and Grace. I took Lucy Allen in to dinner but was forcibly separated from her and sat opposite by Louisa Wyatt who talked Switzerland and saved me much trouble in finding conversation. It was a very nice pleasant dinner. No constraint, plenty of ice. Good champagne and the first salmon I have tasted this year, a nice curry, and the Riflemen strawberries quite magnificent. Everyone in good spirits and tempers and full of talk. Clifford Priory is certainly one of the nicest most comfortable houses in this part of the country. The evening was exquisite and the party wandered out into the garden promiscuously after dinner under the bright moon which shone alone in the unclouded sky. When the party re-assembled in the drawing room there was music, and meanwhile I had a long talk in the recessed window and moonlight with Helen of Troy. She and her sister were dressed prettily in blue, the most elegant and tasteful dresses I have seen this year. Mrs Allen asked me to a croquet party here next Tuesday, and Mr Allen asked me to luncheon at Oakfield on Monday when the Foresters are coming to his house. He brought me as far as Hay in the rumble of his most antiquated most comfortable old yellow chariot on C springs, very large broad and heavy and able to carry 7 people. We had 6 on board, Mrs Allen, Thomas and Pope inside, I preferred the night air and the tramping of the fast mare. Going up the hills we had before us the antiquated figure of the old coachman against the sky and amongst the stars. So we steadily rumbled into Hay and there

was a great light in the North shewing where the sun was travelling along below the horizon, and only just below.

Saturday, 9 July

It is a pretty lane this Bird's Nest lane, very shady and quiet, narrow and overbowered here and there with arching wyches and hazels. Sometimes my darling child Gipsy comes down to school this way, but more often she comes down Sunny Bank when the days are fine, and then over the stile by little Wern y Pentre. Yet often and often must those tiny feet have trodden this stony narrow green-arched lane, and those sweet blue eyes have looked down this vista to the blue mountains and those little hands have gathered flowers along these banks. O my child if you did but know. If you only knew that this lane and this dingle and these fields are sweet to me and holy ground for your sweet sake. But you can never know, and if you should ever guess or read the secret, it will be but a dim misty suspicion of the truth. Ah Gipsy.

As I came up the hill Bengough was playing his harmonium. When I went back he was working in his cowyard. There was something like autumn, a suspicion of late summer, a touch of autumnal stillness and melancholy in the afternoon. A great sultriness brooded over everything and made the air very oppressive and the mountains loomed dark blue.

Savine, the Clyro Court coachman, who is going to be confirmed, came in at 8 o'clock to say that he could not stay tonight for his lecture as he had to go to the 9 o'clock train with a pony to meet his master returning from a cricket match near Hereford, the Wyeside Wanderers against Portway. Savine rather amused me by saying that he had been preparing himself for confirmation by reading Revelations. 'I've read down Timothy too,' said he. How the Bishop would enjoy that.

Monday, 11 July

The view from my bedroom window looking up the dingle always reminds me of Norway, perhaps because of the spiry dark fir tops which rise above the lighter green trees. Often when I rise I look up to the white farm house of Penllan and think of the sweet grey eyes that have long been open and looking upon the pearly morning sky and the mists of the valley and the morning spread upon the mountains, and think of the young busy hands that have long been at work, milking or churning, with the sleeves rolled up the round arms as white and creamy as the milk itself, and the bright sweet morning face that the sunrise and the fresh early air have kissed into bloom and the sunny tresses ruffled by the mountain wind, and hope that the fatherless girl may ever be good, brave, pure and true. So help her God. The sun looks through her window which the great pear tree frames and lattices in green leaves and fruit, and the leaves move and flicker and throw a chequering shadow upon the white bedroom wall, and on the white curtains of the bed. And before the sun has touched the sleeping village in the shade below or has even struck the weathercock into a golden gleam, or has crept down the steep green slope of the lower or upper Bron, he has stolen into her bedroom and crept along the wall from chair to chair till he has reached the bed, and has kissed the fair hand and arm that lies upon the coverlet and the white bosom that heaves half uncovered after the restlessness of the sultry night, and has kissed her mouth whose scarlet lips, just parting in a smile and pouting like rosebuds to be kissed, show the pearly gleam of the white teeth, and has kissed the sweet face and the blue veined silky lashed eyelids and the white brow and the soft bright tangled hair, till she has unclosed the sweetest eyes that ever opened to the dawn, and risen and unfastened the casement and stood awhile breathing the fresh fragrant mountain air as it blows cool upon her flushed cheek and her half veiled bosom, and lifts and ruffles her bright hair which still keeps the kiss of the sun. Then when she has dressed and prayed towards the east, she goes out to draw water from the holy spring St Mary's Well. After which she goes about her honest holy work, all day long, with a light heart and a pure conscience.

Tuesday, 12 July
Walked to Clifford Priory across the fields with Crichton and Barton. Bevan and Morrell walked on before faster and got there before us. I had some pleasant talk with Barton, who is a clever well-read man, about Tennyson, Wordsworth, Mr Monkhouse, the Holy Grail, and at last we got to Clifford Priory, very hot, a few people out in the sun on the lawn, and Lucy Allen came to meet

us. A crowd in the drawing room drinking claret cup iced and eating enormous strawberries. Gradually people turned out on the lawn. Everyone about here is so pleasant and friendly that we meet almost like brothers and sisters. Great fun on the lawn, 6 cross games of croquet and balls flying in all directions. High tea at 7.30 and croquet given up. More than 40 people sat down. Plenty of iced claret cup, and unlimited fruit, very fine, especially the strawberries.

After tea we all strolled out into the garden and stood on the high terrace to see the eclipse. It had just begun. The shadow was slowly steadily stretching over the large bright moon and had eaten away a small piece at the lower left side. It was very strange and solemn to see the shadow stealing gradually on till half the moon was obscured. As the eclipse went on the bright fragment of the moon seemed to change colour, to darken and redden. We were well placed for seeing the eclipse and the night was beautiful, and most favourable, not a cloud in the way. We watched the eclipse till all that was left of the moon was a point of brightness like a large three-cornered star. Then it vanished altogether. Some people said they could discern the features of the moon's face through the black shadow.

Meantime we strolled about in different groups and William Thomas and Crichton ran a race up the steep slippery terrace bank. The ladies' light dresses looked ghostly in the dusk and at a little distance it was almost impossible to tell which was a lady in a white dress and which was a clump of tall white lilies. Mrs and Miss Bridge and Miss Oswald in almost white dresses walked about together arm in arm covered with one scarlet shawl and Jack Dew called them 'the three angels'. When they heard this they said they believed that in reality he had called them 'the three demons'. We wandered up into the twilit garden and there among the strawberries fastened to a little kennel by a collar and a light chain to keep the birds away was a most dear delightful white pussy, very like Polar. He was so delighted to see us that he walked round us purring loudly with his tail erect, rubbing himself against our legs, and he climbed up my leg as if it had been a tree. Three more cats were chained to kennels near the back door.

Wednesday, 13 July

Miss Lynne is a very nice sensible unaffected girl, rather pretty, with dark curls, grey eyes and a rich colour, and pretty little white hands. She is rather short. Her brother Clavering goes in for being comic and ends in being a bit of a buffoon. He has four dogs at the Swan now. His usual complement is thirteen. Miss Lyne told me a good deal about Father Ignatius and his monastery which she called 'his place' at Capel y Ffin.

Friday, St Swithin's Day

Familiar as this place is to me I am always noticing some fresh beauty or combination of beauties, light or shade, or a view from some particular point, where I have never been before at some particular hour and under some particular circumstances.

To Hay Church at 6.30. Afterwards I went to the Castle and found Mrs Bevan sitting in the drawing room in full chat with Miss Wybrow. We had tea and then I went down to the Swan with Fanny and Nelly to fetch Miss Lyne and her brother to play croquet. They were out and we went into the saloon to wait for them. Presently Miss Lyne passed the window with her quick decided step and we went out into the hall to meet her. She came forward and held out her hand so pleasantly, the beautiful little hand just what a lady's hand ought to be, 'small, soft, white, warm and dry'. Then we all tramped up into the town together and walked about with her while she went round to the shops paying their bills as they leave the Swan and Hay tomorrow for Hereford. And I am very sorry they are going, at least that she is going. It is so provoking that just as I have become acquainted with her and like her so much, and just as her shyness and reserve were beginning to wear off, and she had become so friendly and cordial, she goes away and perhaps I shall never see her again.

Clavering Lyne told me some of the extraordinary visions which had appeared to his brother Father Ignatius, particularly about the ghosts which come crowding round him and which will never answer though he often speaks to them. Also about the fire in the monastery chapel at Norwich, that strange unearthly fire which Father Ignatius put out by throwing himself into it and making the sign of the cross. When the Lynes went away I walked with them till our roads parted. One more cordial clasp from the pretty white hand, 'Good night and Good bye.' Shall I confess how I longed to kiss that beautiful white little hand, even at the imminent risk that it would instantly administer a stinging slap on the face of its admirer.

Saturday, 16 July
To-day we heard rumours of war and war itself. Henry Dew brought the news stated in the *Globe* that war had been declared by France against Prussia, the wickedest, most unjust most unreasonable war that ever was entered into to gratify the ambition of one man. I side with the Prussians and devoutly hope the French may never push France to the Rhine. Perhaps the war was a dire necessity to the Emperor to save himself and his dynasty. At all events the war is universally fearfully popular in France, and the French are in the wildest fever to go to the Rhine.

The party at Pont Vaen divided itself into croquet and archery. High tea at 7 just before which someone managed to shoot a chicken with an arrow, or it was said so, and Margaret Oswald told me that as I put my head through the railings to rake a croquet ball out of the field on to the lawn, my head looked so tempting that she felt greatly inclined to shoot at it. Certainly there would have been this comfort that if she had shot at me I should have been very much safer than if she had not, because wherever else the arrow might have gone it certainly would not have hit me.

At tea I sat between Miss and Mrs Oswald and opposite a tongue. May I never sit opposite a tongue again, at least if I have to carve it with a new round-headed small knife as blunt as a fruit knife. I heaved and hacked away at the tongue, cut it up into small bits, and made a complete wreck and ruin of it. The more the knife would not cut and the less tongue there was to give, the more people seemed to want it and asked me to send them some.

After tea Mrs Bridge took us round into the garden to show us her hives. One bee instantly flew straight at me and stung me between the eyes, as I was poking about the hives in my blind way. I did not say anything about it and Mrs Bridge congratulated me on my narrow escape from being stung. All the while the miserable bee was buzzing about entangled in my beard, having left his sting between my eyes. Consequently I suppose he was in his dying agony. Then we walked round the garden and along the water walk, while the water ran out of my eyes. The pretty waterfall did not show to advantage beneath the bridge for the brook ran very low and humble. Then a wild nonsensical game of croquet in the dark, everyone playing at the same time, and screams of laughter which might be heard almost in the Hay.

Tuesday, 19 July
Left Chippenham 11.35 by the down mail with a tourist ticket for Truro. The first few miles of Cornwall looked bleak, barren and uninteresting, the most striking feature being the innumerable mine works of lead, tin, and copper crowning the hills with their tall chimney shafts and ugly white dreary buildings, or nestling in a deep narrow valley, defiling and poisoning the streams with the white tin washing.

The country soon grew prettier, the prevailing feature of the landscape being low rounded hills like those of Radnorshire divided by very deep narrow valleys or ravines which the great timber viaducts crossed continually at a ghastly height in the air. The hill sides were clothed with a rich luxuriance of wood, chiefly oak. A man was mowing oats. Purple heather bloomed in great bunches and bushes along the railway embankments, like broom with us. A sea fog, which enveloped the hills like a mist of small rain and blotted out the distance, crept up the valleys along the streams and rose against the dark green oakwoods. H.[1] met me at Truro (where we changed for Perranwell) and drove me in the pony carriage from Perranwell to Tullimaar. The fulfilment of two years' dream.

Thursday, 21 July
Breakfast 6.45. Mrs H. drove us in the pony carriage to Perranwell Station in time for the 7.35 train to Hayle. The journey lay through a great mining district chiefly tin. The bowels of the earth ripped open, turned inside out in the search for metal ore, the land defiled and cumbered with heaps and wastes of slag and rubbish, and the waters poisoned with tin and copper washings. The Cornish villages bare bleak barren and ugly, whitewashed and

---

1. Hockin.

often unsheltered by a single tree, grouped or scattered about mountainous wastes.

About Godrevy and all along the North coast there are a great many seals. Once at Godrevy the H's saw a fearful battle between a seal and a large conger eel. The seal had got his teeth into the conger and the conger had coiled his folds round the seal's neck and was trying to choke him. The seal kept on throwing up his head and trying to toss the conger up out of the water that he might have more power than the eel. It was a fierce and dreadful fight, but at last the seal killed the conger.

The Vicar of St Ives says the smell of fish there is sometimes so terrific as to stop the church clock.

We did not know it at the time but while we were enjoying ourselves on the beach a poor miner who had gone out to bathe in his dinner hour was drowning in the bay very near us. The sea fog came rolling up from the Atlantic in a dense purple bank, and the sea changed colour to a deep dark green.

Friday, 22 July
Miss Emily and Miss Charlotte Hockin came from Truro to breakfast at 8.30. At 9.30 we all started to drive to Mullion in a nice roomy waggonette, large enough to carry 10 people, drawn by a pair of gallant greys. Drove through St Stithians to Gweek where we stopped to lunch by a hedge side and brook while one of the horses, who had cast a shoe just before, was being shod. A pretty road through woods and fields and across one or two trout streams, but still through a mining country, the mine stacks, works and chimneys rising white on every hill. Soon after this we got into the Serpentine district. The roads were made of marble, black marble, the dust of which looked like coal dust. The country became very wild and timber almost disappeared. Along the roadsides grew large bushes 3 and 4 feet high of beautiful heather, white, pink, and rose colour, growing as freely as gorse grows with us. We stopped the carriage and gathered some fine sprays. The splendour and luxuriance of the heather, I never saw anything like this before.

The strong square tower of Mullion Church stood up before us against the sky on the hill top as we mounted the last rise, and then the glimpse of the bay and the broad blue Cornish sea. Drove through the village to the Old Inn. Kept by Mary Mundy, a genuine Cornish Celt, and a good specimen of one, impulsive, warm-hearted, excitable, demonstrative, imaginative, eloquent. We went into a sitting room upstairs, unpacked the hampers, and ordered dinner to be ready when we came back in an hour's time. The sitting room was over the stable and we heard the horses stamping underneath. The window looked out over a waving field of reddening wheat which grew close up to the cottage wall, and the swaying ears of which were not far below the window sill.

[A walk is described.]

The ladies had not come in when we returned to the Old Inn and we had to wait dinner for them a long time. At length they appeared scarlet and almost exhausted, for the heat was tremendous and they had followed us over the cliffs, finishing up by losing their way, struggling across country over fences and through standing corn. They were almost too much exhausted to eat, and we were delayed until late in the afternoon.

At last we got off and drove to Kynance Cove. The carriage was left on the moors (or 'Croft' as it is called here) above, and we scrambled down into the Cove. The tide was ebbing fast and it was nearly low water. We wandered about through the Dining Room and Drawing Room Caves, and among the huge Serpentine Cliffs and the vast detached rocks which stand like giants guarding the Cove. I never saw anything like the wonderful colour of the serpentine rocks, rich, deep, warm, variegated, mottled and streaked and veined with red, green and white, huge blocks and masses of precious stone marble on every side, an enchanted cove, the palace of the Nereids.

In one of the Serpentine shops at the Lizard there was a stuffed Cornish Chough. He is an elegantly shaped black bird cleanly made with red or orange beak and legs. He is very rarely found now even along the Cornish Cliffs.

Saturday, 23 July
Mrs H. has two pet toads, which live together in a deep hole in the bottom of a stump of an old tree. She feeds them with bread crumbs when they are at home, and they make a funny little plain-

63

tive squeaking noise when she calls them. Sometimes they are from home especially in the evenings.

In the kitchen live a pair of doves in a large cage, and the house is filled with their soft sweet deep cooing.

Wednesday, 27 July

To the Land's End. Early breakfast at 7 and desperate rush to 7.35 train at Perranwell, Mrs H. driving in the pony carriage, H. and I running the short cut by the Church for bare life like rabbits. Caught the Truro train by one minute. From Truro to Penzance by rail. Capt. and Mrs Parker and Miss Lewis got in at Camborne from Rosewarne to join the picnic. By the time we reached Penzance I was becoming rather cooler. St Michael's Mount in mist and the sea very smooth. H. had telegraphed to the Western Hotel, Penzance, for a carriage and pair, and we were met at the station by a small waggonette with a bay and grey. With some difficulty we stowed all the hampers on board and set off driving along the beach for some distance till we turned inland along the pretty road to the cross road made by the meeting of the four beautiful avenues. A little further on an oak arched completely over the road, and the driver, Edward Noy, said that no other oak arched the road between this place and London.

There were some long steep hills on the road but the horses in perfect training took us up and down capitally. Capt. Parker was the life of the party and kept the waggonette in a roar. Egg sandwiches went round and presently we stopped to have sherry all round. When we were ready to go on Capt. Parker said to Mrs H., 'If we wanted a donkey to go on what would you say?' Then he added instantly in a loud voice, 'Proceed, Edward.' There was a roar from the waggonette, everyone was convulsed, and Edward grinned a tremendous grin, looked somewhat red and foolish, and *proceeded* amidst a storm of laughter. It was a very merry party. The Scilly telegraph wire accompanied us along the road.

The horses were put up at the inn and we walked by a narrow pass cut in the cliffs and over steep slippery rock slopes and ledges to the Logan Stone. At the foot of the steep rock on which the Logan Stone is balanced a man stood ready to show the way up, and when he saw me coming he began to run up just like a monkey. His action was so sudden, strange and wild, and so exactly that of a monkey clambering up the bars of his cage, that I looked to see whether he had a tail. He helped me up capitally with knee and hand. I could never have got up by myself for the rock faces were very steep, smooth and slippery. The guide wanted to put me up on to the top of the Logan Stone but I declined. He shewed me the cleft in the cliff into which the Logan Stone rolled when Lieutenant Goldsmith and his crew upset it. The guide first put his shoulder under the stone and rocked it, and then I did the same. It rocks perceptibly though very slightly. But it has never rocked so well and easily since it was wilfully thrown down. The perfect balance of nature could never be restored.

I found the rest of the party waiting for me sitting on the opposite rock. An elderly grizzled man in a blue slop was offering photographs for sale. He was a boy when the Logan Stone was upset 46 years ago, and he remembered its being replaced.

As we returned to the wild granite village along the field paths a rude vulgar crew of tourists (real British) passed us going down to the cliffs, grinning like dogs, and one of the male beasts said in a loud insolent voice evidently meant for us to hear, 'I hope they haven't upset the Logan Rock'. For a moment I devoutly wished that we had.

The village was a paradise of black pigs which lay about in the glare of the sun under the hot granite walls par-roasted but in great content.

At the inn we had some ale and cider. The horses were put to and we drove on to the nearest point which we could reach by carriage. Here H., Captain P. and I alighted, waved adieu to the ladies, who drove on to the Land's End while we walked to the same point along the coast and over the line of magnificent cliffs and headlands which stand between.

[The walk is described.]

Crossing the croft near the Inn while gathering heath Capt. P. killed a snake or viper with his stick, ripped it open with his knife and found three young mice inside. Edward Noy came to meet us, saying the ladies were waiting for us down among the rocks, and sure enough they were waiting and had been waiting for an hour or more. Famished they were and some of them sleeping for hunger.

The Inn and a tent outside the house were occupied by a large vulgar picnic party, so we had our nice dinner among the rocks in aristocratic simplicity and seclusion. A '*duke*' is truly a lordly dish.

I am told that the wind here at times is so furious that four men have been wanted to take a lady out of her carriage and carry her into the Inn. Two young men have been needed to take an old man to his work, supporting him one on each side against the wind. A carriage has been lifted up into the air by the wind with its wheels whirling round. The panels and windows of a carriage have been so cut and scratched by the granite-dust and sand (which when blown by the wind cuts and scores like diamond dust) that the carriage has had to be repainted and the windows replaced because they were so scratched that it was impossible to see through them. Sometimes the Inn windows have to be barricaded as if a storm of rifle balls was expected.

After dinner Capt. P. took Miss Lewis and me down to the Land's End, a little triangular point of rock reached by passing round to the seaward side of a tall upright shaft of cliff. The accomplishment of an old dream.

Coming back we met a noisy rabble of tourists, males and females, rushing down the rocks towards the Land's End as if they meant to break their necks, and no great loss either. The rest of the insufferable snobs had of course been endeavouring to insult the ladies and Capt. Parker suggested that a kicking might tend to mind their manners.

Drive back to Penzance.

I like Penzance.

We drove down the old long Market Jew Street, stopped at the fishmonger's, and then past the Market Jew Chapel under repair where several coffined children have lately been found stopped into holes and corners in the roof. Probably they were unbaptized children.

The Penzance people and especially the women are said to be the handsomest in Cornwall.

Mrs H. drove me to Truro in the pony carriage. Shopping, and then we joined the Truro Hockins and a party of their friends, young people chiefly, for a picnic down the river. We rowed or rather were rowed by boatmen down to Tregothnan, two boatloads of us, the hostess very nervous and fearful lest both boats should go to the bottom. We landed just above Tregothnan and walked up through pretty woods to the beautiful Church of St Michael Pen Kevil, restored by Lord Falmouth at a great expense.

Some of the party waited outside for us in the drive and we walked up to the house, and down the other hill to the boat house, just above which we had tea all across the road completely obstructing the thoroughfare. Our hostess reclined gracefully on her side up the slope of a steep bank and thus enthroned or embedded dispensed tea and *heavy* cake and was most hospitable. The young ladies remarked with severity upon H. and myself for not being sufficiently attentive to their pretty wants. How could we be so inattentive to such fascinating creatures? They suggested it was because we were taking such uncommonly good care of ourselves. Listen to the voice of the Charmers. Is not this a caution to snakes? Charmeth she wisely?

I unhappily mistook butter for cream (Tell it not in Truro) and was much concerned about our hostess lest she roll down the bank into the river. Also I was exceedingly puzzled to find out how it was that she did not so roll, for *what was to hinder it*?

The youngest girl, Agatha, I think, planted herself before me and demanded impetuously and imperiously in a loud voice, 'What do you want?' 'A kiss', said I mischievously, whereat she flung off in high disdain without a word. But being of a forgiving nature she presently returned and brought me some food.

After tea the young ladies rowed us across the river to see Old Quay Tower. The tide was too low to admit of our landing, but the pinnacles of the old tower looked pretty among the trees in the sunset. Young lady affectations, peculiarities, vagaries, &c., &c., unintelligible.

Friday, 29 July

A most delightful expedition and picnic at Gurnards Head. We drove to Camborne in the pony carriage and got to Rosewarne at 11. A large omnibus and pair was waiting to drive us on with the Parkers' party. I preferred going outside to see the country. The road not very bad, but the hills severe and our miserable horses nearly gruelled, almost fainting from thirst and fatigue, all abroad scrambling and staggering all over the place. Once in a narrow part of the road the wheel tottered on the edge of a bank. We yawed about frightfully, the horses were too much done to pull straight or steady. Another lurch and we should have gone head over heels into the field below, such a roly poly, broken bones if nothing worse and the doctor to pay. Happily there was one on board. Then the tyre of the near face wheel almost came off, and had to be inadequately tinkered on again.

Captain Parker came outside with me. We were consulting his map and looking at the country. A sudden shout from the bowels of the omnibus, 'Wo-way-halt hold hard.' 'What's the row?' called Capt. Parker from the top of the omnibus, craning down to see what was the matter inside. 'The sherry's flying all about,' was the reply. 'Miss Lewis has upset every drop of hers.' A roar of inextinguishable laughter, sherry all round, and 'Proceed, Edward'.

The horses were driven into a pond in order to drink and cool their heels and tighten the tyres of the omnibus wheels. (What a beautifully accidental couplet.) Then we came to Zennor, the strange old tower in the granite wilderness in a hollow of the wild hillside, a corner and end of the world, desolate, solitary, bare, dreary, the cluster of white and grey houses round the massive old granite Church tower, a sort of place that might have been quite lately discovered and where 'fragments of forgotten peoples might dwell'.

'*None of your larks*', said Capt. Parker occasionally and reprovingly to the people inside. But he was the most larky of the party.

We were encouraged to hold on tight to the roof of the omnibus by the intelligence that a Captain had fallen from the box seat of this very omnibus a few weeks ago and had been killed.

At last we got to the Gurnards Head Hotel, the gentlemen walking across some fields while the ladies drove swiftly round. Then the scrimmage of unpacking the hampers and everybody of course in everybody's else way. A capital dinner indoors, the Tullimaar *'dukes'* delicious and I actually ate and liked a slice of melon and like Oliver Twist asked for 'more'. Memorable day. How do all the ghosts of those rejected melons now rise up and accuse me.

Dinner over and another scrimmage of repacking got through. We all streamed out down to the Head.

Oh that sunny happy evening gathering ferns among the Cliffs. *Asplenium Marinum,* with its bright glossy green leaves, hiding itself so provokingly in the narrowest crevices of the rocks. I wandered round the cliffs to the broken rocks at the furthest point of the Head, and sat alone amongst the wilderness of broken shattered tumbled cliffs, listening to the booming and breaking of the waves below and watching the flying skirts of the showers of spray. Perfect solitude. The rest of the party were climbing about in the rocks somewhere overhead, but not a voice or sound was to be heard except the boom of the sea and the crying of the white-winged gulls. Not a sign or vestige of any other living thing.

A scramble up among the rocks to search for ferns for Mrs H. Not very successful, and H. had got her some much finer ones, but she did not despise mine, though they were very poor little ones in comparison.

The rest of the party had come down from a scrambling like goats and conies in the high rocks, the ladies having had to mount by means of the gentlemen's backs and knees.

We returned by Penzance hearing it was a better road, and we did not repent of it.

It was getting very chilly on the top of the omnibus. Mrs H. very kindly sent me out her waterproof cloak to put on and oh how warm and comfortable it was. We reached Camborne soon after 11 and sat down to dinner or supper at midnight at Rosewarne, that hospitable house, after depositing some of the party at their own houses in the town. Mrs Parker is an admirable hostess. I took her in to supper and had some talk with her about Wales and Monmouthshire where she used to live. She tells me her brother has lately taken Bronllys Castle in Breconshire. The dining room at Rosewarne is beautifully hung round with horns, antelope, stag, gnu, buffalo, &c. &c. We left the hospitable house at 1 and got home about 3 in the morning. Daylight had not appeared, but it was a clear case of 'We won't go home till morning'. As we passed down the creekside the masts of a vessel showed against the sky. A sailing lighter had come up the creek at high tide with a load of limestone and was lying at the quay waiting to unload and go down again with the next tide.

This morning we met two girls smartly dressed and driving cows to market with parasols up.

Friday, 5 August
The last pleasant excursion. The last happy day. Martin had been sent to Falmouth overnight for a carriage and horse and brought back a grey heavy horse and hooded carriage in which he drove us this morning to Godrevy.

We called at Camborne (Rosewarne) to leave an Inverness cloak which Capt. Parker lent me to drive home in last Friday, and the kind hospitable people made us promise to call on our return and have supper or something.

Redruth Market and people hurrying about with conger eels.
Sorrowful dreams.

We met with several sharp white squalls and had all to crowd for shelter under the hood with an umbrella up in front.

H. suggested that passers by would say, 'There go a lady and gentleman with a child.'

The road led us along the top of the cliffs.

Leaving Mrs H. in the carriage to drive on to Gwythian Church Town, H. and I struck across the down to see the British Church buried in the sand.

We came to the place suddenly and without warning and looked down into the church as into a long pit. The sand is drifted solid up to the very top of the outside walls. The walls are about four feet high measured from the inside. So far they are almost perfect. The material is granite with a good deal of pure felspar, of which I brought away a pretty pink piece. The church is quite a small building, oblong, a door and window place still perceptible, and the faint remains of the rude pillars of a chancel arch still to be made out. Within the memory of persons still living the altar was standing, but the place has got into the hands of a dissenting farmer who keeps the place for a cattle yard and sheep fold and what more need be said. I do wish that some people of influence in the neighbourhood would bestir themselves and rescue from utter destruction and oblivion this most interesting relic of the earliest British Christianity, that which came to us direct from the East.

Probably there was a Christian Church at Gwythian before St Augustine landed in England to bring us the Roman version of Christianity.

These sand hills are very restless, always shifting. They overwhelm ancient buildings and then reveal them after they have been hidden for centuries. The sand passes on in its progress to form hills elsewhere and gives up its prey. Suddenly the monument and relic of an olden world and more primitive ancient simple religion is revealed. The sand and the centuries have been kinder than the dissenting farmer.

We found Mrs H. waiting for us at Gwythian Church, and crossing the moor we caught sight of the top of Godrevy Lighthouse over the line of sand towans, and heard the roaring of the sea.

I took a great fancy to this village by the sea, with its nice Church and schools. The curate complained a good deal about the people and their ineradicable tendency to dissent.

In the churchyard is the grave of a former curate of Gwythian, a Mr Drury, who was drowned amongst the rocks near Godrevy on Palm Sunday evening, 1865. It is supposed that his dog pulled him into one of these horrible deep chasms and crevices amongst the rocks, or that he fell in whilst playing with his dog and pushing him into the water, for he was a beautiful swimmer and would not have been drowned probably in open water. The body was found among the rocks by a man gathering sand or seaweed on the shore, and brought home in his cart.

There is a coloured window in the church to Drury's memory. In the churchyard, overhanging the road, is a magnificent fruit-bearing fig tree, covering a vast space of ground. The figs on the top of the tree only ripen and become fit to eat. The horse was put in the carriage again and we drove heavily through the deep sand to the shore, passing a red river and tin stamping works rattling clanking pounding away amongst the sand hills.

The horse was put up at a farm house and Martin ordered to beg borrow or (not steal, but) take some corn for him, and then bring up the luncheon hamper to the rocks. Martin appeared with the rug and basket and we had luncheon. He amused me by retiring to a respectful distance with his share of the provender and grinning over a rock, nothing but his black head to be seen, like a seal with a tall hat on. After luncheon we went down on the beach to look for sea anemones among the rocks and pools at low water for Mrs H. We found a green one. H. and I went out nearly to the end of the rocks where the waves were plunging and flying in foam over the reef, and presently we saw a large seal a hundred yards off fishing among the rocks near the shore. His black head was like a dog swimming and something like the head of a man. He dived suddenly, then came up again, disappeared again, and once more appeared with his large black shiny head not more than 50 yards from us, stationary, floating and riding easily, rising and falling with the swell, sometimes looking round at us with his great bright eye. It was the first seal I had ever seen wild, and I was delighted.

Grapes and claret on a grassy bank and we drove back to Camborne reaching Rosewarne at 7.

We walked round the pretty flower gardens and fine kitchen garden and visited the ferns and fruit houses. Dinner at 8 and a most admirable conger eel. I had no idea conger was so good, or good at all. As we drove away the church clock struck ten and the granite pillars sparkled in the moonlight.

Home at midnight and hot supper, roast fowl.

Saturday, 6 August
Up at 6. Finished packing and rushed down the Truro drive to get some sprays from the bush of white heather. The trees were all dripping from early showers, the tears of the morning. The morning was fresh cool and lovely and the beautiful place looked more beautiful than ever.

H. drove me and my luggage to the first train, 7.35. A hurried rush but we arrived a minute too late. There was nothing for it but to leave the luggage at the station and return to Tullimaar to wait for the next train at 11.5. After the first feeling of annoyance and disappointment I was glad to have missed the train as it gave me another pleasant morning.

The morning sunshine and shadows of the overhanging trees chequered and dappled the fish pond, and the gold and silver fish gleamed as they sailed from shadow into sunlight. Mrs H. was planting ferns, the Gurnard's Head *Asplenium*, in the potting house, and I leaned on the window sill outside watching her and making her laugh with Cowper's 'Tithing Time'. 'The Parson merry is and blithe' &c.

The second parting.

And so endeth a very happy time.

Monday, 8 August
Today came the news of the two battles of Forbach and Woerth won by the Prussians on Saturday. 'France is reeling under two fearful blows.' I read this sentence in the *Standard* in the High St Chippenham whilst waiting for my Mother at Noyes' shop door, in the carriage.

Tuesday, 9 August
Wharry the Chemist told us he had been in Normandy, found it very uncomfortable, was mobbed, and very glad to get out of the country. He says unless you go all lengths with the French and take their part through thick and thin they consider that you are against them, and accordingly treat you as an enemy.

Thursday, 11 August
The weather has become intensely hot again. There are such quantities of apricots this year and they all ripen so fast together that there is no knowing what to do with them. A great number have been given away.

Old John Bryant told my Father today as they were talking about the War that he remembered the news coming that the King of France's head had been cut off. He was a boy at the time, 13 years old, helping to drain a field near Bull's Copse at Tytherton, and he heard the men with whom he was working talking about the news that had just come.

[The diarist returns to Clyro.]

Monday, 15 August

This being the Napoleon Fête Day it has been supposed that the Emperor would hazard a battle for the sake of French sentiment. Went to see the old soldier and talk to him about the War. I asked him as an old enemy of the French which side he took, French or Prussian. He said he knew nothing of the Germans, the French were more natural to him and he wished them well. They were very kind to him, he said, when he was quartered in the Allied Army at a small village near Arras. He helped them to dig their fields, garden, cut wood or do anything that was wanted. In return they rewarded him by giving him their nice white bread, while the dark hard ration went to the pigs. Morgan said there was often a good and friendly feeling between English and French soldiers when they were in the field. He had often been on picquet duty less than 50 yards from the French sentries. He would call out, 'Bon soir'. The Frenchmen would sing out in return 'Will you boire?' Then they would lay down their arms, meet in the middle space and drink together. Morgan liked drinking with the French sentries because they mostly had something hot. He believes and believed then that if they had been caught fraternizing he would have been shot or hung.

Friday, 19 August

Ben Lloyd of the Cwm Bryngwyn reeling up the steep fields above Jacob's Ladder carrying a horse collar and butter tub. Just as I came up the drunken man fell sprawling on his back. He got up looking foolish and astonished, and I gave him some good advice which he took in good part at first. I asked if he were married. Oh, yes, and had great-grandchildren. A nice example to set them, I thought. When I said how his wife would be vexed and grieved to see him come rolling home, I found I had touched a tender point. He became savage at once, cursed and swore and threatened violence. Then he began to roar after me, but he could only stagger very slowly so I left him behind reeling and roaring, cursing parsons and shouting what he would do if he were younger, and that if a man did not get drunk he wasn't a man and of no good to himself or the public houses, an argument so exquisite that I left it to answer itself.

On the Little Mountain the gorse that glowed and flamed fiery gold down the edge of the hill contrasted sharp and splendid with the blue world of mountain and valley which it touched.

Tuesday, 30 August
Hay Flower Show, the first they have had, a very successful one. A nice large tent, the poles prettily wreathed with hop vine, and the flowers fruit and vegetables prettily arranged. There was an excursion train from Builth to Hay for the occasion. The town was hung with flags. The whole country was there. A row of pretty girls, Bevans and Thomases, were sitting on a form which broke down and left the whole row sprawling on their backs, with their heels in the air. Fanny Thomas was the only one who had any presence of mind about ancles. It was quite a case of being 'on view' and 'open to the public' and 'no reserve'. Twice round the tent was enough and as Trotter of the Bank and I were shaking hands with impressive cordiality our enthusiasm was so great that we tore off the top of an *Osmunda* frond.

Friday, 2 September
At 10.45 started across the fields to walk to Capel y Ffin. I came in sight of the little Capel y Ffin squatting like a stout grey owl among its seven great black yews. I hastened on, and in front of the Capel House farm there was the sunny haired girl washing at a tub as usual by the brook side, the girl with the blue eyes, not the blue of the sky, but the blue of the sea. 'Is Father Ignatius here?' I asked. 'Yes, at least he was here this morning.' I asked a mason at work upon the building if Father Ignatius was there. 'There he is with his brother,' said the mason. A black robed and cowled monk was walking fast along the bottom of the field towards a barn with Clavering Lyne. Clavering came up to me, but the monk walked quickly on without looking round. Clavering took me to his father and mother, who were sitting on a garden seat under a tree in a pretty little dingle. They had just arrived unexpectedly from Pontrilas having driven up the valley as I came down. It was curious, our meeting thus as it were by chance.

Mr and Mrs Lyne came up out of their dingle and Mrs Lyne brought up Father Ignatius and introduced us. He struck me as being a man of gentle simple kind manners, excitable, and entirely possessed by the one idea. He always spoke to his father and mother as 'Papa' and 'Mamma' and called me 'Father'. I could not persuade him that my name was not Venables. His head and brow are very fine, the forehead beautifully rounded and highly imaginative. The face is a very saintly one and the eyes extremely beautiful, earnest and expressive, a dark soft brown. When excited they seem absolutely to flame. He wears the Greek or early British tonsure all round the temples, leaving the hair of the crown untouched. His manner gives you the impression of great earnestness and singlemindedness. The voice and manner are very like Clavering's and it was with difficulty that I could tell which of the two was speaking if I did not see them. Father Ignatius wore the black Benedictine habit with the two loose wings or pieces falling in front and behind, two violet tassels behind, the knotted scourge girdle, a silver cross on the breast, and a brazen or golden cross hanging from the rosary of black beads under the left arm.

We walked round the place and then climbed the steep bank above and looked down upon the building. Mrs Lyne gathered some whinberries and gave them to us to eat. They were very nice. They grew along the ground on tiny bushes among a very small delicately twisted pink heath. We saw the monks and novices below issuing from a barn where they had engaged for an hour or so in an 'examination of conscience'. One of the monks was gazing at us. He had conceived an irrepressible desire to see Mrs Lyne again. He did not wish to intrude upon her approach or address her. He simply wanted to see her at a respectful distance and admire her afar off. Mr Lyne said the monk was a man of few and simple wants, content with a little and thankful for small mercies. Because the monk had said that if he could see Mrs Lyne he would be perfectly happy.

Mrs Lyne not having much faith in the larder or resources of the monastery, especially on a Friday, had wisely taken the precaution of bringing with her an honest leg of mutton and two bottles of wine. The monasterial garden provided potatoes and French beans, very good, and we had luncheon under the tree in the dingle, waited on by the novices also cowled and robed in black like the monks. They addressed Father Ignatius as 'dear Father' whenever they spoke to him and bent the knee whenever they approached or passed him.

Whilst we were at luncheon we heard voices close to us proceeding from the bottom of a deep watercourse or lane, on the other side of the hedge. Then a man looked over the hedge and asked his way to Capel y Ffin. Father Ignatius had been sitting talking freely and at ease with his head uncovered, and his cowl lying back on his shoulders. But directly he heard the strange voices and saw the strange face peering over the hedge he dashed the cowl over his head and face and bolted up the bank among the shrubs like a rabbit. I never saw a man so quick on his legs or so sudden in movement. He was gone like a flash of lightning. He has been much intruded on and persecuted and dreads seeing strangers about the place. Last night some men came up from Llanthony Abbey and rung the monastery bells violently and were very rude and insolent. However he treated them kindly and they apologized for their conduct and went away conquered.

After luncheon we went up to the monastery again and Mr and Mrs Lyne, Clavering and I each laid a stone in the wall. We had to go up a ladder on to the scaffolding and hoarding. Each of us 'walled' our stone for the benefit of the masons. I laid a stone at the particular request of Father Ignatius. The building that the masons are at work on now is the west cloister which is to be fitted up temporarily for the accommodation of the monks. This work was begun in March and ought to have been finished long ago. But there was no one to look after the workmen and they did as much or as little as they pleased. Father Ignatius thinks every one is as good as himself and is perfectly unworldly, innocent and un-suspicious. He gave the contractor £500 at first, took no receipt from him. And so on. The consequence is that he has been imposed upon, cheated and robbed right and left. Father Ignatius took us into the Oratory, a tiny square room in the Cloister, fitted with a lace and silk-covered altar upon which stands a super altar or Tabernacle in which he informed us in a low awestruck voice was 'the Blessed Sacrament'. There was a couch in the room on which he sleeps. The altar lace came from France, and was very expensive. There was a crucifix above the altar. It came from Spain and had been broken, but it was a beautiful figure. Father Ignatius said that once when he was praying Gerald Moultrie who was present saw the crucifix roll its eyes, then turn its head and look at Father Ignatius. Father Ignatius confessed that neither he nor any of the monks had ever seen the crucifix move. He did not know what to think about it, but he could not help believing that Moultrie saw what he declared he saw. He says that Moultrie is not at all an excitable imaginative man. As he was talking about this in a low eager whisper, he looked strange and wild and his eyes were starting and blazing. He apologized for Mr Lyne's not kneeling at the altar by saying that his father did not believe in the Real Presence. He knelt for a moment at the side of the altar.

Mr Lyne was anxious to be going as they had ten miles to drive down a bad road to Pontrilas. So they got their dog-cart. Clavering drove and we parted in the lane. They drove off and I remained in the lane talking to Father Ignatius. I had a good deal of conversation with him then and at luncheon time. He told me that Lord Bute came up to see him and the monastery a few days ago, and to make enquiries. He greatly hopes Lord Bute may help him and send him money. The Order of St Benedict, Father Ignatius says, is now worth about £60. The monks are supported entirely by his preaching. He makes £1000 a year. He gets on much better with the Low Church than with the High Church people he says, best of all with the Dissenters who consider and call him a second Wesley. He allows that a man must be of a very rare and peculiar temperament to become and remain a monk. A monk he says must either be a philosopher or a 'holy fool'. He also allows that monkery has a strong tendency to drive people mad. Out of 50 novices he could only reckon on making 3 monks. The rest would probably be failures. One in seven was a large percentage.

One of the novices was a fine noble looking boy, a gentleman's son, with a sweet open face and fair clustering curly hair. He had been sent to the new monastery by his parents to learn to be a monk. The boy seemed to be devoted to Father Ignatius and came running up with a basket of mushrooms he had just bought to show them to the Father. His cowl was thrown back and his fair young head, bright face and sunny hair made a striking contrast with his black robe. 'Yes, dear Father. No, dear Father.' And off he went in high delight with his mushrooms and the approval of the Father, as happy as a king and much happier. Poor child. I wonder if he will ever become a monk. I hope he is reserved for a better fate. He shook hands with us all before he went off to the barn. His hand was as small, soft and white as a girl's. They called him 'Manny'. Another of the novices, of lower rank in life, one who waited on us at luncheon, had a peculiarly sweet and beautiful face. He is called Brother Placidus.

I stood in the lane near the Honddu bridge for some time talking with Father Ignatius. I asked him if he would not find an ordinary dress more convenient and practical and less open to insult and objection. But he scouted the idea of abandoning his distinctive monastic dress. He said he had once given it up for a few days, but he felt like a deserter and traitor till he took to the habit again. Then he again became happy. The Bishop of Gloucester and Bristol, he said, had suggested the same thing, but he turned the tables on the Bishop by asking him why he did not discard his own foolish and meaningless dress, far more irrational than the Benedictine habit, every part of which has its meaning. The Bishop laughed and said there was a good deal in what Father Ignatius said. He thinks the Bishops are coming round to his side. We shook hands and departed. 'Goodbye, Father,' he said with an earnest kindly look, 'and thank you for your good wish. You must come and see us again when we have our guest house ready.' When we had parted a little way and our roads had diverged he called out through the half screen of a hazel hedge, 'Father ! Will you remember us the next time you celebrate the Holy Communion?' 'Yes,' I replied, 'I will.'

Saturday, 3 September
The news was brought from Hereford this afternoon that Mac-Mahon's army had been surrounded and had capitulated and that the Emperor had surrendered himself in person and given up his sword to the King of Prussia. What a tremendous collapse. We waited and waited dinner and at last it appeared that we were waiting for the Llanthomases. Presently they came in, a little before 8. They had walked from Llanigon, their waggonette having broken down directly they started. I sat next to Mrs Bridge at dinner and we had a very merry time. Coming home at midnight

there was a pitiful thing. At Wye Cliff gate I overtook a little girl taking her tipsy father home. It was dark but I thought I recognized Sarah Lewis' plaintive voice.

Tuesday, 6 September
We went into the green orchard where beautiful waxen-looking August apples lay in the grass, under the heavily loaded trees. Williams gave me a pocket full of apples. The postman came in with the latest news, the *Evening Standard*. Williams tore the paper open and we saw the reports of Saturday confirmed and that a Republic had been proclaimed in Paris under General Trocher. Crichton sent me 1½ brace of partridges. Really people are very kind in sending me game.

Saturday, 10 September
We all left Newbridge for Clyro at 12.20. At Llechrhyd I saw Mary Bevan on the platform waiting to get into our train. Mary of course got into our carriage. At Three Cocks she took Mr Venables aside and told him that a dreadful calamity had happened. On Wednesday morning the turret ship *Captain* went down at sea with 500 men. Capt. Cowper Coles who constructed her was on board and went down with the rest. Mary Bevan thought Capt. Coles was Mr Venables' brother in law and very sensibly refrained from saying anything of what she had heard or seen in the *Western Post* of this morning until she could speak to Mr Venables alone. He waited till they got home to break the news to Mrs V. It is a terrible blow to her and all the family. Poor Mrs Coles and her 9 children. And no one left to tell the tale, or why the ship went down. *The Times* of today confirms the sad news.

Thursday, 13 September
Mrs Venables gave me a letter of Captain Chandos Stanhope to read and letters from Lily and Edmund Thomas with others from Southsea, all about the loss of the *Captain*. We have the gunner's account now. He says the ship turned suddenly bottom upwards in a squall and then went down so. He and some other men scrambled upon her hull and for a minute or two actually stood upon her bottom. What a sight. What a moment. And what a

terrible [   ] for the 500 men entangled and surprised below deck. She was top heavy, had too much 'top hamper' and too low a free board, so that when she heeled over in the squall she had no high broadside to oppose to and press against the water, and so she turned upside down at once.

Wednesday, 14 September

I dined at the Vicarage. Poor Mrs Venables terribly distressed by Capt. Coles' death in the disaster of the *Captain*. She utterly broke down at dinner time and cried quietly and bitterly. I never saw her cry before.

Thursday, 15 September

Hay Fair. Roads lively with men, horses and sheep. We were busy all day dressing the Church or preparing decorations. Mrs Price and Miss Elcox had got a quantity of wild hops from their fields and were arranging bright red apples for ornament. Also they had boughs loaded with rosy apples and quantities of bright yellow Siberian crabs. At the school the children were busy leasing out corn from a loose heap on the floor, sitting among the straw and tying up wheat, barley and oats in small sheaves and bundles. Gipsy Lizzie was amongst them, up to her beautiful eyes in corn and straw. The schoolmaster, the boys and I gathering stringed ivy from the trees in the Castle Clump. The Miss Baskervilles dressing the hoops for the seven window sills with flowers and fruit. Mrs Morrell undertook to dress the reading desk, pulpit, and clerk's desk, and did them beautifully. Then Cooper came down with his men carrying magnificent ferns and plants and began to work in the chancel. One fine silver fern was put in the font. Gibbins undertook the font and dressed it very tastefully with moss and white asters under the sweeping fronds of the silver fern. Round the stem were twined the delicate light green sprays of white convolvulus. The pillars were wreathed and twined with wild hop vine falling in graceful careless festoons and curling tendrils from wreath and capital. St Andrew crossed sheaves of all sorts of corn were placed against the walls between the windows, wheat, barley and oats with a spray of hop vine drooping in a festoon across the sheaf butts and a spray of red barberries between the sheaf heads. Bright flowers in pots clustered round the spring of the arches upon the capital of the pillars, the flower pots veiled by a twist of hop vine. Mrs Partridge returned from Worcestershire this afternoon and brought and sent us two magnificent branches of real hops from the Worcestershire hop yards. These we hung drooping full length on either side of a text Mrs V. had made, white letters on scarlet flannel, 'I am the Vine. Ye are the branches. Without Me ye can do nothing.' And from the corners of this text Cooper hung two bunches of purple grapes. Two texts in corn on green baize. 'Praise ye the Lord' in wheat ears, and 'Thanks be to God' in oats were placed over the doors, inside. Outside the great door branches of apples and pears hung over the door. The gates were dressed with ferns, fruit and flowers. Following the outer arch, within a border of Spanish chestnuts, oak and acorn, elderberries, barberries and apples, was Mr Evans' text in scarlet letters on a bright blue ground, 'Enter into His Gates with Thanksgiving'. An avenue of tall ferns and coleus led up the chancel. A row of the same plants stood along the altar steps, and dahlias were laid on brae fern along the altar rail bars. On either side of the entrance to the altar hung a splendid cluster of purple grapes, and along the rails were tied at intervals small sheaves of wheat and tall heads of Pampas grass. On the altar stood two sheaves of all corn with a paten between them worked in scarlet flannel bordered with corn and IHS worked in wheat ears. Above this hung a cross covered with scarlet flannel and adorned with corn barberries. On the window sill above stood a larger sheaf of all corn in a moss field and upon the moss lay all fruit, plums, apples, pears.

Tuesday, 20 September
The sky a cloudless deep wonderful blue, and the mountains so light blue as to be almost white. The slight mist of an early autumn afternoon hanging over the gorgeous landscape. This morning there was a heavy dense white mist, which hung till noon, a real old fashioned September fog.

Went up the orchard bank in preference to Jacob's Ladder, but found the spiked gate at the top locked and had to climb over it. Just below on the orchard bank grew an apple tree whose bright red boughs and shoots stood up in beautiful contrast against the light blue mountains and grey town and the blue valley. And the grey tower of Clyro Church peeped through the bright red branches. A sack half filled with apples stood under a tree but no one was about. A woodpecker was tapping loud some way down Jacob's Ladder. Partridge shooting on all round.

From the stile on the top of the hill above the plantation watched the sun set in a crimson ball behind the hills or rather into a dense ball of dark blue vapour. It was like seeing a sunset over the sea. He went down very fast. All the country round was full of evening sounds, children's voices, dogs barking, the clangour of geese. Meanwhile the sheep fed quietly round me. Then came the afterglow round the S. and E. Scarlet feathers floated in the sky, and the gorse deepened into a richer redder gold in the sunset light.

Wednesday, 21 September
Another dense white fog which cleared off to cloudless blue and brilliant sunshine at 11. As I sat with my windows open at noon writing, the rustle of the glossy bright poplar leaves filled the room as the leaves twinkled and shimmered up the green poplar spire into the blue.

Went to the Bronith. People at work in the orchard gathering up the windfall apples for early cider. The smell of the apples very strong. Beyond the orchards the lone aspen was rustling loud and mournfully a lament for the departure of summer. Called on the old soldier. He was with his wife in the garden digging and gathering red potatoes which turned up very large and sound, no disease, and no second growth, an unusual thing this year. The great round red potatoes lay thick, fresh and clean on the dark newly turned mould. I sat down on the stones by the spring and the old soldier came and sat down on the stones by me while his wife went on picking up the red potatoes. We talked about the war and the loss of the *Captain*. Mary Morgan brought me some apples, Sam's Crabs and Quinin's. The spring trickled and tinkled behind us and a boy from the keeper's cottage came to draw water in a blue and white jug.

It was very quiet and peaceful in the old soldier's garden as we sat by the spring while the sun grew low and gilded the apples in the trees which he had planted, and the keeper's wife moved about in the garden below, and we heard the distant shots at partridges.

I dug up the half row of potatoes for him which he had left unfinished.

Monday, 26 September
Magistrates' meeting at noon. Two Clyro cases. An unsuccessful attempt by Samuel Evans' daughter and wife of the Bird's Nest to father the daughter's base child upon Edward Morgan of Cwmpelved Green. It came out that Mrs Evans had been shameless enough to let the young man sit up at night with Emily after she and her husband had gone to bed. Mrs V. most properly reprimanded her publicly and turned her out of the Club. Such conduct ought to be strongly marked and disapproved. The other case was the Crowther's Pool fighting case which was burked and settled out of court.

Wednesday, 28 September, Michaelmas Eve
I went out for a walk with Mr G. Venables over the Doldowlod suspension bridge across the Wye and up the Llandrindod road.

We fell into conversation about Wordsworth and the following are some of Mr George Venables' recollections of him.

'I was staying at Ambleside with some people who knew Wordsworth and was introduced to him there. Then I went over to tea at his house, Rydal Mount. Wordsworth's sister Dorothy was in the room, an old woman at that time. She was depressed and took no part in the conversation and no notice of what was passing. Her brother told me he attributed the failure of her health and intellect to the long walks she used to take with him, e.g. from Llyswen to Llanthony.

'He said he met "Peter Bell" on the road between Builth and Rhayader.

'One evening riding near Rydal I saw Wordsworth sauntering towards me wearing a shade over his eyes, which were weak, and crooning out aloud some lines of a poem which he was composing. I stopped to avoid splashing him and apologized for having intruded upon him. He said, "I am glad I met you for I want to consult you about some lines I am composing in which I want to make the shadow of Etna fall across Syracuse, the mountain being 40 miles from the city. Would this be possible?" I replied that there was nothing in the distance to prevent the shadow of the mountain falling across the city. The only difficulty was that Etna is exactly North of Syracuse. "Surely", said Wordsworth, "it is a little N.E. or N.W." And as he was evidently determined to make the shadow fall the way he wanted it I did not contradict him. Wordsworth was a very remarkable looking man. He looked like an old shepherd, with rough rugged weather beaten face, but his features were fine and high cut. He was a grand man. He had a perfectly independent mind and cared for no one else's opinion. I called upon him afterwards at the Stow, Whitney. He was very kind to me there. He used to say that the Wye above Hay was the finest piece of scenery in South Britain, i.e. everything south of himself.'

Friday, October Eve
Reading before luncheon. Read that clever amusing book *A Week in a French Country House*. What an elegant ease and simplicity there is about French manners and ways of domestic country life, and how favourably it contrasts with our social life, cumbrous, stiff, vulgarly extravagant, artificial, unnatural.

Sunday, October Morrow
A heavy cold white mist, very raw and chilly. The poplars rustled loud in the mist with a sound like heavy rain. While we were in Church the fog cleared away and the afternoon was glorious sunshine and unclouded blue. Holy Communion. At the Vicarage I saw one of the first 'Post Cards' that have been sent. It was from Lilian to Mrs Venables, very bright and cheery.

Monday, 3 October
How odd, all the news and letters we get from Paris now coming by balloons and carrier pigeons.

Tuesday, 4 October
Today I sent my first post cards, to my Mother, Thersie, Emmie and Perch. They are capital things, simple, useful and handy. A happy invention.

Dinner at Clifford Priory. A fair haired pretty German girl dressed in blue staying in the house showed us some beautiful drawings and illuminated texts, and at her request I became a subscriber for a six shilling set, of which she has ordered 1000 copies to be printed.

The subject of Germany was started and we were talking about Baden, Strasburg, Heidelberg. 'Ah,' said Miss Schlienz to me, 'it is easy to see which way *your* sympathies lie.' She had (I learnt afterwards) been made painfully aware that other people's sympathies did not all lie the same way, for one afternoon when driving through Hay with Mrs Allen, she met Captain Thomas and Captain Bridge, both strong French partisans. The two Captains naturally turned the talk upon the War and not knowing Miss Schlienz's nationality they both expressed their opinions freely. 'And now,' said Captain T., 'there is one of those beastly German Dukes shot.' 'I don't know if you are aware,' said Katie Allen leaning grimly down from the box, 'I don't know if you are aware that there is a German lady in the carriage.' The Captains routed horse and foot, bowed and fled, one up, the other down street.

Wednesday, 5 October

A dark foggy afternoon. At the Bronith near the Cottage a yellow poplar spire stood out bright against the dark woods above. At the Bronith spring a woman crippled with rheumatism and crying with the pain, had filled her tin pail and was trying to crawl home with it. So I carried the pail to her house.

Saturday, 8 October

Heavy rain in the night and in the morning the mists had all wept themselves away. In the night the wind had gone round from the cursed East into the blessed West. All evil things have always come from the East, the plague, cholera, and man.

Monday, 10 October

All the evening a crowd of excited people swarming about the Swan door and steps, laughing, talking loud, swearing and quarrelling in the quiet moonlight.

Here come a fresh drove of men from the fair, half tipsy, at the quarrelsome stage judging by the noise they make, all talking at once loud fast and angry, humming and buzzing like a swarm of angry bees. Their blood is on fire. It is like a gunpowder magazine. There will be an explosion in a minute. It only wants one word, a spark. Here it is. Some one had said something. A sudden blaze of passion, a retort, a word and a blow, a rush, a scuffle, a Babel of voices, a tumult, the furious voices of the combatants rising high and furious above the din. Now the bystanders have come between them, are holding them back, soothing them, explaining that no insult was intended at first, and persuading them not to fight. Then a quick tramp of horsehoofs and a farmer dashes past on his way home from the fair. Twenty voices shout to him to stop. He pulls up with difficulty and joins the throng. Meanwhile the swarm and bustle and hum goes on, some singing, some shouting, some quarrelling and wrangling, the World and the Flesh reeling about arm in arm and Apollyon straddling the whole breadth of the way. Tonight I think many are sore, angry and desperate about their misfortunes and prospects. Nothing has sold today but fat cattle. No one would look at poor ones, because no one has keep for them during the winter. Every one wants to sell poor cattle to pay their rent and to get so many mouths off their hay. No one wants to buy them. Where are the rents to come from?

Tuesday, 11 October
Visited Edward Evans in the dark hole in the hovel roof which does duty for a bedroom, and a gaunt black and white ghostly cat was stalking about looking as if she were only waiting for the sick man to die, that she might begin upon him.

Thursday, 13 October
On leaving the School I went in to the Vicarage. I met Webb at the stable yard gate and he took me in and showed me how he was getting on. In the evening and night he and his men had opened the cesspool close to the drawing room wall, emptied it, and shot the contents into a deep pit in the garden. Late yesterday evening Richard Williams sent his little boy Johnny into the Vicarage garden to pick up the pears which were falling in the high wind. Some pears had fallen into the pit half full of night soil and lime which was all in a soft slabby state. The boy, not knowing what Webb and his men were doing or what was in the pit, jumped into it to pick up the pears which he saw lying on the lime. Immediately he began to sink and unable to extricate himself was getting deeper and deeper by his struggles. He was too much frightened or too stupid to cry out and in a few minutes he would

have been smothered in the horrible mess, if rain had not come on heavily and driven Webb into the garden to fetch his mackintosh when he found the boy lying on his side half immerged, floundering and struggling deeper and deeper in the slush just like a fly in a basin of treacle. He was struggling silently and holding fast to three pears. With great trouble Webb standing on the brink leaned over to him, got hold of his hand, pulled him out, and sent him down to the brook to wash himself and change his clothes at home afterwards.

Friday, 14 October
Visited Edward Evans and the stench of the hovel bedroom almost insupportable. The gaunt ghastly half starved black and white cat was still sitting on a box at the bed head waiting for the sick man to die.

It is an old custom in these parts for the poor people to go about round the farm-houses to beg and gather milk between and about the two Michaelmasses, that they may be able to make some puddings and pancakes against Bryngwyn and Clyro Feasts, which are on the same day, next Sunday, the Sunday after old Michaelmas Day or Hay Fair, October 10th. The old custom is still kept up in Bryngwyn and at some hill farms in Clyro, but it is honoured at comparatively few houses now, and scarcely anywhere in Clyro Vale. Wern Vawr is one of the best houses to go to, a hospitable old-fashioned house where they keep up the old customs. Besides being given a gallon of milk to be carried away, the poor people are fed and refreshed to help them on their journey to the next farm, for they wander many miles for milk and it is a weary tramp before they reach home.

I turned in to old Hannah's and sat with her an hour talking over old times, and listening to her reminiscences and tales of the dear old times, the simple kindly primitive times 'in the Bryngwyn' nearly ninety years ago. She remembers how, when she was a very little girl, she lived with her grandfather and grandmother, old Walter Whitney (who was about ninety) and his wife. In the winter evenings, some of their old neighbours, friends of her grandfather, used to come in for a chat, especially old Prothero, William Price and William Greenway, contemporaries of her grandfather, and all men born about the beginning of the 18th or the end of the 17th century. These old people would sit round the fire talking on the long winter evenings, and Hannah then a child of 8 or 10 would sit on a little stool by her grandfather's chair in the chimney corner listening while they told their old world stories and tales of 'the fairies' in whom they fully believed. There was the 'Wild Duck Pool' above Newbuilding. To this pool the people used to come on Easter morning to see the sun dance and play in the water and the angels who were at the Resurrection playing backwards and forwards before the sun. There was also the 'sheep cot pool' below Wernwg, where Hob with his lantern was to be seen, only Hannah never saw him. But when people were going to market on Thursday mornings they would exhort one another to come back in good time lest they should be led astray by the Goblin Lantern, and boys would wear their hats the wrong way lest they should be enticed into the fairy rings and made to dance. Then the story of the girl of Llan Pica who was led astray by the fairies and at last killed by them, and the story of the old man who slept in the mill trough at the Rhos Goch Mill and used to hear the fairies come in at night and dance to sweet fiddles on the mill floor. Hannah living in 'the Bryngwyn' wore a tall Welsh hat till she was grown up.

Saturday, 15 October
I found the old soldier sitting by his black fireplace and the door open, but soon a spark of fire showed and the flame leapt up, and soon we had a glowing fire. We talked about the War and he amused me by telling me his remembrances of the wolves in Spain, how they were very large and fierce, much larger than any dog he had seen. 'We frightened them,' he said 'by making a flash of powder in the pan of our muskets. When the wolves saw it they went away. They did not like to see that.' It is nothing to write, but the old man said it so quaintly as if the wolves disapproved of the proceeding and did not wish to countenance it, so they walked away.

Tuesday 18 October
Old James Jones was breaking stones below Pentwyn. He told me how he had once cured his deafness for a time by pouring hot eel

oil into his ear, and again by sticking into his ear an 'ellern' (elder) twig, and wearing it there night and day. The effect of the eel oil at first was, he said, to make his head and brains feel full of crawling creatures.

A wild rainy night. They are holding Clyro Feast Ball at the Swan opposite. As I write I hear the scraping and squealing of the fiddle and the ceaseless heavy tramp of the dancers as they stamp the floor in a country dance. An occasional blast of wind or rush of rain shakes my window. Toby[1] sits before the fire on the hearthrug and now and then jumps up on my knee to be stroked. The mice scurry rattling round the wainscot and Toby darts off in great excitement to listen and watch for them.

Wednesday, 19 October
Mrs Chaloner told me this morning that when the Harrises, now living at the Wine Vaults at Hay, kept the Baskerville Arms, at one of the Clyro Feast Balls the Whitcombs of the Bronith got in. A fight followed, the house was in an uproar, the company were fighting all night instead of dancing, and in the morning all the respectable people had black eyes. At that time the inn was very badly conducted, people sat up drinking all night and fought it out in the morning in the road before the inn. Frequently they were to be seen at 11 o'clock in the morning stripped and fighting up and down the road, often having drunk and vomited and wallowed in the inn all night.

Went in to see Richard Meredith the Land Surveyor and sat talking to him for some time. He said the old folks used to rise very early, never later than five even in winter, and then the women would get to their spinning or knitting. His grandmother was always at her spinning, knitting or woolcarding by 6 o'clock in the morning. It was fashionable to breakfast just before daylight in winter and 9 o'clock at night was a very late hour for going to bed. When people rose very early it was a saying that they were 'beating for day', because it was supposed that they went out and knocked on the earth for day to come.

---

1. The diarist's cat.

Saturday, 22 October

I went up the common to White Ash, the air blowing fresh and fragrant on the open hill side green. Read to Sarah Probert, the story of the Raising of Lazarus. Hannah came in and sat by the fire listening with grunts of assent between the whiffs of her short pipe. She said she had been 'tugging and tearing firewood up the old dingle'. A squirrel's skin hung over the hearth. The cat killed the squirrel and several others a month ago. 'I couldna think,' said Hannah, 'what she was a-tushing down the fold.' Hannah had preserved for me some Columbine seeds and some seed of the blue flower Scabious called 'Kiss at the garden gate'.

Tuesday, 25 October

At Maesllwch Castle last week four guns killed seven hundred rabbits in one afternoon.

Wednesday, 26 October

Carrie Gore let me in to the Mill kitchen through the meal room and loft over the machinery, and there was Mrs Gore making up the bread into loaves and putting them into the oven. Good-natured nice Carrie, with her brown hair arranged in a bush round her jolly broad open frank face, and her fine lusty arms bare, entertained me by playing on the jingling old harpsichord, sitting very stiff and straight and upright to the work with her chair drawn in as near as possible to the key-board so that she was obliged to lean a little back quite stiff. She played some hymn tunes correctly, but what I admired most was her good nature, good breeding and perfect manners in sitting down to play directly she was asked without any false shame or false modesty, without shilly-shallying or holding back that she might be asked again, but just sitting straight down, doing what she was asked and doing her best at once without any nonsense, in a good-tempered cheerful way that many young ladies might copy with advantage. She is as nice and good a girl as you will meet in a day's march.

A pretty little girl sat in an armchair by the fire reading. Mrs Gore had made her some apple hop-abouts, but forgot to put them in the oven till I reminded her of them. Mrs Gore wanted me to have some gin and when I declined offered me tea as an alternative. I accepted the tea. While they were getting it ready Mary came

back from a long round among the hills on horseback, collecting
bills and money for her father. The Gores of Whitty's Mill are
very well-off, make at least £200 a year, the schoolmistress says,
and have a matter of £300 in the bank. Carrie had gone upstairs,
and I heard Mrs Gore calling in a loud voice, 'Carrie dear, there's
Mary come back, go to the door and take the mare off her'. I rose
and looked through the window into the yard below. Carrie was
leading a bay mare to the stable and a pretty girl who had just
dismounted, the Miller's daughter, was coming towards the house
with her riding whip in her hand, dressed in a dark riding habit
which she was holding up as she walked, and a black jaunty pretty
hat with a black feather sat upon her flowing fair hair. It was a
pretty picture. She came into the kitchen straight, with the
manners, bearing and address of a lady, shook hands and welcomed
me cordially. 'Well, Miss Mary, you've had a cold stormy ride.'
Her little hand was cold with riding. She began to tell me where
she had been, then went upstairs, took off her riding habit, and
came down in a pretty maize print dress, and sitting in an armchair by the fireside went on with the account of her ride. The dog
and cat fawned on her and jumped into her lap. Everybody and
everything seemed glad when 'Mary' came home. She appeared to
be the strong gentle ruling spirit of the house. Oh the dear old
Mill kitchen, the low, large room so snug, so irregular and full of
odd holes and corners, so cosy and comfy with its low ceiling,
horse-hair couch, easy chair by the fire, flowers in the window
recess, the door opening into the best room or parlour. Oh these
kindly hospitable houses about these hospitable hills. I believe I
might wander about these hills all my life and never want a kindly
welcome, a meal, or a seat by the fireside. And the kindness and
earnest gratitude one meets with when one calls at the houses is
quite touching. Mary brought me a small round table to my side
of the fire. Mrs Gore herself brought me tea and bread and butter
and preserves. So we sat round the hearth and talked about the
War. And when I rose to go, 'Goodbye, Sir,' said the Miller's
daughter, with a warm hearty clasp of the hand. 'I'm *very* glad to
see you here.' Blessings on the dear old Mill, and the brook that
turns the wheel, and on the hospitable kitchen and the rooftree of

the Gores, and blessings on the fair brave honest girl, the Miller's daughter of Whitty's Mill.

Friday, 28 October

Hot coppers, too much wine last night and an ill temper this morning. Reading *Puck* by 'Ouida', a bock Morrell lent me. The authoress seems to have a rabid hatred of women and parsons.

Saturday, 29 October

Reading *Puck*. Last night we heard that Metz has fallen and that four Marshals of France and 150,000 men have surrendered as prisoners of war.

Today I found in a book a red silk handkerchief worked with the words 'Forget me not', and I am sorry to say that I have entirely forgotten who gave it to me. One of my many lovers no doubt. But which?

Tuesday, 15 November

Letters from my Father and Mother enclosing a nice letter from Augustus Hare,[1] describing to my Father his 'Mother's'[2] illness. He gives the following affectionate words to his reminiscences of dear old Harnish and Harnish days. Speaking of Aunt Mary, he says, 'I remember Mrs Matthews so well and going to tea there, for consolation, the first day I was left with you. It all seems very long ago, but so vivid still, the garden with its laurel hedges and the large elm tree, the dusty hot little courtyard, the romantic adventures of climbing down by stealth into the vault under the church, persuading Mary the cook to give us little hot cakes of bread out of the window when she was baking. Asking the French master with Walter Arnold, "Who won the battle of Waterloo?" and being well punished for it too, the odious Gumbleton who always pinched and pricked me under the tablecloth, the eccentric Proby, the affectionate little Henry, the nice Percival, Deacon Coles (who always seemed more than grown up when he was 12 years old) and all his maiden aunts, the delights of Kellaways, our

1. Augustus Hare (1834–1903), author of *The Story of My Life*, &c., had been a pupil of the diarist's father at Hardenhuish Rectory.
2. The lady was Hare's adoptive mother.

"museum" of bits of tobacco pipe picked up in the roads, the dressings-up on the 5th of November, the geography book which taught us about Crema and Cremona (such extraordinary obscure places!) and, oh, a hundred thousand other things.'

Wednesday, 16 November
Last night the waning moon shone bright and cold in the East and I had a horrible dream that I was married to Mrs Danzey and living as curate at Gwythian. I woke up in a cold sweat. This morning I learnt from Mrs Venables of the death of Mrs Augustus Hare. She heard of it from Miss Higginson. Mrs Augustus Hare was one of Lady Frances Higginson's oldest friends. My Father I know will feel her death, and poor Augustus, what will he do without her? She has been his object in life. It was a very beautiful attachment on both sides. Augustus has written a book in 2 Vols. called *Walks in Rome*. Miss Higginson sent a notice of it to Clyro. They want Mr G. Venables to review it in 'the Saturday'.

Thursday, 17 November
The trees blazed with the diamonds of the melting hoar frost. The wet village roads shone like silver below, and the market folk thronged past the Vicarage and School. A railway engine shot up a bright white jet of steam over the bank from Hay Station, the oaks were still tawny green and glittering with diamond dews, Hay Church in a tender haze beyond the gleaming of the broad river reach and rapids above the Steeple pool. How indescribable, that lovely brilliant variegated scene. A rook shot up out of the valley and towered above the silver mist into the bright blue sky over the golden oaks, rising against the dark blue mountains still patched and ribbed with snow.

Friday, 18 November
Went into the Tump to see young Meredith who has had his jaw locked for six months, a legacy of mumps. He has been to Hereford Infirmary where they kept him two months, gave him chloroform and wrenched his jaws open gradually by a screw lever. But they could not do him any good.

Next to the Pant, where Mrs Powell was entertaining a sister-in-law from Huntingdon at tea. We were talking about parishes and boundaries. 'I'm sitting in Brilley (England and Herefordshire) now,' said I, feeling for the boundary notch in the chimney. 'It's further this way,' she said. 'I suppose,' she said, 'there have been some curious disputes about the boundary running through this house.' 'Very odd indeed,' I said, remembering the extraordinary story which old Betty Williams of Crowther used to tell me about the birth of a child in this house (the Pant) and the care taken that the child should be born in England in the English corner of the cottage. 'Stand here, Betsey, in this corner,' said the midwife. And the girl was delivered of the child *standing*.

At Cae Noyadd in its black yews and hedges covered white with drying linen Mrs Harley was washing, the floor was littered with dry fern, and a big girl had of course 'cracked a commandment', run away from her place ('started', as they call it) and come home in this fashion, i.e. in the family way. The usual old story.

Sunday, 20 November
I went back with Mrs Venables to the Vicarage to tea and we had a long confidential talk between the lights and far into the dark, sitting by the drawing room fire, talking about the prevailing scepticism of the day. I said if I had children I should teach them to believe all the dear old Bible stories. She said she hoped to see me some day with a number of children about me, my own children. Never, I said, adding I did not believe that I should ever marry. Then came out by degrees my attachment to C. She was very much surprised when she guessed the right name after trying Mary Bevan, Fanny Higginson, Flora Ross, Lily Thomas. 'She'll never marry,' she said gravely. 'I know it,' I said.

Wednesday, 23 November
I dined at the Vicarage with Lord and Lady Hereford who came today and stay till Saturday for the shooting at Clyro Court.

Thursday, 24 November
A wild rainy night and the rain poured all day so that the Clyro Court party could not shoot and played battledore and shuttlecock in the hall, gentlemen and ladies.

Monday, 28 November

A plaintive mew outside the door. I open the door and tabby Toby comes trotting in with his funny little note of affection.

Walked up the Cwm and found old James Jones stonebreaking. He told me how he was once travelling from Hereford to Hay by coach when the coach was wrecked in a flood by Bredwardine Bridge because the coachman would not take the bearing reins of the horses off. The bearing reins kept the horses' noses down under water, they plunged and reared and got the coach off the road and swimming like a boat, and an old lady inside screaming horribly. 'Don't keep such a noise, Ma'am,' said old Jones, throwing himself off the roof into a hedge-row against which the coach was swept by the fierce current. 'We won't leave you before we get you out somehow.' He was followed by most of the passengers on the roof, though one very tall man fell into the water on his face all along like a log, and waded through the flood out on to the Bredwardine side. One outside passenger was a miller of the neighbourhood who had a boat on the river. This was sent for and the old lady pacified and pulled into it through the coach window. The coachman was prayed and entreated to loose the bearing reins, but refused to do it. Two horses were drowned, one wheeler went down under the pole. The other, a leader, broke loose and plunged and pawed and reared at the bridge out of the flood till he was exhausted, and then fell over backwards into the stream and was rolled away by the current.

Tuesday, 29 November

A letter from my mother enclosing one from Perch. She tells me that Maria Kilvert of Worcester died last week after a few days' illness. Mr Hooper, her Worcester lawyer, wrote to ask my Father to come immediately. He and my Mother went to Worcester yesterday. My Father said on reading Mr Hooper's letter that he thought she had probably left all the bulk of her property to the Cathedral. Curiously enough my Mother opened immediately afterwards Perch's letter which she forwarded to me, and he says, 'I see in the *Illustrated London News* that Miss Kilvert of Worcester had just given £300 to the clock and bells of the Cathedral'. Perch gives a good account of his own position in the Inland

Revenue which he considers now to be safe and he thinks he will shortly have an increase of salary.

Wednesday, December Eve
A letter from my Mother from College Green, Worcester — Maria Kilvert's house, where they are staying. When my Father and Mother arrived, the servants were crusty and evidently did not intend them to stay there, saying there was no spare bed and nothing to eat in the house. Mr Hooper, the acting executor, was out of town, so not liking to take any step without his sanction they went to the Star for the night, until they could see him. Next morning he told them, 'Certainly, they had a perfect right to go to the house, and stay there'. So armed with his authority they went to College Green and took up their quarters there. My Mother sent a rough sketch of the will which Mr Hooper read over hastily to them. £15,000 left to charities, Clergy widows and orphans, Home Missions and S.P.G., by a right but by no moral right and a most unprincipled unnatural act and piece of ostentation and a most erroneous injustice. Still more monstrous, £600 had been left by the will to Lord Lyttelton and his son. Happily this had been revoked by codicil. Her beautiful prints she left to the Bishop of Worcester and the magnificent volumes of engravings were left to the executors. To my Father she left her *rose trees* and to my Mother her furs and lace, which my Mother thinks may be worth a few shillings. There are many legacies to old servants etc., some of them heavy ones. After the sale of the house everything in it, including the fine old plate with the family arms engraved upon it, is to be sold, and after all legacies, debts and expenses have been paid what remains of the property, which will probably be a mere trifle, is to be equally divided between my Father, Aunt Marianne and the Motherwells. A most iniquitous will, not a shilling was left to any of the Francis Kilverts, the old grudge and malice against Uncle Francis for writing Bishop Hurd's life ruling strong in death.

My Mother has been very busy making inventories and lists for Mr Hooper as a check on the servants, as everything was left to their mercy. The funeral is to be on Friday after Cathedral morning service. The funeral service is to be choral. The six pall bearers to be the Canons. My Father and Mother the only mourners. I decided to go over tomorrow and stay over the night and see the funeral and Worcester, and wrote to offer to attend the funeral.

Thursday, December Day

[The diarist arrives at Worcester and a girl, of whom he has asked his way, offers to guide him.]

We passed along an irregular quadrangle formed by the N. side of the Cathedral on one hand and houses on the other sides. A carriage drive swept round an iron-railed grass enclosure within which were some ancient elms with almost all their limbs lopped or broken off. This was the Cathedral Close or College Green. Most of the houses were red brick, some stuccoed white, all irregular and unlike each other. 'There,' said the girl with the baby, 'that is Miss Kilvert's house, the last house, red brick with white blinds down.' It was a curious looking house in an inner recess of the Close, red brick, white window frames, a conical roof with tiles, and a small front. In the middle of this inner recess was a smaller open grass plot. The Close may be pretty in summer but it looked bare and dreary in December. The Cathedral Tower close by, just restored by Lord Dudley, is a grand rich object. The first impression the Cathedral exterior gave me was one of plainness, bareness, newness, produced by the new grey sandstone with which it has been cased, not yet weather-fretted or lichen-grown.

The maid-servant announced me at the library door where my Father and Mother were sitting, as 'a visitor for Mrs Kilvert'. My Mother, who was writing at a table between the two windows, rose and took off her spectacles, expecting to see a stranger, as I had written that I was coming by a later train. Dinner had just gone out but a charwoman brought me in a tray of luncheon. The three servants are too grand to wait upon us so they employ a charwoman. Then my mother related all their adventures. I had a particular wish to see Miss Kilvert though I usually loathe and abhor the sight of a corpse, so Charlotte Haynes, the ladies' maid, was summoned and she gladly conducted us upstairs into the bed-room and drew up the blinds. It was a small room very plainly furnished, but some exquisite engravings hung on the walls. The bed stood in the middle of the room and the room was full of chloride of lime. It was a four post curtained bed, covered with a white sheet. Charlotte drew back the sheet. The dead woman 80 years old lay in her coffin, a lead coffin fitted into an outer one of dark oak and lined with white satin. The coffin lid with its brass breastplate leaned upright in a corner of the room. The face that lay still, frozen down into silence, in the coffin was a very remarkable one. It was a distinguished face with aristocratic features. A firm mouth, fine highly formed nose delicately and sharply cut. There was a slight frown and a contraction of the brows. It was the face of a person of considerable ability, stern, severe, and perhaps a little contemptuous, an expression which with the contraction of the brows was so habitual that death had smoothed neither away. It did not look like the face of a woman of fourscore. The 'likeness to some one of the race' had 'come out'. There was a strong family resemblance to my Father, and there was a look which brought back a vague fleeting dim recollection which I could not catch or define. It was the least repulsive dead face I have seen. My Father went downstairs to bring my Mother up, as she had at first declined accompanying us to the bedroom. I think we were all glad that we had visited the room and seen the noble face of the dead uncovered. She must have been very handsome in her youth. My Father says she was more than this, 'she was bewitching'. She seems to have been a singularly clever accomplished person of refined and elegant tastes. She played and sang exquisitely and one of the canons compared her to Jenny Lind. The drawing room upstairs was hung round with beautiful proof prints, some of the most exquisite engravings I ever saw, so soft and clear. There also lay on a side table the noble volumes of engravings of the ancient Mansions of England. These were brought down by a servant for us to look at.

I went out into the town for a walk with my Father. As we were returning we were met by the charwoman saying she could get no fowls for the funeral breakfast tomorrow. 'Should she get a small turkey?' – 'Yes, she should get a small turkey.'

Friday, December morrow
I had a comfortable dry warm bed and nice bedroom at the Star. I walked up to College Green and my Father and Mother drove up

to 8.30 breakfast. At 10.30 the canons and prebendaries who were to be pall-bearers began to assemble with the other people who attended the funeral. Cathedral morning prayer at 10.15 and as it was Litany Day they were not over till 1.30. Meanwhile breakfast, scarves and hatbands. Mr Hooper the lawyer and Mr Wheeler the Cathedral Precentor were there. The former reminds me much of Haman of Boatside. There was an old Mr Gresley who knew my great uncle and said he remembered often being blessed by Bishop Hurd. It was not on the whole a distinguished looking company. They met in the dining room where over the mantlepiece hung a nice portrait of old Doctor Green, Chancellor of the Diocese, in his scarlet D.D. robes, old Mrs Kilvert's father, or brother. Opposite hung a Paul Potter, and on the side wall a quaint view of Rome in a very long narrow picture. There was a piano in the dining room and another upstairs, and there was a little funny old-world picture of two children playing together, one of them being old Mrs Kilvert. The coffin had been brought downstairs and was waiting in the hall covered with the black velvet sweeping soft pall, white bordered. Boom went the great bell of the Cathedral. Church was over, and someone said they ought to have used the tenor bell, but they were using the great bell and no mistake. Boom went the bell again. The coffin went out immediately and the pall bearers filed out in pairs after it, taking their places and holding each his pall tassel on either side. My Father and I followed as Chief mourners in crape scarves and hatbands. All the rest in silk. The bearers had been selected not at all with reference to their fitness for the task, but with reference to the friendship entertained for them by the servants of the house. One of the bearers on the right side was very short, so short that he could not properly support the coffin level. The coffin seemed very heavy. As the procession moved across College Green to the Cloister arch, the men staggered under the weight and the coffin lurched and tilted to one side over the short bearer. One very fat man had constituted himself chiefest mourner of all and walked next the coffin before my Father and myself. The bearers, blinded by the sweeping pall, could not see where they were going and nearly missed the Cloister arch, but at length we got safe into the narrow dark passage and into the Cloisters. The great bell boomed high over-

100

head and the deep thrilling vibration hung trembling in the air long after the stroke of the bell.

So the clergy and choir came to meet us at the door, then turned and moved up the Cathedral nave chanting in solemn procession, 'I am the Resurrection and the Life saith the Lord'. But meanwhile there was a dreadful struggle at the steps leading up from the Cloisters to the door. The bearers were quite unequal to the task and the coffin seemed crushingly heavy. There was a stamping and a scuffling, a mass of struggling men swaying to and fro, pushing and writhing and wrestling while the coffin sank and rose and sank again. Once or twice I thought the whole mass of men must have been down together with the coffin atop of them and some one killed or maimed at least. But now came the time of the fat chief mourner. Seizing his opportunity he rushed into the strife by an opening large and the rescued coffin rose. At last by a wild effort and tremendous heave the ponderous coffin was borne up the steps and through the door into the Cathedral where the choristers, quite unconscious of the scene and the fearful struggle going on behind, were singing up the nave like a company of angels. In the Choir there was another dreadful struggle to let the coffin down. The bearers were completely overweighted, they bowed and bent and nearly fell and threw the coffin down on the floor. When it was safely deposited we all retired to seats right and left and a verger or beadle, in a black gown and holding a mace, took up his position at the head of the coffin, standing. The Psalm was sung nicely to a very beautiful chant. The Dean had the gout and could not appear, so Canon Wood read the lesson well and impressively in a sonorous voice. The Grave Service was intoned by the Sacristan Mr Raisin and sung by the choir, standing on the planking round the vault whilst a crowd of people looked in through the cloister windows.

It must have been an expensive funeral. Everyone had hatbands down to the Choristers who wore them round their college caps. And there was a heavy fee to the Choir for the Choral service. Canon Wood floated down College Green from the cloisters to his own house next to Miss Kilvert's, and we went home with the two executors, Mr Wheeler and Mr Hooper, to read the will. Mr H. gave Mr W. and myself each a copy of the will and read it aloud.

The estate proved to be £36,000, and about £7000 will come to my Father. When he left Langley he did not even know if he should have enough left him to pay his expenses. The cook was entirely ignored, except £5 for mourning like the others. The other two servants had £100 apiece. Charlotte, the ladies' maid, asked Mr Hooper to announce this fact to the cook himself. She was summoned and he broke the news to her. She retired in dudgeon and I expect the other servants had a breezy time of it as the cook was said to be a bad-tempered woman. Luncheon off the turkey and other funeral baked meats and Mr Wheeler went away to another funeral, exhorting me first to see his son's church. We went down into the rose garden to choose the roses that are to go to Langley. Then we went out into the town to see Hobbs the auctioneer near Foregate St Station, to tell him to come and value the furs, laces, etc., for the legacy duty and probate.

We passed a very cosy evening and about 7 o'clock Mr Hobbs made his appearance with an assistant laden with a box containing a pair of scales, which we had ordered him to bring to weigh the plate. When he arrived we discovered the plate ought not to be weighed now. But the scales were solemnly produced to weigh a silver seal which Hobbs pronounced worth 2/6 and which I immediately stole from the estate in consideration of my having come from Clyro to lend my support and countenance on the occasion. I should like to have stolen a great many things, books, plate, etc., but I did not dare. The deep soft muffled tones were still echoing the grand pealing of the bells from the lighted Tower and the dark night was all in a tremble from the sweet vibration. 'That is for Miss Kilvert,' whispered the officious ladies' maid to me in the porch.

Saturday, 3 December
I am 30 years old today. Well, well.

We went to breakfast to College Green. We went back to the Star to pick up our luggage and there we parted, my Father and Mother going to the Shrub Hill and I to the Foregate St Station. But first I had my hair cut and I told the man to cut my beard square. 'Now,' he said, 'this is very inconsistent. Your features are round and you want your beard cut square.' 'Still,' I said, 'I prefer it.' My Mother had given me some money, five shillings, to buy a book as a birthday present. Part of it, 2/–, I spent on buying a copy of *Faust*, an English translation, one of Tischendorf's series, at the Foregate St Station, as a remembrance of Worcester.

Saturday, 17 December

That liar and thief of the world Sarah Thomas, Mrs Chaloner's servant, is gone. The evening she went no one knew what had become of her all the early part of the night. Probably she passed it under some hedge and not alone. At a quarter before midnight she asked for a bed which Mrs Price very properly refused. I hope she has cleared out of this village. Beast.

Sunday, 18 December

I could not get out of my head a horrible story Wall was telling me this evening of a suicide committed by an old man named William Jones in the old barn, now pulled down, which stood close by Chapel Dingle cottage. The old man used to work for Dyke at Llwyn Gwillim, but becoming helpless and infirm he was put upon the parish. It is supposed that this preyed upon his mind. He was a very good faithful servant and a man of a sturdy independent character who could not bear the idea of not being able any longer to maintain himself and hated to be supported by the parish. 'I used to bake his bit of meat for him that was allowed him by the Board', said Mr Wall, 'for Rachel Williams with whom he was lodging at the Chapel Dingle was out at work every day. My baking day was mostly Friday. On Friday he had been up with his meat and I did not notice anything more than usual about him. At noon on Saturday Rachel's step-children missed him. They had seen him go towards the barn some hours before. They went and looked through a lance hole of the old building and saw the old man lying on the floor, and they came back saying that old William Jones was lying in the barn dead. The master and I went down to the barn. Inside the barn there was a door leading into a beast house. The old man could not shut the barn door from the inside, so he had gone into the beast house and had shut himself in. Then he had leaned his stick up in a corner quite tidy. He had then taken out a razor, unsheathed it, putting the sheath back into his pocket. He was lying on the floor on his face when we saw him. The master turned him over. Heaven send I never see such a sight again. His head was nearly cut off, both arteries were cut through, the tongue was unrooted and, (perhaps in his agony), he had put his hand into the wound and torn his "keck" and everything out.'

Wednesday, 21 December

Coming into the Vicarage from the school I found Sir Gilbert Lewis pacing round the gravel walk round the lawn in gloves and stick and great coat trying to get warm before starting on his cold journey to Harpton. He told me a good deal about Maria Kilvert of Worcester whom he knew, as he is a Canon of Worcester. He said she was tall and thin. She used to come rapidly into Church (into the Cathedral) to receive the sacrament two or three times a month, but for the last three years she had not attended the other services. She used to come in a respirator. She shut herself up almost entirely ever since he had been Canon of Worcester, 15 years. Lady Lewis used to call and was sometimes admitted. Sir Gilbert had not called for three years. The house looked most melancholy and dreary, like a house of the dead, no movement, the blinds never drawn up, no carriage ever stopping at the gate, scarcely any one ever going out or in at the door. Sir Gilbert does not believe she had the slightest acquaintance with Lord Lyttelton, or that she even knew him by sight. He said mad people are apt to come to Cathedrals. There was a mad woman who came to Worcester Cathedral and gave him a great deal of trouble by screeching out. There was a Mr Quarrell who used to make antics at the time of the Communion. At a certain point in the service this man would bow down till he got his head on the pavement and his movements were so extraordinary that all they could do was to look at him and watch him. The authorities did not know what to do with him. They could not say, 'You shall not be a Communicant', but they let him know indirectly that they thought his proceedings very ridiculous. 'Ah,' said Sir Gilbert, 'you don't know all the little games that go on in Cathedrals.'

Sunday, Christmas Day

As I lay awake praying in the early morning I thought I heard a sound of distant bells. It was an intense frost. I sat down in my

bath upon a sheet of thick ice which broke in the middle into large
pieces whilst sharp points and jagged edges stuck all round the
sides of the tub like chevaux de frise, not particularly comforting
to the naked thighs and lcins, for the keen ice cut like broken
glass. The ice water stung and scorched like fire. I had to collect
the floating pieces of ice and pile them on a chair before I could
use the sponge and then I had to thaw the sponge in my hands for
it was a mass of ice. The morning was most brilliant. Walked to
the Sunday School with Gibbins and the road sparkled with
millions of rainbows, the seven colours gleaming in every glittering point of hoar frost. The Church was very cold in spite of two
roaring stove fires. Mr V. preached and went to Bettws.

Monday, 26 December
Much warmer and almost a thaw. Left Clyro at 11 a.m.
  At Chippenham my father and John were on the platform.
After dinner we opened a hamper of game sent by the Venables,
and found in it a pheasant, a hare, a brace of rabbits, a brace of
woodcocks, and a turkey. Just like them, and their constant kindness.

Tuesday, 27 December
After dinner drove into Chippenham with Perch and bought a
pair of skates at Benk's for 17/6. Across the fields to the Draycot
water and the young Awdry ladies chaffed me about my new
skates. I had not been on skates since I was here last, 5 years ago,
and was very awkward for the first ten minutes, but the knack
soon came again. There was a distinguished company on the ice,
Lady Dangan, Lord and Lady Royston and Lord George Paget all
skating. Also Lord and Lady Sydney and a Mr Calcroft, whom
they all of course called the Hangman. I had the honour of being
knocked down by Lord Royston, who was coming round suddenly
on the outside edge. A large fire of logs burning within an enclosure of wattled hurdles. Harriet Awdry skated beautifully and
jumped over a half sunken punt. Arthur Law skating jumped
over a chair on its legs.

Wednesday, 28 December

An inch of snow fell last night and as we walked to Draycot to skate the snow storm began again. As we passed Langley Burrell Church we heard the strains of the quadrille band on the ice at Draycot. The afternoon grew murky and when we began to skate the air was thick with falling snow. But it soon stopped and gangs of labourers were at work immediately sweeping away the new fallen snow and skate cuttings of ice. The Lancers was beautifully skated. When it grew dark the ice was lighted with Chinese lanterns, and the intense glare of blue, green, and crimson lights and magnesium riband made the whole place as light as day. Then people skated with torches.

Thursday, 29 December

Skating at Draycot again with Perch. Fewer people on the ice today. No quadrille band, torches or fireworks, but it was very pleasant, cosy and sociable. Yesterday when the Lancers was being skated Lord Royston was directing the figures. Harriet Awdry corrected him in one figure and he was quite wrong. But he immediately left the quadrille and sat down sulking on the bank, saying to one of his friends, 'Those abominable Miss Awdrys have contradicted me about the Lancers'. This was overheard and repeated to Harriet by a mutual friend, and the next time she saw him she said meaningly, 'Lord Royston, sometimes remarks are overheard and repeated', or something to that effect. However soon after he wanted to make it up and asked her to skate up the ice hand in hand with him. 'Certainly *not*, Lord Royston,' she said. Lady Royston skates very nicely and seems very nice. A sledge chair was put on the ice and Lady Royston and Lady Dangan, Margaret, Fanny, Maria, and Harriet Awdry were drawn about in it by turns, Charles Awdry pushing behind and Edmund and Arthur and Walter pulling with ropes. It was a capital team and went at a tremendous pace up and down the ice. A German ladies' maid from Draycot House was skating and making ridiculous antics.

1871

New Year's Day

My Mother, Perch and I sat up last night to watch the old year
out and the New Year in. The wind was in the North and the
sound of the bells came faintly and muffled over the snow from
Chippenham and Kington. We opened the dining room window to
'loose in' the sound of the chimes and 'the New Year' as they say
in Wales. It was bitter cold, but we went to the door, Perch and I,
to hear better. I was carrying my travelling clock in my hand and
as we stood on the terrace just outside the front door, the little
clock struck midnight with its tinkling silvery bell in the keen
frost. We thought we could hear three peals of Church bells,
Chippenham, St Paul's, and very faintly Kington. 'Ring happy
bells across the snow.'

When Perch came back from skating at Draycot last night, he
amused us with an account of Friday's and Saturday's doings on
the ice. On Friday they had a quadrille band from Malmesbury,
skated quadrilles, Lancers, and Sir Roger de Coverley. Then they
skated up and down with torches, ladies and gentlemen pairing off
and skating arm in arm, each with a torch. There were numbers of
Chinese lanterns all round the water, blue, crimson and green
lights, magnesium riband, and a fire balloon was sent up. Maria
Awdry, forgetting herself and the passage of time, inadvertently
spoke to Perch calling him 'Teddy' instead of 'Mr Kilvert'.
Having done which she perceived her mistake, turned 'away and
smote herself on the mouth', while Perch 'looked at her with a
face like a stone'. While people were standing about in groups or
skating up and down gently young Spencer skated up suddenly
with outstretched arm to shake hands with Teddy. At the critical
moment his skate hitched and he lost his balance and made a deep
but involuntary obeisance before Perch, describing 'an attenuated
arch', with his fingers and toes resting on the ice. People hid their
faces, turned and skated away with a sour smile or grinning with
repressed laughter. Perch stood still waiting for the 'attenuated

arch' to unbind itself and retrieve its erect posture, 'looking on with a face like a stone'. Gradually the 'arch' rose from its deep obeisance. The arch was the arch described by an attenuated tom cat. During the torch skating Harriet Awdry hurled her half-burnt torch ashore. Lord Cowley was walking up and down the path on the bank watching with great impatience the skaters whom he detests. The fiery torch came whirling and flaming through the dark and hit the noble diplomatist sharply across the shins, rebounding from which it lay blazing at the foot of a tree. Lord Cowley was very angry. 'I wish these people wouldn't throw their torches about here at me,' grumbled his lordship. 'Come away and hide behind the island or he'll see you,' said Perch to Harriet. So they glided away and from the cover of the island they watched Lord Cowley angrily beating the blazing torch against the ground to try to put it out. But the more he beat it, the more the torch flamed and showered sparks into his face. Harriet described the incident thus, 'I hit old Cowley such a crack over the shins'.

Last week Mr Greenwood, the Calne organist, fell on the Bowood ice and broke his nose. The next day his son, a boy of 15, fell while sliding, struck his head against a stone, fractured his skull and died in an hour and a half by the lake side.

Tuesday, 3 January
I went to see old Isaac Giles. He lamented the loss of his famous old pear tree. He told me he was nearly 80 and remembered seeing the Scots Greys passing through Chippenham on their way to Waterloo. They looked very much down, he said, for they knew where they were going.

Wednesday, 4 January
At 8 p.m. I went out on the terrace. There was a keen clean frost and the moon was bright in a cloudless sky. Some men were beating the holly bushes along the old bridle lane at the top of Parson's Ground. They probably had a clap net and were beating for black-birds, &c. 'Look out,' cried one man. I could hear their voices quite distinctly across the fields in the silence of the frost. Children's voices seemed to be calling everywhere. I heard them from the

village and across the common. A number of children must have been out. Perhaps they were sliding in the moonlight.

[The diarist goes to stay at Claygate in Surrey.]

Thursday, 12 January
Sam, Perch and I went up to Town together, walking to Thames Ditton station, 3 miles, as the roads were too icy for the horse to travel.

A little before one o'clock I called at 9 Wilton Crescent by Miss Higginson's desire, but she was out of Town and not being sure whether Lady Frances would remember me I did not go in. I wandered back along Piccadilly to a pastrycook's and then up the Burlington Arcade. In the Arcade I went into a photograph shop to get some scraps and asked if he had a photograph of the picture 'Rock of Ages' or 'Clinging to the Cross'. A dark French-looking bearded man was reading a paper behind the counter. He got up and looked at me steadily and then backed towards the fire to get away as far as possible. 'No, Sir', he said sternly after scrutinizing me narrowly. I asked him to show me some other photographs. 'No, Sir,' he said again sternly. 'I never will show anything to persons who ask me for the "Rock of Ages".' 'Why?' I said. 'Is there any harm in asking for the photograph?' He said it was copyright and any one selling the photograph was liable to a penalty of £2. I said I was quite unaware of the fact and was sorry I had asked him for the picture. Then I asked him again to show me some more photographs. 'No, Sir, thank you,' he repeated. His manner was very curious and he was evidently very uneasy and anxious to get me out of the shop as quickly as possible without letting me see anything. I saw there was something wrong, but could not make out what was the matter. I was sorry afterwards that I had not insisted on seeing his goods as I might have done, for he was legally bound to show them. Opposite the Charing Cross Hotel I met Sam and we walked along the Strand to Waterloo. He explained the mystery of the shop in the Arcade. The man is notorious for selling obscene French photographs. The police have long been watching him, but have never caught him yet. He thought I was a spy. I got some scraps in another shop in Piccadilly. We walked home to Claygate from Thames Ditton in a brilliant hard frost.

Tuesday, 17 January

Sam, Emmie and I went up to Town. In the street outside one of the police courts there was a dense crowd, great excitement and inextinguishable laughter. The prison van stood at the door and a prisoner had just been put in. Two handsome fair-haired girls, bare-armed and bare-headed, were shouting derisively to the person inside, who seemed to have incurred the popular hatred and contempt. The girls approached the van closely and yelled insulting words to the miserable creature inside while the people stood round and grinned applause. Then the great long black van drove rapidly off through the crowd, followed by the shouts & yells of the people.

[The diarist returns to Langley Burrell.]

Wednesday, 18 January

A soft sunny showery morning and it felt like spring as we walked to Claremont (Sam and I) soon after noon. Mr Macdonald's[1] quarters are the same as those of the equerries over the handsome stables. Before luncheon he took us round the gardens and stables. (In his rooms is the log of Herne's oak from which he cut a wedge for Emmie.) There is a great deal of glass, but the place was sadly neglected during the residence of the French Royal Family who let the gardens and glass houses to a market gardener. Mr Macdonald is gradually reducing things to order and the shrubberies and lawns and all the grounds are much improved during the year and a half that he has been in power at Claremont.

There is stabling for some 40 horses at Claremont. When the Queen stays here 7 or 8 policemen are on duty and live on the premises. Mr M. took us across the finely timbered park down to the home farm where there is a tall column crested with a stone statue of a peacock, the bearing of the Earls of Clare to whom the property formerly belonged, before it was bought by Lord Clive. Round the base of the column are several inscriptions, one commemorating the marriage of Prince Leopold with Princess Char-

---

1. The Queen's factor.

lotte, another the building of Claremont House and the laying out of the grounds by 'Capability Brown'.

Mr M. took us over the equerries' quarters and showed us the comfortable rooms usually occupied by Sir Thomas Biddulph, Lord Alfred Paget and Col. Ponsonby. Lord Alfred Paget hates fire-guards and the housemaids always insisted on putting one on his fire. Whenever he came into his room the fire-guard was sure to be on. He tried to hide it in every corner of the room, but the housemaid always found it and put it on again. One day Lord Alfred was found on his knees to the great surprise of one of his friends who came in suddenly, for it was not a posture which was familiar to Lord Alfred. But it was discovered that he was striving to pack away the fire-guard into his portmanteau and so effect-ually hide it from the careful search of the housemaid. When the Queen comes over from Windsor to Claremont she drives at a great pace all the way, 12 miles an hour. The distance is 18 miles and she changes horses at Chertsey, but the equerry in attendance is obliged to ride the same horse all the way. A short time ago she came over for the day, Lord Alfred in attendance riding 16 stone and riding by the carriage door covered with mud from the wheels. They came at the grand trot all the way, and when they reached Claremont the Queen said alighting, 'I hope you are not tired, Lord Alfred.' 'Well, Ma'am', drawled Lord Alfred, 'we had all our work to do to keep up.' The Queen is always addressed in private as 'Madam' to save 'Your Majesty' which is not allowed.

From the passage of the equerries' quarters we descended a stair-case into the stables immediately below. The equerries try to get the horses put under each other's rooms that they themselves may not have their sleep broken by the stamping and neighing of the horses and the rattling and ringing of their chains. There is not room for the equerries usually in the house so they are sent down here to sleep. Mr M. gave us an admirable luncheon of roast mutton and claret followed by an excellent Gloucestershire wild duck. Also he made us drink some very powerful mountain dew. After which we sallied out towards the house which we entered by a back door after passing through a tunnel well managed so that tradesmen and servants can approach the back entrance without being seen from the house. We went through the large dark

111

kitchen with its immense fire and admirable hot plate dresser. In the back kitchen a boiler had just burst and the ruin of the boiler was standing surrounded by debris, waiting for repairs. Mr M. had been very busy in the house all the morning giving orders and superintending the preparations for Lord Lorne and the Princess Louise who are to pass their honeymoon here in March.[1]

We went up a staircase into the Grand Hall, which is oval and paved with white and black marble. There are some busts in the hall, of Prince Leopold and the Princess Charlotte.

The rooms lie en suite all round the grand hall and staircase. The first we went into was the drawing room furnished and coloured with blue, with some handsome orange-yellow Japanese or Chinese folding screens. The window seats of white marble. In this room are two beautiful pictures, one of the Duchess of Kent with the Princess Victoria as a child in her lap. The other has only lately been placed at Claremont and is a copy of the original picture of Princess Charlotte painted by her command and at her expense, and intended by her to be a birthday present to her husband for his birthday which happened just after her own death.

The face is a singularly beautiful one. The original picture is at Brussels. We saw also the room and bed in which the French Queen Marie Amélie died. In this room there are several portraits of the French family, including pictures of the French Queen herself and of her husband Louis Philippe. Next door was her dressing room with a deep large bath, almost concealed, in which the old French Queen was nearly drowned. Her attendant had left her for a few minutes and when she returned the old Queen was struggling and plunging about in the bath almost at her last gasp. Her picture gives the impression of a very handsome aristocratic person, of decided character, with a sweet and dignified face. Next is the room and bed in which the Princess Charlotte died. The room has remained almost undisturbed since then. At the time of the Princess's confinement the ministers of State were assembled in the dressing room adjoining.

Next is the Ball Room, a fine room some 60 feet by 30, carpeted with a richly coloured superb deep Persian carpet which was

---

1. The wedding took place on 21 March.

brought over by Lord Clive and which has been in use ever since. It had hard wear during the occupation of the French Royal Family for they used the room as a chapel and were always having prayers and mass in it. The carpet however has been scoured and looks entirely bright and new. This grand suite of rooms runs completely round the house and this and some others of the rooms look out towards Esher over the terrace and what is called the garden front of the house.

There are several more family portraits (English) in the dining room, but it was almost too dark to see them. There is a fine expanding table, and between the table and the fire stands a folding screen covered with pictures which Princess Charlotte used to cut out and colour and paste on to it as an amusement on wet days. The Queen (Victoria) sits at the round table with her back to the fire. When the French people were here they used to sit down to dinner every day 70 in number, the whole household assembling together and the upper servants sitting below the salt.

We went upstairs and got out on to the leads on the top of the house, from whence there is a splendid view on clear days. The Grand Stand at Epsom looks quite near. It began to rain and we came in again and went into the room now occupied by Sir W. Jenner. It is a room in the roof, low but large and comfortable. It was Lord Clive's bedroom, the room he chose in preference to all the rest of the house, and he never occupied any other. When the S.W. gales blew and rattled the windows Lord Clive used to get up in the night to wedge them tight and guineas being more plentiful with him than anything else he always used them. The housemaids used to transfer these guineas to their own pockets in the morning and prayed with reason for a S.W. storm. The room is said to be haunted and was not used for some time, but when Dr Jenner heard of this he said, 'Put me there', and he has been in possession ever since. The rooms are appropriated by cards with the names of the occupants written on them placed in brass card frames on the doors, e.g. 'Sir J. Biddulph', 'Sir W. Jenner', &c., &c.

Then we went out of doors to see the grounds.

Close to the corners of the house stand some noble ancient cedars, one with gigantic horizontal arms, one of them, the lowermost, supported by props. On a high mount clothed with wood rises the ruined tower built by the Earls of Clare. This mount gives the name of the Lords of Clare to Claremont. In their time the dwelling house stood lower down in the park. Below the mount there is a lake and beautiful alleys and glades of rhododendrons amongst the woods. Looking down upon the lake through a screening fringe of trees is the old summer arbour of the Princess, a place which she was very fond of and which the King of the Belgians after her death converted into a memorial temple. It was opened and unshuttered for us. It is a circular building with small high stained windows emblazoned with the arms of the Royal Houses. Before the door runs a small terrace with a low iron railing ornamented now with the monogram L.L. From the terrace you look down through the trees upon the lake.

The Camellia house was very beautiful, the trees loaded with white and crimson buds shining like stars among the glossy dark green foliage.

We wandered about the beautiful paths and glades under the great oaks and firs, till we came round again under the Claremont ruined tower peeping from the top of the steep high mount through the trees and so by the great cork tree to the front of the house adorned by the grand portico supported by massive and lofty Corinthian columns.

[The diarist returns to Langley Burrell]

Wednesday, 25 January

Mrs Daniell was at home and I sat some time talking to her. She told me about their 5 Japanese pupils, all noble, and one of royal blood, who has gone to the seat of war with an official deputation from Japan to make notes and take observations for the benefit of his country. Some of these young Japanese gentlemen live across the way at Miss Salters' old house. Mrs Daniell said that during the time they have had these Japanese the young men have never given them an uncomfortable moment, and their manners are perfect, so courteous and kind and so loving to each other. The Daniells had a very short notice of their coming. Fred Lowden wrote to ask Daniell to receive them whilst he was on the voyage with them, bringing them over. They go to Church, but they have no particular religion of their own. Only Saturday nights seemed to be a solemn time with them. One Saturday evening one of them was found in a dark room alone on his knees. Today it was rumoured that Paris was about to capitulate. How prophetic was the old Welsh country dance taught to men by the fairies and called (why?) 'The Downfall of Paris'. .

A fly took Fanny, Dora and myself to dinner at Langley House at 7.30. The Ashes were very agreeable and Thersie Ashe was in the drawing room before dinner sitting on an ottoman in a white dress, white boots and gloves, almost a grown-up young lady and looking exceedingly nice with her dark long hair and brilliant colour. I took Mrs Welsh into dinner and sat between her and Mrs Winthrop, whom I congratulated on her daughter Annie's engagement to a lieutenant in R.N. Mrs Winthrop jumped right round on her chair and stared at me as if she had heard the subject mentioned then for the first time. She said at last that she could not deny it, but the engagement was not publicly declared. It was a regular facer but her extraordinary manner was owing to her extreme nervousness. Mr Winthrop said that all the water he and his family had to wash in was some filthy black water full of black beetles stagnant on the leads.

[The diarist returns to Clyro.]

Wednesday, February Day, Candlemas Eve
Sarah Whitney came to my rooms this evening for an old pair of trousers I had promised her. She told me that Mrs Jones, the jockey's wife at the corner, had a fortnight ago left some linen drying out on the churchyard hedge all night having forgotten to take it in. By morning Mrs Jones declared two pairs of drawers and a 'shimmy' had been stolen, and her suspicions fell on some of the neighbours. She and her husband consulted the ordeal of the key and Bible (turning the key in the Bible). The key said, 'Bella Whitney'. Then Jones the jockey went to the brickyard and got some clay which he made into a ball. Inside the ball he put a live toad. The clay ball was either boiled or put into the fire and during the process of boiling or baking the toad was expected to scratch the name of the thief upon a piece of paper put into the clay ball along with him. Some other horrible charm was used to discover

115

the thief, the figure of a person being pricked out on a piece of clay. It is almost incredible.

Friday, 3 February

This evening we had our 4th Penny Reading. The room was fuller than ever, crammed, people almost standing on each other's heads, some sitting up on the high window-seats. Many persons came from Hay, Bryngwyn and Painscastle. Numbers could not get into the room and hung and clustered round the windows outside trying to get in at the windows. The heat was fearful and the foul air gave me a crushing headache and almost stupefied me. I recited Jean Ingelow's 'Reflections' and my own 'Fairy Ride'.

Saturday, 4 February

I hear that last night there were some 60 people standing outside the school during the whole time of the Readings. They were clinging and clustering round the windows, like bees, standing on chairs, looking through the windows, and listening, their faces tier upon tier. Some of them tried to get through the windows when the windows were opened for more air.

Monday, 6 February

I looked out at dawn. The moon was entangled among light clouds in the North and made a golden maze and network across which the slender poplars swayed and bowed themselves with a solemn and measured movement in the west wind.

The afternoon was so beautiful that I walked over to Broad Meadow to see old David Price again. David Price's young good-humoured-looking slatternly wife opened the door to me. The old man was in bed and weaker than when I saw him last. Price said, 'One day a lady was walking on a hill in Flintshire when she met Prince Caradoc who wanted to be rude with her but she spurned him. Whereupon he drew his sword and cut off her head. And a monk coming by at the moment clapped her head on again and she lived 15 years afterwards'.

Tuesday, 7 February

Finished reading *Puck*, clever, bitter, extravagant, full of repetitions and absurdities and ludicrous ambitious attempts at fine writing, weak and bombastic. The great blot is the insane and vicious hatred of women. Evidently written by a woman.

Monday, St Valentine's Eve
Mrs Vaughan told me that Mrs Irvine whom I used to see at Gilfach-y-rheol and the Harbour is still at the Harbour. She is a daughter of old Squire Beavan of Glascwm, who is a magistrate the deputy lieutenant. She married against his will one Lieutenant Irvine (I believe). When her husband died Mrs Irvine returned to her father's house at Glascwm. He refused to take her in, saying that her husband had left her £500 a year and that she had made away with it. She said this was all a wrong tale. Squire Beavan, who has some £1500 a year, then put his daughter upon the parish, and for some time she lived on 2/6 a week like a common pauper. Then the parish said her father should keep her. But her father wouldn't and sent her back to the parish. She soon got disgusted with being a pauper and was half starved. Out of pity the David Vaughans took her in on the condition that she should teach their children. But they soon found that she could teach them nothing, for she did not know anything about anything. Moreover she was of no use in the house for she would not turn her hand to a thing or make herself of the slightest use. They soon got very tired of her and she was a great burden and a heavy expense to them, taking the bread out of their many children's mouths. She stayed there *three years*. When they got her to go she went to the Joneses at the Cloggau where she stayed a year, and they could not get rid of her till in an unguarded moment she went one Sunday evening to Colva Church. When she came back she found the door locked and was earnestly recommended through an upstairs window to ask Mrs Jones of the Harbour for a night's lodging. She has been at the Harbour ever since, more than a year, and no one knows when she will go. She does not give them a chance of locking her out for she never leaves the house.

Friday, 24 February
Villaging about to Mrs Jones at the Infant School, Jo Phillips and Margaret Griffith, who told me that in the old-fashioned farm houses a steen of butter and something particularly good was

always kept till March and not touched because March was reckoned a very severe trying month and people were thought to want some special support then. Old-fashioned folks called March 'heir-loun' or some such name.

Saturday, 25 February
Sophy told me of the murder of 'Sammy', son of Rees Pritchard, the Great Vicar of Llandovery. He was murdered by the two half-brothers of the heiress of Maes y Felin whom Sammy was courting. They did not wish the property to go with her away from them and out of the family, so they waylaid their sister's lover, murdered him, put him in a sack, and threw him into the Towy. Ever after that 'the ill will of God' was upon Maes y Felin and nothing grew, trees nor grass.

A servant girl living at Pant y weil near Llandovery 150 years ago was told by her mistress overnight to get up very early in the morning and go to the town to fetch something. She got up at midnight and thinking the full moonlight was dawn started for Llandovery without looking at the clock. When she came to the bridge over the Towy she met four men carrying a dead man whom they threw into the river. The girl went home and died of the fright in two days. 'They murdered him,' said Sophy in her broken English, 'according to money.'

Monday, 27 February
Tossing about with face ache till 3 o'clock this morning. Clyro Petty Sessions. Fifteen people summoned for neglecting to have their children vaccinated, but they got off by paying costs. A full bench of magistrates, 5, and the Chief Constable was present. An old magistrate, Mr Bold, came in late and in long riding leggings, very dirty, for he had ridden from Boughrood. He amused himself during a dull part of the proceedings by combing his grey hair with a pocket comb. Then he lay back in his chair with his hands clasped behind his head.

I hear the Rifle Volunteer Corps Concert at Hay last Wednesday was moderately successful. In the middle of the performance the Rifle Corps band played 'Vital Spark', and a man named Clement skated round the platform upon wheel skates, and fell off into the front row of ladies. Every one rose, the ladies were very much frightened, and one lady's dress was irretrievably damaged. Can any one conceive a more senseless piece of buffoonery?

Wednesday, March Day

After dinner last night Mr V. kindly anxious to cure my face ache made me drink four large glasses of port. The consequence was that all night and all today I have been groaning with a bursting raging splitting sick headache.

Thursday, March Morrow

I went up the lane to see the old soldier and read him from *The Times* a notice of Lord Palmerston's tours in France in 1814 and 1818, mentioning the occupation of Paris by the Allies, and giving some anecdotes of the Duke and his opinion of the British soldiers, especially of the Peninsular regiments. The Duke's kind words pleased the old Peninsular Veteran. He remembered the time so well. He had seen them all in their pride. Emperors, King, Duke. Then I read to him by the fast fading light Matthew ix and after some talk he asked to receive the Sacrament shortly. As I came home alone in the dusk the banks above and the meadows below the road were filled with the sweet last singing of innumerable birds.

Monday, 6 March

I like wandering about these lonely, waste and ruined places. There dwells among them a spirit of quiet and gentle melancholy more congenial and akin to my own spirit than full life and gaiety and noise.

Sunday, 12 March

After evening service I went in to see Joe Phillips and read some of the Evening Prayers for him. He told me that on the night when Anne Phillips, Jane Phillips' daughter, ran down from Clyro Court, threw herself into the river and was drowned, some of the Sheep House lads across the river who were out in the meadows late looking after the sheep and cattle, heard loud and repeated screams from the river. It was getting dark, and they could see nothing. The poor girl's father was in prison and some of her fellow servants had been twitting her with this and saying, 'When your father comes out of prison there will be a place for you'. She jumped up, ran straight down to the river and plunged in. Her grandmother hung herself at the Burnt House, behind the door.

Tuesday, 14 March

The afternoon had been stormy but it cleared towards sunset. Gradually the heavy rain clouds rolled across the valley to the foot of the opposite mountains and began climbing up their sides wreathing in rolling masses of vapour. One solitary cloud still hung over the brilliant sunlit town, and that whole cloud was a rainbow. Gradually it lost its bright prismatic hues and moved away up the Cusop Dingle in the shape of a pillar and of the colour of golden dark smoke. The Black Mountains were invisible, being wrapped in clouds, and I saw one very white brilliant dazzling cloud where the mountains ought to have been. This cloud grew more white and dazzling every moment, till a clearer burst of sunlight scattered the mists and revealed the truth. This brilliant white cloud that I had been looking and wondering at was the mountain in snow. The last cloud and mist rolled away over the mountain tops and the mountains stood up in the clear blue heaven, a long rampart line of dazzling glittering snow so as no fuller on earth can white them. I stood rooted to the ground, struck with amazement and overwhelmed at the extraordinary splendour of this marvellous spectacle. I never saw anything to equal it I think, even among the high Alps. One's first involuntary thought in the presence of these magnificent sights is to lift up the heart to God and humbly thank Him for having made the earth so beautiful. An intense glare of primrose light streamed from the west deepening into rose and crimson. There was not a flake of snow anywhere but on the mountains and they stood up, the great white range rising high into the blue sky, while all the rest of the world at their feet lay ruddy rosy brown. The sudden contrast was tremendous, electrifying. I could have cried with the excitement of the overwhelming spectacle. I wanted someone to admire the sight with me. A man came whistling along the road riding upon a cart horse. I would have stopped him and drawn his attention to the mountains but I thought he would probably consider me mad. He did not seem to be the least struck by or to be taking the smallest notice of the great sight. But it seemed to me as if one might never see such a sight again. The great white range which had at first gleamed with an intense brilliant yellow light gradually deepened with the sky to the indescribable red tinge that snow-fields assume in sunset light, and then the grey cold tint crept up the great slopes quenching the rosy warmth which lingered still a few minutes on the summits. Soon all was cold and grey and all that was left of the brilliant gleaming range was the dim ghostly phantom of the mountain rampart scarce distinguishable from the greying sky.

Saturday, 18 March
A heavenly day, reminding one of Wordsworth's 'March Noon', larks mounting, bees humming in the hot afternoon, lambs playing. Children in the lanes gathering violets and primroses, and the mountain streaked and striped and ribbed with snow.

Mothering Sunday, 19 March
And all the country in an upturn going out visiting. Girls and boys going home to see their mothers and taking them cakes, brothers and sisters of middle age going to see each other. As I walked to Bettws it was so sultry that I thought it would thunder. The sun was almost overpowering. Heavy black clouds drove up and rolled round the sky without veiling the hot sunshine, black clouds with white edges they were, looking suspiciously like thunder clouds. Against these black clouds the sunshine showed the faint delicate green and pink of the trees thickening with bursting buds.

Brothering Monday, 20 March
Miserable news from Paris. Another Revolution, barricades, the troops of the line fraternizing with the insurgent National Guards, two Generals shot, two more in the hands and tender mercies of the beastly cowardly Paris mob. Those Parisians are the scum of the earth, and Paris is the crater of the volcano, France, and a bottomless pit of revolution and anarchy.

Friday, 24 March
After luncheon I spent a happy half hour in the lovely warm afternoon wandering about Clyro churchyard among the graves. I sat awhile on the old Catholic tomb of the 'Relict of Thomas

Bridgwater' under the S. Church wall, near the chancel door. This is my favourite tomb. I love it better than all the tombs in the churchyard with its kindly 'Requiescat in pace', the prayer so full of peace, with its solemn reminder 'Tendimus huc omnes' and the simple Latin cross at the head of the inscription. There is something much more congenial to my mind in these old Catholic associations than in the bald ugly hideous accompaniments which too often mark the place of Protestant or rather Puritan burial. The Puritans of the last century seem to have tried to make the idea and place and associations of death and burial as gloomy, hideous and repulsive as possible, and they have most signally succeeded.

A small and irreverent spider came running swiftly towards me across the flat tombstone and scuttling over the sacred words and memories with most indecent haste and levity. Here it was very quiet and peaceful, nothing to disturb the stillness but the subdued village voices and the cawing of the rooks nesting and brooding in the tops of the high trees in the Castle clump. Somewhere near at hand I he⸱ ⸱d the innkeeper's voice behind the church and across the brook giving orders to a workman about planting some quick and privet.

Wednesday, 29 March
Went down the meadows to Mrs Tudor's. Handsome Tudor was working in his garden. By the door lay a salmon rod on the ground, so I knew the Squire was having luncheon in the cottage. I went round and there he was with old Harry Pritchard. He brought out his telescope and we had a look at Crichton and Mrs Nicholl both wading in the river and fishing under the red cliff. I crossed the ditch, climbed the bank and went along the beautiful cliff walk on the edge of the cliff looking over the edge at Mrs Nicholl standing on a rock fishing far below till I came to a steep path leading down the rocks to where Crichton was fishing. 'Henry,' called Mrs Nicholl's voice faintly down the river. 'She has got a good fish,' said Crichton, winding up his line after looking at her a moment. We scrambled over the rocks to her, but she had landed her fish before we reached her. I was amazed to see

Mrs Nicholl coolly wading more than ankle deep in the river with her ordinary lady's boots on. She walked about in the river as if she were on dry land, jumped from rock to rock, slipped off the rocks into the river, scrambled out again, splashed about like a fish. March water is cold. Mrs Nicholl must be an uncommonly plucky woman. Crichton says she rides to hounds and nothing stops her. She does not care what she does. He hooked a salmon the other day and his boy was clumsy in landing the fish, so Mrs Nicholl plunged into the water on the edge of a deep hole, embraced the great fish round the body, and carried him out in her arms.

Friday, April Eve
A letter from Emily Dew asking me to go to Whitney Rectory either tomorrow or next Tuesday to meet Miss Hutchinson, the niece of William Wordsworth by marriage and the god-daughter of his sister Dorothy, for whom I have a great admiration. I shall certainly go. I remember seeing this Miss Hutchinson at Whitney Rectory with her sister years ago, but then they were very shy and hid behind a hedge.

Saturday, April Day
I went to Whitney by the 2.6 train. Miss Hutchinson was at home at the Rectory. She is the niece of Mary Hutchinson, the wife of William Wordsworth the poet. And she was the god-daughter of Dorothy Wordsworth, William's sister. We had some interesting talk about the Wordsworth family. She showed me first a large brooch she was wearing containing on one side a beautiful coloured photograph of the poet, and on the other side two locks of grey hair from the heads of the poet and his wife. This photograph is far the best and most pleasing likeness I have seen of the poet. It was taken from a picture painted by H—[1] almost entirely from memory. The poet had written to the painter telling him with pride that he had ascended Helvellyn when he was 70 years old, and sending him a sonnet on the occasion. The painter was extremely pleased with the letter and the sonnet and immediately

---

1. Presumably Haydon.

drew Wordsworth in a meditative mood composing the sonnet.

Miss Hutchinson said that once, when she was staying at the Wordsworths', the poet was much affected by reading in the newspaper the death of Hogg the Ettrick Shepherd. Half an hour afterwards he came into the room where the ladies were sitting and asked Miss Hutchinson to write down some lines which he had just composed. She did so, and these lines were the beautiful poem called the Graves of the Poets. He was very desultory and disinclined to write. His ladies were always urging him to do so however. And he would have written little if it had not been for his wife and sister. He could not bear the act of writing and he wrote so impatiently and impetuously that his writing was rarely legible. He was very absent and has been known to walk unconsciously through a flock of sheep without perceiving them. He had many books read to him in his later years when his eyesight grew weak. He did not care much for society and preferred the society of women to that of men. With men he was often reserved.

When William Howitt was at Rydal Mount looking about after Wordsworth's death he fell in with old James the gardener and asked him which was the poet's study. 'This,' said James pointing to the arbour and the grass mound from which Rydal Mount takes its name. William Wordsworth was a tall man. Dorothy was short and spare. She was a great walker in her youth and suffered physically and mentally as she grew old for having overtaxed her strength when she was young with excessively long walks. When she was middle aged and growing elderly she thought nothing of walking from Brinsop into Hereford, six miles and back, if she wanted a thimble. When she was staying at the Hutchinsons' farm in Radnorshire she would walk into Kington and back on the smallest excuse. During her imbecility she had frequent intervals when all her old brightness, liveliness and clearness of mind returned. Then she relapsed into her sad state. She and her brother used often to stay at Mrs Monkhouse's at the Stow farm, Whitney. Dorothy had a lucid interval at her brother's death. She was deeply affected at his loss, left her room and came to his bedside when he was dying.

Tuesday, 4 April

A letter from my mother brings the astonishing news that Mr Ashe wishes to have a stove in Langley Burrell Church, will offer no opposition to the gallery being taken down to admit of the stove being placed at the West end of the church, and has actually been going about the Church to see where additional seats can be contrived. Also he is going to cut down a tree worth £10 and will devote the proceeds towards the stove erection. Wonders will never cease.

Easter Monday, 10 April

After lunch Mrs Venables came down and asked me to drive to Boughrood with her and the Miss Halls. No one was at home at Boughrood Castle for which reason Mrs V. called there, and knowing beforehand the reply to the question we could scarcely keep our countenances while the servant solemnly asked if Mrs Bold was at home. Mrs V. said that one afternoon late she drove up to the door of Boughrood Castle to call and heard Mrs Bold's voice from an upper window saying aloud, 'I can't think what makes people come at this time of day'.

Friday, 14 April

In the cross lane below Tybella old deaf Tom Gore was mending a ruined dry stone wall. He said he had only one pair of boots in the world, they were cracked and full of holes and he had asked in vain of the relieving officer to beg the Board of Guardians to give him a new pair. He told me his wife was ill and he hoped he should not lose her. He remembered what it was after he lost his first wife, how he often came home wet through to the skin and no fire and no food cooked. Four little children of his lay side by side in Bryngwyn Churchyard. He had seen trouble. He didn't know but he thought it was a fate. I could scarcely make him understand a word. He went on building up his stone wall at half a crown a perch and I went on to see his wife.

Hetty Gore was very indignant with Mainwaring, who keeps a school on the Rhos Goch, and removed her children from his school because he said that she and three Bryngwyn women ought to be and he wished they were hung up all together to balance each other. When this neighbourly wish and saying was inquired into and he was asked his reason he said that Hetty Gore was starving him, the fact being that she had owed him sixpence for a week. Hannah Gore was born with six fingers on each hand but not with six toes. Her feet were all right. The sixth finger was cut off each hand.

Saturday, 15 April

Last night like a fool I drank strong tea and in consequence I tossed from side to side the livelong night and never closed my eyes till five o'clock this morning, with the additional comfort of being in a frantic state of nervous energy.

The Miss Halls left the vicarage this morning at 9.45 to catch the 10.13 train for Neath. I had promised to go and wish them goodbye but when I got to the Vicarage stable yard at 11 o'clock the carriage was gone. William Pugh was chaffcutting in the barn. 'They are at Hay by now,' he said consolingly. And I like an idiot thought the train went at 11.26. Provoking, vexing. I would have given a sovereign to see them and speak to them once more. And what must they have thought? That I would not take the trouble to come to see them off in spite of my promise. I crossed the lawn, seeing Mrs Venables and the baby in the drawing room. But in spite of them how cold blank dull and empty the room looked. There was the table at which they used to sit writing letters. Ten days ago I scarcely knew of their existence nor cared. And now. Mrs V. said they had left a kind message for me. They were all disappointed when I did not come in time. I am so vexed. I should have loved dearly to take another look at their bonnie faces. Especially Kathleen's. How well I remember her standing at the head of the grave on Easter Eve and making up the primroses into bunches for the primrose cross. Her little foot peeped out from under her dress. I thought it was the prettiest foot I ever saw. Then there was Church on Good Friday (just as Petrarch first saw Laura 'in the Cathedral on Good Friday' when and where was 'kindled that world-renowned flame'). And there was the drive to Boughrood, the call at Cae Mawr, the dinner party in the evening, and the place where she sat by the Maiden's Stile. Ah they are nice sweet girls, so natural and genuine, so pleasant and so kind. Well. Well. Such is life, comings and goings and meetings and partings.

I thought I was not going to care for any one again. I wonder if there is any receipt for hardening the heart and making it less impressible.

I went sadly back to my room, took down and went sorrowfully on with my sermon for tomorrow, feeling as if all was dull and blank and as if some light and interest had suddenly gone out of life. It was pleasant to see Mrs Nash downstairs again in the cosy little warm parlour. I went to read to Sackville Thomas. Being tub night Polly with great celerity and satisfaction stripped herself naked to her drawers before me and was very anxious to take off her drawers too for my benefit, but her grandmother would not allow her. As it happened the drawers in question were so inadequately constructed that it made uncommonly little difference whether they were off or on, and there was a most interesting view from the rear. Then her grandmother washed her head with soft soap and hot water in a tub, the little image kneeling down in her drawers on the cold stone floor with her head in the tub close to the open door into the road.

Wednesday, 19 April
Mr Venables heard this morning from Chelsea Hospital. The authorities have granted a pension of ninepence a day to our old Peninsular veteran John Morgan of the Bronith with arrears from February. Mr V. went to the old man's house to announce the good news.

Monday, May Day
Up early, breakfast at 7 and the dog cart took me to the station for the 8 train. It was a lovely May morning, and the beauty of the river and green meadows, the woods, hills and blossoming orchards was indescribable. At Hereford two women were carrying a Jack in the Green about the High Town. In the next carriage a man was playing a harp and a girl a violin as the train travelled. At Chippenham no one was at the station. I left my luggage and walked up to Langley.

Sunday, 7 May
I went to church early, soon after ten o'clock, across the quiet sunny meadows. There was scarcely any one about – only one boy

loitering by the stile in Becks by the road under the elms. The trees are in their most exquisite and perfect loveliness. There is usually one day in the Spring when the beauty of everything culminates and strikes one peculiarly, even forcing itself upon one's notice and a presentiment comes that one will never see such loveliness again at least for another year. This is the day that Robert Burns delighted in, the first fine Sunday in May. He had a peculiar love for such a day as this. The great elms shaded the road from the glowing sunshine and everything was still and beautiful and green.

I went into the churchyard under the feathering larch which sweeps over the gate. The ivy-grown old church with its noble tower stood beautiful and silent amongst the elms with its graves at its feet. Everything was still. No one was about or moving and the only sound was the singing of birds. The place was all in a charm of singing, full of peace and quiet sunshine. It seemed to be given up to the birds and their morning hymns. It was the bird church, the church among the birds. I wandered round the church among the dewy grass-grown graves and picturesque ivy- and moss-hung tombstones. Round one grave grew a bed of primroses. Upon another tall cowslips hung their heads.

The hour for service drew on. The clerk coughed in the church. Two girls in grey dresses passed quietly through the church and moved about among the graves on the N. side bending over a grave beneath the elm. Then a woman in deep mourning moved slowly down the path of the churchyard, and the clerk began to ring the bell for service. My Father read prayers and I preached on the Master washing the disciples' feet.

Monday, 8 May
It was very hot this morning, burning hot as I was in the garden tying up 3 or 4 dozen lettuces. A cuckoo sat in the broken elm overhead, moaning and chuckling and making an odd noise like a dove. The two cows stood up to their udders in the pond in the little field under the shade of the high hawthorn hedge that almost encircles the pond. I took a book to the white gate and stood in the shade of the trees reading and watching the people crossing the sunny common to and fro by the several paths.

Tuesday, 9 May

I went to Hannah Hatherell's. Hannah told me of a dream Jane had shortly before she died which comforted her very much. She dreamt she saw a man lying down and a snowdrop was growing out of his breast. Then she heard a voice saying, 'Wash me and I shall be whiter than snow'. She thought it was a very comfortable dream. Sometimes she had frightful dreams which terrified her.

Wednesday, 10 May

Fanny and I walked to Harnish house to dinner at 7.30. After the ladies had left the dining room Mr Winthrop and Mr Bolden got into a warm theological discussion. Mr Winthrop, anxious to refute all High Church arguments and repudiate all High Church tendencies, threw over the Church altogether, denied the gift of the Holy Spirit at Ordination and Baptism, denied the presence of the Saviour with His Ministers, denied everything in short, and there was nothing left. He said a man became a clergyman just as he became a gardener by taking up that particular line of life.

Friday, 12 May

My Mother's birthday. I gave her a travelling brass inkstand. Please God that she may long be spared to us.

[The diarist returns to Clyro.]

Wednesday, 17 May

The great May Hiring Fair at Hay, and squadrons of horse came charging and battalions of foot tramping along the dusty roads to the town, more boys and fewer girls than usual. All day long the village has been very quiet, empty, most of the village folk being away at the fair. Now at 8 p.m. the roads are thronged with people pouring home again, one party of three men riding on one horse.

Sunday, 21 May

After Church visited some of the cottages. Elizabeth Pugh told me that when she was living at Little Pen-y-fforest she used to go to the Baptist and Independent Chapels at Painscastle. Stones were frequently thrown into the Chapels among the congregation during service, and once a dog was hurled in. There was a great laugh when the dog was seen flying in.

Monday, 22 May

[The diarist walks to Glascwm.]

First I went to the Vicarage. A pair of shears lay on the door step and a beautiful luxuriant sweet briar[1] climbed a trellis by the door and filled the whole porch with fragrance. I met the old Vicar magistrate in the hall with his stout frame, ruddy face, white hair, stern long sweeping eyebrows and a merry odd twinkle in his eye. One of the last of the old-fashioned parsons. He gave me some splendid Herefordshire cider and some bread and butter and there came in with him a very small black and tan terrier named Ti (or Tiger I suppose), a waddling wheezing gasping mass, a ball of fat.

'I am bishop here,' said the Vicar. Then fetching the church key he added, 'Come and see the Cathedral'.

The Cathedral lay a little distance down a pretty lane over-arched and avenued with sycamores and limes. It was one of the very large Welsh Churchyards, 2 acres in extent and thinly peopled. The church long low and whitewashed, an unbroken line of roof without a tower or bell-turret of any kind. An immense chancel and an equally large belfry and a small nave. The belfry is the village school, fitted up with desks, forms and master's desk and a fireplace. The village clerk is village schoolmaster. In a huge deep Church chest were an old parish accounts book, an enormous flagon of pewter and pewter paten and a fragment of one of the Church bells. There used to be three good bells in Glascwm Church brought by the enchanted bisons from Llandewi Brefi. Just before the present Vicar came there was a tremendous wedding of a farmer's daughter. There was great enthusiasm and excitement and the bells were required to ring very loud. One bell did not ring loud enough to satisfy the people so they took an axe up to the bell and beat the bell with the axe till they beat it all to pieces.

At the west end of the churchyard almost hidden in trees is the Yat, Squire Beavan's house, or as the Squire tries to have it called, Glascwm Court. Just outside the churchyard the Beavan family have a private burial ground, unconsecrated, where a number of them are buried.

---

1. Some pressed leaves of the briar are inserted in the MS. at this point.

Mr Marsden entertained me with some reminiscences of his own. 'A public house in the village, haven't we?' he said. 'We just have, and they keep a fearful noise there sometimes. Then I put my head out of my bedroom window and holla to them and they fly like the wind. When I was curate of Llangorse,' he said, 'the Vicar of Talgarth was ill and I had to procure an assistant curate. So I wrote to Llewellyn, now Dean of St David's – then Principal of Lampeter – to send me a man who wanted a title for orders and could speak Welsh and English. Llewellyn wrote that he had the very man for me, *doctus utriusque linguae*. The man came. I saw his Welsh was very shaky.

Once he was publishing Banns. He meant to say, 'Why these two persons may not lawfully be joined together in holy Matrimony'. But what he did say was, 'Why these two backsides may not lawfully be joined together in Holy Matrimony'. Everyone in Church hid their faces. When we came out of Church I said, 'Well, you *have* done it now'. 'What?' said he. I told him. 'God forbid,' said he. 'It is true,' I said.

Wednesday, 24 May
Dined at Cae Mawr and we had a capital stuffed and roasted pike. Baron Meyer Rothschild's Favonius has won the Derby today.

Thursday, 25 May
Today we read in the paper that the Assembly troops are in possession of Paris, but that Paris is on fire, the Communists having yesterday drenched with petroleum the Tuileries, the Louvre, Nôtre Dame, the Hôtel de Ville and La Sainte Chapelle and set them in flames. When the telegram left Paris at 6.30 last night the Tuileries were a heap of ashes, the Louvre not much better and no hope of saving anything, the petroleum flames were so furious.

Saturday, 27 May
At the top of Jacobs Ladder met Miss Sandell with the Morrell children carrying home from their ramble a beautiful rich nosegay of wild flowers. They had found the bog bean, the butterwort, milk-wort in four varieties, butterfly orchis, mouse ear, marsh valentine, marsh buttercup, hawkweed fumitory, yellow pim-

pernel, yellow potentilla. The children showed me what I never found out for myself or knew before, that the bog bean grows in the wern below Great Gwernfydden. And I have walked 14 miles for that flower, when it grew close by. Miss Sandell taught me more about these flowers in ten minutes than I have learnt from books in all my life. She knows a great deal about flowers. She did not know the comfrey or the yellow hill-violet, some of which I promised to bring her from the Warren Hill today.

Saturday, 3 June
Mrs Griffiths told me that a few days ago a man named Evans kicked his wife to death at Rhulen. He kicked her bosom black and her breasts mortified.

Monday, 12 June
At 1 o'clock I started with my Father for North Wales. Just before we reached Barmouth Junction the train was hailed and pulled up and a party of people came tumbling into our carriage. It was Strong, Mary and Freddy and two Misses Davies. They were staying at Barmouth and had been out into the country to visit a friend who had influence enough to hail the train as if it were an omnibus and pull it up for them. From Barmouth Junction leaving the sea we travelled up the beautiful valley to Dolgelly beside the noble estuary of the Mawddach, mountains standing close on either side of the river.

We drove to Miss Roberts' Hotel, the Golden Lion. 'Did you had your luggage?' asked the omnibus driver. I was very much struck and taken with the waitress at the Golden Lion. She said her name was Jane Williams and that her home was at Bettws y Coed. She was a beautiful girl with blue eyes, eyes singularly lovely, the sweetest saddest most weary and most patient eyes I ever saw. It seemed as if she had a great sorrow in her heart. Into the soup the cook had upset both the salt cellar and the pepper box. After dinner we went out and strolled round the town. Wombwell's menagerie had just come in and town was all alive and swarming with people. The caravans were drawn up in the 'Marian Mawr', the marshy meadow at the back of the Hotel just outside the Golden Lion garden. It seemed so strange to hear the little children chattering Welsh. I have always had a vision of coming into a Welsh town about sunset and seeing the children playing on the bridge and this evening the dream came true.

Tuesday, 13 June

Up at 5.30. Not a soul stirring in the house, the front door locked and the key gone. I got out by the garden door and through the wicket into the Marian Mawr. There was the caravan. The people were all asleep, but the lions were rustling and growling about their dens hungry for breakfast. The caravans were full of strange noises of the different beasts. I knocked at the lions' door and at the door of the ostriches, gnus and antelopes, eliciting divers roars, groans, howls, hoots and grunts. In the town I met the guide, old Pugh, coming to meet me. He took me to his house and furnished me with an alpenstock while his good wife gave me some tea and bread and butter for I could get nothing at the inn.

As we went towards the mountain my old guide told me how Mr Smith (Tom Colborne's clerk at Newport), was lost on Cader Idris some 6 years ago. He was on a tour in N. Wales, walking with his knapsack and had come to Machynlleth. He wanted the guide on the Machynlleth side to go over the mountain with him and offered him 2/6. The guide refused, saying his fee to go to the top of the mountain was 5/- and if he went on down the other side it was 10/-. Moreover the guide strongly advised Mr Smith not to attempt the ascent alone that evening, for night would soon fall and the weather was bad. However Mr Smith persisted in going on and the guide went a little way with him to put him in the right road. Two days after this guide was in Dolgelly and meeting my guide, old Pugh, he asked if he had seen anything of the gentleman who had crossed the Cader from Machynlleth to Dolgelly two days before. Pugh said he had neither seen nor heard anything of him although he had been up Cader Idris twice that day, one time being late in the evening. So they supposed Mr Smith had changed his mind and had gone down from the top of the mountain to Towyn. But 6 weeks passed. Nothing was heard of him and his wife grew very uneasy. His brother came to Machynlleth, Towyn, and Dolgelly to make inquiries but could hear nothing, and the mountain was searched without result. Mr

Smith disappeared in September, and in the following May a man was up on Cader Idris looking for a quarry. He heard his dog bark suddenly and looking over a precipice he saw a dead body. He hurried back to Dolgelly and fetched a doctor and policeman and the coroner, and Pugh came along with them. When the body was turned over Pugh was horrified. He said he never saw such a sight and he hoped he should never see such another. It was what had been Mr Smith. It was a skeleton in clothes. The foxes and ravens had eaten him. His eyes were gone. His teeth were dashed out by the fall and lay scattered about the mountain. His head was bent double under him and crushed into his chest so that his neck was broken. The only piece of flesh remaining on the bone was where the coat buttoned over the chest. One leg was gone and one boot. Pugh looked up and saw something white lying on a ledge above where the body lay. It was his knapsack. When it was brought down there were his things, his papers, his money. Then his stick was found. And some months afterwards Pugh found his hat. Pugh said he had probably tried to come down a short way to Dolgelly and must have fallen down a precipice in the mist and growing darkness. He showed me the place where the body was found. He found the marks the body had made in falling and knew exactly the point it had fallen from. He had carefully measured the distance and declared the body must have fallen 440 yards.

My old guide comes of a family of Welsh harpers. His brother is now harper to [   ] Sir Watkin's sister. Another brother who is dead won a silver harp at an Eisteddfod and was one of the best harpers in Wales. Pugh said there was a harper at Corwen and another at Llangollen and he knew an old bard at Corwen. He told me he had once been up Cader Idris 4 times in one day for a £10 wager against a reading party of 4 or 5 Cambridge men who declared he could not do it. On the last day of September a pouring wet day he did it and won the wager easily. He could have gone up the 5th time. A man on each side was posted on the top of the mountain and a man on each side at the bottom to see fair play and that Pugh did not ride up. It was stipulated that he should go up by the pony road and come down any way he liked. Coming down the first time he nearly came to trouble and was delayed 20 minutes in this way. He had noticed often when on the mountain that at a particular place his dog usually put up a fox and that the fox always disappeared down a cleft in the rocks. When walking for the wager he thought of this fox path and thought it would take him down quicker. Supposing that he could go where a fox went he slid down the narrow chasm and found that it led to the brink of a precipice. He could not go back and he was obliged to go on so taking off his boots and slinging them round his neck he clambered down. He did not try that way again.

By this time we had come to a place where was a lake by the roadside and in a boat on the lake were two men fishing. Leaving the road here we turned up a rough lane and crossing a little brook by a farm house were on the open mountain. As we sloped up the mountain side we had beautiful views of the Harlech mountains opposite, blue Cardigan Bay and dim Snowdon. The zig-zag path was steep in parts and a great wind blew over the mountain so that I had to sit down in a sheltered place and tie the band of my hat to my button-hole with the old guide's neckerchief, for, said the old man, 'Many hats have been lost on this ridge'. We aimed for a great stone on the top of the first ridge. After this the climbing was not so severe. The old man came up very slowly. Soon after we passed the great stone we passed through a gateway the posts of which were large basaltic pillars. Here we saw a mountain standing apparently close by waiting upon Cader Idris. It was Plynlimmon. Here we passed round over the back of the mountain and began ascending the summit from the S. We came to a little round pool or rather hole full of water. The old man pulled a little tumbler out of his pocket rinsed it and gave me a glass of the clear bright water. It was delicious. Then he drank himself. He said the pool was the head water or spring of the Dysyni River. He had never known it dry in the driest summers. We saw from the spring the winding gleam of the Dysyni wandering down a desolate valley to join the Dyfi, its sister stream.

About this time the wind changed and flew suddenly round into the S. The head of Idris, which had been cowled in cloud, had cleared for a while, but now an impenetrable dark cloud settled down upon it and the mist came creeping down the mountain. The sky looked black and threatened rain. Now there lay before us vast tracts and belts of large stones lying so close together that

135

no turf could be seen and no grass could grow between them. It was broken basalt, and huge lengths of basalt, angled, and some hexagonal, lay about or jutted from the mountain side like enormous balks of timber and with an unknown length buried in the mountain. We passed quarries where some of the great columns had been dug out to be drawn down the mountain on sledges. Cader Idris is the stoniest, dreariest, most desolate mountain I was ever on. We came now to the edge of a vast gulf or chasm or bason almost entirely surrounded by black precipices rising from the waters of a small black tarn which lay in the bottom of the bason. Here the guide showed me the place at the foot of an opposite precipice where Mr Smith's body had been found. Then we stumbled and struggled on again over rough tracts and wildernesses of slate and basalt. The sun was shining on the hills below, but the mist crawled down and wrapped us as if in a shroud blotting out everything. The mists and clouds began to sweep by us in white thin ghostly sheets as if some great dread Presences and Powers were going past and we could only see the skirts of their white garments. The air grew damp and chill, the cloud broke on the mountain top and it began to rain. Now and then we could discern the black sharp peak which forms the summit looming large and dark through the cloud and rain and white wild driving mist, and it was hidden again. It is an awful place in a storm. I thought of Moses on Sinai.

The rain grew heavier. The old guide could not get on very fast and told me to go on alone to the top and shelter in the hut as I could not miss the path. So I went on up the last sharp peak looming black through the dark mist and cloud, by a winding path among the great rocks and wildernesses of loose stone. For a few minutes I was alone on the top of the mountain. The thought struck me, suppose the old man should be seized with cramp in the stomach here, how in the world should I get him down or get down myself in the blinding mist? The cloud and mist and rain swept by and drove eddying round the peak. I could hear the old man chinking his iron-shod staff among the rocks and stones, as he came up the path, nearer and nearer, but till he got close to me I could not discern his white figure through the dense mist. 'This is the highest point of *Cader Idris*', he said, laying his hand upon a peak of wet living rock, 'not *that*', looking with contempt at the great conical pile of stones built upon the peak by the sappers and miners during the Ordnance Survey. He said, 'The Captain of the surveying company had his tent pitched on the top of Cader Idris for 3 summer months and never left the place. He had 18 men to wait upon him. And how many clear views do you think he got in that time?' 'Twelve', I hazarded. 'Nine', he said.

He took me down to a rude 2-roomed hut built of huge stones by his father just under the shelter of the peak, and produced for my benefit a hard-boiled egg and some slices of bread and butter. Also he gave me a woollen comforter to wrap round my neck. Then he vanished. The mist drove in white sheets and shapes past the doorless doorway and past the windows from which the window frames had been removed and the wind whistled through the chinks in the rude walls of huge stones. A large flat block of stone in the middle of the room on which I sat formed the table. It is said that if any one spends a night alone on the top of Cader Idris he will be found in the morning either dead or a madman or a poet gifted with the highest degree of inspiration. Hence Mrs Hemans' fine song 'A night upon Cader Idris'. The same thing is said of the top of Snowdon and of a great stone at the foot of Snowdon. Old Pugh says the fairies used to dance near the top of the mountain and he knows people who have seen them.

Presently I heard the old man clinking his stick among the rocks and coming round the hut. He came in and lighted his pipe and we prepared to go down by the 'Foxes' Path'. And indeed it was a path fit only for foxes. After leading me a few steps he began to go over what seemed to me to be the edge of a precipice, depth unknown and hidden in the mist. The side of the mountain was frightfully steep here and required great care in going down. Suddenly the old man stopped at a beautiful little spring in the almost perpendicular bank, pulled out his tumbler and gave me a draught of the clear sparkling water, much colder than the water from the spring of Dysyni. About the spring the grass grew brilliant green and there was a long winding riband of bright green where the waters overflowing from the spring trickled down through the grass stems to feed the lake at which the foxes drink just below. Next we came to a broad belt of loose rocks lying close together which the guide cautioned me to beware of and not without reason saying they were as slippery as glass and that a sprained ankle was an awkward thing on the mountain. Down, down and out of the cloud into sunshine, all the hills below and the valleys were bathed in glorious sunshine – a wonderful and dazzling sight. Above and hanging overhead the vast black precipices towered and loomed through the clouds, and fast as we went down the mist followed faster and presently all the lovely sunny landscape was shrouded in a white winding sheet of rain. The path was all loose shale and stone and so steep that planting our alpenstocks from behind and leaning back upon them Alpine fashion we glissaded with a general landslip, rush and rattle of shale and shingle down to the shore of the Foxes' Lake. The parsley fern grew in sheets of brilliant green among the grey shale and in the descent we passed the largest basaltic columns of all protruding from the mountain side. In the clefts and angles of the huge grey tower columns grew beautiful tufts and bunches of parsley fern. We passed another lake and after some rough scrambling walking over broken ground at the mountain foot we came back into the turnpike road at the lake that we had passed in the morning. As we entered Dolgelly the old man said, 'You're a splendid walker, Sir', a compliment which procured him a glass of brandy and water.

[The diarist and his father continue their tour.]

Friday, 16 June

As we crossed the bridge [at Bangor] and were approaching the Anglesey shore we overtook a quaint humorous old man with a tall white hat, a merry twinkle in his eye, and a huge cancer in his face. I fell into talk with him. 'Now', he said as we left the Bridge and walked into Anglesey, 'now you are like Robinson Crusoe, you are on your island. How should you like to live in that house all the year round, winter and summer?' he said pointing to a white house on a little rock island in the straits. I said I thought there might be worse places. 'They live like fighting cocks there', winked the old man with the merry twinkle in his eye and his tall white hat nodding from side to side. 'They have got a weir there and they catch all the fish.'

At 6 o'clock we left Chester for Llangollen. We walked up through the town to the Hand Hotel, stopping a moment on the fine quaint old grey stone bridge of Dee with its sharp angled recesses, to look down into the clear rocky swift winding river, so like the Wye. As we came near the Hand we heard the strains of a Welsh harp, the first I ever heard. The harper was playing in the hall the air 'Jenny Jones'. I would have come all the way to Llangollen on purpose to hear the Welsh harp. This is the only hotel in Wales where a Welsh harper can be heard. I stood by him entranced while he played Llwyn-on and the Roaring of the Valley, and several of the other guests in the house gathered round the harp in the corner of the hall. The harper was a cripple and his crutch rested by his side against a chair. He was a beautiful performer and he was playing on a handsome harp of sycamore and ash, which he had won as a prize at an Eisteddfod. I had a good deal of talk with him after he had done playing. He told me there were very few people now who could play the Welsh harp, and the instrument was fast going out of use. The young people learn the English harp which is much easier being double stringed instead of treble stringed. The Welsh harp has no silver string and it is played from the left shoulder while the English harp is played from the right shoulder. Sir Watkin keeps no harper. His sister does, and her harper is the brother of old Pugh of Dolgelly who took me up Cader Idris. The Llangollen harper said he knew him and thought him a good harper, but his brother whom he also knew and who is dead was much better, the first harper in Wales.

Presently the harper covered his harp and limped away to his own house in the town, saying he should come and play again at 9 o'clock. He plays in the hall at several stated hours every day. He gets nothing from the Hotel and subsists entirely on what visitors give him. At 9 o'clock he came again and played while we were at supper. It was a great and strange delight to listen to the music of this Welsh harp. The house was full of the melody of the beautiful Welsh airs. No wonder when the evil spirit was upon Saul and when David played upon the harp, that Saul was refreshed and was well and that the evil spirit departed from him.

Meantime we walked down to the gardens belonging to the Hotel on the other side of the road, and sat on the garden seat and river wall watching 'the cataract flashing from the bridge' and the quiet stream and pools below the fall dark under the trees opposite and dimpling with the rising of innumerable fish, in the warm damp evening. My Father took a fancy to throw a fly, so I got a rod for him from the billiard marker and he fished till supper time.

After supper I was going to my room to fetch my hat for a stroll and forgot my number. Going to the door which I thought was mine I took the precaution to knock before opening and was answered by a man's voice, coming to the door. Turning in the dark passage to escape I stumbled over two pair of boots and found I was invading a room where a man had retired to bed with his wife.

We walked up and down before the Hotel laughing over this adventure and three of the pretty saucy girls of Llangollen were driving each other about in a wheelbarrow.

[The diarist returns to Clyro.]

Monday, 19 June
Palmer, the new Cae Mawr gardener, and his wife have moved down from the Vineyards Cottage to the Old Mill. Mrs Palmer could not bear the Vineyards. She said it was so lonely. Miss Bynon, to whom the cottage belongs, took great exception to Mrs Palmer and the fault she found with the cottage. 'Lonely indeed ! What does the lady on the hill want?' asked Miss Bynon. 'She can see my backdoor.'

Tuesday, 20 June
An angel satyr walks these hills.

Wednesday, 28 June
I went to the Walls' new farm house where they have been settled a week. The two nice girls Lucretia and Eliza were at home and quite unspoilt by the Bristol school and as simple and nice as ever. Their mother was gone to Hereford to buy furniture for the new house, but their father came in from the farm. Pretty Lucretia was burning to show me over the new house and do the honours. The father and children took me all over the new house. Lucretia showed me her bed, a French bed, blue and gold, the prettiest piece

of furniture I saw. Wall pointed out to me with satisfaction the door with a lock which separated the sleeping rooms of the servant boys and girls.

Thursday, 29 June

Annie Corfield is better but we fear that she and her sisters, the twins Phoebe and Lizzie, are very miserable and badly treated by their father since their dear mother's death. What would she say if she could see them now, ragged, dirty, thin and half-clad and hungry? How unkindly their father uses them. The neighbours hear the sound of the whip on their naked flesh and the poor girls crying and screaming sadly sometimes when their father comes home late at night. It seems that when he comes home late he makes the girls get out of bed and strip themselves naked and then he flogs them severely or else he pulls the bedclothes off them and whips them all three as they lie in bed together writhing and screaming under the castigation. It is said that sometimes Corfield strips the poor girls naked holds them face downwards across his knees on a bed or chair and whips their bare bottoms so cruelly that the blood runs down their legs.

Tuesday, 4 July

Hannah Jones told me about the madwoman of Cwmgwanon. They keep her locked up in a bedroom alone, for she will come down amongst them stark naked. She has broken the window and all the crockery in the room, amuses herself by dancing naked round the room and threatens to wring her daughter-in-law's neck. Then she will set to and roar till they can hear her down the dingle at John Williams's house, nearly half a mile.

Wednesday, 5 July

This morning Edward Morgan of Cwmpelved Green brought his concubine to Church and married her. She was a girl of 19, rather nice looking and seemed quiet and modest. She had a pretty bridesmaid and they were both nicely prettily dressed in lilac and white. After the ceremony I saw the stout dwarf Anne Beavan pinning on bright nosegays.

Friday, 7 July

As I was sitting in my room reading this afternoon with the tabby cat Toby sitting in the back of the easy chair just above my shoulder and her white tortoiseshell kitten sitting at my feet, who should walk in but Teddy Bevan. He had come over on his donkey with a note from Mrs Bevan and was enchanted with my cats and our happy family appearance.

I went up the Bird's Nest dingle calling at Bowen's and old Meredith's and Richard Jones' and then across the wern to Cross Foot where Mrs Watkins told me the scandal about the daughter of Shene of the Lane Farm and the child found dead in the water closet at the Three Cocks Station.

Sunday, 9 July
April Storms. Shower and shine chasing each other swiftly. The little clerk coming down the road in his mackintosh cape to chime the bells at 9 o'clock. The galloping and pattering up and down the passage. The old cat bringing in a young blackbird dead for the kitten. The red roses in the garden bright against the sunny light blue mountains. Mr Venables preached morning and evening and I was glad to go to Bettws.

It was sultry hot climbing the hill though there was the blowing of a wind from the west. In the Chapel field the tall brown and purple grasses were all in billows like the sea, as the wind coursed over the hill driving one billow after another, sheen and dusk, up against the Chapel wall. And the Chapel in the grass looked like a house founded upon a rock in the midst of a billowy sea.

How quiet and sunny and lovely the village was this evening as I went to the Vicarage to dinner. There was not a person in the roads or moving anywhere. The only living creature I saw was a dog. An intense feeling and perception of the extraordinary beauty of the place grew upon me in the silence as I passed through the still sunny churchyard and saw the mountains through the trees rising over the school, and looked back at the church and the churchyard through the green arches of the wych elms. Then the glowing roses of the Vicarage lawn and the blue mountains beyond broken by the dark Castle Clump.

Wednesday, 12 July
There came begging through the village today three girls tall dressed in ragged black with naked legs and feet. The eldest was a

142

straight girl with a profusion of curling chestnut hair. The second girl was slighter. Her tattered black frock hardly covered her knees, her delicate beautiful slender limbs were bare and whiter by contrast with her black dress, and her pretty white feet small and shapely were bruised and worn with travel.

Thursday, 13 July

As I sat at breakfast I heard the drone of bagpipes. A man was playing at the New Inn. He came playing down the road and stopped in front of the forge droning on while the blacksmith's children danced before him. He could not complain that he had piped to the Clyro children and they had not danced. He was a wild swarthy Italian-looking man, young, with a steeple-crowned hat, and full of uncouth cries and strange outland words. He moved on from the forge to the inn still playing while the children still danced before him. I could see the group through the screen of chestnuts.

Poor Captain Brown used to say he could go anywhere and do anything under the influence of the bagpipes. It seems to me that I could go anywhere and do anything to get out of the sound of them. He found them warlike, exciting, inspiring. I find them intolerable. A droning wailing whine, no tune. I had far rather go into battle to the sound of a barrel organ.

Friday, 14 July, St Swithin's Eve

I went to Hereford to see the dentist McAdam. He showed me the apparatus for giving people the new anaesthetic laughing gas which he thinks much safer than chloroform, indeed quite safe. In the street two or three French or Italian boys were singing the Marseillaise to a beautiful harp and violin accompaniment. The afternoon became lovely, very hot, and being early for the 3.15 return train I strolled across the meadows near the Moorfields Station. I got out at Whitney and went to the Rectory. I dined with the girls and their father. He told me of the sermons which old Mr Thomas the Vicar of Disserth used to preach as they were described to him by the Venables. He would get up in the pulpit without an idea about what he was going to say, and would begin thus. 'Ha, yes, here we are. And it is a fine day. I congratulate you on the fine day, and glad to see so many of you here. Yes indeed.

Ha, yes, very well. Now then I shall take for my text so and so. Yes. Let me see. You are all sinners and so am I. Yes indeed.' Sometimes he would preach about 'Mr Noe'. 'Mr Noe, he did go on with the ark, thump, thump, thump. And the wicked fellows did come and say to him "Now, Mr Noe, don't go on there, thump, thump thump, come and have a pint of ale at the Red Lion. There is capital ale at the Red Lion, Mr Noe." For Mr Noe was situated just as we are here, there was the Red Lion close by the ark, just round the corner. Yes indeed. But Mr Noe he would not hearken to them, and he went on thump, thump, thump. Then another idle fellow would say, "Come Mr Noe — the hounds are running capital, yes indeed. Don't go on there thump, thump, thump." But Mr Noe he did never heed them, he just went on with his ark, thump, thump, thump.'

Miss E. Hutchinson had sent to Whitney for me to keep for my very own a relic very precious to me, a little poem of her aunt Dorothy Wordsworth in her own handwriting.

Tuesday, 18 July
I went to Wern Vawr. The sun burnt fiercely as I climbed the hills but a little breeze crept about the hill tops. Some barbarian — a dissenter no doubt — probably a Baptist, has cut down the beautiful silver birches on the Little Mountain near Cefn y Fedwas.

Wednesday, 19 July
After morning school I went to Cae Mawr and Mrs Morrell told me about the picnic at the Nydd yesterday. At luncheon Mr de Winton the host said to one of his guests, Llanthomas, 'Thomas, you'll be sick'. 'Why?' 'Because you eat so much.' When the tipsy cake came round Llanthomas said viciously, 'We call this *tipsy squire*.' 'That'll do for you then,' retorted the host. 'No,' said the guest meaningly, 'I never get drunk.' These were some of the amenities.

Saturday, 22 July
I went up to Cross Foot, turned down the farm lane to the huge Gospel Oak which overshadows the farm, and across the meadow to the beautiful green lane which leads down to Cwmpelved and Cwmpelved Green. At Cwmpelved Green the low garden wall

was flaming with nasturtiums which had clambered over it from the garden. Their luxuriant growth had almost smothered the gooseberry trees under the wall. Along the narrow garden border nodded a brilliant row of gigantic sweet williams.

Within the cottage sat old Richard Clark and the pretty girl lately Edward Morgan's concubine, now happily his wife. I had thought Edward Morgan had a comfortless, miserable home. I was never more mistaken or surprised. The cottage was exquisitely clean and neat, with a bright blue cheerful paper and almost prettily furnished. A vase of bright fresh flowers stood upon each table and I could have eaten my dinner off every stone of the floor. The girl said no one ever came near the house to see it, and she kept it as clean and neat and pretty as she could for her own satisfaction. The oven door was screened from view by a little curtain and everything was made the most and best of. I don't wonder Edward Morgan married the girl. It was not her fault that they were not married before. She begged and prayed her lover to marry her before he seduced her and afterwards. She was very staunch and faithful to him when she was his mistress and I believe she will make him a good wife. She was ironing when I came in and when I began to read to old Clark she took her work and sat down quietly to sew. When I had done reading she had me into the garden and shewed me her flowers with which she had taken some pains for she was very fond of them. No one ever came to see her garden or her flowers she said. The only people she ever saw passing were the people from the farm (the Upper Bettws where her husband works). They come on Market days along a footpath through the field before the house. The girl spoke quietly and rather mournfully and there was a shade of gentle melancholy in her voice and manner. I was deeply touched by all that I saw and heard. With a kind carefulness she put me into the footpath to the Upper Bettws farm, which passes by the solitary barn and over the lofty bridge across the brook and deep dingle. Miss Allen was at home and kindly brought me some cider. Sitting in the window seat she told me of the almost sudden death after three days' illness of the daughter of Mrs Davies of the Pentre aged 17 – inflammation of the bowels. I went on up to Pentwyn Forge and had a long chat with Mrs Nott the blacksmith's wife. She told me her next door neighbour Mrs Williams was 'a wicked woman' and prostituted herself to her lodgers, while her husband as bad as herself took the money and asked no questions.

Mrs Nott told me that Louie of the Cloggau was staying in Presteign with her aunt Miss Sylvester, the woman frog. This extraordinary being is partly a woman and partly a frog. Her head and face, her eyes and mouth are those of a frog, and she has a frog's legs and feet. She cannot walk but she hops. She wears very long dresses to cover and conceal her feet which are shod with something like a cow's hoof. She never goes out except to the Primitive Methodist Chapel. Mrs Nott said she had seen this person's frog feet and had seen her in Presteign hopping to and from the Chapel exactly like a frog. She had never seen her hands. She is a very good person. The story about this unfortunate being is as follows. Shortly before she was born a woman came begging to her mother's door with two or three little children. Her mother was angry and ordered the woman away. 'Get away with your young frogs,' she said. And the child she was expecting was born partly in the form of a frog, as a punishment and a curse upon her.

Sunday, 23 July

This morning Mr Bevan went up to the Volunteer Camp above Talgarth, on the high common under the Black Mountain. He is Chaplain to the Forces and attended to hold an open air service and preach a sermon to the Volunteers. When the Chaplain arrived on the Common, the Builth Volunteers were already well drunk. They were dismissed from the ranks but they fought about the common during the whole service. The officers and the other corps were bitterly ashamed and scandalized.

Thursday, 27 July

In the afternoon I took the old soldier the first instalment of his pension, £8 0 4 for half a year. Mr Venables has got the pension for him at last after a long correspondence with the War Office. The old soldier told me some of his reminiscences. In the Battle of Vittoria as they were rushing into action his front rank man, a big burly fellow, was swearing that 'There wasn't a bloody Frenchman who had seen the bullet yet which should strike him'. A few minutes after he was shot dead. After the battle when old

Morgan was shaking out his blanket to wrap himself up at night in the bivouac he shook three or four bullets out of it, and one ball had gone through his cap, so close as almost to graze his head

Friday, 28 July

Gipsy Lizzie was at the School. Again I am under the influence of that child's extraordinary beauty. When she is reading and her eyes are bent down upon her book her loveliness is indescribable.

Sunday, 30 July

I lay awake sleepless almost all night and had a vision of myself as Vicar of Builth, to the accompaniment of the rushing and roaring of torrents of rain.

[On the next day the diarist leaves Clyro for a holiday.]

Wednesday, 23 August

'It began with a lass and it will end with a lass.'

In the evening before sunset while the sun was yet warm and bright I went across the golden common and meadow to the Three Firs to call on Hannah Britton. I had not been long in the house when Hannah's beautiful seven year old child Carrie gradually stole up to me and nestled close in my arms. Then she laid her warm temples and soft round cheek lovingly to mine and stole first one arm then the other round my neck. Her arms tightened round my neck and she pressed her face closer and closer to mine, kissing me again and again. Then came the old, old story, the sweet confession as old as human hearts, 'I do love you so. Do you love me?' 'Yes,' said the child, lovingly clinging still closer with fresh caresses and endearments. 'You little bundle,' said her mother laughing and much amused. 'I wish I could take you with me.' 'You would soon grow tired of her,' said her mother. 'No', said the child with the perfect trust and confidence of love, 'he said he wouldn't.' An hour flew like a few seconds. I was in heaven. A lodger came in and sat down, but I was lost to everything but love and the embrace and the sweet kisses and caresses of the child. It seemed as if we could not part we loved each other so. At last it grew dusk and with one long loving clasp and kiss I reluctantly rose to go. It was hard to leave the child. When I went away she brought me the best flower she could find in the garden. I am exhausted with emotion.

147

Thursday, 24 August, St Bartholomew's Day

Edward Awdry walked up with us to Easton Pierse, by the old paths which I used to travel and which seemed so familiar to me. From the meadows above Lower Easton we caught the first glimpse of the grey gables. The old manor house has fallen into sad ruin since I used to come here to see old Mrs Buckland seven years ago. The great hall and the grand staircase both gone. All the back of the house tottering and the tall carved chimney stack trembling to its fall. From the huge oak beam which runs across and supports the vast ruined kitchen chimney, we stripped off large pieces of the bark which had never been removed and which looked as fresh as when the beam was placed there, perhaps hundreds of years ago. The house seemed empty and deserted. Heaps of stone and rubbish lay round the yards. The orchards were tangled and overgrown, the garden run wild with weeds, rank and neglected. Pink stone-crop and some straggling Virginia Stock ran over the heaps of waste and rubbish stone. There was not a sound or sign of life or living thing about the ruinous deserted place. Nothing but silence and desolation. A shepherd lives in a part of the house which still stands but as the staircase has fallen he is obliged to go out of doors and across a rude scaffolding stage before he can reach his bedroom.

Saturday, 26 August

I left Langley for Clyro.

Thursday, September Eve

I went up to Lower Cwmgwanon to see the old madwoman Mrs Watkins. Her son was out in the harvest field carrying oats, and I had to wait till he came in to go upstairs with me. While I waited in the kitchen the low deep voice upstairs began calling, 'Murder! John Lloyd! John Lloyd! Murder!'

The madwoman's son, a burly tall good-humoured man with a pleasant face, came to the garden gate and thought I could not do any good by seeing his mother. So I went away. But when I had got half way down the meadow Cwmside on my way to the Burnt House he shouted to me to come back and asked me to go up and see her. He led the way up the broad oak staircase into a fetid room darkened. The window was blocked up with stools and chairs to prevent the poor mad creature from throwing herself out. She had broken all the window glass and all the crockery. There was nothing in the room but her bed and a chair. She lay with the blanket over her head. When her son turned the blanket down I was almost frightened. It was a mad skeleton with such a wild scared animal's face as I never saw before. Her dark hair was tossed weird and unkempt, and she stared at me like a wild beast. But she began directly to talk rationally though her mind wandered at moments. I tried to bring some serious thoughts back to her mind. 'Whom do you pray to when you say your prayers?' 'Mr Venables.' It was the dim lingering idea of someone in authority. I repeated the Lord's Prayer and the old familiar words seemed to come back to her by degrees till she could say it alone. When I went away she besought me earnestly to come again. 'You'll promise to come again now. You'll promise,' she said eagerly.

I went to the Homme where John Meredith's sister has been taken in a very queer way and seems to have gone out of her mind.

Friday, September Day
I dined at Hay Castle. The Fanshawes were staying in the house. Last night Arthur Crichton amused them all after dinner by dressing, acting and singing 'The Grecian Bend'. While his brother and sister-in-law were away he amused himself with cutting down the trees at Wye Cliff by bed candle light.

Sunday, 3 September
I went to Bettws in light rain and preached extempore on the Good Samaritan from the Gospel for the day. A red cow with a foolish white face came up to the window by the desk and stared in while I was preaching.

Tuesday, 5 September
The day was lovely and I went over to Newchurch. A solitary fern cutter was at work on the Vicar's Hill mowing the fern with a sharp harsh ripping sound. From the Little Mountain the view was superb and the air exquisitely clear. The Clee Hills seemed marvellously near. The land glittered, variegated with colours and gleams of wheat, stubble and blue hill. The yellow potentilla jewelled the turf with its tiny gems of gold and the frail harebell

trembled blue among the fern tipped here and there with autumn yellow. The little lonely tree bowed on the mountain brow, and below lay the tiny village deep in the valley among the trees embosoming the little church with its blue spire and Emmeline's grave.

Friday, 8 September

Perhaps this may be a memorable day in my life.

At 2 o'clock I walked to Llan Thomas. A gentleman was carrying chairs out of the house on to the lawn, a stranger to me, deeply sunburnt, but I soon recognized him as Lechmere Thomas, the Ceylon coffee-planter, from his likeness to Henry and Charlie. It was some time before the party began to arrive. The 3 Crichtons, 2 Miss Baskervilles and Miss Howard, Col. Balmayne and his niece Miss Baldwin, Mr and Mrs Webb and 2 Miss Estcourts of Gloucestershire, Tom Williams and Pope.

Some played croquet. Some went to archery. There were two croquet games going. I played with Daisy and a Miss Estcourt against Miss Baldwin, Tom Williams and Mrs and Major Thomas alternately. Daisy was very kind and charming, just home from school for good, she said. I sat next her at supper at the bottom of the side table in the window and we were very merry. Her father wanted me to sit elsewhere, but she overruled him, saved my place, and kept me by her. I was telling her about Alice Davies of Cwm Sir Hugh. She became interested and when she heard what a treat fruit was to the sick child she sent the footman for a dish of grapes. 'Here,' she said, taking two bunches and putting them on my plate, 'take her these.' 'I do like you for that,' I said earnestly, 'I do indeed.' She laughed. I think she was pleased.

To-day I fell in love with Fanny[1] Thomas.

I danced the first quadrille with her and made innumerable mistakes, once or twice running quite wild through the figure like a runaway horse, but she was so goodhumoured and longsuffering. It was a very happy evening. How little I knew what was in store for me when I came to Llan Thomas this afternoon.

---

1. Fanny was evidently Daisy Thomas's nickname.

Saturday, 9 September

I thought Mrs Oswald looked ill. She showed us a copy book sent over from Africa and written by a native boy whom she supports there at school and whom she has named Arthur Drummond, which has so disgusted and enraged her own son Arthur Oswald that he threatens to shoot Arthur Drummond if he should ever dare to come to England.

Sunday, 10 September

I have been in a fever all day about Daisy, restless and miserable with uncertainty.

Monday, 11 September

This morning I went to Mrs Venables and unburdened my mind to her and asked her advice. She was enchanted to hear of my attachment and wish to marry, though I did not tell her it was Daisy. She gave me a great deal of good kind advice and encouraged me very much. Still I was very restless and feverish all day.

Tuesday, 12 September

A wretched restless feverish night. This morning I went to Mrs Venables in the drawing room bow-window and told her that it was Daisy I was in love with. She liked the idea extremely. Then she went to discuss the matter with Mr Venables. I went away, but soon she came down to tell me that he was very glad, highly approved of it and would talk to me about the matter at ten o'clock tomorrow morning.

Wednesday, 13 September

An ever memorable day in my life. I went to the Vicarage at 10 o'clock and had a long talk with him on the lawn about my attachment to Daisy. Ways, means and prospects. I started off for Llan Thomas on foot rather nervous. As I crossed the bridge over the Digedi I wondered with what feelings I should cross the bridge an hour later. The whole family at home came into the drawing room to see me and I was wondering how I could get Mr Thomas away for a private talk, when he said suddenly, 'Come out into the garden.' Daisy came into the room. I thought she coloured and looked conscious. Then we went out into the garden, her father and I. I said, 'You will be very much surprised but I hope not displeased at what I am going to say to you.' 'What is it?' he said eagerly, 'have you got the living of Glasbury?' 'No, something much nearer to you than that.' 'What is it?' I was silent a minute. I was frightfully nervous. 'I-am-attached-to-one-of-your-daughters,' I said. Just as I made this avowal we came suddenly round the corner upon a gardener cutting a hedge. I feared he had heard my confession, but I was much relieved by being assured that he was deaf. Mr Thomas said I had done quite right in coming to him, though he seemed a good deal taken aback.

He said also a great many complimentary things about my 'honourable high-minded conduct', asked what my prospects were and shook his head over them. He could not allow an engagement under the circumstances, he said, and I must not destroy his daughter's peace of mind by speaking to her or showing her in any way that I was attached to her. 'You have behaved so well that I don't know which of them it is, unless it is Mary.' 'No, it is your youngest daughter.' 'Poor little girl, she is so young.' 'She is nineteen.' 'Yes, but a mere child, and so guileless and innocent. She would be so fond of you. If I were a young man I should have done just what you have done and chosen her out of the rest. When you were here on Friday I saw she liked you. I said to my wife after you were gone, "That little Fanny likes Mr Kilvert". Long engagements are dreadful things. I cannot allow you to be engaged but I won't say "Don't think of it". Go on coming here as usual, if you can put constraint on your feelings and not show her that you like her more than the others. It is a cruel thing for you, I know, but it would be a still more cruel thing to tell her and destroy her peace of mind.'

Well, I thought to myself, whatever I suffer she shall not suffer if I can help it.

We had been walking along the path between the house and the garden and down the middle garden walk. The place is inextricably entwined in my remembrance with the conversation and the circumstances. I felt deeply humiliated, low in spirit and sick at heart. But it was a great deal to learn from her father that he had observed her liking for me. I believed she liked me before. Now I am sure of it. But it was hard to know this and yet not to be able to tell her or show her that I loved her. I was comforted by remembering that when my father proposed for my mother he was ordered out of the house, and yet it all came right. I wonder if this will ever come right. The course of true love never does run smooth. What has happened only makes me long for her more and cling more closely to her, and feel more determined to win her.

On this day when I proposed for the girl who will I trust one day be my wife I had only one sovereign in the world, and I owed that.

I went back across the brook with a sorrowful heart. At Clyro Vicarage every one was out. I left a note for Mrs Venables. 'He was very kind but gave no encouragement.' At Cae Mawr I found my sisters and Tom Williams playing croquet and just driven into the verandah by the rain. The afternoon had been grey, dull and dismal with an E. dark wind. Everything seemed gloomy and cold and the evening was irksome. I could not feel able to join in the Bezique at Cae Mawr.

Thursday, 14 September
I went to the Vicarage after breakfast and told them the result of my visit and proposal yesterday. They were much pleased and very hopeful and thought the answer was as favourable as I could have expected at first. Somehow things seem to look brighter and more cheerful this morning. I wrote to my father to tell him of my attachment and ask what my prospects were as far as he knew.

Friday, 15 September
Lying in bed this morning dozing, half awake and half asleep, I composed my speech of thanks at my wedding breakfast, a very affecting speech, and had visions of myself with Daisy at Langley and other places.

Thersie and Dora in the churchyard sketching the Church from different points. Fanny in the Church practising on the harmonium.

Saturday, 16 September
I went to see Mrs Lewis and old Mrs Watkeys at Whitcombe's. She began talking about Daisy. She said she liked her best of all

the sisters though they were all very kind to her. She remembered Miss Fanny when the family first came to Llanigan, a bright pretty little thing coming into Church with her long hair falling over her shoulders. She was always such a kind friendly humble young lady. Mrs Watkeys said she should never forget how Daisy would come to see her with some of her sisters. Too shy to speak herself she would whisper to one of her sisters to tell Mrs Watkeys to send down to the house for some meat. It reminded me irresistibly of 'the grapes'. I loved to hear the old woman talking so fondly of her.

Sunday, 17 September

I preached in the morning from Psalm xv, 1, 2, and went to Bettws with Dora who skipped about like a goat.

I had to-day very kind letters from my Father and Mother about my attachment to Daisy. They say if they had inherited their natural share of the Worcester money they might have retired from Langley in my favour, but now that is impossible. They cannot afford it. My mother is very curious to know the young lady's name. I believe she thinks it is Mary Bevan. I am told by my father that I shall have one day £2700.

Monday, 18 September

I went to the Vicarage with Mrs Venables and had a talk with Mr Venables about my prospects. He most kindly promised to write to the Bishop to ask him for a living for me.

At 2.30 we all drove to Llan Thomas with Mrs Hilton, meeting Major Thomas, Lechmere and Charlie at the Brecon turnpike coming into Hay on foot to pay calls. Mrs Thomas and Mary came into the drawing room first. I was very nervous when Mrs Thomas came in, but she received me very kindly and cordially just as usual. The croquet things were got out, two sets playing on the same ground across from either peg. The girls gradually came out on to the lawn. I began to fear Daisy was not coming. She was the last of all, I was horribly afraid she had been advised not to appear, because I was there. Presently I turned and there she was in a black velvet jacket and light dress, with a white feather in her hat and her bright golden hair tied up with blue riband. How bright and fresh and happy and pretty she looked.

She stood by me all the game watching us. I talked to her a good deal and she was so nice and sweet.

I love her more and more each time I see her. I think she loves me a little. I hope so. God grant it. I am sure she does not dislike me, and I believe, I do believe, she likes me and cares for me. I fancy I can see it in her clear loving deep grey eyes, so true and fearless and honest, those beautiful Welsh eyes that seem to like to meet mine. I think she likes to be with me and talk with me, or why did she come back to me again and again and stand by me and talk to no one else? I wish I could tell her how dearly I love her but I dare not. I must not, because of my promise. Perhaps I am deceiving myself and mistaken after all. Perhaps what I think is love is only her innocent childlike affectionate way with all, and she might be the same with anyone else. I cannot believe it. I will not believe it. How proud and glad I felt every time she came and stood by me. And I thought she seemed proud and fond too. How fond we should be of each other. I wonder what she thinks of my poor disfigured eyes, whether she loves me better or worse for that. She must know. She must see. Yet it does not seem to make any difference against me with her. Perhaps she is sorry for me. And they say pity is akin to love.

My own dear girl. My own precious love. May God give her to me in His own good time. What should I do if anyone else were to come and take her from me? I believe this is one of the matches that are made in Heaven. All is hers now. It is all for her, life, talents, prospects, all. All for her sake, valuable only that they may be laid at her feet, with fond pride. I look at everything now only in relation to her. If I am and have anything that is good I prize it and rejoice in it for her sake, that it may be hers.

She and Mrs Thomas and I were walking together. With what different feelings I walked down this same path last Wednesday with her father. How miserable I was then and how happy I have been this afternoon. Daisy went to her own little garden which she had when she was a child and has still and gathered from it a scarlet geranium and a geranium leaf which she put into her own dress. We went down the broad middle garden walk and presently came to a large bed of mignonette which scented the whole air. Daisy asked me if I would like some flowers. 'Yes,' said Mrs

Thomas, 'gather him some.' So she gathered me some mignonette, took the geranium out of her dress, and made up a nosegay which she gave to me. 'It is from my own garden,' she said. 'I shall value it all the more,' said I.

Wednesday, 20 September

I went to the Vicarage to speak to Mrs Venables and settle the Psalms and Lessons with Mr Venables for the Harvest Festival next Tuesday. As I was coming down the steps he tapped his study window and came out on to the lawn to have a talk. He said he thought he ought to caution me not to think my prospects better than they were and not to do anything precipitate.

At 2.30 I walked across the fields to Hay Castle to a croquet party. Daisy was at the Castle already with Charlotte and Charlie. Part of the people went out into the archery field. She went with them, inseparable from her friend Fanny Bevan. I and some of the rest played a slow game of croquet. Presently Daisy came on to the lawn again. I thought her manner was altered, more quiet, guarded and reserved. Perhaps it was only that she was more shy in a strange place than at home. But it seemed to me as if she had received a hint not to be too forthcoming.

Friday, 22 September

After luncheon walked with Mrs Venables to Cusop Church to attend the Harvest Thanksgiving Service. By the way we had a long nice talk about Daisy. Mrs Venables thinks her so nice and grown so nice looking. I don't know what I should do without Mrs Venables. She encourages and does so comfort and help me at this time.

Saturday, 23 September

A letter came from Mr Thomas. Kindly expressed and cordial, but bidding me give up all thoughts and hopes of Daisy. It was a great and sudden blow and I felt very sad. The sun seemed to have gone out of the sky. I wrote a courteous reply saying that I must abide by his decision, but that an attachment would not be worthy of the name which could be blown out by the first breath of difficulty and discouragement and that I should be more unworthy of his daughter than I was if I could give her up so lightly and easily. I

156

said that all that was left me was to hope and quietly wait for her, but I could not conceal from myself that the lapse of years and a long unbroken separation might alter feeling which at present appeared to be unalterable.

In the afternoon we went to Cae Mawr to shoot and play croquet. The Priory people were there, Mrs Allen, Lucy, Katie, Miss Draper, and lovely little May Oliver with her bewitching face, beautiful dark eyes and golden curls. She was shooting and had no quiver, so I acted as quiver for her, holding her arrows, picking them up, and being her slave generally.

Sunday, 24 September
Mr George Venables told the following story at dinner the other day. The Bishop of Worcester (Philpot) who is singularly spare and attenuated, was staying in a house. He observed a child looking at him very attentively for some time, and when the Bishop left the room the child asked, 'Is the Bishop a spirit?' 'No, the Bishop is a very good man, but he is not exactly a spirit yet. Why do you ask?' 'Because,' said the child gravely, 'his legs are so very thin, I thought no one but a spirit could have such very thin legs.'

Saturday, October Eve
A glorious morning after the dark hopeless rain of yesterday. The land was rejoicing in the sunshine, the jewelled green of the meadows, the brilliant blue of the Beacons. The river swollen by yesterday's rain was tumbling and rushing brown and tumultuous under Hay Bridge and sweeping round the curves below where the yellowing trees leaned over the brown water hurrying along the winding shore.

Then to see John Williams the gardener and old Sarah Probert. As I sat by their fireside old Hannah Jones lighted her pipe, began to smoke, and told me the tragic story of Mary Meredith's suicide. She lived at New Barn and a son of Juggy (Joan) Price, Bill Price, lived close by at Sunny Bank. They went together and he got her with child. She had a little money of her own in the bank but she could not draw it out without her brother John's consent for their money was mixed up together. Mary thought that if she could get her money her lover would marry her for the sake of the money. But her brother would not yield to let Mary draw her money.

Moreover he and his father were very angry with Mary for being with child and disgracing them. Whereupon poor Mary seeing no hope of marriage became melancholy mad. 'Often,' she said to Hannah Jones my informant, 'often I have gone out on moonlight nights and sat down by the spring and cried for hours, thinking that I would drown myself in the river.' What a picture. The solitary figure of the weeping girl sitting by the well in the moonlight. The many bitter tears shed on many a cold night by the moonlit well.

Then her father died and she grew worse and worse. At last there came an outbreak. One day she suddenly declared she would do no more for her brother, left the bacon half salted and the meat was spoilt. Not long after she was seen walking and 'prancing' about down by the river on Boatside. But she left the river and in the evening she was seen 'prancing' about in the Bron. John her brother went down and brought her up home to New Barn. He suspected she was up to something, for she asked him to let her little boy who always slept with her sleep with him that night, and when they went to bed he locked the front door and put the key in his pocket forgetting that the backdoor had no fastening but a bolt on the inside. In the night Mary got up and left the house and was seen by people who were abroad very early in the morning dodging and ducking behind the hedges and going down the Cwm. The carter boys at Boatside were at plough that morning when they saw a woman coming up from the river with her head buried in her breast. She was a long way from them and they thought it was Mary Pugh who lived then at Tump House. They called out, 'Mary, you are out early this morning'. They thought she had been down gathering wood by the river. The woman lifted her head, looked at the teams, turned and ran down to the river as hard as she could go and plunged headlong in. It was a fortnight before she was found, and then a flood cast her body up near Whitney Court. It was surmised that she would be buried as a suicide without any service on the 'backside of the Church', but she was buried by Mr Venables with the usual ceremony.

Tuesday, 3 October

A note from Jane Dew of Whitney Rectory asking me to attend their Harvest Festival this afternoon. The service began at 2.15. After Church the whole parish, men, women and children, dined in the Rectory yard under a pent-house of beams and tarpaulin, near 200 people. After dinner all the men played or rather kicked football at each other and then till it grew dark, when the game ended in a general royal scuffle and scrummage. Cold supper at 7. I took Lizzie Thomas of Winforton Rectory and her pretty eyes into supper, and tried to catch the 8.45 train but while Henry Dew and I were running along the line to the station we heard the train coming behind us and it glided past close blazing with lamps into the station where it stopped half a minute and was off again to Hay in spite of Henry Dew's running and hooting. So I walked home. Past and left behind one roaring brook after another, Brilley, Rhydspence, Cabalva. Over the border out of England into Wales in the dark, and one man was bringing another deadly sick out of the Brilley Rhydspence Inn, the old timbered house, into the road.

Thursday, 5 October

A letter from my Mother this morning says that my Father had been to Dr Fox's to see Aunt Emma. She did not use quite so many oaths and curses as usual. But Dr Charles Fox sat by all the time, and she did not scruple to say in his presence that his house was a hell upon earth.

Saturday, 7 October

The *Hereford Times* has misprinted our report of the Clyro Harvest Festival as follows, 'The *widows* were decorated with Latin and St Andrew's crosses and other beautiful devices in moss with dazzling flowers.' This was irresistible and the schoolmaster roared with delight.

There was a murderous affray with poachers at the Moor last night. Two keepers beaten fearfully about the head with bludgeons and one poacher, Cartwright, a Hay sawyer, stabbed and his life despaired of.

Monday, 9 October

There was a frost in the night and this morning the tops of the poplar spires are touched, are turned to finest gold. A letter from my Father saying he is coming to Clyro this afternoon. I went to the station to meet him and Miss Sherriff was there waiting for the train to go back to Glan Usk, and with her were Miss Rhoda and her intended, Mr Timmins. When the train came he put them into a first class smoking carriage. 'Do you smoke?' I said to Miss Sherriff. 'No,' she said laughing, and got out again, while the lover was covered with confusion at having put his betrothed into a smoking carriage.

Wednesday, 11 October

My father brought back 4 nice jack from Llangorse, one 6 lbs, some 18 or 20 pounds of fish altogether, and the best day's fishing he has ever had.

Friday, 13 October

After school about 12.20 I started to walk over the hills. The fern cutters were hard at work on the Vicar's Hill mowing the fern with a sharp ripping sound. The mountain and the great valley were blue with mist and the sun shone brilliantly upon the hill and the golden fern. I had put a flask of ginger wine in my pocket and a sandwich of bread and bacon which I ate by the Milw Bridge at the meeting of the three parishes and wished I had another for I was as hungry as a hunter.

Up the long Green Lane the heather bloom was long over and the heather was dark, speckled with the little round white bells. I looked for Abiasula along the green ride narrowing between the fern and heather, and looked for her again at the Fforest, but the great dark heather slopes were lonely, nothing was moving, the cottage was silent and deserted, the dark beautiful face, the wild black hair and beautiful wild eyes of the mountain child were nowhere to be seen.

Round the great dark heather-clothed shoulder of the mountain swept the green ride descending steeply to the Fuallt farm and fold and the valley opened still more wide and fair. The beautiful Glasnant came leaping and rushing down its lovely dingle, a flood of molten silver and crystal fringed by groups of silver birches and alders, and here and there a solitary tree rising from the bright green sward along the banks of the brook and drooping over the stream which seemed to come out of a fairy land of blue valley depths and distances and tufted woods of green and gold and crimson and russet brown.

At last I found my way up a rich green orchard and through a gate into the fold sheltered by some noble sycamores. The farm house, long, low and yellow-washed, looked towards the N.E. The house is said to be the oldest inhabited building in these parts. It stands high above the Arrow on its green mount, embosomed and almost hidden by its sycamores and other trees. In a dark secluded recess of the wood near the river bank an ice-cold never-failing spring boils up out of the rock. Mrs Jones said it makes her arms ache to the shoulder to put her hand into the water from this spring in the hottest day of summer. In the hot summer days Louie and the other girls take the butter down the steep bank, across the Arrow and make up the butter in the wood by the icy spring. Then they bring the butter up and it remains as if it had been iced. There are beautiful trout in the river and large eels. Mrs Jones talked much of the wicked old Squire, Beavan of the Yat Glascwm and of Mrs Irvine and his two other poor daughters [   ] into idiots.

Sunday, 22 October
Coming home in the dusk I turned into the school house to tell the schoolmaster I was going out to-morrow for a few days and that I should not be at school this week. The schoolmaster is learning to play the violin. He produced the instrument and began to play upon it. It had a broken string, and there was something wrong with all the rest, and the noise it made 'fairly raked my bowels' as old Cord used to say at Wadham of Headeach's violoncello. The schoolmaster however did not appear to notice that anything was wrong. His wife held the book up before him. 'Glory be to Jesus', sang the schoolmaster, loudly and cheerfully sawing away at the cracked and broken strings, while the violin screeched and shrieked and screamed and groaned and actually seemed to writhe and struggle in his arms like a wild animal in agony. There was something so utterly incongruous in the words and the noise,

the heart-rending bowel-raking uproar and screams of the tormented violin, that I smiled. I could not help it. Shriek, shriek, scream, groan, yell, howled the violin, as if a spirit in torment were writhing imprisoned within it, and still the schoolmaster sawed away vigorously and sung amid the wailing, screeching uproar, 'Glory be to Jesus' in a loud and cheerful voice. It was the most ludicrous thing. I never was so hard put to it not to laugh aloud.

Monday, 23 October
A wedding at 9 o'clock, fixed most conveniently for me by the people themselves. The man was one of the most Boeotian clowns I ever saw. He made an unusually extraordinary hash of 'I thee endow' and 'thereto I plight thee my troth'. Plainly he had not the least idea of the meaning of what he was saying. And the woman was naturally foolish and childish and did not even know her right hand from her left.

Wednesday, November Day
Mrs Venables wrote to me yesterday. She is terribly bothered again about Gibbins' affairs. Young Lewis, the Hay tailor, has once more suddenly appeared on the scene and all is ablaze again when we thought the attachment had died away at least on her part and been forgotten. Mrs Venables wants some reliable information about the young man. So I had to consult Evans the schoolmaster yesterday and to go to Hay this morning to the Castle to ask Mrs Beavan's advice.

The old soldier Morgan sent me by his wife a basket of Quince apples, the only ones that grew on his tree this year.

Thursday, November Morrow
The morning opened with a fine sky of brown and dark hard steel-blue.

Old Sarah Williams and a few more of the old people still salute one with 'Your servant, sir', 'Your servant, ma'am'. In the next generation and after a few more years this will never be heard. Some of the old fashioned folks still call me 'your honour' and 'your reverence'.

Monday, 6 November

Such a happy day. Thank God for such a happy day. I have seen my love, my own, I have seen Daisy. She was so lovely and sweet and kind and the old beautiful love is as fresh and strong as ever. I never saw her more happy and affectionate and her lovely Welsh eyes grew radiant whenever they met mine. She was looking prettier than ever and the East wind had freshened her pretty colour and her lovely hair was shining like gold. She wore a brown stuff dress and white ribbons in her hat.

I wonder if Daisy and I will ever read these pages over together. I think we shall.

As I went to Llan Thomas this afternoon I met the Tregoyd travelling carriage with imperials on the roof dashing along the road to Hay and round the turn by Victoria Cottage. Lady Hereford and De Bohun Devereux (my old St Leonard's pupil at Thatch Cottage) were inside and on their way to Whitfield.

Saturday, 11 November

Mr George Venables sent me a brace of Llysdinam pheasants and a rabbit. Baskerville shot 3 woodcocks this afternoon near the Llainau.

This morning Catherine Price of the New Inn was married to Davies, a young Painscastle blacksmith, before the Hay registrar. What I call a gipsy 'jump the broom' marriage. The wedding feast was at the New Inn which is now shut up as an inn and abolished. As I passed the house I heard music and dancing, the people dancing at the wedding. They were dancing in an upper room, unfurnished, tramp, tramp, tramp, to the jingling of a concertina, the stamping was tremendous. I thought they would have brought the floor down. They seemed to be jumping round and round. When I came back the dance seemed to have degenerated into a romp and the girls were squealing, as if they were being kissed and tickled and not against their will.

Sunday, 12 November

In the evening as I was sitting by my fire thinking, just after I had lighted the candles came a tap at the door and Mrs Venables. She sat down and put her feet up on the fender and we had a long cosy talk together about Daisy, and Gibbins' love affairs. She says she

163

and Mrs Henry Venables consulted together about the expediency of the step and then she read aloud to Gibbins my letters about her lover young Lewis. I asked if Gibbins did not hate me for what I had said, for I had no idea that she would ever hear the contents of the letter or know that I had written on the subject. No, Mrs Venables said, not at all. Gibbins thought it very kind and friendly of me to take so much trouble about the matter. I must give her a copy of *Stepping Heavenward*. I think it will do her good.

Monday, 13 November
'What a fine day it is. Let us go out and kill something.' The old reproach against the English. The Squire has just gone by with a shooting party.

Tuesday, 14 November
Tom Williams of Llowes, Pope and Clouston dined with me this evening. Mrs Venables sent some soup from the Vicarage and we had a leg of mutton roasted and a couple of boiled chickens and bacon and a brace of pheasants from Llysdinam, an apple pie and an apricot jam tart.

Thursday, 16 November
Yesterday Mr and Mrs Venables drove to call at Llan Thomas. This morning Mrs Venables told me that Mr Venables likes Daisy very much. He thinks her very nice-looking and admires her nice open face. Mrs Venables was very much disappointed to see so little of Daisy. Mrs Thomas sent her on an errand out of the room and she did not come in again.

Sunday, 19 November
At the school this morning I had a grateful word and glance and clasp of the hand from Gibbins in return for the book I gave her, *Stepping Heavenward*.

Saturday, 25 November
I went up to Cwm Sir Hugh. A heavy dark mist from the East brooded over the country and the trees dripped drearily in the fading light. A screaming romp with Lucretia who in rolling about upon the bed upset the candle on to the coverlet and burst

into peals of inextinguishable laughter while a strong smell of burning rose from the singed woollens and I snatched up the candle in a way which redoubled Lucretia's mirth.

Advent Sunday, 3 December. My Birthday
Holy Communion. Sadly few communicants. Almost the smallest number I ever saw here.

Champagne at dinner at the Vicarage and a capital plum pudding in honour of my birthday.

Monday, 4 December
The sun went down behind the dark round of the Old Forest filling the air with a strange yellow splendour and brightness as of the colour of shining brass.

Called on Hannah Whitney. I told her of the tomb of Walter Whitney. She had never seen the tomb and did not know of it, but she said she thought it must be the tomb of her grandfather's cousin. 'You are of a better family than many of the gentlemen round here,' I said. 'I know it,' said the old woman proudly. 'If I were any the better for that,' she added with a half sigh. 'Thank God for my bit of breed,' she said cheerfully.

She was sitting at her frugal tea at her little table by the fire in her humble cot, this descendant of a line of squires. I told her I could see her good blood in her face. She replied that she had no cause to be ashamed of her family. The old woman was daily, hourly, expecting a load of club coal from Hay for her scanty store was nearly exhausted and the weather is sharp.

Knocked all to pieces to-day with face ache, feeling miserable, stiff, sick and nohow.

Friday, 8 December
News came to Hereford to-day that the Prince of Wales is much worse, dying it is thought.

Sunday, 10 December
The blue mountains were silver-ribbed with snow and looked like a dead giant lying in state – a Titan.

Thursday, 14 December
The anniversary of the Prince Consort's death ten years ago, and people were very anxious about it for it was said the Prince of

Wales was conscious of the day, but to-day the Prince is better.
Thank God.

Sunday, 17 December
Before he began his sermon this morning Mr Venables read from
the pulpit the latest telegram from Sandringham which is very
comfortable. 'The Prince has passed a tranquil day and the
symptoms continue to be favourable.' Dated last evening. What a
blessed happy contrast to the suspense and fear of last Sunday.
How thankful we all are. I love that man now, and always will
love him. I will never say a word against him again. God bless
him. God bless him and keep him, the Child of England. In the
afternoon I alluded to the Prince's illness in an old Advent sermon
on John the Baptist from Matthew xi, 10 and nearly broke down.

Monday, 18 December
Came from Clyro to Langley.

Wednesday, 20 December
Miserable all day with an attack of cholera and diarrhoea.

Wednesday, 27 December
At noon went to call upon old John Bryant. A grandson and a
great grandson were spending Christmas with him, young men
employed in the Derbyshire iron works. They told me of a new
invention, iron paper, as thin as the thinnest tissue paper. The
sheets of iron are rolled so thin that 3000 sheets together are only
an inch thick. The patriarch lay in his bed looking merry and
hearty, and ever ready with a joke. He said it was the ninety-first
Christmas he had seen in this world, and he had never seen such a
mild and green Christmas, but he never felt better in his life.

After dinner I went with Dora to call at the John Knights' at
the farm on the common. At the cross roads we met Mrs Ashe
with Thersie and Syddy going round to the cottages giving the
invitations to the New Year's supper at Langley House. Syddy is
magnificent entirely, splendidly handsome. I never thought her so
beautiful before. Her violet eyes, her scarlet lips, the luxuriance of
her rich chestnut curling hair, indescribable. She is said by my
mother to be very like her great-grandmother, especially in her
chestnut curling hair.

Saturday, 30 December
To-night Fanny, Dora and I dined at Langley House. Mr Ashe was particularly agreeable. He gave me a bottle of superb 1847 port which we finished together.

Sunday, New Year's Eve
Thersie was at Church twice to-day. A few days ago she was teaching Florence and asking her who died for us on the Cross. 'Lord Chesterfield', replied Florence promptly, having heard a good deal lately about his death in connection with the Prince of Wales and Londesborough Lodge.

I was going to bed but Dora came down on tiptoe in a loose wrapper with her hair falling on her shoulders, soon followed by Thersie in the same state. We sat round the fire talking of domestic matters in whispers, not to disturb my Mother who was immediately overhead sleeping the sleep of the just. At 5 minutes to midnight the bells of Chippenham Church pealed out loud and clear in the frosty air. We opened a shutter and stood round the window listening. It was a glorious moonlit night.

1872

New Year's Day
I went to London by the midday mail.

Wednesday, 3 January
During the most critical days of the Prince's illness a friend of
Perch's was present one night amongst a great crowd, when an
unfavourable bulletin came from Sandringham. The crowd had
been patiently waiting some time and when the sad bulletin was
posted and read a groan of dismay ran through the people. One
man exclaimed, 'Serve him right!' Immediately the infuriated
crowd seized him, stripped him naked, knocked him down and
kicked him up and down the street like a football till the police
burst in and rescued him just in time before he was killed.

Thursday, 4 January
Sam and I went down to Dulwich by rail to see the picture Gallery
at the College. I was delighted with the beautiful picture of
Rembrandt's pretty servant girl immortalized by himself. There
is also a fine martyrdom of St Sebastian and the Madonna and
child. But the gems of the collection are the two superb and
famous Murillos, the two Spanish peasant boys and the Spanish
flower girl. The Crystal Palace at Sydenham glittered upon the
hill in the sunshine like an enormous diamond and seemed to be
close to Dulwich.

I went to see the Doré Gallery in Bond Street, a few fine
pictures. There was a noble picture of Paolo and Francesca.

[A gap in the MS. at this point.]

The beautiful girl stripped naked of her blue robe and stabbed in
the side under the left breast is sailing through the air and reclines
half standing, half lying back, supported tenderly in the arms of
her lover who has been stabbed in the same place. They are
passing over the fiery gulf. The naked girl is writhing and drawing
up one of her legs in an agony – but her arms are thrown back and

168

clasped passionately round her lover's neck. Her head lies upon his breast, her face is turned back up to his, and her eyes are looking into his eyes. She seems to look up to him and through him to another for comfort and help and strength and an example of suffering patience, and he looks down upon her with infinite pity and sadness and tenderness and love. The anguish of death is stamped upon her white and sharpening yet still lovely features, but her soul is rapt above her pain in an ecstasy of love. The longing loving yearning look in her eyes grows more intense. Her arms are tightening with a last loving effort and clasp round her lover's neck. She feels she is going, but she knows that he will follow her soon, and that they will meet again before long at the Master's feet. Love is stronger than death.

Saturday, Twelfth Night
Came down to Langley.

Tuesday, 9 January
Went to see old Caroline Farmer and read to her the latter part of Luke vii. On my way thither I fell in with a boy in the lane named George Wells. He was going to beg a bit of bread from a woman who lived at the corner of the Common under the Three Firs. He said he did not know the name of the woman but she knew his mother and often gave him a bit of bread when he was hungry. His mother was a cripple and had no parish relief, sold cabbage nets and had nothing to give him for dinner. The boy's face looked pale, pinched and hungry. Then a very different figure and face came tripping down the lane. Carrie Britton in her bright curls and rosy face with a blue cloak, coming from the town with a loaf of bread from the baker's for her grandmother.

Wednesday, 10 January
This morning at prayers the pretty housemaid Elizabeth with the beautiful large soft eyes was reading aloud in Luke i how Zacharias saw a vision in the Temple, but for the word 'vision' she substituted 'venison'.

Thursday, 11 January
The air early this morning was as warm as the air of a hot-house and the thrushes singing like mad thinking that spring had come

Saturday, 13 January

Left Langley for Clyro by the usual early beastly train.

Dined at the Vicarage.

I hear Daisy came out at the Hereford Hunt Ball last Tuesday, looked very pretty and danced a great deal and was very much admired.

Tuesday, 16 January

Lucretia and I had a splendid romp.

Called on Lewis the policeman, who was in a difficulty to know what to do with some Clyro boys who had been playing football on Sunday.

Saturday, 20 January

Took old Sylvanus Whitcombe a note from the Registers showing that he was baptized January 1st, 1783.

A warm golden afternoon and the mountains white with snow. The frosty sun set on the snowy mountains, their great white slopes and snow fields. A party of the young men of the village have just gone past my window in the clear bright frosty moonlight with an accordion well played and sweet voices singing 'Though hardy Norsemen'.

One day some of the schoolchildren came rushing into the School house to tell Mr Evans that Sarah Chard Cooper, the gardener's little granddaughter, was running about the school as if she were mad and they could not stop her. The children added that they believed Sarah was drunk. Mr Evans went out immediately to see what was the matter and he found the little girl running wildly round and round the school with her hair streaming, and her eyes glaring and starting out of her head. They could not stop her, she slipped through their hands and rushed past them, running round in circles plainly quite beside herself. It was true the child was drunk. Her grandmother Mrs Cooper confessed afterwards laughing that she had been drinking brandy herself and had given the child some.

Tuesday, 23 January

Visited Edward Evans, old Price the paralysed keeper, Mrs Lacy, Catherine Ferris, James Smith, and Mrs Price of the Swan who showed me preserved in a box part of one of Price's whiskers pulled out by the Clyro women in the late row at the Swan. Price told some one at the time that he had one of his whiskers in his pocket.

The Penny Readings to-night went off admirably, one of the very best we have ever had. A crowded room, nearly 250 people.

Wednesday, 24 January
Visited John Morgan. The old soldier had another epileptic fit on Sunday. Came home in a wild storm of rain. A waterspout of rain burst in the night about midnight and the Dulas and Cwmbythog brook are in full roar, rushing through the dark with a wild strange stormy foam light. The Cwmbythog brook burst its banks and came through the Lower House, in at the back door and out at the front. Mrs Williams said she had only known this happen once before since they had lived there. The same thing happened at Wern Vawr, and at the Lower Bettws, and at Lower Cabalva a sudden rush of water, from a drain blown up by the wet, poured down the hill and flooded the house so that when the servants came down in the morning they suddenly found themselves up to their middles in water. Happily a great portion of the flood escaped into the cellars or they thought the rooms might have filled and the windows been blown out by the pressure of the water. A thick deposit of yellow mud was left upon the carpets. The great white mountains this afternoon loomed ghostly through the rain clouds and the thick dark mist.

Thursday, 25 January
A beautiful gleam of sunshine lit the rainy mountains into tender showery lights of blue and green. At 3 o'clock walked to Hay with Mr Venables and Captain Adam and met Mary, Grace and Charlotte Thomas walking to call at Wye Cliff after the ball. I have not seen Daisy since November. It seems a long, long time, and I do so yearn after her at times. She went with Edith and Henry to a private ball near Hereford on Tuesday and enjoyed it very much I hear.

Saturday, 27 January

Banging of guns, rabbit shooting at Wye Cliff. Then the Radnor-shire postman coming from Llowes blew his horn.

I set out for Pwlldwrgwy to get some wild snowdrops along the river side by the Otter's Pool for Mrs Venables.

Friday, Candlemas Day

At the Vicarage I found the servants taking down the awnings from outside the drawing room window. The cords had got twisted and would not work. The morning was superb, warm and brilliant, like a May morning, and the hundreds of yellow stars of the Cape jessamine between the drawing room and dining room windows were full of bees.

Wednesday, 7 February

I walked to Hay. The afternoon was brilliant in its loveliness. The sun was under a cloud from behind which streamed seven broad rays on to the variegated mountain and valley, river and meadow, striking out brilliant gems of sunlit emerald green on the hill sides.

Teddy Bevan walked with me to Pont Vaen. In the street we met Mrs Allen's carriage with Mrs Allen and Mrs Oswald. Mrs Allen was dressed as I told her like a duchess in a magnificent ermine cape. The Bridges were at home, gave us tea and showed us all their poultry, the white Brahmas, the golden-pencilled and silver-spangled Hambros, and that ferocious wild beast the silver pheasant who has at length been tamed by having his long spurs cut, and has at last consented to allow his wife of the period to live. He killed all the rest.

I had a great business at Owen's getting some crackers. The people seemed to me to be all mad or drunk. A chorus of boys in the street was singing and enquiring in loud strains, 'Where is now the prophet Daniel? Where are now the Twelve Apostles?' A lady bowed to me across the street and evidently wished to speak to me. I approached her and bowed and she began, 'Oh, Dr Clouston' – I explained that she had made a mistake, whereat she fell into great confusion and profuse apologies. But I begged her not to regard the matter for I was used to being mistaken for Dr Clouston.

Home across the river roaring in the dark.

Before I settled down for the evening I went into old Hannah Whitney's and sat awhile with her. She spoke of the two extraordinary sermons she heard preached in Llanbedr Church by 'Parson Button', Parson Williams of Llanbedr. 'He was a good Churchman but he was a very drunken man.' 'How then being a very drunken man could he be a good churchman?' 'Oh, he read the Lessons very loud and he was a capital preacher. He used to say to the people in his sermons, "My brethren", says he, "don't you do as I do, but you do as I say".' He was very quarrelsome, a fighting man, and frequently fought at Clyro on his way home from Hay. One night he got fighting at Clyro and was badly beaten and mauled. The next Sunday he came to Llanbedr Church bruised black and blue, with his head broken and swollen nose and two black eyes. However, he faced his people and in his sermon glorified himself and his prowess and gave a false account of the battle at Clyro in which he was worsted, but in which he represented himself as having proved victorious. The text was taken from Nehemiah xiii, 25. 'And I contended with them and cursed them and smote certain of them and plucked off their hair, and made them swear by God.' Another time he was to preach a funeral sermon for a farmer with whom he had quarrelled. He chose his text. Isaiah xiv, 9. 'Hell from beneath is moved for thee to meet thee at thy coming.'

Thursday, 8 February
To-night there is a dinner party at Llan Thomas. Some officers from Brecon are to be there, but all married men, as Mrs Bevan pointedly informed me. I wonder if she suspects anything. Sat up late writing some blank verse in honour of Daisy.

Shrove Tuesday, 13 February
Dined at the Vicarage at 5.30 and at 7 drove with the Venables and Crichton to the Rifle Volunteer Concert in the National Schoolroom at Hay. We had tickets for the first row, and in the third row I immediately espied Daisy and Charlotte. I had the good fortune to get a chat with Daisy before the seats were filled up, and she was so nice and I was so happy. She told me she had been to two balls and I told her how disappointed I was not to meet her at the Crichtons' ball. She said she had enjoyed her balls

very much, and I said I heard that the young ladies who 'came out' at the Hereford Hunt Ball (of whom she was one) had all looked very pretty and been very much admired. She smiled and blushed and looked pleased. I told her how well I remembered the last time I saw her nearly 3 months ago. 'It's a long time since you have been over to Llan Thomas. I suppose you have been very busy. If you come over you will find some of us at home. We don't usually go out till half past three.' 'I am afraid,' I said, 'that you have all quite forgotten me.' 'Oh, no,' she said.

I was so happy talking to her. I had been hoping and thinking all day that I might meet her at the concert this evening. But now the seats began to fill. Fanny Bevan her great and inseparable friend sat on one side of her and her father on the other. I sat in the row before them. Henry sang.

Oh Daisy.

When the concert was over rain was pouring and there was a long way to go to the carriages. Daisy took Lechmere's arm but they had no umbrella and were standing in the porch waiting for one of their party to come back with an umbrella. She was dressed entirely in white, a white dress and long white cloak, and she looked so pretty standing there with her fair golden head uncovered. I ran back into the room, got Cooler's umbrella for them and accompanied them to the carriage. 'Thank you', she said gratefully. When we reached the door of the school yard their covered waggonette was standing in the middle of the road. It was very dark. 'Where's Fanny?' said Henry. 'Oh here you are, I was just coming back for you. I'll carry you to the carriage.' 'Can you?' she said. 'Yes, put your arms round my neck.' She clasped her arms round her brother's neck, and he took her up in his strong arms and carried her safe and dry to the carriage. It was the prettiest sight in the world and reminded me irresistibly of Huldbrand carrying Undine through the flood.

Wednesday, 21 February

One day Perch skinned an owl in London and from midnight till one o'clock he roamed about the streets seeking where he might bestow the body of the owl, fearing that the carcase of the owl might be found and described in the papers as the body of a fine full grown male child. Eventually he whirled the corpse over a garden wall.

Leap Thursday, 29 February
There is a general belief amongst the Clyro and Langley people that I cannot travel from Radnorshire to Wiltshire without going over the sea.

Sunday, 3 March
Supper at the Castle and home under the clear sky brilliant flashing moving with the quick lights of the stars and the bands of Orion, the sweet influences of the Pleiades and Arcturus with his sons.

Monday, 4 March
What a superb day it has been, almost cloudless, brilliant, hot as late May and the warm south wind blowing sweet from the Black Mountains. Cwmgwanon Wood is being murdered. As I walked along the edge of the beautiful dingle and looked sadly down into the hollow, numbers of my old friends of seven years standing lay below on both banks of the brook prostrate and mutilated, a mournful scene of havoc, the road almost impassable for the limbs of the fallen giants.

At the Homme the door was unlocked but the downstairs rooms empty and the only sounds in the silent house were the scratching of a little fox terrier shut up in a closet and the horrible moaning and growling of the madwoman upstairs.

She was in service more than twenty years as a housemaid at Kensington with some people named Collinson I think, an agent of Lord Bute's. In their service she saved £500 and came home to her own country to *enjoy* her money. This is how she is enjoying it.

Wednesday, 6 March
The night was superb, glittering with stars in a cloudless sky. As I came down the Long Lands Pitch I met a man in the dark coming up. It was old Richard Meredith the land-surveyor who stopped and began to talk about all things in heaven and earth, planets and fixed stars, philosophers and heretics, Mahometans and their creed. Amongst other things he asked me if I considered that

animalculae had the power of suffering. He was inclined to think not.

Friday, 8 March
At the Scripture Lesson at the School this morning asking Eleanor Williams of Paradise, 'What happened on Palm Sunday?' she replied, '*Jesus Christ went up to heaven on an ass*'. This was the promising result of a long struggle to teach her something about the Festivals of the Church.

Sunday, 10 March, Mothering Sunday
And a fine day for the young people to go Mothering.

Monday, 11 March
In the afternoon I walked over to Llan Thomas. Mrs Thomas better but not downstairs. Mr Venables came soon after me, then the Bridges, and then Mr Allen. I had a good deal of talk with Daisy. The coming of the other visitors created a confusion and diversion in our favour and being screened and our voices drowned in the Babel of tongues we were not noticed so much. She said that she and her sisters had been looking for birds' nests. 'I hope you didn't take any,' said I. 'Do you *think* we would?' answered she indignantly with a pretty flash of spirit. She told me that three of the six bells of Llanigan Church were stolen by dissenters who carried them away across the mountain and put them up in their own chapel. She was going for a walk with her father and sisters and said it was 'Such fun'. Rest, happy child, content with a few simple innocent delights. Rest, happy child, guileless and unspoilt. God keep thee, dear.

Wednesday, 13 March
Rain was creeping over the hills from the west and blotting out the mountains. Below lay the black and gloomy peat bog, the Rhos Goch, with the dark cold gleam of the stagnant water among its mawn pits, the graves of the children. This place has always had a strange singular irresistible fascination for me. I dread it yet I am drawn to it. As I returned I paused at the stonen stile above Llanshifr to look down upon the strange grey dark old house lying in the wet hollow among the springs, with its great

dismal solitary yew and the remains of the moat in which the murdered Scotch pedlar was buried.

Thursday, 14 March

After dinner to-day I was seized with a strange fit of nervous restlessness such as I never felt before. I should think it must have been something like the peculiar restlessness that comes shortly before death. I could not sit still or rest for a minute in any posture. The limbs all kept jumping and twitching and I should have liked to set to a run only I felt so weak and wretched. It was a strange uncomfortable feeling and with it came a twinge of neuralgia and toothache. I stood, I knelt, I sat, I lay back in my chair, I got up and walked about but nowhere could I rest. After a while I fell asleep or dozed in my chair and afterwards I awoke better.

Sunday, 17 March

After dinner Mr Venables told me that I must write next week to the Bishop to give notice that I mean to resign the curacy of Clyro on July 1. He asked me what I should do if the living of Clyro were offered to me. 'I should refuse it,' I said. 'Then you would be mad,' he said. But I don't want the living of Clyro, I don't want to be vicar of Clyro.

Wednesday, 20 March

By the great oak of Cross Foot and the green lane to Cwmpelved Green, where the idiot girl Phoebe sat laughing by the fire while her grandfather was groaning in bed and a black cat rushed in and out through a broken window pane, through which also the keen E. wind rushed in upon my head.

Thursday, 21 March

Dora writes, 'Father Ignatius and his monk caused a great sensation in Bath last week. They were staying at rather a grand house where there were some pretty fashionable girls and the unfortunate monk was bound by his vow not to look at a woman. They live on vegetables and dates entirely in Lent and look very ill. On Sunday they came into Bathwick Church for the Communion and Thersie said they looked so odd coming very fast up the aisle against the stream of people just pouring out of church.

177

All the young ladies eyes were on them but the monk's were never raised from the ground.'

Saturday, 23 March

In the afternoon called on Miss Bynon. She asked me about Emmie and her voyage to India, and declared that she should dread the 'Musketoos' more than anything. She said that when she came home from Kington last summer her house was filled with such swarms of flies that she sat down and cried to think wherever all the flies could come from.

I had a long talk with Mrs Venables this morning about my prospects. Pointing to a letter on the mantelpiece she said smiling, 'From your father-in-law'. She thinks I am quite right in wishing to decline the living of Clyro if it is offered to me. I devoutly hope it will not be. She says what is quite true, that I could scarcely keep the poor old vicarage in repair. Carpenters and masons are almost always there now to prevent its falling down.

Palm Sunday, 24 March

A snowy Palm Sunday. Mr Venables went to Bettws in a dense snowstorm. In the afternoon I had the happiness to have all the poor people to myself. None of the grand people were at Church by reason of the snow. So of course I could speak much better and more freely.

After service I went up to the Bird's Nest to see old Meredith. Further up I stopped and turned to look at the view. I saw what I thought was a long dazzling white and golden cloud up in the sky. Suddenly I found that I had been gazing at the great snow slopes of the Black Mountain lit up by the setting sun and looking through the dark storm clouds. It was a sublime spectacle, the long white rampart dazzling in its brilliancy and warmed by a golden tinge standing high up above the clear dark line of the nearer hills taking the sunshine, and bathed in glory. Then in the silence the Hay Church bell for evensong boomed suddenly out across the valley.

Monday, Lady Day

Snow storms again, and Hay Fair.

At 5 o'clock I went up the Bron and by the field path to little

Wern y Pentre. The old people talked over some of the parish tragedies which I have heard of, the supposed murder of Price of Cwmrafan by Burton, his would-be son-in-law, by day on the high road near Cabalva, and the digging up of Jane Whitcombe's baby at the Bronith, a baby which was supposed to have met with foul play. 'It's bad to get them,' said old Williams shaking his head, 'but it's worse to do away with them.'

When I rose to go the snow was still falling thickly in enormous feathers and was growing deep upon the ground. I had not brought an umbrella and kind Mrs Williams insisted upon my having her shawl to put over my shoulders. What kindly people these are. The leaden sky was awfully dark and low and seemed loaded with snow. I went down by the fields and wandered over the fields wide of the stiles, so much in a few minutes had the snow changed the look of everything. The sheep and lambs were running about in confusion crying piteously and all taken aback by the sudden storm. When I got to Penllan I could not help being struck by the change in the village. I had left it bright and sunny and green smiling under a blue sky. Now [after] an hour and a half it lay apparently deep in snow, snow on the village roofs, snow on the Church and Churchyard, snow on the green trees, snow everywhere. And over the village stooped low the terrible black leaden sky like a pall drooping lower and lower. Nothing could be more dark and dreary and depressing. But the trees were a beautiful sight. They were loaded thick with soft feathery snow in the most fairylike and fantastic shapes.

Tuesday, 26 March
To-day I wrote to the Bishop of St David's to give notice that I intend to resign the Curacy of Clyro on the 1st of July next, 'when' (I added by Mr Venables' advice, but against my own wish) 'I shall have been a licensed curate in the same parish in your Lordship's diocese for seven years and a half'.

The New Barn meadows are fearfully cut up by the timber carriages which are hauling away the fallen giants, ash and beech. The shouts of the timber haulers were ringing hollow and echoing through the wasted murdered dingle. My beautiful favourite Cwm is devastated and laid waste.

179

Good Friday, 29 March

For the first time I heard to-day the sweet bells of Clyro chiming down in the valley just before I reached the Chapel. I could even hear the three bells chime change for the single bell. The west wind brought the sound of the bells up the hill so clearly that it arrested me even while I was walking.

After Chapel I learnt that Mrs Wall had been happily brought to bed of a son at half past one this afternoon. She and her husband had been very anxious about it for it is four years since their last child Eleanor was born. And Mrs Wall was rather ashamed of her condition I suppose, though I am sure I don't know why she should have been, for she denied to her neighbour Mrs Nott, the blacksmith's wife, that she was in the family way. 'Then,' said Mrs Nott oracularly to Mrs Wall, 'I am sorry to hear it, Mrs Wall. I am sorry for you, for it is something worse.'

I went down to the Chapel Dingle to see sweet Emma Griffiths and to give her a cross Bun I had brought up for her. There was a smile in her sweet sky-blue eyes as she came to the door, but her voice and manner were very sad and quiet and I soon found she was suffering from face-ache. She said she should so much have liked to come to Chapel but her child kept her at home. She was scarcely ever able to leave home and went nowhere and heard nothing. She could not go to Chapel to-day because her husband Evan was at work at Llwyn Gwillim. Emma told me she was married when she was between nineteen and twenty, nineteen and a half. 'Too early,' she said, 'too early,' with a sad shake of the fair young girlish head, wise by sad experience before its time, that sorrowful touching thing, a grey head on green shoulders. 'It was much too early,' she repeated. 'I've often been sorry since that I married so young. I have been at service ever since I was ten years old. I have not been in a sight of places. My first place was at Bron Ddu at Mr Williams'. One morning all the men were away and the two missises were in bed and I had to fetch the cows in to be milked. There was a bull with the cows. I left the bull in the field with one cow and brought the other cows on to the gate. I saw the bull coming after me. He had come after me before but he had never caught me. I saw him now coming on towards me through the cows. I tried to get through the gate, but the bull caught me and struck [me] down. I felt no pain then or afterwards though he had me down on the ground punishing me for half an hour. I know it was half an hour the bull had me for I had looked what time it was when I went out and they told me what time it was when I came into the house afterwards. No one came to help me or to drive the bull away. No one knew about it. He "punned" me with his head mostly, but he ran his horn into my side and into one of my legs. After he had knocked me about on the ground a long time he got me up and pushed me through a pleached hedge that had been newly tined. He did not come after me. Many folk wondered he didn't come through the hedge after me and kill me. When I came to myself and stumbled into the house I was bruised all over and covered with blood, almost naked, with my clothes torn nearly off me, and the doctor couldn't tell whether I had any eyes or not for they were quite closed up. I was half unconscious all the time the bull had me on the ground and I felt no pain, at the time. But I have never been so strong or well since. I have gatherings on my side and the bull hurt something within me. I was at home for three months but after I got well I went back to Bronddu and finished my time till the May Fair though my friends tried to persuade me not to. But I always finished my time if I could. I never liked to break my time. I was not afraid of other cattle afterwards, but I was afraid of that bull. He was a two-year-old. Master fatted him and killed him. It was a great mercy the bull did not kill me, but my time was not come. The Lord was very merciful to me and saved me from him,' said the girl reverently and humbly. 'The Lord had something else for me to do.'

And this was one of the sorrowful and hard experiences in that her young life. A child between eleven and twelve years old.

An election of a Guardian for the parish is coming on and the place is all in an uproar of excitement. Church versus Chapel and party feeling running very high. The dissenters are behaving badly.

Easter Sunday, April Eve

A soft warm spring morning of changing sunshine and shower.
I never was so hard put to it as in Church this morning to resist
untimely and inextinguishable laughter. It was almost irresistible.
The sun was beating fiercely through the southern windows upon
the heads and books of the devout Hodgson party in the Cabalva
seat. Mrs Chinnock tried to draw down the blind, but the blind
was broken and would not draw or be drawn. Mrs Venables then
signed to the clerk to come and pull the blind down. The little man
came and pulled and pulled till at last with a more violent tug
smash went the wooden bar with a loud report and hung in ruins
in the air with a broken back. I knew the crash was coming when
I saw the clerk pulling, and when it came it was almost too much.
I was nearly choked. There came into my mind suddenly my
Father's old story of the clergyman waiting for the hymn before
the sermon to be finished and meanwhile looking through the
church window and seeing an old woman pulling up a stubborn
carrot. At last up came the carrot all at once, over went the old
woman on her back head over heels. 'I thought so!' exclaimed the
delighted clergyman aloud, to the astonishment of the expectant
congregation who had finished the hymn and were waiting for
him to begin the prayer.

Easter Monday, 1872

Crichton said when he lived at Boughrood Castle with his uncle
Mr Clutterbuck, old Boughrood Church was a most miserable
place. The choir sat upon the altar and played a drum.

Friday, 5 April

I dined at the Vicarage at 6.30 and went with the Venables to the
ball at Clifford Priory at 8. There were 52 people at the party.

Daisy promised to dance the 5th dance – a quadrille – with me
and gave me her card and pencil to write her name. Morrell and
Miss Child were vis-à-vis to us, but I am afraid we did them out of
their fair share of dancing, for Daisy and I were soon absorbed in
conversation and each other – I at all events was absorbed in her –
and became quite oblivious of the figure and the whole thing.

'You never come to Clyro,' I said, 'and it is such a pretty place.'
'Talking of flowers,' I said, 'do you remember once last September

giving me some flowers out of your own garden?' 'Yes,' she said
blushing prettily and looking down. 'I have those flowers now,' I
said, 'I have kept them carefully ever since, and I prize them more
than I can tell you.' 'I am sure,' she said, 'they can't be worth
keeping now. They must be withered long ago.' 'No,' I said, 'I
kept them in water a long time and then I dried them, and they
are as sweet as ever, especially the mignonette. I shall keep them
until you give me some more.' She blushed and smiled and I don't
think she was displeased. I ought not to have said so much, but I
could not help it. She was so pretty and sweet and kind and she
made such gentle and kind allowance for my awkwardness and
mistakes in dancing, and I did love her so. She was dressed in
white almost entirely, with a faint sweet suspicion of blue, a
white flower in her bright hair and a quantity of dainty frilling
and puffing almost hiding her fair shoulders. I thought I had never
seen her look prettier.

When the quadrille was over – much too soon – she took my
arm and we went out into the cool hall. I found her a comfortable
chair screened from general observation by a beautiful azalea. She
sat down and we began to talk again. But alas, 'the course of true
love never did run smooth'. We had not been talking long, when
our seclusion was broken in upon and our happiness marred – at
least mine was – by hearing her father's voice behind us. As soon
as she heard his voice she rose, I thought in a slight and pretty
confusion. Then he called to her to know if she were engaged for
the next dance, and I saw she was obliged to go. So we went back
together to the ball room and I scarcely saw her to speak to her
again the whole evening, except once in the gallery when we were
drinking claret cup and we had a few words together about the
Wen Allt. I should have dearly liked to ask her to dance again,
but I was afraid of getting her into a scrape and attracting people's
attention, and she was much too kind to refuse if she were not
engaged, and much too honest to pretend to be engaged when she
was not.

I got to bed at 4.30 just as dawn was breaking.

Saturday, 6 April

To-day I feel good for nothing, from the reaction after the excitement of the ball last night and seeing Daisy. All the old feelings of last September have revived again as keenly, as vividly, as ever. The old wounds are all open and bleeding again and I can rest nowhere in my misery.

In the afternoon I went to the Vicarage. Mrs Venables seeing in a moment what I wanted — God bless her — came out into the garden with me and sitting under the great double-headed fir tree we talked over the evening of yesterday with reference to Daisy and myself. She told me I owed it to myself to speak to her father again before I left the country, and get something settled. But my position is no better now than it was 6 months ago and I cannot humiliate myself before him again for nothing. I don't know what to do. Mrs Venables asked me if I saw any one I liked better should I still consider myself bound in honour to Daisy. 'Yes,' I said, 'but I don't think I shall ever see any one I like better. I daresay I shall never marry, but if I do marry I shall marry her.'

Sunday, 7 April

Colonel Pearson gave us some of his Crimean reminiscences. Most of the English officers could speak French. Hardly one of the French officers could speak English. The Russian officers could speak both French and English fluently. Colonel Pearson was on Sir George Brown's staff. The old General was not much of a linguist and knew but little French. One night an Aide de Camp came from Marshal Canrobert with a message about an attack that was to be made or expected in the morning. The French officer was grinning, bowing, scraping, grimacing and gesticulating. Sir George could not understand a word. He used some strong language and turned to Colonel Pearson. 'What does he say, Master Dick? Give him a glass of sherry and tell him to go away.' *Tell him to go away!* As if he had been an organ-grinder! 'And,' said Colonel Pearson with an expressive shrug, 'perhaps next morning a hundred lives might depend upon that message.'

Saturday, 13 April

The two old women Hannah Jones and Sarah Probert were both lying in bed and groaning horribly. I gave them some money and their cries and groans suddenly ceased.

Sunday, 14 April

The beauty of the view, the first view of the village, coming down by the Brooms this evening was indescribable. The brilliant golden poplar spires shone in the evening light like flames against the dark hill side of the Old Forest and the blossoming fruit trees, the torch trees of Paradise blazed with a transparent green and white lustre up the dingle in the setting sunlight. The village is in a blaze of fruit blossom. Clyro is at its loveliest. What more can be said?

Sunday, 21 April

I hear that Houseman at Bredwardine wishing to drape the Communion table with black on Good Friday and having no black drapery suitable for the purpose was misguided enough to put over the Table the old filthy parish pall. Everyone was disgusted and shocked at what they considered a piece of indecency. It is the talk of the country and Miss Newton is up in arms.

Monday, 22 April

Held a consultation with Mrs Venables about my love affairs, plans and prospects. I see how it will all end. Alas, who could have believed that I could be such a villain?

> Alas for the breaking of love
> And the lights have died out in the West,
> And, oh, for the wings of a dove,
> And, oh, for the haven of rest.

Wednesday, 24 April

I went up the Cwm this afternoon. I went on to Fairlands to see the sick blacksmith Bayliss. He said his son the wantcatcher was very good to him. There were 5 dozen of prepared moleskins hanging up to the cratch, to make somebody a waistcoat.

Wednesday, May Day

I stayed to dinner[1] and Armine and Helen played very nicely.
The night was cool and pleasant as I walked home under the stars.
About midnight I passed over the Rhydspence border brook, and
crossed the border from England into Wales. The English inn was
still ablaze with light and noisy with the songs of revellers, but
the Welsh inn was dark and still.

Monday, 6 May

Got into an argument with Mr Latimer Jones about people's legal
and moral rights over their property and he spoke in such an
insolent overbearing contemptuous way that my blood was up,
and Mrs Bevan said afterwards she feared we should have fought.

Holy Thursday, 9 May

This morning I conceived the idea of a poem in the style of Tam
o'Shanter — the scene to be laid in the ruined Church of Llanbedr
Painscastle. Two lovers who had made an assignation in the
churchyard to be terrified by seeing through the windows an
assembly of devils, ghosts, lawless lovers and murdered children.

Visited old Price as usual. He was lying on his bed which has
been moved downstairs. He invited me to sit down. I was afraid to
because of the lice. I read to him Psalms cxxi and cxxx.

Friday, 10 May

An Indian letter from Emmie at Hyderabad was forwarded to me
from Langley. It describes their journey up country from Bombay
and their arrival at the Residency, Hyderabad, in their bullock
transits, their horses having jibbed and broken down. There was a
capital description of the moment when the horses struck work in
the midst of a violent thunderstorm at midnight, the pouring
rain, the intense stifling heat of the carriage, the wailing hungry
baby, the lightning-lit barren dreary landscape and the motionless
figures of the Sowar horsemen who were escorting them.

Above Pentwyn old James Jones the sawyer was breaking stones.
We fell into discourse. He said the ground ivy or Robin-run-in-
the-hedge is called Hay Maids in Herefordshire. 'That's hemlock,'
said he severely, taking the white blossom from me. 'That's poison

---

1. At Whitney Rectory.

186

for Christians.' He said wild garlic, called Jack-in-the-Bush, is a famous pot herb. The old man's work was done, he put up his tools, took me home with him, and lent me Culpeper's *Herbal*.

Saturday, 11 May
This is the bitterest bleakest May I ever saw and I have seen some bad ones. May is usually the worst and coldest month in the year, but this beats them all and out-herods Herod. A black bitter wind violent and piercing drove from the East with showers of snow. The mountains and Clyro Hill and Cusop Hill were quite white with snow. The hawthorn bushes are white with may and snow at the same time.

Late in the afternoon walking from the Lower House to the Bronith I met Morrell returning from fishing his water at Cabalva. His keeper Whitcombe was carrying with justifiable pride a beautiful 9½ lbs salmon, the first he has killed. Morrell asked me to dine with him and we discussed part of the salmon which was delicious, a bottle of port, and some fine strawberries from Cabalva as well flavoured as if they had been ripened out of doors.

Whitsun Monday, 20 May
To-day I came to Langley.

Monday, 27 May
As I sat in my bedroom window seat with the window open towards Jerusalem in the early beautiful May morning, the nightingale was singing and a cuckoo was calling, a cushat was cooing, and a turtle dove was trilling.

Went to London by the mid-day mail. Put up at Perch's rooms, 68 Westbourne Park Villas. Visited the Academy and saw Mr Venables' portrait. Perch met me there. The poorest Academy Exhibition I ever saw and full of uninteresting portraits. Dined at the Gaiety rooms and went to see *Pygmalion and the Statue* played at the Haymarket. The Statue scenes where the statue becomes a woman and the woman becomes a statue were admirable. The Statue was played by Mrs Kendall (Miss Robertson). Old Buckstone as Chrysos the art critic and in the preceding farce was inimitable.

One picture in the Academy Exhibition was fascinating.

Fauchette, the half-length picture of a dark-haired girl, the dark eyes full and large with tears, mournful, beseeching, imploring, and sad with a wistful despairing sadness too sad for words.

Tuesday, 28 May

The eve of the Derby and London very full. Walked through Kensington Gardens to the International Exhibition. Some good pictures, especially in the Belgian gallery. I was much struck by some snow scenes, and Undine rising from the fountain. At one o'clock the Row was a stirring sight, the Ladies' Mile crowded with riders. At 5 and 5.30 the Drive at Hyde Park Corner was dazzling, the throng tremendous.

Wednesday, 29 May

London very empty, everyone gone to the Derby, the Row deserted. We came down by the evening express. How delicious to get into the country again, the sweet damp air and the scent of the beanfields. I do loathe London. I walked up by Cocklebury through the cool fresh damp lane, green and fragrant.

Friday, June Eve

Left Langley for Clyro for the last time. To-day is Minna Venables' birthday and I went back to Clyro on purpose to celebrate it. Flags were flying at Clyro School and children were swarming in and out like bees. Over the school gate the schoolmaster and mistress had made a pretty triumphal arch of greenery and flowers with 'Long Live Miss Venables'. As we dashed up to the Vicarage door the bells pealed out. They had been ringing since early morning and the ringers had dined at the Vicarage. The blacksmiths also had been firing anvil cannons since 5.30 a.m.

The children had their tea on the lawn between 5 and 6 o'clock and then went to play on the Lower Bron. It seemed as if the night would never get dark and we could not begin the fireworks till nearly ten. They were the first fireworks ever seen in Clyro and the village and the Bron were swarming with people.

Saturday, June Day

I went up to the Wern below Gwernfydden this afternoon to see if the bog beans were yet in flower. I found a few here and there standing with their feet in the water and with their delicate lace-like flowers shining like stars about the swamp. I think it is one of the loveliest flowers that grows, the exquisite fret and filigree work of the white lace blossom surrounded by the cluster of bright pink buds.

Monday, 3 June
At 1.30 the omnibus and my Father drove up to the door. He went out fishing at Cabalva immediately.

Tuesday, 4 June
The news of my leaving Clyro is spreading through the village. These people will break my heart with their affectionate lamentations.

Friday, 7 June
Dined at Llan Thomas. A family party. Major Thomas showed me his stereoscopic slides 'The Diversions of Satan' which he bought in India. They were made for an Indian Prince, but were not pronounced enough to suit his taste.

Saturday, 8 June
A pouring wet morning. Nevertheless my Father and I started in the rain for the Vale of Arrow, he riding the Vicarage pony sheltered by two mackintoshes and an umbrella and I on foot with an umbrella only. We plodded on doggedly through the wet for 6 miles, casting wistful glances at all the quarters of the heavens to catch any gleam of hope. Hope however there seemed to be none. The rain fell pitilessly. The Harbour below us in the Vale of Arrow was a welcome sight, a haven of refuge.

In spite of the wild weather on the open mountain we could not help noticing the beautiful effect produced upon the steep slopes by the vast sheets of brilliantly green young fern spreading amongst the old black heather. The mountain ashes were still in full blossom in the Fuallt fold and the meadows round the old farm house and the graceful trees were covered with the bunches of white bloom.

We reached the Harbour more like drowned rats than clergymen of the Established Church.

The boy took the pony to the stable and Mrs Jones came to the door. And now here is a fine specimen of Radnorshire manners.

She was in her working dress and in the midst of her Saturday cleaning but quite unconscious of herself and her dress she simply and naturally came forward at once and welcomed us to the Harbour with her grand courteous manner as if she had been a queen in disguise or in full purple and ermine. Then at the time when the work was done the mistress of the house took her place at the head of her table with all the natural grace and simple quiet dignity of a woman in the best society. Mrs Irvine came down and Watkeys Jones, the master of the house, appeared like a wounded soldier with his head bound up in a rèd handkerchief. The good people were most kind to us, providing us with dry coats, hats and leggings and hot brandy and water and when the rain had a little abated we went down to the little river to fish under the guidance of the master of the house. The stream was too muddy for the fly and too clear for the worm. But the water was rising fast. We crossed a swampy meadow to the Glasnant above the meeting of the waters, a little stream flowing swiftly under alders. Then we followed the Glasnant down to its meeting with the Arrow. Some willows grew here and there was a likely hole with deep smooth still water under a bush sheltered by a sudden curve in the bank. Out came two trout. From the next pool four trout came out fast one after another. 'Well done, well done!' cried the good farmer with delight, clapping my Father on the back, 'I've never seen better work than that.'

Sunday, 9 June

I went to see Mrs Prosser at the Swan, a young pretty woman dying I fear of consumption which she caught of her sister, Mrs Hope of the Rose and Crown in Hay. It was a sad beautiful story. She was warned not to sleep with her sister who was dying of decline and told that if she did she herself would probably be infected with the disease. But her sister begged her so hard not to leave her and to go on sleeping with her that she gave way. 'What could I do?' she said. 'She was my only sister and we loved each other so. I have been married seven years,' she said, 'and now my first child has just come, a little girl, and it does seem so hard to go away and leave her. But if it is the Lord's will to take me I must be content to go. My left lung is quite gone,' she said look-

190

ing at me with her lip trembling and her beautiful eyes full of tears.

Margaret Griffith, speaking of Mrs John Vaughan of Llwyn Gwillim, who has just been confined with her fourth child, said, 'Mrs Vaughan will have a good family soon. Her children come fast. But the harder the storm the sooner 'tis over. Every one will have her number.' She described how she had washed and cleaned Old Price and how she had 'combed out of his head a score platefuls of "bocs" (lice)'.

Monday, 17 June
Went to Bockleton Vicarage.

Wednesday, 19 June
Left Bockleton Vicarage for Liverpool. At Wrexham two merry saucy Irish hawking girls got into our carriage. The younger had a handsome saucy daring face showing splendid white teeth when she laughed and beautiful Irish eyes of dark grey which looked sometimes black and sometimes blue, with long silky black lashes and finely pencilled black eyebrows. This girl kept her companion and the whole carriage laughing from Wrexham to Chester with her merriment, laughter and songs and her antics with a doll dressed like a boy, which she made dance in the air by pulling a string. She had a magnificent voice and sung to a comic popular air while the doll danced wildly,

> 'A-dressed in his Dolly Varden,
> A-dressed in his Dolly Varden,
>   He looks no neat
>   And he smells so sweet,
> A-dressed in his Dolly Varden.'

Then breaking down into merry laughter she hid her face and glanced roguishly at me from behind the doll. Suddenly she became quiet and pensive and her face grew grave and sad as she sang a love song.

The two girls left the carriage at Chester and as she passed the younger put out her hand and shook hands with me. They stood by the carriage door on the platform for a few moments and Irish Mary, the younger girl, asked me to buy some nuts. I gave her sixpence and took a dozen nuts out of a full measure she was going to pour into my hands. She seemed surprised and looked up with a smile. 'You'll come and see me,' she said coaxingly. 'You are not Welsh are you?' 'No, we are a mixture of Irish and English.' 'Born in Ireland?' 'No, I was born at Huddersfield in Yorkshire.' 'You look Irish – you have the Irish eye.' She laughed and blushed and hid her face. 'What do you think I am?' asked the elder girl, 'do you think I am Spanish?' 'No,' interrupted the other laughing, 'you have too much Irish between your eyes.' 'My eyes are blue,' said the elder girl, 'your eyes are grey, the gentleman's eyes are black.' 'Where did you get in?' I asked Irish Mary. 'At Wrexham,' she said. 'We were caught in the rain, walked a long way in it and got wet through,' said the poor girl pointing to a bundle of wet clothes they were carrying and which they had changed for dry ones. 'What do you do?' 'We go out hawking,' said the girl in a low voice. 'You have a beautiful voice.' 'Hasn't she?' interrupted the elder girl eagerly and delightedly. 'Where did you learn to sing?' She smiled and blushed and hid her face. A porter and some other people were looking wonderingly on, so I thought it best to end the conversation. But there was an attractive power about this poor Irish girl that fascinated me strangely. I felt irresistibly drawn to her. The singular beauty of her eyes, a beauty of deep sadness, a wistful sorrowful imploring look, her swift rich humour, her sudden gravity and sadnesses, her brilliant laughter, a certain intensity and power and richness of life and the extraordinary sweetness, softness and beauty of her voice in singing and talking gave her a power over me which I could not understand nor describe, but the power of a stronger over a weaker will and nature. She lingered about the carriage door. Her look grew more wistful, beautiful, imploring. Our eyes met again and again. Her eyes grew more and more beautiful. My eyes were fixed and riveted on hers. A few minutes more and I know not what might have happened. A wild reckless feeling came over me. Shall I leave all and follow her? No – Yes – No. At that moment the train moved on. She was left behind. Goodbye, sweet Irish Mary. So we parted. Shall we meet again? Yes – No – Yes.

Maria Gwatkin took me down to Mr Gwatkin's office (wine and

ship's stores) and introduced me to him, an elderly man, grey, with a pleasant goodhumoured face and kindly eye. We went to the Exchange, one of the finest buildings of the kind in the world, and passing upstairs into the gallery and leaning upon the broad marble ledge we looked down upon a crowd of merchants and brokers swarming and humming like a hive of bees in the floor of the vast area below. All round the enormous hall were desks or screens or easels or huge slates covered with the latest telegrams, notices of London stock and share lists, cargoes, freights, sales, outward and homeward bound ships, times of sailing, states of wind and weather, barometer readings. Mr Gwatkin did not seem to have a high opinion of the solvency or honesty of Liverpool merchants. Pointing to the great crowd buzzing and surging below he said, 'I don't believe there are ten men there who could pay 15/- in the pound.' He pointed out to me however three honest men. It was a case for Diogenes and his lantern, and one felt uncomfortably like being in Sodom and ten righteous men nowhere to be found. The quadrangle outside called 'the Flags' is where the cotton merchants meet and the pavement was white with the fluff of the cotton samples.

Thursday, 20 June
At ten o'clock Mr, Mrs, Miss Gwatkin and I went down to the Landing Stage and embarked on board a steamboat for New Brighton on the Cheshire side of the Mersey, a suburb of Birkenhead. The morning was lovely, all was fresh and new, the salt air and the wind exhilarating and I was in dancing spirits. The Mersey was gay and almost crowded with vessels of all sorts moving up and down the river, ships, barques, brigs, brigantines, schooners, cutters, colliers, tugs, steamboats, lighters, 'flats', everything from the huge emigrant liner steamship with four masts to the tiny sailing and rowing boat. From the river one sees to advantage the miles of docks which line the Mersey side, and the forests of masts which crowd the quays, 'the pine forest of the sea, mast and spar'.

At New Brighton there are beautiful sands stretching for miles along the coast and the woods wave green down to the salt water's edge. The sands were covered with middle class Liverpool folks and children out for a holiday, digging in the sand, riding on horses and donkeys, having their photographs taken, and enjoying themselves generally. Some of the lady and gentlemen riders upon the hired horses were pitiable objects, bumping up and down upon their saddles like flour sacks, and even requiring their horses to be led for them. The ladies as a rule rode without riding habits and with crinolines. The effect was striking.

As we came down the river this morning several large emigrant ships lay in the river getting up steam and the Blue Peter, the signal for sailing, flying at the fore. They were going down the river this afternoon. They seemed crowded with Irish and German emigrants and small steam-boats kept bringing fresh loads of passengers alongside the big ships. One could not help thinking of the hundreds of sorrowful hearts on board and ashore and the farewells and partings for ever, so many of them, on this side of the grave.

Eventually we came back to Liverpool, got luncheon and went to see the Docks. Nothing gives one so vivid an idea of the vast commerce of the country as these docks, quays and immense warehouses, piled and cumbered with hides, cotton, tallow, corn, oil-cake, wood and wine, oranges and other fruit and merchandise of all kinds from all corners of the world. I admired the dray horses very much, huge creatures 17 or 18 hands high, more like elephants than horses. Liverpool boasts the finest breed of Flemish draught horses in the world.

Mrs Gwatkin said that 15, 10 and even 5 years ago there was much more trade and wealth in Liverpool and much larger fortunes more rapidly made than now. There has been of late and there still is a stagnation of trade, a depression and deterioration of credit. Formerly the streets were blocked by the enormous business and the mountains of merchandise passing about, but there is plenty of room now.

Friday, 21 June
Liverpool left upon my mind an impression of ragged Irish bare-footed women and children. Enormous wealth and squalid poverty, wildernesses of offices and palatial counting houses and

warehouses, bustling pushing vulgar men, pretty women and lovely children.

Saturday, 22 June
I was very sorry to leave Liverpool this morning. Theodore went with me in the cab to the Lime St Station at 9.15. The cab was driven by an old gentleman named Gwynne who was once a man of good estate and county magistrate. He married a woman of family, but he dissipated his fortune and now he has sunk to be a common cabman and his wife makes him an allowance.

When I reached Clyro about 5 o'clock I found on my table a red leather case containing a beautiful gold watch and chain with two most kind letters from Mr and Mrs Venables saying in the nicest way that the watch was from him, the chain from her, and the little chain supporting the Braquet Key from the baby. I went immediately to the Vicarage to thank them as well as I could, for my heart was full.

Monday, Midsummer Day
The cuckoo was still singing this morning. As I was getting up I heard the drone of the Italian bagpipes advancing and two men with dancing children, poor little wretches, came playing through the village.

In the afternoon Tom Williams came and carried me off to Llowes to dine with him. At dinner he told the following story. A soldier who did not want to go to church told his officer that he was neither Catholic nor Protestant, Church of England nor Presbyterian, nor Dissenter. The officer asked what he did belong to. The soldier said he belonged to the Yarmouth Bloaters. He meant the Plymouth Brethren.

Thursday, 27 June
Mrs Baskerville sent me a kind letter this evening saying that she and her daughters wished me to carry away some remembrance of them and begging me to take my choice of an oaken stationery cabinet, a large musical box, a time piece or a fitted travelling bag, or to mention any thing else that I liked better.

Friday, 28 June

I promised Mr Venables in answer to his request that I would stay here through August till September 1st inclusive and go home for July if my Father wants me. I hope this will be the last of the many changes and postponements that have been made in our plans. Going down the village I fell in with old James Jones the sawyer. 'I hear you are going away,' he said in a broken trembling voice. And he walked down the village with me weeping as he went.

Saturday, 29 June

Called at Hay Castle and went with the four pretty girl archers to shoot and pick up their arrows in the field opposite the Castle.

This evening I went out visiting the village people. The sinking sun shone along the Churchyard and threw long shadows of the Church and the tombstones over the high waving grass. All round the lychgate and the churchyard wall the tall purple mallows are in flower and the banks and hedges about the village are full of them. Old Hannah Witney was sitting in her cottage door at work as usual with her high cap and her little red shawl pinned over her breast, her thin grey-bearded nutcracker face bent earnestly upon her knitting till she glanced sharply up over her spectacles to see who it was that was passing.

Wednesday, 3 July

Tom Williams of Llowes and I had long been talking of going up to Llanbedr Hill to pay a visit to the eccentric solitary, the Vicar, and we arranged to go this morning. The day promised to be fine and after school at 10.30 I walked over to Llowes. When the postman, who followed me closely, had arrived we started up a steep stony narrow lane so overgrown and overarched with wild roses that it was difficult for a horseman to pass, but a lane most beautiful and picturesque with its wild luxuriant growth of fern and wild roses and foxgloves. The foxgloves were wonderful. They grew on both sides of the lane, multitudes, multitudes in long and deep array.

Tom Williams was on horseback, I on foot. As we mounted the hill, beautiful views of mountains and valley opened gleaming behind us, and Tom Williams pointed out to me some of the

Llowes farmhouses scattered over the hills. The road seemed deserted as we went on our pilgrimage. All the folk were busy in their hay fields. Here and there my fellow pilgrim from his point of vantage in the saddle spoke to a labourer or small farmer over the hedge.

As we went up the steep hill to Painscastle the huge green Castle mound towered above us. A carpenter came down the hill from the village. I asked him where the grave of Tom Tobacco lay upon the moor, but he shook his head. He did not know.

In the village, a Post office had been established since I was last here and the village well, the only one, which was formerly common and open to ducks and cattle had been neatly walled and railed round. We went to Pendre, the house of the Mayor of Painscastle, but the Mayor was not at home.

At last Mr Price the Mayor was discovered in the centre of a group of village politicians before the alehouse door where

> While village statesmen talked with looks profound
> The weekly paper with their ale went round.

Tom Williams talked to the Mayor about quarrying stone for the Painscastle school while the blacksmith leaned over the wall taking part in the conversation and the rest of the village statesmen lounged in the inn porch. The Mayor came up with us on to Llanbedr Hill to show us the best quarry.

He said Painscastle was an old broken borough, one of the Radnorshire boroughs, and they still went through the form of electing one of the chief men of the village as Mayor. Sometimes the office ran in one family for some time. Williams asked the Mayor if he had any power. 'No', answered that dignity, 'I dinna think I have much power.' We stopped to look at the stone of the ruined village pound. With a touch of dry humour the Mayor told us that at the last Court Leet the village authorities and tenants of the Manor had made a present to the Lord of the Manor (Mr de Winton) of the pound, the stop gate and the village well, that he might keep them in repair. Pointing to one of his fields, whose boundary had lately been moved and enlarged, he said with a merry twinkle in his eye, 'Because the Lord had not land enough before I have taken in a bit more for him off the waste'. The

Mayor said there was a small school kept near Llanbedr Church by an old man, who taught the children well. 'But I do consait he do let them out too soon in the evening, he do', said the Mayor disapprovingly.

The Mayor took us to the quarry and discoursed without enthusiasm and even with despondency on the badness of the roads, the difficulty of hauling the stone and the labour of 'ridding' the ground before the stone could be raised. After some talk at the quarry about ways and means, we parted, the Mayor returning to his mayoralty which had no emolument, no dignity, and no powers, he 'didna think', and we going on over the hill towards the abode of the hermit.

At length we came in sight of a little hollow, a recess in the hills at the foot of Llanbedr Hill, a little cwm running back into the mountain closed at the end and on both sides by the steep hill sides but open to the South, and the sun and the great valley of the Wye and the distant blue mountains. A sunny green little cwm it was secluded deep among the steep green hills, and until you came close to it you would not be suspecting the existence of the place. A well watered little cwm with sweet waters from the upper and lower springs which welled up through the turf and peat and fern and heathers, and joining their rills trickled away in a tiny stream down the cwm to form a brook.

In this green cwm stood a little grey hut. It was built of rough dry stone without mortar and the thatch was thin and broken. At one end of the cabin a little garden had been enclosed and fenced in from the waste. There was one other house in sight where the cwm lay open to the west, Pencommon which used to belong to Price, the old keeper, who died lately in Clyro Village. Not a soul was stirring or in sight on the hill or in the valley, and the green cwm was perfectly silent and apparently deserted. As we turned the corner of the little grey hut and came in sight of the closed door we gave up all hope of seeing the Solitary and believed that our pilgrimage had been in vain. Then what was my relief when I knocked upon the door to hear a strange deep voice from within saying, 'Ho! Ho!' There was a slight stir within and then the cabin door opened and a strange figure came out. The figure of a man rather below the middle height, about 60 years of age, his head covered with a luxuriant growth of light brown or chestnut hair and his face made remarkable by a mild thoughtful melancholy blue eye and red moustache and white beard. The hermit was dressed in a seedy faded greasy suit of black, a dress coat and a large untidy white cravat, or a cravat that had once been white, lashed round his neck with a loose knot and flying ends. Upon his feet he wore broken low shoes and in his hand he carried a tall hat. There was something in the whole appearance of the Solitary singularly dilapidated and forlorn and he had a distant absent look and a preoccupied air as if the soul were entirely unconscious of the rags in which the body was clothed.

The Solitary came forward and greeted us with the most perfect courtesy and the natural simplicity of the highest breeding. 'And now', he said thoughtfully, 'how shall we do? My landlord promised at 2 o'clock to meet me in an hour's time on the hill with a gambo to bring home my mawn.' It was now 3 o'clock.

I asked if he would allow us to accompany him up to the mawn hill. 'Would you like it?' he said eagerly. 'Would you like it?' Then he went off with Williams to Pencommon to stable 'the mare' begging me to wait and sit down in his house till he returned. 'The house' was a sight when once seen never to be forgotten. I sat in amazement taking mental notes of the strangest interior I ever saw. Inside the hut there was a wild confusion of litter and rubbish almost choking and filling up all available space. The floor had once been of stone but was covered thick and deep with an accumulation of the dirt and peat dust of years. The furniture consisted of two wooden saddle-seated chairs polished smooth by the friction of continual sessions, and one of them without a back. A four-legged dressing table littered with broken bread and meat, crumbs, dirty knives and forks, glasses, plates, cups and saucers in squalid hugger-mugger confusion. No table cloth. No grate. The hearth foul with cold peat ashes, broken bricks and dust, under the great wide open chimney through which stole down a faint ghastly sickly light. In heaps and piles upon the floor were old books, large Bibles, commentaries, old-fashioned religious disputations, C.M.S. Reports and odd books of all sorts, Luther on the Galatians, etc. The floor was further encumbered with beams and logs of wood, flour pans covered over, and old chests. All the other articles of food were hung up on pot hooks some from the ceiling, some in the chimney out of the way of the rats. The squalor, the dirt, the dust, the foulness and wretchedness of the place were indescribable, almost inconceivable. And in this cabin thus lives the Solitary of Llanbedr, the Revd John Price, Master of Arts of Cambridge University and Vicar of Llanbedr Painscastle.

Presently I heard the voices returning from Pencommon where they had stabled 'the Mare'. We had not gone many steps before Williams called the attention of the Solitary to a man with a horse and cart moving along the top of the hill high above us and standing out clear against the sky. 'It is my landlord,' said the Solitary. 'He is as good as his word.'

The hermit told us the name of his house was Cwm Cello, and that he had been much perplexed and exercised in mind about the meaning of the latter word. He was Welshman enough to know that there was no such word in Welsh as Cello. But in a dictionary which he took up one day in a farm house he found that the word 'Ceilio' meant a retreat or enclosure, or shelter or pen from cattle. 'And indeed,' said the Solitary plaintively, 'when I first came to live here I did find that all the sheep and cattle took shelter in my garden as if they had always been used to retreat there, to that very place in a storm. So I called it "the Shepherd's Dingle".'

By this time we had reached the crest of the hill side which was almost as steep as the wall of a house and at a little distance we saw waiting a horse and gambo and a peasant whom the Anchorite described as his landlord and addressed as 'Mr James'. On the whole the landlord was better dressed than his tenant. Some low conical heaps of peat turf were scattered about among the heather. They were large flat thin pieces skimmed off the surface with the heather upon them. The Solitary and his landlord and a little boy, the son of the landlord, began loading and piling the peats upon the gambo first removing the outer turves which had been thrown over the rest to keep them dry. I helped the hermit in loading his mawn while Tom Williams looked on with a benevolent smile. When the gambo was loaded heavily enough for the steep descent the Solitary sent it down to the cabin of Cwm Ceilio in charge of his landlord while he walked further over the hill with us to show us the famous Rocks of Pen Cwm and Llanbychllyn Pool. Suddenly we came in sight of the precipitous grey rocks which are so like the Rocks of Aberedw and which were the last haunt of the fairies, the last place where the little people were seen. Then there was a gleam of silver over the dark heather stems and Llanbychllyn Pool lay in its hollow like a silver shield. The view was beautiful and we all lay down upon the dry heather just budding into pink blossom to enoy the fair and 'delicate prospect' in full view of the grey rocks and the silver lake. And the curlews called and the plovers whistled with their strange wild whistle about the sunny hill. The Solitary was infinitely pleased to learn that the grey rocks which looked at us across a cwm from the opposite hill side had been observed and admired by other people than himself. 'I said to myself,' he observed, 'that those were very beautiful rocks.'

He told us that he had been very ill with internal inflammation, whether of liver or lungs he did not know. He had gone to Builth for some medicine which he thought he had chosen very judiciously, camomile pills, and he believed they had done him much good. It was touching to hear the Solitary man say rather mournfully and despondingly, 'And I thought I was as strong as ever again, but when I walked to Hay and back yesterday I found my mistake.' To be ill and to grow old in that lone hut without a soul to care for him or to turn his head. How wretched a prospect for the poor Solitary.

It was touching too to find that in his loneliness the hermit had been employing his time in inventing without help or sympathy, and perfecting, two new systems of shorthand which he had published in Manchester and London. 'I said to myself', he remarked, 'that I thought I might find out a new way.'

The Solitary told us that he had two little bounty farms in Llandeilo Graban. He kept a few fields in his own hands and occasionally went over the hill to see his land. The Anchorite and the Mayor of Painscastle had both heard of Tom Tobacco's grave, but neither knew the mysterious story of the lonely grave on the open hill, and only the Mayor could tell me the place of the grave, on the top of the ridge where Llanbedr Hill marches with the Hill of Llandeilo Graban.

When we came down from off the hill the Solitary compelled us to come into his hut again and sit down for a while. The gambo stood at the door with its load of mawn but the landlord and his horse and son were gone home. At our request the anchorite hunted among his piles of rubbish with a candlestick covered with the thick grease of years, trying unsuccessfully to find one of his shorthand pamphlets in print. But to give us an idea of his system he drew to the table a flour pan covered with a board, and sitting down on it he produced a pencil and a piece of paper and for our benefit wrote in shorthand the following verse which he had seen in a sampler lately in a farm house and which had taken his fancy :

> A little health,
> A little wealth,
> A little house and freedom,
> And at the end
> A little friend
> And little cause to need him.

This verse the Solitary wrote with extraordinary rapidity and conciseness. A dozen strokes and the thing was done. He said he had no opportunity of trying the new system of shorthand he had discovered except by writing his sermons in it. Looking round his habitation it seemed suddenly to occur to him that it was not just like other people's. 'I am afraid', he said, 'that I am not very tidy to-day.' A little girl, he told us, came to make his bed and tidy up, four days a week. Going to a dark corner he routed out three wine glasses which he washed carefully at the door. Then he rummaged out a bottle of wine and drawing up his flour pan to the table and taking his seat upon it he filled our glasses with some black mixture which he called I suppose port and bade us drink.

The Solitary accompanied us to Pencommon to get the horse and then showed us the way down the lanes towards the Church. The people who met him touched their hats to his reverence with great respect. They recognized him as a very holy man and if the Solitary had lived a thousand years ago he would have been revered as a hermit and perhaps canonized as a Saint. At a gate leading into a lane we parted. There was a resigned look in his quiet melancholy blue eyes. The last I saw of him was that he was leaning on the gate looking after us. Then I saw him no more. He had gone back I suppose to his grey hut in the green cwm.

The evening became lovely with a heavenly loveliness. The sinking sun shot along the green pastures with a vivid golden light and striking through the hedges here and there tipped a leaf or a foxglove head with a beam of brilliant green or purple. Down the steep stony lane by the ruined Church of Llanbedr, a team of horses came home to Llandeviron from plough with rattling chains.

I crossed the Bach Wye by the short cut at Trewilad leaving Williams to ride round the longer way by Rhyd Ilydan and to cross the brook at the Broad Ford lower down. I stood upon the stepping stones at Trewilad to watch the little herd of cows undriven coming lazily through the brook home to Trewilad to be milked. The water, darkly bright, came flowing down and filling the cool shadowy lane, and the red and white cows loitered slowly down to the brook, standing still often in the shallow water as they forded the stream, and the air was full of sunshine and the honey scent of the charlock, and the hedges were luxuriant with the luscious sweetness of woodbine and the beauty of the stars of the deep red rose.

Monday, 8 July

Reports coming in all day of the mischief done by yesterday's flood. Pigs, sheep, calves swept away from meadow and cot and carried down the river with hundreds of tons of hay, timber, hurdles and, it is said, furniture. The roads swept bare to the very rock. Culverts choked and blown up, turnips washed out of the ground on the hillsides, down into the orchards and turnpike roads. Four inches of mud in the Rhydspence Inn on the Welsh side of the border, the Sun, Lower Cabalva House flooded again and the carpets out to dry. Pastures covered with grit and gravel and rendered useless and dangerous for cattle till after the next heavy rain.

Tuesday, 9 July

To-day I have been much moved. Just after we had finished lessons at the school at noon, the children deputed little Amy

Evans the schoolmaster's daughter (of whom they know I am very fond) to present to me a little box in which I found a beautiful gold pencil case to hang at my watch chain. My own precious lambs. They had of their own will saved up their money to give me this costly and beautiful present. They would not go to the fair and spend the money upon themselves. It was all to be 'for Mr Kilvert'. I tried to speak to tell them what I felt, but my heart was full.

'Please not to forget us,' said the children. Dear children, there is no danger. I did not want this to help to keep you in mind.

Thursday, 11 July
Took 3 bottles of Attar of Rose to Clyro Court for the three Miss Baskervilles.

'There is great mourning for you at Pen y cae,' said Mrs Harris. 'Why, do the children really care so much?' 'Ay, that day they gave you the pencil case the girl was crying and dazed all the evening. We could do nothing at all with her, and the boy is worse than her. "There'll be no one to come and teach us now," he says, "Mr Kilvert do come and tell us about all parts."' I showed her the beautiful pencil case. But oh, Gipsy Lizzie dear, my own love, it doesn't make up to me for losing you.

Friday, 12 July
Daisy gave me a rose.

Saturday, 13 July
Left Hay. Reached Langley at 3 o'clock.

Friday, 19 July
Emily Ashe came here yesterday and to-day. This afternoon she got Fanny out under the acacia on the lawn, and suddenly demanded of her 'dear Christian sister' her spiritual experiences.

Katie and the Monk[1] were in the habit of calling over the balusters 'Bigglesy-buggles' to everyone who came up. They were told not to do it as it was not a nice word for them to use. Soon after Fanny was reading to them the story of David and Goliath

---

1. The children of Kilvert's sister, Emily.

and how Goliath 'cursed David by his gods'. The Monk asked what this meant. Fanny said Goliath said some naughty words. 'Do you think,' asked the Monk in a solemn and awestruck voice, 'do you think, Auntie Fanny, the giant said "Bigglesy-buggles"?'

Sunday, 21 July
I took the whole morning and afternoon service and sermon, but my Father took part in the Holy Communion. I was very much annoyed at seeing the black bottle put upon the Table again by George Jeffries.

One of the Langley Burrell school children being asked, 'Who made the World?' replied, 'Mr Ashe'.

Tuesday, 23 July
Perch and I went to spend the day at Brinkworth Rectory with the De Quettevilles. As we approached the Rectory door, we were seized with inextinguishable laughter which returned at intervals during the day.

Mrs De Quetteville pointed out to Terry with great pride the pond of delicious water which supplied the house with drinking water. At that moment, as she was assuring him that the water was perfectly pure, a large evet rose to the surface and stared at them while water spiders and amphibious beetles rowed about the pond.

Monday, 5 August
Left Langley and came to Clyro. I dined at the Vicarage and received a present of a magnificent writing desk, which I am writing upon now, the most beautiful and perfect I ever saw, of coromandel wood bound with brass, fitted with polished mahogany and containing two most secret drawers.

Tuesday, 6 August
Mrs Pring was married to James Rogers last Thursday as quietly as possible. She would not allow the church bells to be rung, though the ringers entreated her to let them ring a peal, and she openly wished for rain that no one might be able to come to the wedding. Moreover she invited as few people as possible to the wedding dinner (not even her own mother-in-law) that she might not cause Mr and Mrs Venables any needless expense. It was

with great difficulty that she was prevailed upon to go to Brecon for the night and to let her husband accompany her. Her own wish was that the bridegroom should return to his own house while she slept at the Vicarage as usual. She said she did not want any of that fuss and nonsense. She looked upon marriage as a religious thing. But Mrs Venables represented to her what a talk would be caused by such a proceeding, so she consented to go as a bride to Brecon for one night and to let the bridegroom go too.

Thursday, 8 August
This afternoon Thomas Beavan of Bryn yr hydd came to call, and directly he was gone a servant came from Clyro Court with a magnificent present from the Baskervilles, a travelling bag beautifully fitted, accompanied by a most kind and cordial letter from Baskerville himself.

Saturday, 10 August
This afternoon I went up the Old Forest road bidding the people Farewell. At the Well Cottage an old spinning wheel stood in the bow window, one of the few spinning wheels that are to be seen at work now.

Dear Sophy Ferris, the warm-hearted Carmarthenshire woman at the old Forest farmhouse, overwhelmed me with bitter lamentations at my departure. 'If gold would keep you with us,' she said, 'we would gather a weight of gold.' What have I done? What am I that these people should so care for me? How little I have deserved it. Lord requite these people ten thousand fold into their bosom the kindness they have showed to the stranger.

Monday, 12 August
This morning came an envelope by post containing a Bank of England note for £5 and an anonymous line on a scrap of paper 'For the Revd F. Kilvert's private use'. I don't know who sent it. Emily and Jenny Dew gave me a most kind and beautiful present, *Wordsworth's Complete Works*.

Friday, 16 August
The stories about the baboon of Maesllwch Castle grow more and more extraordinary. It is said that when visitors come to the

Castle the creature descends upon their heads, clambering down the balusters of the staircase. He put Baskerville and Apperley to flight, routed them horse and foot, so that they clapped spurs to their horses and galloped away in mortal fear, the baboon racing after them. He carries the cats up to the top of the highest Castle Tower, and drops them over into space, and it is believed that the baboon seeks an opportunity to carry the young heir up to the top of the Tower and serve him in the same way.

Saturday, 17 August

Once more for the last time I skirted the dear old Common carrying a great bunch of the purple heather blossoms to take to Wye Cliff to-night for Mrs Crichton. The sun shone hot and bright down into the little valley among the hills, upon the wild white marsh cotton and the purple heather and the bright green Osmunda ferns with their brown flower spikes, and upon the white shirt sleeves of the peat cutters working amongst the mawn pits on a distant part of the Common. It is a bad mawn harvest this year in consequence of the wet summer and what with the dear coal and bread and meat and the diseased potatoes, I don't know what the poor people will do.

Monday, 19 August

To-day I went to Llysdinam to spend a week.

Saturday, St Bartholomew's Day

This morning I left Llysdinam for Clyro with Mr Venables. As soon as we got to Clyro we were in the full swing of the School feast. My last in the dear old place. It all seemed very sad. And in the midst of the tea drinking on the Vicarage lawn the new curate Mr Irvine arrived in the omnibus from Hay. It gave me a bitter pang, but I went down to Mrs Chaloner's at once to see and welcome him.

After the usual sport in the Cae Mawr Crichton sent up a most successful fire balloon which curiously enough went home again, descending in the garden at Wye Cliff, though to us watching its course from Cae Mawr the balloon seemed to have crossed the river and to have travelled at least as far as Llydyadyway. After the balloon had gone up I received a hint to go to the school which immediately after was thronged with people gentle and simple. Wall the Churchwarden mounted the schoolmaster's desk platform and made an admirable speech presenting me in the name of the parishioners with a testimonial of a magnificent silver cup.

Then Holding, the butler at Clyro Court, came forward. He also made a very nice speech and gave me a beautiful inkstand from the servants and workmen at Clyro Court. I was deeply touched. I tried to say a few words, but my heart was full and I could not speak what I would.

Along with the inkstand was given me a short written address followed by the autograph signatures of the subscribers, and with the cup was presented a thin green leather book with my initials stamped in gold on the cover. On the title page Mrs Crichton had painted an exquisite picture of Clyro Church and School and illuminated an address after which came the as far as possible autograph signatures of the subscribers to the testimonial.

Sunday, 25 August

I read prayers in the morning. Irvine preached and Mr Venables sat in his pew. Irvine and I walked to Bettws. It was my last visit to the dear old Chapel. Every tree and hill and hollow and glimpse of the mountains was precious to me, and I was walking with a stranger to whom it was nought, and who had no dear associations with the place. I took the whole service and preached a farewell sermon from Philippians i, 3. 'I thank my God upon every remembrance of you.'

It was for the last time. I could not help it. I burst into tears.

After Chapel I went to the Chapel Farm and Llwyn Gwillim and to the Forge and sweet Emma of the Chapel Dingle to say Good-bye and then to Whitty's Mill, the dear old Mill, to see sweet dying Margaret.

It was a sad sad day.

Wednesday, 28 August

Dined at Hay Castle. Mrs Bevan and the girls gave me a splendid photograph album, and Cousie had painted me with kind and beautiful thoughtfulness a garland of heartsease encircling this text from Exodus xxxiii, 14: 'My Presence shall go with thee and I will give thee rest.'

My last evening at Hay, a home to me for nearly 8 years, and its inmates like brothers and sisters. Good-bye and God bless and keep you all.

Sunday, September Day
My last day at Clyro.

I read prayers in the morning and Irvine preached. Holy Communion. Irvine went to Chapel in the rain and would not put on leggings as I advised him. He came back wet and weary, saying there were a man, a woman and a boy in Chapel. In the afternoon I preached my farewell sermon at Clyro, the same that I preached at Bettws last Sunday. Though the afternoon was so rainy there were a good many people in Church. I don't know how I got through the service. It was the last time. My voice was broken and choked by sobs and tears, and I think the people in the Church were affected too. Richard Brooks in the choir was crying like a child.

The last round through the village in the evening. 'To-morrow to fresh woods and pastures new.'

Monday, September Morrow
Left Clyro for ever. A chapter of life closed and a leaf in the Book of Life turned over. The day I came to Clyro I remember fixing my eyes on a particular bough of an apple tree in the orchard opposite the school and the Vicarage and saying to myself that on the day I left Clyro I would look at that same branch. I did look for it this morning but I could not recognize it. All the dear people were standing in their cottage doors waving their hands as I drove away.

As the train went down the valley of the Wye to Hereford I waved my handkerchief to all the old familiar friendly houses, to Mrs Bridge at Pont Vaen, to Annie Dyke at Upper Cabalva, to Rosie Hodgson at Lower Cabalva, and to Louisa Dew at Whitney Rectory.

Tuesday, 3 September
When I opened my window at Langley Burrell Rectory this morning the first sound I heard was the tapping of a nuthatch in

an acacia. There had been a little rain in the night but the morning was fine.

At 9.20 I left Chippenham to join the rest of the party, my mother, Dora, and the children Katie and Monk, at 1 Prince's Buildings, Weston, leaving my Father and Fanny alone at Langley.

In the evening I had a bathe in the open sea for the first time for ten years and enjoyed it thoroughly.

At 7.30 my Mother and I went to the Assembly rooms to a lecture on craniology and phrenology and mesmerism. A table full of skulls was set out and the lecture was given by a Mr Hume. We had seen it advertised on the pier. He talked a good deal of wild nonsense and examined the heads of two or three of the audience whose moral and mental qualities he appraised highly. Then began the mesmerism. A number of men came up on the platform from the body of the room and offered themselves to be operated on. They were placed in a semi-circle on chairs sitting with their faces to the wall and their backs to the audience. A young lady went to the piano and began playing low soft dreamy music. The Mesmerist passed between his victims and the wall and after making a few passes over their faces and arms and looking intently into their eyes he soon had 8 out of the 10 prostrate on the floor in a mesmeric sleep. He took them by the hand and drew them after him, holding his hand against the side of their heads. 'Come, come,' he said authoritatively, and they followed as it seemed to me unwillingly, but unable to help themselves, though the Mesmerist used no violence but appeared to draw them after him by the influence of a stronger will.

I noticed that out of the 10 there were two middle-aged men whom the Mesmerist could make nothing of. But he had previously warned them and the audience that if the men resisted him and made up their minds they would not be mesmerized he could do nothing with them.

The young men and lads (all apparently of the shopkeeper class) were now lying asprawl upon the floor in all attitudes and wrapped in a deep mesmeric sleep. They lay like dead men and as still as death, with a ghastly unnatural look in their faces and at the mercy of the Mesmerist. One by one he raised them up, stiffened them by a pass and wave of the hand and stamp of the foot and left them swaying to and fro, unable to fall down or lift a foot from the ground, telling them sternly as he turned away that they could not move. Then he bade them look at the stars and they all stood with their ghastly faces turned up gazing steadfastly at the ceiling. Suddenly he assured them they were cocks and commanded them to crow and flap their wings. Instantly they flapped their arms violently and crowed in every key. One man was then put up on a chair and ordered to sell an imaginary clock. He did it admirably. When in his senses he was apparently a lad of some humour. He took the bids quickly from the audience and was selling the clock smartly when the Mesmerist said, 'That isn't a clock. It's a donkey.' The lad looked unfounded for a moment and then brightened up and leading an imaginary donkey by an imaginary halter began to sell him. What he was really holding was a shawl bundled up. 'That isn't a donkey,' said the Mesmerist. 'It's a child, nurse it.' The lad began to nurse the supposed child. But here a curious trait in his character came out. No sooner had the Mesmerist left him than a fury of hatred seemed to seize the lad and he dashed the child's head against the back of the chair. Perhaps he had a real hatred to infants which he could not conceal.

Then the Mesmerist set them all waltzing in pairs, then rowing, then swimming for their lives, the imaginary boat having met with an imaginary upset. It was curious to watch the different modes of rowing and swimming. The Mesmerist invited one of the lads to strike at his hand, telling him he would not be able to strike him and strike him the lad could not though he tried his best and struck on all sides of the hand.

At length the Mesmerist waved his hand in passes over the heads of the lads and shouted, 'Wake, all of you!' In a moment the boys were all awake, rubbing their eyes, yawning, and stretching themselves, as if they had just arisen from a sound sleep. One of them on being asked by the Mesmerist complained that his eyes were heavy and being called back to the platform as he was going down the room to his place had the oppression taken off his eyes by a pass and wave of the hand. The Mesmerist said that now the young man was awake he could prevent him from lifting his feet from the floor and make him unable to strike, and though the young man laughing and struggling tried to do both, he could do neither. Hume said he had sometimes found this power very useful in street rows in preventing people from striking him.

He asked the lads if they had ever seen him before or had any collusion with him and in the face of the audience they openly denied any knowledge of him. It seems they were all well-known young men from the town. The lads said they were perfectly aware all the time what they were doing, but they had no power to resist.

Hume showed us afterwards a curious instrument for gauging the intellect of the human head by taking an angle and measuring from it.

Wednesday, 4 September

Bathing in the morning before breakfast from a machine. Many people were openly stripping on the sands a little further on and running down into the sea, and I would have done the same but I had brought down no towels of my own.

At 7 o'clock this evening my Mother, Dora and I walked up to Trinity Church and heard Mr Hunt preach. During the service the lightning looked in at the windows and shamed the gas while from the town far below came up on the still sultry air the strains of the Italian band.

Thursday, 5 September

I was out early before breakfast this morning bathing from the sands. There was a delicious feeling of freedom in stripping in the open air and running down naked to the sea, where the waves were curling white with foam and the red morning sunshine glowing upon the naked limbs of the bathers.

[Kilvert returns to Langley Burrell.]

Monday, 16 September

At 6 o'clock this evening a large balloon, striped red and blue, passed over this house very high in the air, almost a mile high it was said. It looked very small and we could not see the car. There was one man in it and he kept on sending down parachutes and emptying sandbags. The balloon was rapidly travelling eastwards in a straight line, but it had previously been veering about a good deal in various currents of air, passing over the Plough before it came to us. The balloon started from Bristol where there was a great Conservative demonstration and came down at Yatesbury.

The Yatesbury people were terrified when they saw the balloon descending and some ran away and some stared. But the aeronaut could get no one to help him or catch hold of the grappling ropes to steady the balloon, so it came down bump and bounced up again. At last it was secured and packed, and the aeronaut found board and bed at the Parsonage. It was said that he had made 30 ascents before.

Friday, 27 September
Maria told us the story of Anne Kilvert and the cat, and the Epiphany Star. It seems that when Aunt Sophia was dying Anna thought some mutton would do her good and went to fetch some. When she came back the nurse said, 'She can't eat mutton. She's dying'. Anna put the mutton down on the floor and rushed to the bed. At that moment Aunt Sophia died and Anna turned round to see the cat running away with the mutton and the Epiphany Star shining in through the window.

Wednesday, 9 October
Mrs Haddrell showed me a brown linnet in her room and she said she had a lark 'but he makes no *charm* now'.

Monday, 14 October
Last night I had a strange and horrible dream. It was one of those curious things, a dream within a dream, like a picture within a picture. I dreamt that I dreamt that Mr and Mrs Venables tried to murder me. We were all together in a small room and they were both trying to poison me, but I was aware of their intention and baffled them repeatedly. At length, Mr Venables put me off my guard, came round fondling me, and suddenly clapping his hand on my neck behind said, 'It's of no use, Mr Kilvert. You're done for'. I felt the poison beginning to work and burn in my neck. I knew it was all over and started up in fury and despair. I flew at him savagely. The scene suddenly changed to the organ loft in Hardenhuish Church. Mr Venables, seeing me coming at him,

burst out at the door. Close outside the door was standing the Holy Ghost. He knocked him from the top to the bottom of the stairs, rolling over head over heels, rushed downstairs himself, mounted his horse and fled away, I after him.

This dream within a dream excited me to such a state of fury, that in the outer dream I determined to murder Mr Venables. Accordingly I lay in wait for him with a pickaxe on the Vicarage lawn at Clyro, hewed an immense and hideous hole through his head, and kicked his face till it was so horribly mutilated, crushed and disfigured as to be past recognition. Then the spirit of the dream changed. Mrs Venables became her old natural self again. 'Wasn't it enough,' she said, looking at me reproachfully, 'that you should have hewed that hole through his head, but you must go and kick his face so that I don't know him again?' At this moment, Mr Bevan, the Vicar of Hay, came in. 'Well,' he said to me, 'you *have* done it now. You have made a pretty mess of it.'

All this time I was going about visiting the sick at Clyro and preaching in Clyro Church. But I saw that people were beginning to look shy at me and suspect me of the murder which had just been discovered. I became so wretched and conscience-stricken that I could bear my remorse no longer in secret and I went to give myself up to a policeman, who immediately took me to prison where I was kept in chains. Then the full misery of my position burst upon me and the ruin and disgrace I had brought on my family. 'It will kill my father,' I cried in an agony of remorse and despair.

I knew it was no dream. This at last was a reality from which I should never awake. I had awaked from many evil dreams and horrors and found them unreal, but this was a reality and horror from which I should never awake. It was all true at last. I had committed a murder. I calculated the time. I knew the Autumn Assizes were over and I could not be tried till the Spring. 'The Assizes,' I said, 'will come on in March and I shall be hung early in April.' And at the words I saw Mrs Venables give a shudder of horror.

When I woke I was so persuaded of the reality of what I had seen and felt and done in my dreams that I felt for the handcuffs on my wrists and could not believe I was in bed at home till I heard the old clock on the stairs warn and then strike five.

Nothing now seems to me so real and tangible as that dream was, and it seems to me as I might wake up at any moment and find everything shadowy, fleeting and unreal. I feel as if life is a dream from which at any moment I may awake.

Sunday, 20 October
A dark wet day. I read prayers in the morning and a Declaration of Assent to the Prayer Book and Articles on being licensed to the Curacy of Langley Burrell. I think this proclamation rather astonished the people.

Thursday, 24 October
A wild wet morning. Charles Awdry of Draycot came over to call on me this afternoon, and I walked back with him as far as Cold Harbour. He told me he once said to Lord Cowley at Draycot House, 'My ancestors owned this estate when yours were peasants'. 'It is true', Lord Cowley said. 'We are only a hundred years old.'

Sunday, 27 October
I have rarely seen Langley Church and Churchyard look more beautiful than they did this morning. The weather was lovely and round the quiet Church the trees were gorgeous, the elms dazzling golden and the beeches burning crimson. The golden elms illuminated the Church and Churchyard with strong yellow light and the beeches flamed and glowed with scarlet and crimson fire like the Burning Bush. The place lay quiet in the still autumn sunshine. Then the latch of the wicket gate tinkled and pretty Keren Wood appeared coming along the Church path under the spreading boughs of the wide larch, and in the glare of yellow light the bell broke solemnly through the golden elms that stood stately round the Church.

To-day we had one of those soft, still, dreamy, golden afternoons peculiar to Autumn.

Monday, 28 October
This afternoon I cleaned the harness entirely myself and sent it out smarter and brighter than it has been I think for years.

Wednesday, 30 October

Called on the Dallins, the new people at Langley Lodge, and found both Captain and Mrs Dallin were out riding.

Monday, 25 November

The old Manor House of Langley Burrell used to stand on the knoll just beyond the fishpond below the terrace walk, where an oak stands now. The new Manor House was built about 100 years ago by Robert Ashe, Rector of the Parish and Lord of the Manor, my great-great-grandfather. The stones for the new houses were hewn by an old man named Old Chit Chat. When he got his pay he would go down the ancient footpath by Pen Hills House tossing a coin with himself to see whether his belly or his back should get the benefit of his wages. If the back won the toss Old Chit Chat would toss again to give the poor belly one more chance. The game generally ended by his going to the public house.

Friday, 29 November

The Irvingites are all in a flutter of expectation and excitement. They believe that Christ has already come and is at Glasgow working miracles.

Miss Mewburn whom I met at the Kerrys' this evening lent me a pamphlet by Edward Hine on the identity of the English nation with the ten lost tribes of Israel. It is a grand idea and an interesting and exciting surmise. We 'stared at each other with a wild surmise'. I only hope it is true. It would be a glorious truth.

Miss Mewburn went to the Agricultural Meeting at the Town Hall at Chippenham yesterday and came away furious at the patronizing manner in which the labourers were preached at and the way in which the poor old people were kept standing during the whole meeting, while 'their betters'(?) were comfortably seated in cushioned chairs. She wished she could have lifted up her voice and borne witness against the proceedings. And I very heartily sympathize with her feelings.

Monday, December Morrow

To-day we had a luncheon party to meet the Dallins. Mrs Dallin looked very nice. She was exquisitely dressed in rich black silk with loose open sleeves. Poor child, she confided to Fannie that she was very dull. Hardly anyone had been to see her.

Tuesday, 3 December
My thirty-third birthday.

Friday, 6 December
Dined with the Dallins at Langley Lodge. A handsome and most hospitable entertainment and a very pleasant friendly evening. Two soups, champagne and curaçao.

Sunday, 8 December
The morning had been lovely, but during our singing practice after evening Church at about half past four began the Great Storm of 1872. Suddenly the wind rose up and began to roar at the Tower window and shake the panes and lash the glass with torrents of rain. It grew very dark. The storm increased and we struggled home in torrents of rain and tempests of wind so fearful that we could hardly force our way across the Common to the Rectory. All the evening the roaring S.W. wind raged more and more furious. It seemed as if the windows on the west side of the house must be blown in. The glass cracked and strained and bent and the storm shrieked and wailed and howled like multitudes of lost spirits. I went out to see where the cows were, fearing that the large elms in the Avenue might fall and crush them. The trees were writhing, swaying, rocking, lashing their arms wildly and straining terribly in the tempest but I could not see that any were gone yet. The twin firs in the orchard seemed the worst off, they gave the wind such a power and purchase, with their heavy green boughs, and their tops were swaying fearfully and bending nearly double under the tremendous strain. The moon was high and the clouds drove wild and fast across her face. Dark storms and thick black drifts were hurrying up out of the west, where the Almighty was making the clouds His chariot and walking upon the wings of the wind. Now and then the moon looked out for a moment wild and terrified through a savage rent in the storm.

The cows were safe in the cowyard and the door shut, though how I cannot tell. They must have gone there for shelter and it seemed as if the Lord had shut them in. As I stood at the cowyard gate leading into the field I was almost frightened at the fury of the wind, the blasts were so awful that I feared one of the great elms must fall. Sometimes the tempest rose to such a furious and ungovernable pitch as if hell had been let loose, that it seemed as if something must go, and as if the very world itself must give way and be shattered to atoms. The very beasts seemed frightened and the dog lay close in his kennel and would not come out. I went round to the front of the house and stood on the stone steps and wondered at the wind and thought of the poor people on Clyro Hill and prayed for those at sea. 'For at his word the stormy wind ariseth which lifteth up the waves thereof.' The whole world seemed to be groaning and straining under the press of that dreadful wind. All the evening the wind roared and thundered and the tempest grew wilder and more wild, and if damage was done we could not hear it. Everything was drowned in the roar and thunder of the storm. The wind howled down the chimney, the room was full of smoke and every now and then the fire flaught out into the room in tongues of flame beaten down with a smother of sparks and smoke.

Monday, 16 December

Dame Matthews used to live at the Home Farm at Langley Burrell. She was a member of the family, but she must have lived a long time ago, as Mrs Banks remarked, because she called cows 'kine'. The Dame used to sit in the chimney corner and near her chair there was a little window through which she could see all down the dairy. One evening she saw one of the farm men steal a pound of butter out of the dairy and put it into his hat, at the same moment clapping his hat upon his head.

'John,' called the Dame. 'John, come here. I want to speak to you.' John came, carefully keeping his hat on his head. The Dame ordered some ale to be heated for him and bade him sit down in front of the roaring fire. John thanked his mistress and said he would have the ale another time, as he wanted to go home at once.

'No, John. Sit you down by the fire and drink some hot ale. 'Tis a cold night and I want to speak to you about the kine.'

The miserable John, daring neither to take off his hat nor go without his mistress's leave, sat before the scorching fire drinking his hot ale till the melting butter in his hat began to run down all over his face. The Dame eyed him with malicious fun. 'Now, John,' she said, 'you may go. I won't charge you anything for the butter.'

Tuesday, New Year's Eve
My Mother says the old Langley people always used to say that the Langley Burrell bells rang these words, 'My cow's tail's long, my cow's tail's long.'

1873

Tuesday, 7 January

At 8 o'clock Fanny, Dora and I went to a jolly party at Sir John Awdry's at Norton House. Almost everybody in the neighbourhood was there. There had been a children's party with a Christmas Tree at 5 o'clock, but when we drove up the harp and the fiddles were going.

I danced a Lancers with Harriet Awdry of Draycot Rectory, a quadrille with Sissy Awdry of Seagry Vicarage, a Lancers with Louise Awdry of Draycot Rectory, a Lancers with Mary Rooke of the Ivy, and Sir Roger with dear little Francie Rooke of the Ivy. How bright and pretty she looked, so merry, happy and full of fun. It was a grand Sir Roger. I never danced such a one. The room was quite full, two sets and such long lines, but the crush was all the more fun. 'Here,' said Francie Rooke to me quietly, with a wild, merrie sparkle in her eye, and her face brilliant with excitement, 'let us go into the other set'. There was more fun going on there, Eliza Stiles had just fallen prostrate. There were screams of laughter and the dance was growing quite wild. There was a struggle for the corners and everyone wanted to be at the top. In a few minutes all order was lost, and everyone was dancing wildly and promiscuously with whoever came to hand. The dance grew wilder and wilder. 'The pipers loud and louder blew, the dancers quick and quicker flew.' Madder and madder screamed the flying fiddle bows. Sir Roger became a wild romp till the fiddles suddenly stopped dead and there was a scream of laughter. Oh, it was such fun and Francie Rooke was brilliant. When shall I have another such partner as Francie Rooke?

An excellent supper and we got home about one o'clock, on a fine moonlit night.

Thursday, 9 January

The earthly troubles of the exiled Emperor are over. At eleven o'clock this morning Napoleon III passed away at Camden House,

Chislehurst. He died very suddenly and quietly. He had undergone several severe operations by Sir Henry Thompson for crushing the stone in the bladder. Another operation, the last, was contemplated, and the symptoms and condition of the patient were all favourable when suddenly at 10 o'clock this morning to the surprise of the doctors the pulse fluttered and in a few minutes Napoleon breathed his last quietly and without pain. It is supposed that a clot of blood rose to the heart and suffocated him.

It has been a life of marvellous vicissitudes and the most wonderful romance since that of Charles Edward.

Saturday, 11 January
Dora went to Langley House and found poor Syddy Ashe in agonies of grief at the Emperor's death.

Sunday, 12 January
When I came out the night was superb. The sky was cloudless, the moon rode high and full in the deep blue vault and the evening star blazed in the west. The air was filled with the tolling and chiming of bells from St Paul's and Chippenham old Church. The night was soft and still and I walked up and down the drive several times before I could make up my mind to leave the wonderful beauty of the night and go indoors. To be alone out of doors on a still soft clear moonlit night is to me one of the greatest pleasures that this world can give.

Monday, 13 January
Susan took a great interest in the Emperor and his death. The post mortem shows the kidneys to have been so extensively diseased that life could not have been much prolonged.

Wednesday, 15 January
A satisfactory lecture. I spoke about Noah's vineyard and drunkenness, the Tower of Babel, Babylon and the confusion of tongues, the Tongue Tower, the death of the Emperor Napoleon III and the Great Coram Street Murder.

Wednesday, 22 January
Visited the Goughs. Gough came in. He is a pensioner. He was in the 19th Regiment and directly after landing in England after

the Crimean War volunteered to go to India at the time of the
Indian Mutiny. He landed at Calcutta and his regiment marched
through Cawnpore 48 hours after the Massacre. He said the scene
was horrible, so horrible, shocking and disgusting that it could not
be explained or described. Women's breasts had been chopped
and sliced off and were still lying about with their other parts
which had been cut out. Women were cut to pieces and mutilated
in a vile and shocking manner. The most devilish and beastly
ingenuity had been at work in mutilating the persons and violat-
ing and dishonouring the parts of the poor creatures. A child's
head had been cut off and was lying on the ground with the lips
placed by a devilish jest as if sucking the breast of a woman which
had also been chopped off. Numbers of the poor women had
jumped down the great well with their children to avoid the
horrors which were being perpetrated on the bodies of women all
over the place. The soldiers were furious, almost ungovernable, as
they marched through Cawnpore and saw those shameful sights.
If they had caught the rebels then no mercy would have been
shown to those who showed none. The scene of shameful horror
was indescribable. Gough saw 500 mutineers executed at once, the
rank and file shot by musketry, the ringleaders blown from guns.
One stout fellow stepped lightly up to his gun as unconcernedly,
said Gough, 'as you or I would go into Service'. 'I have killed the
English,' said the ruffian, 'and I don't care for death.' Those who
were blown from guns were tied with their arms fastened tightly
to the wheels and their chests pressing against the muzzles of the
cannon. A small square piece of wood was hung round their necks
and came between the chest of the men and the muzzle of the
gun. At the discharge the man was blown all to fragments but his
arms remained tied to the wheels of the gun.

To-night the starlit sky was a glorious spectacle.

Thursday, 23 January

After I had been at the school I went at ten o'clock to Langley
House to beard the lion in his den. I found Mr and Mrs Ashe in
the dining room. She had just finished reading *The Times* to him.
I plunged at once *in medias res*. He said that he wished the money
could be procured in the old-fashioned way by the ancient

machinery of Church rate, and so much the worse for those who refused to pay. The Squire begged that the Church should not be washed with yellow ochre. I got his consent to the Communion Service being read from the altar, and Mrs Ashe backed me up staunchly and proposed that two chairs should be got to stand within the rails. The Squire seemed rather surprised at the idea of a clergyman sitting within the rails during the service and thought that he should not 'lounge' in a chair.

Friday, February Eve
When I came home last night at half past twelve I was surprised by seeing lights still burning in the house and Dora let me in. I never saw my dear sister look so pretty. A black cloak was thrown round her and her bright hair fell like a cloud over her shoulders. She had been playing chess with my Father. The fire was still burning in the dining room. We stood a few minutes to warm ourselves. Then a shower of sweet kisses and I sent the dear pretty girl to bed.

Tuesday, 4 February
Sat an hour with John and Hannah Hatherell at tea. I read to them and they told me the story of the terrible faction fight between the men at Chippenham and the men of the two Langleys [   ] years ago, in which two Chippenham men were killed, Hall the saddler and Reynolds the tinman. The quarrel between Chippenham and the Langleys had been long brewing and there was bad blood and a bitter feud between the town and the two villages. It was the fault of Chippenham. They began it. A lot of Chippenham blackguards had been in the habit of ill-using and beating the Langley men whenever the country folk came into the town on the market day which was then Saturday. Things came to such a pass that the Langley people could not enter the town without being abused and knocked about and they were afraid to go to market. This state of things was not to be borne and the men of Langley Fitzurse arranged to go into Chippenham in force on a certain market day and avenge their insults and injuries. A number of Langley Burrell men joined them and the united force armed with sticks and bludgeons and numbering perhaps from 30 to 40 men entered the town on a market day, Saturday afternoon.

223

Some folk say it was a cunning plot and that the whole scheme was preconcerted, but at all events what happened was this. After some fierce fighting in the streets with fists, sticks and stones, after many heads had been broken and some blood had been spilt the Langley men retreated up the hill in a body as far as the Little George where a turnpike then stood. Here they stood. The Chippenham men taunted and reviled them and called to come on like men and not to run home like women. The Langley men having gained their purpose and having drawn their enemies out of the town now turned fiercely and charged upon them down the hill. The stones flew like hail. Strong men were beaten down. Eyes were knocked out and the road ran with blood. The Chippenham blackguards were driven back pell-mell in wild confusion into the town, the 30 or 40 Langley men driving a mob of 200 before them like sheep. The scene in the streets was fearful. One of the Chippenham blackguards had his eye knocked out with a stone. But unhappily innocent men suffered with the guilty. Hull the saddler and Reynolds the tinman came out to quell the riot. They got into the mob and were irresistibly and helplessly borne away by the crowd down the Bath road by the Ivy, in which direction the fight was surging. They were never able to regain their houses and were both killed. Hull was set up dead upon the 'turn train' (turnstile) going to Beck Avon Bridge between Chippenham and the Ivy where the posts stand now. A Langley man found Reynolds lying on the ground with his head almost beaten to pieces and raised the poor fellow's head on his knee, but the hair and skin and flesh came off in flakes when it was touched. Reynolds only spoke one word. 'Mountjoy,' he muttered. Mountjoy was a Langley man and it was always supposed that he gave the fatal blow but no one knows.

Jerry Knight, the carpenter at the top of Huntsman's Hill, was Constable and Mr Sheppard of the Brewery was 'Tyddyman' of the parish. On this Saturday night John Hatherell had been brewing for Mr Sheppard and on Sunday morning as he was at the Brewery he suddenly saw the courtyard filled with people from Chippenham and the constables were going about among the cottages making arrests of the Langley men who were suspected of having been engaged in the riot overnight. Old John Thomas the carpenter, then a lusty young man, ran down to John Hatherell's cottage and leaned up against the dresser as white as a sheet. Hannah asked him if he had been in the fight. 'No,' he said. But he had, and he was arrested, tried, and sent to jail. Farmer Matthews of Rawlings and Henry Knight were both in the riot and had to go to jail.

The prisoners were kept at a public house in Chippenham waiting their turn for examination and trial and Hannah Hatherell looked through the window and saw them all chained to a long iron bar.

Scarcely any of the Chippenham men were arrested and examined. Most of the blackguards got off scot-free. And this was most unjust because they began the quarrel and the Langley men would never come into Chippenham to fight unless they had been terribly provoked. The poor Langley fellows too were beaten black and blue and fearfully knocked about.

John Hatherell said that old Langley Common was once a great play place on Sunday, and on Sunday afternoons football and hockey and other games went on all over the common. The Revd Samuel Ashe, then Rector of Langley Burrell, used to come round quietly under the trees and bide his time till the football came near him when he would catch up the ball and pierce the bladder with a pin. But some of the young fellows would be even with the parson for they would bring a spare bladder, blow it, and soon have the football flying again.

Wednesday, 5 February
A scanty audience at the lecture but it was a wet, dirty night. I spoke of heroism and self-sacrifice instanced by the stories of Tom Flynn of Virginia, Jim Bludso the engineer of the Mississippi steam boat, the *Birkenhead* and the drunken private of the Buffs.

Friday, 7 February
Coal still rising. £2.11. a ton in London now. We are burning coke with wood and find it answers very well. The poor people are very badly off for coal. The coal famine is becoming most serious. And the colliers' strike in South Wales seems to have entered upon a desperately bitter and obstinate struggle with the masters, a struggle to be fought out now to the death and till one party or

the other is utterly exhausted. Meanwhile innocent men, non-unionists, and women and children are dying of cold and hunger.

Monday, 10 February
My Mother says that at Dursley in Gloucestershire, when ladies and gentlemen used to go out to dinner together on dark nights, the gentlemen pulled out the tails of their shirts and walked before to show the way and light the ladies. These were called 'Dursley Lanterns'.

Tuesday, 11 February
A letter from Mr Venables from Clyro asking me if my Father could spare me to come to Clyro and take charge of the Parish from March 3rd to March 22nd as Irvine leaves at the end of February and he himself wants to be in London during part of March. I wrote immediately to say 'yes'. How pleasant it will be seeing the dear old place and people again.

Wednesday, 19 February
At 2 o'clock came up to London third class with a foot warmer to stay till next Tuesday with the Venables at 35 Eaton Square.

Thursday, 20 February
A thick yellow fog all day. London very dark and it was of no use to go to see pictures.

Went to Somerset House. Found Jack in his room in the Legacy Duty Office. Mr Venables asked him to dinner on Saturday next. I gave him my musical box to take to Metzler's to be mended and as I pulled it out of my pocket the box began to play to my dire confusion and could not be stopped till it had finished its tune.

Mr Venables took me over the Oxford and Cambridge Club where I saw Mr Franklin Lushington.[1]

At 9 o'clock I went to a debate at the House of Commons. An Irish member complained bitterly that when Irish affairs came on the English and Scotch members absented themselves from the House.

---

1. A fellow of Trinity College, Cambridge, and a friend of Tennyson and of Edward Lear.

Monday, 24 February

Some inches of snow fell this morning early and the travelling in the streets was bad and heavy, the cabs charging double and even treble fares. I went to the Bethnal Green Museum and was delighted with the beautiful collection of pictures and china belonging to Sir Richard Wallace. Went to Bethnal Green and returned in heavy snow. As we went the omnibus wheels stuck fast in a drain and we all got out to lighten the load. Came back on the top of an omnibus on the box seat alongside of a pleasant good-natured soldier who was grateful for the shelter of my umbrella.

Shrove Tuesday, 25 February

Returned to Langley.

Ash Wednesday, 26 February

My dear Father's birthday. My Father read the Commination from the pulpit.

Friday, March Eve

I went to Hardenhuish House. Between St Paul's Church and the Lodge an old man stood by the way-side begging. He was quite blind, and beside him stood a pretty girl, his granddaughter, with curling chestnut hair and beautiful roguish merry eyes. She had gathered some primroses and stuck them in her brown straw hat. And when I came up the child pretended to be shy, got behind her grandfather and seemed to be looking along the bank for more flowers. I stopped and spoke to the old man. 'I am fourscore,' he said. 'For sixty years I worked at the blast furnaces and the fire was too strong for my eyes. I came out here to stand and try if I could gather a few coppers as it is market day.'

Monday, 3 March

Returned to Clyro to take charge of the parish for three weeks, two Sundays for Mr Venables.

Reached Hay at 1.18 and going to the Castle joined the Bevans at luncheon. As I walked over to Clyro I overtook Mrs Williams of Little Wern y Pentre hobbling home with her stick, and Hannah. She was almost overcome and besought me to stay with them and never to leave them again. 'You know what we want,' she said. 'We want you to live at the Vicarage.' Alas, it is not in my power. At the school the dear children were on the look out for me. Afternoon school was just over and they were clustering in the playground and some walking along the road towards the Hay – such exclamations of delight and smiles of loving welcome and faces lighted up and flushed with pleasure. It was very touching to be so welcomed back. Mrs Rogers (Pring) makes me most comfortable at the Vicarage and quite spoils me.

Tuesday, 4 March
I have the bedroom at the Vicarage looking towards the south and the mountains. How sweet once more to see the morning spread upon the mountains.

Mrs Chaloner says I must put myself in a cage to-day or the old women will tear me to pieces for joy. I have been villaging all day. The welcome of the people is very touching.

There are changes in Clyro since I left. Six or seven of the old familiar faces have passed away in those six months. Dear little Lily Crighton, aged 7 years, and the patriarch William Williams of Crowther's Pool, aged fourscore years and ten, William Price of the Stocks House, aged 85 years, and sweet Margaret Gore of Whitty's Mill in the bloom of her youth and 20 years. Edward Evans has left us, having just fulfilled his three-score and ten. The troubles of poor mad Margaret Meredith (entered in the Burial Register of the Parish as Margaret Mulready) have ended in her 62nd year. And the sufferings of John Powell the blacksmith closed when he wanted but two years to complete the 'day of our age'.

There are changes too in the landscape of Clyro for the trees have all been felled on the Castle mound which now looks bare and dreary.

Wednesday, 5 March
After Church I went to see Hannah Whitney and she received the Holy Communion for the first time at the age of fourscore years and ten.

Friday, 7 March

In the afternoon I drove to Whitney Rectory in the dog-cart to dine and sleep. An April day and showers and shine with exquisitely clear views of the mountains and two beautiful rainbows. Before dinner Emily, Jane and Armine Dew walked with me up through the steep hanging wood above the railway, carpeted with primroses upbreaking through the earth. After dinner Henry Dew told us some of his old hunting reminiscences of the days when he rode with the Maesllwch fox-hounds.

Charles Lacy was out with the Radnorshire and West Herefordshire fox-hounds when they met at Cabalva last Wednesday. He gave an amusing description of the run. Old Tom Evans, the tailor, of Cwm Ithel on Clyro Hill, was once a running huntsman with the Clyro harriers, and very keen after the sport. When he heard the hunting horns along the hill on Wednesday the old hunting instinct in him awoke like a giant refreshed. He scrambled on to his old pony and rode furiously into the middle of the pack hat in hand hooping and holloing and laying the hounds on to the scent as of yore. Colonel Price the M.F.H. was greatly enraged. 'Man! Man!' he shouted. 'Where are you going, man? Come from those hounds!' But the tailor maddened with the chase was deaf to all entreaties and commands. He careered along among and over the hounds, hooping, holloing and waving his hat till the enraged M.F.H. charged him and knocked tailor and pony head over heels. Nothing daunted however the tailor scrambled on to his beast again and he and his pony were second in at the death, close at the heels of the M.F.H.

Charles Lacy said the bag fox had been kept in a dark cellar so long that he was dazed and half blind when he was turned out. After they had killed the bag fox they tried for a wild one at Dolbedwyn, where some poultry had been stolen by a fox.

Saturday, 8 March

At eleven o'clock the dog-cart came for me with the chestnut old Rocket, and I returned to Clyro.

Amelia Meredith tells me that at Llanhollantine people used to go to the church door at midnight to hear the saints within call over the names of those who were to die within the year. Also they heard the sound of the pew doors opening and shutting though no one was in the church.

Tuesday, 11 March
To-night was the last Clyro Penny Reading of the season. The programme was fair but the attendance small, only 14/5 taken at the door. Charlie Powell had proposed to sing two songs, one perfectly unobjectionable and even nice, the other low and coarse. To the latter I objected strongly, refused to sit by and hear it sung, and threatened to leave the choir and the platform. Charlie Powell turned rusty and sulky when I proposed that he should substitute another song for the objectionable one and refused to sing either. Not only so, but he tried to raise a disturbance at the Readings by calling out, romping, and making insulting remarks. John Vaughan very properly went down the room to the policeman who very quietly and ignominiously put Master Charlie out of the room and now Charlie is the laughing stock of the village.

Saturday, 15 March
I caught a chill yesterday in the snow at Emmeline's grave and tossed all night in a fever.

I had heard that William Meredith of the Tump just above Whitty's Mill was very sick, and going to the house I found him dying. As I sat talking with the dying man and as we knelt round the bed the tempest shook the old house and roared in the roof so as almost to drown my voice, and the dying man rolled his eyes wildly in the darkness of the curtained bed.

A bitter east wind blew furiously over the hills as I stood at the exposed door of Llwyn Gwillim.

At the lone cottage in the Chapel Dingle my dear friend sweet Emma Griffiths was almost beside herself with delight when I opened the door. But her joy was soon turned into sorrow. I had not many minutes to stay and when I rose to go poor Emma clasped my hands in both of hers, gave me a long loving look and turned away with a burst of weeping, in a passion of tears. What is it? What is it? What do they all mean? It is a strange and terrible gift, this power of stealing hearts and exciting such love.

At the new Chapel Farm I found Wall and his wife at home and little Nellie lay lovingly in my arms.

I ran down to Cabalva and called at Whitcombe's at the Bronith. Saw Mrs Watkeys and kissed her two beautiful grandchildren as the girls sat together by the fire.

Found Mrs Potts the keeper's wife among the tubs surrounded by naked girls and boys whom she was washing and putting to bed. Spent a quarter of an hour, my last, with the old soldier John Morgan and his wife Mary, and reached home just in time for dinner at Cae Mawr with the Morrells, almost worn out with running, talking, and different emotions. I had been obliged to run almost all the way between the various houses.

Sunday, 16 March

The bitter cold east wind yesterday ended in a heavy fall of snow this morning about 4 inches on the level of the Vicarage lawn. Scarcely any people were at Church at either service.

The madness, cloud and delirium I trust has passed away at length. 'And it came to pass that when the devil was gone out the dumb spake.' I can write again now.

At Gipsy Castle I found Sally Whitney sitting with Mary Jones and Caroline Price. Sally said she remembered the old Clyro stocks and whipping post which stood by the village pound in front of their door. She had often seen people in the stocks and once she saw a sweep whipped by the parish constable for using foul language at the Swan. When people were put in the stocks it was generally for rioting and using bad language at the Swan, and fighting. Sally does not remember if the sweep was stripped naked to be whipped.

Monday, 17 March

Old James Jones the sawyer of the Infant School told me that he remembers a reprobate drunken fellow named James Davies, but nicknamed 'Jim of the Dingle' being put in the stocks at Clyro by Archdeacon Venables and the parish constable. This Jim of the Dingle had a companion spirit as wicked as himself. And both of them belonged to the Herefordshire Militia. So when the Archdeacon and the Constable had gone away leaving Jim in the stocks, Jim's friend brought an axe and beat the stocks all to pieces and let the prisoner out. The two worthies fled away to Hereford to the militia and never returned to Clyro. But the Clyro people, seeing the stocks broken, demolished and burnt the stocks and the whipping post, and no one was ever confined or whipped at Clyro after that.

Wednesday, 19 March
I drove to Llan Thomas to dine and sleep. Daisy was very good to me all the evening. She taught me to play Commerce, and thinking the lamp hurt my eyes as I shaded them a moment with the cards to look across the table she rose at once and brought the lampshade. She asked anxiously if my cough hurt me and whenever I coughed she seemed to suffer pain herself.

[The diarist returns to Langley Burrell.]

Wednesday, 9 April
While we were sitting at supper this evening we were startled by a sound under the sideboard as if a rat were tearing and gnawing at the wainscot or skirting board. The noise ceased and then began again. Suddenly Dora uttered an exclamation and a strange look came over her face. She seized the lamp and went to the sideboard pointing to a white handled knife which lay under the sideboard and which she said she had seen a moment before crawling and wriggling along the floor-cloth by itself and making the tearing, gnawing, rending noise we had heard. No one knew how the knife had got under the sideboard. As four of us stood round looking at the knife lying on the floorcloth suddenly the knife leaped into the air and fell back without anyone touching it. It looked very strange and startled us a good deal. We thought of spirit agency and felt uncomfortable and compared the time expecting to hear more of the matter, until Dora observed a very tiny grey mouse taking the buttered point of the knife in his mouth and dragging it along and walking backwards. Then all was explained.

Friday, 18 April
My mother says she remembers to have heard as an old village tradition that the street of Kington St Michael was green with grass during the Great Plague for there was scarcely any passing in those dreadful months.

Sunday, 27 April
Visited old Sally Killing. She said when she was young women never wore their gowns out haymaking. If a farmer saw one of his women working in her gown he would order her to take it off. She herself had been weeks without putting on her gown from Monday morning till Saturday night, in the hay harvest. The women had loose sleeves which they pinned on to their 'shift sleeves' and which covered their arms to the wrist from the sun. 'But now,' said Sally contemptuously, 'now they are all ladies. They wear *dresses* now, not *gowns*.'

Monday, 19 May
Went to London by 11.15 train. At half past four I met Jack in the vestibule at Burlington House. The Exhibition seemed to me to be an unusually good one, and I was much struck by some of the pictures especially sweet Imogen, and the Turning Point, the beautiful face and eyes of the wife looking up to her husband's stern sullen countenance as she leans on his breast, beseeching him, pleading with him, oh so earnestly and imploringly, to give up drinking. It went to my heart.

Wednesday, 21 May
I went to Doré's Picture Gallery in New Bond Street. There was a new picture there, an Andromeda, a handsome graceful girl life size, well painted, the flesh tints very natural. The slender girlish form is bowed and shrinking from the monster, the white feet are washed by the lap of the green waves, the manacled hands and wrists are straining at the chain and the rich brown hair is blown wildly forward from the bowed back and beautiful shoulders across the horror-stricken face.

Holy Thursday, 22 May
I went to the International Exhibition and saw the silk looms weaving and bought some medals of the Queen, Prince of Wales and the Exhibition which I saw being struck. One of the most beautiful pictures was one of a lovely girl reaper. At 5 o'clock I went into the Park. At Hyde Park Corner the crush was incredible.

Friday, 23 May
How delightful to get down into the sweet fresh damp air of the country again and the scent of the bean blossoms.

Wednesday, 11 June
Drove my Mother to Kington St Michael in a shandry dan which was lent to us by Hart Porter while he is repainting and repairing our own carriage. In Gander Lane we saw in the banks some of the 'Midsummer Men' plants which my Mother remembers the servant maids and cottage girls sticking up in their houses and bedrooms on Midsummer Eve, for the purpose of divining about their sweethearts.

Sunday, 15 June
A beautiful peaceful summer Sunday morn such as Robert Burns would have loved. Perfect peace and rest. The sun and the golden buttercup meadows had it almost all to themselves. A few soft fleecy clouds were rising out of the west but the gentle warm air scarcely stirred even the leaves on the lofty tops of the great poplars. One or two people were crossing the Common early by the several paths through the golden sea of buttercups which will soon be the silver sea of ox-eyes. The birds were singing quietly. The cuckoo's notes tolled clear and sweet as a silver bell and a dove was pleading in the elm and 'making intercession for us with groanings which cannot be uttered'.

Wednesday, 18 June
This evening the Shah of Persia arrived in England from Brussels and Ostend, escorted by the British fleet, and got wetted through by a heavy shower as he drove from the Railway Station to Buckingham Palace. The Shah is the first Persian monarch who ever left his own dominions except for conquest.

Saturday, the Longest Day
Near the keeper's cottage the setting sun made a green and golden splendour in the little open glade among the oaks while the keeper and two other men walked like three angels in the gilded mist.

Tuesday, Midsummer Day

Walter Brown of the Marsh says that his grandfather once saw some fairies in a hedge. But before he could get down out of the cart they were gone.

Saturday, 12 July

This afternoon I went to see Mrs Drew and if possible to comfort her concerning the death of her child. She was filled with sorrow and remorse because when the child had mouched from school last Monday and had wandered about all day with scarcely any food she had whipped him as soon as he came home in the evening and had sent him supperless to bed, although he had besought her almost in an agony to give him a bit of bread. 'Oh Mother, oh Mother, do give me one bit of bread.' Her heart smote her bitterly now that it was too late, when she remembered how the child had begged and prayed for food. The next morning soon after rising he fell down in a fit and he died at even. The mother asked me to go upstairs and see the child. He lay in his coffin looking very peaceful and natural with the flowers on his breast and the dark hair curling on his forehead.

Wednesday, 16 July

As I walked along the field path I stopped to listen to the rustle and solemn night whisper of the wheat, so different to its voice by day. The corn seemed to be praising God and whispering its evening prayer. Across the great level meads near Chippenham came the martial music of a drum and fife band, and laughing voices of unseen girls were wafted from farms and hayfields out of the wide dusk.

Monday, 21 July

A splendid summer's day, burning hot, sitting under the linden reading *Memorials of a Quiet Life*, Augustus Hare's book. As I sat there my mind went through a fierce struggle. Right or wrong? The right conquered, the sin was repented and put away and the rustle of the wind and the melodious murmurs of innumerable bees in the hives overhead suddenly seemed to me to take the sound of distant music, organs. And I thought I heard the harps of the angels rejoicing in heaven over a sinner that had repented.

Then I thought I saw an angel in an azure robe coming towards me across the lawn, but it was only the blue sky through the feathering branches of the lime.

Tuesday, 22 July
To-day the heat was excessive and as I sat reading under the lime I pitied the poor haymakers toiling in the burning Common where it seemed to be raining fire.

Wednesday, 23 July
Came to Hawkchurch for three days. A pleasant and lovely journey with the air cleared and cooled by the storm. Uncle Will met me at Axminster Station with Polly and the dog cart.

After tea Dora and I went up the high field in front of the cottage to look for mushrooms and glow worms in the dusk.

Thursday, 24 July
This morning Uncle Will, Dora and I drove to Seaton with Polly and the dog cart. It was a lovely morning. At Seaton while Dora was sitting on the beach I had a bathe. A boy brought me to the machine door two towels as I thought, but when I came out of the water and began to use them I found that one of the rags he had given me was a pair of very short red and white striped drawers to cover my nakedness. Unaccustomed to such things and customs I had in my ignorance bathed naked and set at nought the conventionalities of the place and scandalized the beach. However some little boys who were looking on at the rude naked man appeared to be much interested in the spectacle, and the young ladies who were strolling near seemed to have no objection.

Saturday, 26 July
Up at 6.30 and out at 7 o'clock in a lovely bright breezy morning, the dew shining after rain. I stole out at the back door to avoid disturbing anyone and I believe Rawlings the gardener thought I was gone mad or going to commit suicide for he ran anxiously out of his shoe house and looked after me to see which way I was going. The meadows were clean swept and washed and the lattermath from which the hay had been cleared gleamed brilliant green after the rain. I followed the lanes past West Hay, and presently came to the dry bed of a brook crossing the road. Before I could

pass over it however I heard a sudden sound of water and saw a stream beginning to trickle and wind amongst the stones. The stream broadened and deepened till with a swift rush of brown turbid water the brook bed was filled and the stream poured under a little foot bridge and roared down, a small cataract, into the meadows beyond. I thought at first it was a little flood caused by the day and night's rain and just came down the valley, but a merry-faced peasant, who was on his way to a rustic festival of sheep dipping, said that the sudden stream I had seen was the water fresh loosed from the mill pound of Zealey's Mill at Phelley Holme. The man said there were a good many trout in the brooks from ½ lb. to 2 lbs. and told me they should probably end their sheep dipping with a trout-netting frolic in the evening after the work was done.

At the bottom of the hill in the sunny hollow where we crossed a little stream of limpid water clear as crystal, dazzling and gleaming over its yellow pebbles, we met a woman who in answer to my companion's enquiries directed him to the sheepwashing. And presently we came to the gate of the meadow where the rural festival was being held. A group of men whose clothes were splashed and dyed by the red wash were plunging sheep and lambs one by one into a long deep trough. The sheep went in white and came out red, protected by their dipping against the attentions of the fly, and walked away across the meadow to join the flock, shaking the red wash in showers from their close-shorn fleeces.

The lane grew more and still more lovely. The morning sunlight slanted richly across the road between the trees, or struck here and there through a break in the foliage and tipped a frond of fern with brilliant green light. Broad alternate bars of sunshine and shadow lay across the lane, the sunlight shone on the polished grey silvery stems of a row of beeches, and a tender morning mist hung dreamily over the wooded hollow of the dingle below the road.

The lane opened up into a high open common across which the morning breeze from the sea stirred freshly with a cool light after the warm shelter of the hollow lanes. Beyond the common a gate let into a shady road cool and damp, dark and quiet as a cloister. It was completely overhung by trees, and the air was filled with the fragrant aromatic scent of the fir trees and the soft carpet of fir needles with which the ground was thickly strewn. The fields of ripening wheat began to glow golden along the slopes of the blue hills and the ferns, fresh washed by the rain of the night, beamed clear and brilliant green where the sun slanted silently through the windows of the wood.

Monday, 4 August
To-day I took Annie Jefferies[1] to her new place at Llysdinam. We arrived at Llysdinam in pouring rain.

Wednesday, 6 August
This afternoon Mr and Mrs Venables and Mary Bevan and I went by train from Builth road to Garth to attend the Garth Flower Show, Dog Show, Poultry Show, Bazaar and Athletic Sports, all in one. Mrs Welby was holding a bazaar in one of the tents for the benefit of poor old Llanlionfel Church now in ruins, but which they hope to get restored. While the athletic sports were going on I wandered away by myself into congenial solitude for a visit to the ruined Church of Llanlionfel. Passing by the quaint old house of Garth, formerly one of the numberless possessions of the great Gwynne family, I descended by a cart road into the meadows. The ruined Church tottered lone upon a hill in desolate silence. The old tombstones stood knee-deep in the long coarse grass and white and purple flowers nodded over the graves. The door stood open and I went in. The window frames and seats were gone. Nothing was left but the high painted deal pulpit bearing the sacred monogram in yellow letters. Some old memorial tablets bearing Latin inscriptions in remembrance of Marmaduke Gwynne and his family were affixed to the East Wall. The place was utterly deserted, there was not a sound. But through the ruined windows I could see the white tents of the flower show in the valley beneath. I ascended the tall rickety pulpit and several white owls disturbed from their day sleep floated silently under the crazy Rood Loft on their broad downy wings and sauntered sailing without sound through the frameless east and west windows to take refuge with a graceful sweep of their broad white pinions in the

---

1. A maid for whom Kilvert had obtained a place with Mrs Venables.

238

ancient yew that kept watch over the Church. It was a place for owls to dwell in and for satyrs to dance in.

It is long since the Church has been used, though weddings were celebrated in it after it was disused for other services. There is a curious story of a gentleman who was married here. Some years after his marriage his wife died, and it happened that he brought his second bride to the same Church. Upon the altar rails she found hanging the lace handkerchief which her predecessor had dropped at the former wedding. The Church had never been used nor the handkerchief disturbed in the interval of years between the two weddings.

Friday, 8 August
This morning I left Llysdinam with Mr Venables and Mary Bevan. Before I went I sent for Annie Jeffries into the library to wish her Goodbye. She said she was happy and getting on nicely with her work and the servants were kind and friendly to her. But poor child when we came to part, sever the last link that bound her to home, she burst into tears and left the room crying bitterly.

We travelled in great state from Newbridge to Hay in a magnificent saloon carriage, in which Lady Baily had come down from London yesterday and which was on its way home.

[Kilvert returns to Langley.]

Tuesday, 19 August
Went to see Mrs Pearce at Landsend, Mrs James Knight's sister. She told me her sad story. Born in better circumstances, the daughter of a substantial but litigious farmer, her mother died while she was yet a child. Then her husband died young leaving her with two children and a farm at Shaw to struggle with. Her cows caught the distemper and she was forced to drench them with her own hands. Next the rent of her farm was suddenly and greatly raised by her own brother-in-law and she was in consequence thrown out of business and reduced to comparative poverty. 'Twas a sad history and when she had asked me about my own family and had learnt that my Father and Mother were both living, she said with a sigh, 'How different some people's circumstances are'. 'I used', she said, 'to look across the road to the

churchyard where my husband was sleeping and think how he was lying at rest while I had all the cares of the farm and the family to struggle with. And I thought my heart would break.'

Saturday, 30 August
Driving into Chippenham with Fanny this morning we saw the headquarters of the 13th Hussars who had just marched in, band playing. They were on their way up from Dartmoor to Colchester. They had been taking part in the disastrous manœuvres. Horses and men looked thin, worn, weak, dirty and jaded and as if the best manœuvres they could accomplish would be a manœuvre into their barracks. They have had a sad time on Dartmoor, incessant rain and bottomless swamp and no rugs for the horses who stood fetlock deep in the bogs. Capt. Dallin was in the town, delighted to see soldiers again and quite in his element. There was a good deal of excitement and movement in the town. Officers riding about billeting the men and men seeking their billets.

Tuesday, September Morrow
In the evening Dora went to Langley Lodge to see Mrs Dallin and as she did not come back by dark I went to fetch her. A soft moonlight was flooding the common as the moon sailed out from behind a net of heavy clouds and the cattle looked ghostly in the weird silver light. At Langley Lodge I found two dashing Hussars dining with Captain Dallin who was in his glory. Captain Truman and a subaltern in his troop, Lieutenant Burne I think. The Lieutenant found his dress Hussar boot very tight at dessert and in great agony he begged my pen knife. Then while I held a candle from the branches he by Captain Truman's advice slit his boot up the side and found immediate relief, though with some compunction for the boots were his best and last pair.

Wednesday, 3 September
This morning punctually at 7.30 the bugle sounded the trot at the top of Huntsman's Hill and the last troop of the 13th Hussars clanked along the common. Captain Truman was as good as his word. They took the road down the village and stopped at Langley Lodge where Captain Dallin regaled the officers with brandy and

soda. One morning before he gave them brandy and soda on the Common.

Friday, 19 September

At Rawling's I was talking to old Mrs Matthews about the great number of railway accidents that have happened lately. 'It's shocking to be ushered out of the world in that way,' exclaimed Alice Matthews indignantly. John Couzens foretells a revolution in English society. 'I know it's coming,' he said, 'as sure as this prong is in my hand.'

Tuesday, 23 September

In the afternoon as I was sitting under the shade of the acacia on the lawn enjoying the still warm sunshine of the holy autumn day it was a positive luxury to be alive. A tender haze brooded melting over the beautiful landscape, and the peaceful silence was only broken by the chuckling and grumbling of a squirrel leaping among the acacia boughs overhead, and the clear sweet solitary notes of a robin singing from the copper beech.

Wednesday, 24 September

Another glorious day added to this beautiful Michaelmas summer. As I walked before breakfast across the Common I met Herriman the porter returning through the lovely morning from his night work at the station, and I could not help thinking of the difference between my lot and his, and how much more enjoyment I have in my life than he has in his. How differently we both spent last night, but how much better he spent it than I did. He was doing extra night duty that a fellow porter might enjoy a holiday, while I –. Herriman has only three days' holiday during the whole year, while to me every day is a holiday and enjoyment and delight. And for no desert of mine. Surely there will be compensation made for these things hereafter if not here.

Sunday, Michaelmas Eve

Dora said Syddy Ashe is fairly mad with disappointment at not having seen the 13th Hussars when they passed through Langley on their way to Colchester. 'I would have given a great deal to have seen one', she said, 'it would have been happiness to have seen one soldier, but to have missed the chance of seeing them all! It is too much.' And she nearly cried with vexation.

Sunday, 5 October

This morning [name rubbed out] came privately to church at 10.30 with [name rubbed out] to be churched after the birth of her son, which took place three months after her wedding. This has been a great scandal and grief to us.

Tuesday, 7 October

This morning I went to Bath with my Father and Mother to attend the Church Congress Service at the Abbey at 11. Dr Alexander the Bishop of Derry preached an admirable sermon nearly an hour long.

The swarming city was filled with the ringing of bells. At 2 my Mother, Thersie and I went to a meeting in the new temporary Congress Hall, where we heard more good papers and speeches from the Bishop of Bath and Wells, the President of the Congress, the Bishop of Oxford, Lord Bath, Lord Nelson, Beresford Hope, and Canon Girdlestone on 'the duty of the Church with regard to strikes and labour'.

Wednesday, 8 October

This morning I came down to Bath from Chippenham to stay for the rest of the Congress. I reached Bath just in time to go up to the new wooden Congress Hall, admirably arranged for sound and ventilation, and attended two sections, the first on Foreign Missions and the second on the Union of Church and State. In the first section Sir Bartle Frere[1] spoke admirably. Last night and this afternoon George Anthony Denison[2] spoke and excited a storm.

---

1. Sir Bartle Frere (1815–1884), though best known as a statesman, was a zealous churchman. In 1872 he had published a work entitled *Christianity suited to all Forms of Civilization*.

2. George Anthony Denison (1805–1896), archdeacon of Taunton, originated, according to the *Dictionary of National Biography*, 'the now popular festival of "harvest home"'. He was a high Churchman much addicted to controversy, and published a violent diatribe against Gladstone which was widely read.

Thursday, 9 October
Lunched at 1 Sion Hill with Miss Armine Furlong, Miss Reece and Jane Dew and went to three sections of the Church Congress.

Friday, 10 October
Attended three sections of the Church Congress at the Congress Hall. The subjects were the Life of Godliness, the Religious wants and claims of children, and Church Music. In the morning, as Bishop Ryan was speaking, an angel came into the Congress Hall and stood near the door listening. It had taken the form of a very beautiful young girl in a long grey cloak and a shower of golden-brown hair. I watched her intently and as she bowed her fair head and knee at the Name of Names she assumed exactly the attitude and appearance of the angels that overshadowed with their wings the ark and the Mercy seat. In the perpetual struggle between the powers and principles of good and evil the obeisance rebuked and put to flight an evil thought.

After the last section on Church Music I went with Miss Armine Furlong, Miss Reece and Jane Dew to the Mayor and Mayoress's reception at the Assembly Rooms. Some 3000 people were present and yet there was plenty of space to walk about in these noble rooms. We arrived at 9 and left at midnight. There was a band, tea, coffee, ices, champagne cup, claret cup, sandwiches, and speeches by the Bishop of Peterborough, the Bishop of Manchester, the Rector of Bath, and Mr Randall, Vicar of All Saints, Clifton.

It was stated that the Bath Congress was the most successful and the largest Church Congress yet held, 1400 more tickets having been sold than last year at Leeds. Altogether between 6000 and 7000 tickets were sold.

Wednesday, 22 October
This evening I had a letter from Josiah Evans, my friend the Clyro schoolmaster. His letter makes me laugh and almost cry at the same time. The parish he says is all in a muddle from end to end, and the sooner the new Vicar comes the better. My poor Clyro. My beloved Clyro.

Wednesday, 29 October

Dined at Chippenham Vicarage with Fanny. The Jacksons were there, Georgie and George Awdry with Miss Lucy Peck and the Frederick Awdrys with Capt. Hill, their cousin, a tall handsome powerful man who when tiger hunting once in India was seized by a tiger by the back of his neck. But he so pommelled the tiger's face over his shoulder that the beast let go, leaving Capt. Hill however with a stiff neck for life.

Monday, 17 November

At ten o'clock this morning, after school, I went on to Langley House to consult Mr Ashe about the advisability of publicly observing the Special Day of Prayer for Missionaries which the Archbishop of Canterbury has recommended for December 3. I found the Squire and Mrs Ashe in the upper drawing room. She was reading aloud to him. He asked whether I thought it wise to have lectures on winter evenings for mixed audiences of men and women, and to bring out the girls and their sweethearts for a moonlight walk.

Thursday, 20 November

Edward Humphries married a young woman when he was 83 and had a son within the year. 'Leastways his wife had,' said Mrs Hall.

Friday, 28 November

Dined at Langley House. Only the Dallins were there. The Squire was very agreeable, and gave us some of his splendid old '51 port and some priceless Madeira thirty-five years old, imported when Emma Clutterbuck was at Madeira.

Sunday, 7 December

Called on old Sally Killing after Church. She asked me the usual and indeed invariable question whether I remembered her old thatched cottage, near the road, by the lilac bush, and the old house in Westfield. I asked her how she passed her time. 'Aw ther,' she said, 'I do rock and sway myself about.'

Tuesday, 9 December

A brilliant white frost and the hoary meadows sparkling with millions of rainbows and twinkling with diamonds.

From the gate of Langley House, while waiting for Dora and Georgie to come out, I saw the Squire in his white hat cantering his bay pony across the park and charging the phalanx of his daughters on the gravel in front of the house to see how they would 'resist cavalry', his usual joke. The infantry scattered right and left and Thersie flew off to a safe distance.

Mrs Coates told me of her son Reuben's noble conduct to his dying sweetheart Sarah Hains. He would not be ashamed of her nor cease walking with her though her dropsical size drew all eyes and many suspicions upon him.

Wednesday, 10 December

Sad accounts reach me of the neglected state of my poor Clyro. 'My sheep wander through the mountains'.

Thursday, 11 December

There has been another disgraceful uproar in the Tichborne Trial between Dr Kenealy and the Lord Chief Justice.

Friday, 12 December

Walked with Dora to Langley Fitzurse. Called at the Manor Farm and had a long chat with Alice Banks about old times.

When Miss Long became heiress of Draycot and Wanstead and came of age there were great rejoicings. An ox was roasted whole in the park and a troop of yeomanry cavalry guarded it, riding round the roasting ox to keep the people off. When the ox was cut down half of it was burnt and charred and the other half was raw.

Thousands of people gathered from far and near to see the rejoicing. While the cavalry were at dinner in the house the kitchen chimney caught fire. The cavalry rushed out to see what was the matter, and the crowd immediately rushed in and cleared the tables. There was no food to be got in Sutton, all the provisions were swept off. Many of the strangers were nearly starved and came to the Home farm, where Mrs Banks was visiting her grandfather, to ask for some dry bread and cold water for which they were ready to pay anything. But the house was nearly empty of food. There was a ball in the great barn too and horse racing in the Park with all sorts of games and fireworks in the evening.

Then came the courtship and marriage of Miss Long, the great heiress, with the scamp Wellesley. Lady Catherine set her face against the marriage, but her daughter was weak and obstinate, the servants were bribed and the courtship was carried on clandestinely. Wellesley used to drive his tilbury down to the Langley Brewery, leave it there, and come and hide himself in the sunk fence in front of this house, what is now Langley Rectory. When he had watched Lady Catherine drive across the common into Chippenham with her four or six long-tailed black horses, leaving Miss Long the heiress locked up at home, he would run down to the Brewery, get into his tilbury, and gallop over to Draycot, where he saw Miss Long by the connivance of the servants.

She was infatuated and would not listen to those friends who told her that he was a villain and only wanted her money. Afterwards he brought down a hired carriage and horses from London and drove from the Angel at Chippenham to Draycot four-in-hand. At length Lady Catherine gave way and consented to the marriage, which Miss Long never ceased to regret, for her husband treated her in the most brutal manner and squandered the estate.

Mrs Banks said that one night her father came home from Chippenham very much disgusted because Long Wellesley had said in an election speech when he was standing for the county, 'Now gentlemen, all of you who are husbands, I advise you to go home and be as good husbands to your wives as I am to mine'. The impudent scoundrel.

Isaac Giles says he remembers hearing Long Wellesley make an election speech from the Angel in the course of which he told the people how he had 'got up the old lady's legs and married her daughter'. Isaac Giles was then working next door to the Angel and saw Long Wellesley drive away to Draycot four-in-hand every morning courting, and return at night. As he left Church with his bride after the wedding he was tapped on the shoulder for £20,000. And my mother remembers the wretched wife not long afterwards coming up to Langley Fitzurse, to my grandfather's, to borrow money, for the bailiffs were in Draycot House and her scamp of a husband had left her destitute. She was a mean-looking little woman, as weak as water.

Monday, 15 December

Fanny went to luncheon at Langley Fitzurse. I called there at 1.30 and walked to Draycot with her to see Draycot House. Miss West the housekeeper showed us over the house. The entrance hall was matted with fallow deer skins from the chase. The walls were ornamented with fallow bucks' heads and horns from every branch tip of which sprung a jet of gas.

To-day Captain Wellesley was married to the daughter of Lord Augustus Loftus. The bride and bridegroom were expected down by the 5 o'clock train to spend the honeymoon at Draycot. About an hour and a half before they arrived we were being shown through their bedroom, dressing and sitting rooms and looking at their photographs. Coming home I met Mrs Ashe and as I stood talking to her in the dusk, there came a flashing of lights and a rattle of horse-hoofs and the bride and bridegroom whirled past to Draycot with four greys and postilions.

1874

Wednesday, 14 January

To-night my Father told me his reminiscences of my grandfather, old Squire Coleman. 'He was a man of middle height,' he said, 'thin and spare. His hair was grizzled when I knew him. He had a good profile and a fine nose, but his face was the colour of a kite's foot, yellow and unwholesome looking, and his address was rendered unpleasant by a set unmeaning smile. He always said "Sir" to everyone. He dressed in a remarkable way, and looked like a clergyman of the old school in a very large white neckcloth, black coat, white cord breeches, grey gaiters and shoes. He rode a black horse and stooped a good deal over its neck.' (I have heard Edward Little of Lanhill say that my grandfather had the saddle put very far back on the horse and then sat very far back in the saddle). 'I used to go over to Langley occasionally to see your grandfather. Your Aunt Sarah used to ask me to come over and talk to him. One Sunday evening I was sitting with them and Sarah quietly pushed a book towards me. It was a book of sermons. "Shall I read to you?" I asked, opening the book. "If you please, Sir," said the old gentleman with a low and sudden bow and his peculiar set smile. He listened to me but made no remark.'

He was a good and easy landlord, and an upright honourable man in all his dealings. He was a regular attendant at his parish Church, Kington St Michael's, and he was so punctual that the village folks at Kington used to set their clocks by the Squire.

Tuesday, 20 January

Visited John and Hannah Hatherell. Hannah was telling me about an execution. Two young men of Bremhill named Powney saw the mother of the murderer striding across the fields to be in time to see her son hung.

Friday, 30 January

Drove my Mother to Chippenham. A Radical Candidate has taken us all by surprise. Handel Cossham was nominated this morning.

Before daylight the town had broken out with a bad eruption of poisonous yellow bills. We thought Goldney was going to walk over the course without opposition.

Thursday, 5 February
This afternoon I went to see the young dragoon Frank Vincent. He is in the 1st Royals and home on furlough of a month from Edinburgh after an illness. He is a fine handsome young fellow as you shall see in a day's march. He said he was fond of Burns, and I read aloud to him Burns' Epistle to a young friend, Andrew Aiken.

Friday, 6 February
To-day the papers brought us good news from Cape Coast Castle. Sir Garnet Wolseley was within a march of Coomassie. The King of Ashantee had sent in his submission and agreed to pay the £200,000 demanded by Sir Garnet.

As I crossed the Common on my way home a form loomed through the thick mist, a labouring man going home from his work, and a voice hallooed, 'Stop there till I see who you be. Is that Mr Frank Kilvert?' It was poor George Bourchier staggering along the worse for drink. I took his hand. 'George,' I said sadly and gently, 'you have had too much.' 'I have, Sir,' he said. 'God forgive me. I cry about it night and morning. I will try to leave it off. God bless you.' The poor wandering sheep.

Saturday, St Valentine's Day
This afternoon I went to see Frank Vincent, the handsome young Dragoon, once more before he leaves to rejoin his regiment, the 1st Royals at Edinburgh. He is a noble young soldier and singularly attractive and lovable.

Monday, 16 February
Greatly troubled by the licentiousness of the school children, especially Harriet Ferris, Mary Grimshaw and Lucy Halliday.

Friday, 20 February
Visited old John Hatherell the sawyer. He began sawing for the Manor the year my great-grandmother old Madame Ashe died in 1823, more than half a century ago, and he has been at the call of the Manor ever since. He had known sore hardships, he said, when

the bread was so very dear and he was bringing up a large family. Often he had worked all day up to his knees in water and gone to bed hungry that his children might have bread, and he thought they always had enough.

Tuesday, 10 March

I found John Gough returned from the Bath United Hospital last Saturday. He was twenty-one years in the army, and fought at Alma and Inkerman where he was wounded. 'No one but themselves who went through it,' he said, 'will ever know what our soldiers endured in the winter of 1854–1855. No firewood but what they cut down or the roots they grubbed up under the fire of the enemy's guns. The coffee served out green to be roasted as the men could over their miserable fires in fragments of shell, and then when burnt or blackened a little pounded with two stones in a piece of canvas or coarse cloth, just something to flavour the water. A little grog and plenty of salt meat, but often no biscuit, and they were afraid to eat much of the salt meat for fear of scurvy. When they came in from the trenches or night fatigue duty, no fire, no straw to lie down on, only a blanket and greatcoat and the mud ankle-deep. On Christmas Day a little piece of butter and two ounces of "figgy pudding" were served to each man out of casks. Tobacco was more precious than gold. If a man was lucky enough to have a pipe he doted on it as if it were Almighty God coming down upon him. Tobacco was so scarce that he hardly dared to put it into the pipe, only a very little bit, and then just two or three draws at a time. Then he stopped the pipe with a bit of rag and put it into his pocket. He could not afford himself more than that at once. If I had had tobacco I could have done with one meal a day. The French soldiers were in plenty while we were starving. The French managed everything well. In our lines there was nothing but shameful mis-management. As many men died of neglect, mis-management, cold, starvation and needless disease as died in battle. The French were four miles nearer to Balaclava and the provision stores, then they had hardy mules, while the English horses dropped under their loads and died by the roadside.'

John Gough said, 'On the Sunday morning November 5th 1854

I was sleeping in the tent. I had been on fatigue duty that night till midnight. About 6 o'clock before daylight a man who slept next me touched me and said, "Jack, the Rooshians are firing into the camp". I said, "Nonsense, who cares? Let me sleep." However he wouldn't let me be. "It's true," he said with an oath. I wanted to sleep and rapped out a nasty word. It was true enough however and the cannon balls soon came hopping through the camp. Then the bugle sounded "Stand to your arms" and I said, "There is something up then after all". We stood to our arms. It was not daybreak yet and we waited in the shelter of the 4-gun battery that defended our division. Our battery was blazing away at the flashes of the Rooshian guns. This is how we were surprised. There were double sentries on outlying picket duty that night, one to stand and listen while the other walked about and warmed himself. Then he took a turn at listening and the other walked about. When the guard was relieved at 4 o'clock in the morning one of the sentries reported to a captain of the 47th that he could hear a noise like the rattling of waggons coming out of Sebastopol. The sergeant confirmed his report and added that he could hear also that the wheels were muffled. He said the Captain might hear the noise himself if he went down into the ravine. But the Captain laughed at it and took no notice. These waggons were the field pieces and ammunition waggons coming out of Sebastopol to surprise the English and fight the battle of Inkerman. It was the longest battle fought in the war and lasted all day from dawn to dusk.'

Friday, 13 March
Charles Awdry told a good story which he said the Archdeacon of Sarum told him. The Archdeacon on a Visitation tour came to a small upland parish in the diocese of Salisbury. He asked the clerk how often the Holy Communion was administered in the year. The clerk stared. 'What did you please to say?' he asked. 'The Holy Communion,' repeated the Archdeacon. 'How often do you have it in the year?' The clerk still stared open-mouthed in hopeless bewilderment. At length a suspicion of the Archdeacon's meaning began to dawn faintly upon him. 'Aw,' he blurted out. 'Aw, we do never have he. We've got no tackling.'

Monday, 16 March
To-day there was a great gathering at Chislehurst of friends of
the exiled Napoleon dynasty to celebrate the coming of age of the
Prince Imperial at the age of 18.

Started for Llysdinam by the 8.30 express.

At Three Cocks we waited some time and I fell into talk with
one of the Bridgwaters of one of the Porthamal farms who told me
about the elections and how at Talgarth Mr de Winton of
Maesllwch had been insulted by men kicking round him as a
football a rabbit stuffed with bran, in allusion to his propensity
for ruining his tenants by keeping vast hordes of rabbits on his
estate.

When the train came in from Brecon a tall girl with a fresh
colour dressed in deep mourning got out of the train and came
towards me. It was Daisy, and her brother John was with her.
There was a half sweet, half sad look, a little reproachful in the
beautiful kind eyes as she said in a low voice, 'I have been looking
out for you such a long time'. Poor child, my poor child.

Saturday, 21 March
Left Llysdinam and came to Whitney Rectory.

Monday, 23 March
One of the dear old bright happy mornings which seem peculiar
and sacred to Whitney Rectory. The sun shone brightly in at the
southern window bowered in roses and beautiful creeping plants
and the birds chirped and sang in their bowers and I opened my
eyes on the old familiar view as I looked up the valley of the Wye
to the heights of Clyro Hill. Muirbach Hill dawned a soft azure
through the tender morning mists. Pretty Louisa Dew bounded up
the stairs to meet me with a bright rosy morning face and a lovely
kiss, when she heard me leave my room. She will be a noble-
looking girl one day and will make somebody's heart ache. She is
a very fine girl for her age now and as wild as a hawk but as good
as gold, in spite of her dancing spirits. After breakfast a ramble in
the garden to see the fruit trees. A white nectarine was in a blaze
of purple blossom.

I rode with Henry Dew senior to Clifford Priory to see how
Haigh Allen was. We had a scamper back to Whitney Rectory to

catch the 1.8 train which was to take me to Hay to stay at Hay Castle.

In the afternoon Mrs Bevan, Mary and I drove to Clyro. As we passed along the old familiar road that I have journeyed over so many times a thousand memories swept over me. Every foot of Clyro ground is classical and sacred and has its story. When we reached the dear old village the children had just come out of school. I kissed my hand to them, but they seemed as if they could hardly believe their eyes and it was not till after we had alighted at the lodge under the old weeping willow and were walking up the steep drive to Cae Mawr that a ringing cheer came up from the playground.

Mr Morrell was not at home, but Reginald and Winifred came downstairs. They had both forgotten me. Baskerville came to the door and we sat down in the drawing room for a chat.

As we walked down the drive to the carriage renewed cheers came ringing from the school. Mrs Bevan was much amused and Baskerville said to me, 'It is a pity you don't stand for the county. You would have the suffrages of every one here.'

The dear children crowded round the school door. They were a little shy and much grown since I saw them this time last year, but my sweet little Amy was unmistakable and so were the frank sweet eyes of Eleanor Hill.

When we returned to Hay I walked to the almshouses beyond the Brecon turnpike with Mrs Bevan, Alice and Cousie.

The daffodils were nodding in bright yellow clumps in the little garden plots before the almshouse doors. And there a great ecstasy of happiness fell upon me. It was evening when I met her and the sun was setting up the Brecon road. I was walking by the almshouses when there came down the steps a tall slight beautiful girl with a graceful figure and long flowing fair hair. Her lovely face was delicately pale, her features refined and aristocratic and her eyes a soft dark tender blue. She looked at me earnestly, long-ingly and lovingly, and dropped a pretty courtesy. Florence, Florence Hill, sweet Florence Hill, is it you? Once more. Thank God. Once more. My darling, my darling. As she stood and lifted those blue eyes, those soft dark loving eyes shyly to mine, it seemed to me as if the doors and windows of heaven were suddenly opened. It was one of the supreme moments of life. As I stood by the roadside holding her hand, lost to all else and conscious only of her presence, I was in heaven already, or if still on earth in the body, the flights of golden stairs sloped to my feet and one of the angels had come down to me. Florence, Florence Hill, my darling, my darling. It was well nigh all I could say in my emotion. With one long lingering loving look and clasp of the hand we parted and I saw her no more.

Tuesday, 24 March, Lady Day Eve
I went down to the almshouses hoping to see Florence Hill again. Alas, the daffodils were still blowing in the little garden plot, but Florence Hill was gone.

I walked to Clyro by the old familiar fields and the Beacon stile, and when I looked down upon the dear old village nestling round the Church in the hollow at the dingle mouth and saw the fringes of the beautiful woods and the hanging orchards and the green slopes of Penllan and the white farms and cottages dotted over the hills a thousand sweet and sad memories came over me and all my heart rose up within me and went out in love towards the beloved place and people among whom I lived so long and so happily.

I saw a number of the old people. Hannah Whitney was going to the well as of old in her rusty black bonnet tilted on to the top of her head. Mrs Richard Williams was in the churchyard. She had come down from Paradise to trim Mr Henry Venables' grave. Poor Lizzie Powell, a wreck and shadow of the fine blooming girl she was when I saw her last, was crouching up in the sunny window opposite the Vicarage, pale, wasted, shrunken, hollow-eyed and hollow-cheeked, dying of consumption, but with the sanguine and buoyant spirit of that mysterious and fatally deceptive disease, hoping still against hope even with the hand of death upon her. She seemed pleased to see me. She was amusing herself by watching the men at work at the Vicarage building the new garden wall and her brother Charlie among them.

I went to the school to see Evans and his wife and the children. 'We will never forget you,' said one of them. 'I wish,' said Mr Higgins of Clyro Court Farm to me, 'I wish to goodness you were going to stay amongst us. We all love you. We do indeed.'

Thursday, 26 March

I slept at Whitney Rectory last night and came to Hay this morning with Henry Dew by the ten o'clock train.

I walked over to Llanthomas to luncheon with Captain John Thomas. Howarth Greenly was there at luncheon and they played quoits after lunch while I walked to the gardens with Charlotte and Fanny. I went back to Whitney Rectory to sleep as Mr Venables is staying at the Castle. My poor, poor Daisy. When we parted the tears came into her eyes. She turned her face away. I saw the anguish of her soul. What could I do?

Friday, 27 March

After breakfast I walked with Jane and Helen Dew for a charming walk. We loitered through some lovely woods and dingles starred thick with primroses, and across a rushing brook upon the stepping stones. There was a sweet stirring of new life among the woods and a dawn of green upon the larches and hawthorns. We passed by a cottage inhabited by the peasant descendants of the famous and ancient family of De La Haye. The wife of the present De La Haye came to the garden gate to speak to us, a pleasant comely woman.

Saturday, 28 March

Left Hay Castle and returned to Langley after a very pleasant holiday.

Tuesday, 21 April

At noon I attended a Ruridecanal Conference at the Town Hall in Chippenham.

The Rural Dean, Gray Lawson, unwisely introduced the subject of Contagious Diseases and the enforced surgical examination of suspected women, to ventilate the matter, as he said.

Monday, 27 April

This morning came a letter from Mr Henry Moule, Vicar of Fordington, enclosing a note from the Poet, the Revd William Barnes, Rector of Winterbourne Came, near Dorchester, whom I have long wished to see. The Poet says he will be happy to receive a visit from me.

Thursday, May Eve

This will always be a happy and memorable day in my remembrance.

To-day I visited and made the acquaintance and I hope the friendship of William Barnes, the great idyllic Poet of England. Up at 6 o'clock, breakfast at 6.30, and left Chippenham by the 7.15 train. It was a glorious morning, fresh and exhilarating, as I started on my journey and the unclouded sky shone with a splendid blue over the brilliant green elms and the rich warm golden brown of the oaks. The elms performed a solemn dance circling round each of the fine Church Towers of Somerset as we sped down into Dorset by the windings of the Frome and the elms of Castle Cary. And then the high downs began to rise and we seemed to breathe the sweet salt air as soon as we saw the bold white chalk cliffs that look to the blue sea.

Mr Henry Moule, the Vicar of Fordington for nearly half a century, met me at the Dorchester Station, pointed out to me the great Roman amphitheatre, Maiden Castle, the vallum of the Roman camp, and took me round the beautiful avenues of luxuriant sycamore and chestnut which surround and adorn the town with delightful boulevards foursquare and exquisite shaded walks over-arched by trees which give the place the look of a foreign town.

As we passed along the beautiful water walk and over the hatches between the crystal streams of the Frome and the bright water-meadows below and looked up at the picturesque old high town bosomed in its groves of sycamore and chestnut and tufted with lofty trees we met a lovely girl dressed in deep mourning and walking with her lover, probably a bold handsome artilleryman from the barracks, splendid in blue and gold.

The Vicar told me part of the history of the politics of Fordington, his troubles with the Dorchester people and his struggles with the Council of the Duchy of Cornwall to which the parish of Fordington belongs and from which with great difficulty he has at length wrung some acknowledgement and help in money and improvements.

When the Vicar first came to Fordington he was instrumental, he said, in putting down some low bad races held near Dorchester.

This made him very unpopular. For five years none of his family or flock could go into Dorchester without being insulted and baa-ed after like sheep. Twenty or thirty young men stood at the Church gates each Sunday and insulted the pastor and his congregation as they went into Church. And every year all the shrubs and flowers in the garden were rooted up and placed together in the middle of the lawn. All the opposition however had been lived down long ago and now the Vicar seems universally and deservedly respected.

We walked together to the Poet's house, Winterbourne Came Rectory, about a mile from Fordington. The house lies a little back from the glaring white high road and stands on a lawn fringed with trees. It is thatched and a thatched verandah runs along its front. The thatched roof gives the Rectory house the appearance of a large lofty cottage. As we turned in at the iron gates from the high road and went down the gravel path the Poet was walking in the verandah. He welcomed us cordially and brought us into his drawing room on the right-hand side of the door. He is an old man, over seventy, rather bowed with age, but apparently hale and strong. 'Excuse my study gown,' he said. He wore a dark grey loose gown girt round the waist with a black cord and tassel, black knee breeches, black silk stockings and gold buckled shoes.

I was immediately struck by the beauty and grandeur of his head. It was an Apostolic head, bald and venerable, and the long soft silvery hair flowed on his shoulders and a long white beard fell upon his breast. His face was handsome and striking, keen yet benevolent, the finely pencilled eyebrows still dark and a beautiful benevolent loving look lighted up his fine dark blue eyes half hermit, half enchanter.

He is a very remarkable and a very remarkable-looking man, half hermit, half enchanter.

The Poet seemed pleased with my visit and gratified that I had come such a long way to see him. I told him I had for many years known him through his writings and had long wished to thank him in person for the many happy hours his poems had given me. He smiled and said he was very glad if he had given me any pleasure. Frequently stroking his face and his venerable white beard the Poet told me he had composed his poems chiefly in the

257

evening as a relaxation from the day's work when he kept a school in Dorchester.

He was born at [   ] Newton,[1] a son of a small farmer, and in after life when he sat down to amuse himself by writing poetry all the dear scenes and well-remembered events and beloved faces of his youth crowded upon his memory. 'I saw them all distinctly before me,' he said, 'and all I had to do was to write them down. It was no trouble to me, the thoughts and words came of themselves.' He said that some of the names of people and places mentioned in his poems are fictitious, but they all represented real places and persons. The real name of Ellen Brine of Allenburn, he said, was Mary Hames, and the poem was true to the life.

In describing a scene he always had an original in his mind, but sometimes he enlarged and improved upon the original. 'For instance,' he explained, 'sometimes I wanted a bit of water or wood or a hill, and then I put these in.' 'Pentridge by the river,' he said, was a real place, and so were some others. The river was the Stour.

'Once,' said the Poet, 'I had a curious second-sight about a house. It was a farm house in a hollow that I had passed by some time before. I knew nothing about the house or the people, but it haunted me. I saw the place in a vision. Two children, a boy and a girl, were playing in the courtyard. I noticed their features distinctly. The girl ran very swiftly. Afterwards I learnt that just such a boy and girl did live in that house and I am sure that if I were to see these children I should know them by the faces of the children I saw in the vision.'

The Poet is a self-taught man, a distinguished philologist, and is said to understand seventeen languages.

As we walked from Fordington to Came in discussion like friends in council Mr Moule repeated to me some beautiful and touching verses which he had composed when he was in the depths of his great trouble about his poor son Horace. The verses began, 'Lord, I love Thee'. He had sent a copy of them to the Poet

1. William Barnes (1801–1886) was born at Rushay in the parish of Bagber, but was christened at Sturminster Newton and went to school there. He came of yeoman stock, and his mother was a woman of some culture.

who was delighted with them and said it was 'a goodly song from a golden lyre'. Now Mr Moule, who is an universal genius, sat down to the piano in the Poet's drawing room and sang these verses in a sweet deep melodious voice, accompanying himself with a beautiful and appropriate air which he had composed himself and which came to him, he said, like an inspiration. Meanwhile the Poet sat by on an ottoman, stroking his long white beard and glancing round occasionally at me, and clapping his hands softly. He is very musical himself. The walls of the drawing room were almost entirely covered with small oil paintings from floor to ceiling.

At the earnest request of the Vicar the Poet read aloud to us his admirable poem describing how worthy Bloom the Miller went to London to see the great 'glassen house' and how he could not get into the omnibus by reason of his bulk, though he declared he was a poor starved Dorset man. We were all three in roars of laughter. Then to please me he read his beautiful poem called 'Happiness'. It is one of my favourites. He said that 'No So's' means 'No Souls', i.e. friends, neighbours. 'No So's.' 'No my friends.' He read in a low voice, rather indistinct and with much feeling. 'I like your pathetic pieces best,' said the Vicar. 'So do I,' said the Poet.

He spoke of Tennyson's *Northern Farmer*. 'Tennyson,' he said, 'even if he did not mean to ridicule the Northern Farmer, at least had no love for him and no sympathy with him.' Which is probably true and a just criticism. The Poet went on to say that in all which he himself had written there was not a line which was not inspired by love for & kindly sympathy with the things and people described. And this is wholly true. All his poems are overflowing with love and tenderness towards the dear scenes and friends of his youth.

He said the cattle calls used to call the cows home at milking time on the Wilts and Dorset dairy farms are the same as those used in Scandinavia.

Then the Vicar of Fordington told us of the state of things in his parish when he first came to it nearly half a century ago. No man had ever been known to receive the Holy Communion except the parson, the clerk and the sexton. There were 16 women communicants and most of them went away when he refused to pay them for coming. They had been accustomed there at some place in the neighbourhood to pass the cup to each other with a nod of the head. At one church there were two male communicants. When the cup was given to the first he touched his forelock and said, 'Here's your good health, Sir'. The other said, 'Here's the good health of our Lord Jesus Christ'.

One day there was christening and no water in the Font. 'Water, Sir!' said the clerk in astonishment. 'The last parson never used no water. He spit into his hand.'

Friday, May Day
This morning I had a nice letter from the Parshill Barracks from my dear young dragoon Frank Vincent. He says he is trying to follow my advice and to do right though there is a good deal of joking and laughing in the troop at his expense.

Walking up and down the terrace with my Father telling him about the Poet Barnes and discussing with him the advisability of publishing a book of my own poems. I wish to do so. He rather discourages the idea.

Saturday, May Morrow
Went to Peckingell. Found Austin a little better. He and his wife told me things about the parish which drew aside the veil from my eyes and showed me in what an atmosphere and abyss of wickedness we are living and how little many people are to be trusted whom we thought respectable and good. As the evening sunlight shone bright and searching across the lawn upon the lime the shadows of the leaves were cast strongly upon the tree trunk. The leaves were so brilliant that even their shadows showed a pale faint ghostly green. The shadows looked like the spirits of leaves without the body.

Wednesday, 6 May
Though I be tied and bound with the chain of my sin yet let the pitifulness of Thy Great mercy loose me.

Tuesday, 12 May
At the door of the White Lion Hotel in Bath we found a large crowd gathered round the donkey and cart of the nobleman organ-

grinder. The disguised nobleman and his organ were putting up at the Hotel and the people were waiting for him to finish breakfast and to come out. No one knows who he is. There are many reports. Some say he is an Irish baronet, some that he is a Lord. It is believed that he has made a wager for £30,000 that he will go about for three years with the same donkey, and live by his earnings. People give him gold in the street and some days it is said he makes as much as £15. Perhaps he has run through one fortune and taken this means of getting another. Or perhaps a fortune of £30,000 was left him to be inherited on this condition.

Holy Thursday, 14 May
I met in the drive this morning a poor Frenchman, pale, thin and lank. He said he was a soldier and had been taken prisoner at Sedan in September 1870 and sent to Schleswig Holstein. He was coming up to the Rectory to ask if there were any French people in the neighbourhood who would help him on his way to London. He had been sick and in the Bristol Infirmary and was now on his way home to Strasbourg, his native city. 'My father lived there,' he said, 'but I fear he has gone away now.' I told him I had been to Strasbourg and talked to him about some of the people and places there. A bright pleased look came into his wan sorrowful face for a moment as his old home and native city and the great Cathedral rose before his eyes. But they were far away. He had many a weary mile to limp before he could see the old place again. The eager light faded and the sorrowful wistful suffering look came back into his eyes. He had been twice wounded with a bullet through the thigh and gash down the jaw. He asked me if I had heard 'the chicken cry' (the cock crow) on the clock in Strasbourg Cathedral when he saw St Peter come round with the eleven apostles. He recognized with delight my description of the beautiful woman who kept a photograph shop in the corner house near the front of the Cathedral. 'Ah,' he cried, 'Madame Tournon. But,' he said sadly, 'it is all gone now. It was bombarded in the siege.' 'I hope,' said the poor broken soldier with a sad and deep sigh, 'England will never see such a war as that.'

Saturday, 16 May
This day ten years ago I walked to Bath and back. This afternoon

I drove with my Father to Seagry through the snowy May bushes and golden brown oaks and lovely hedgerows of Sutton Lane. Charles Awdry went with us to the river and Seagry Mill, and we lay back on the river bank talking while my Father fished. It was a glorious afternoon, unclouded, and the meadows shone dazzling like a golden sea in the glory of the sheets of buttercups. The deep dark river, still and glassy, seemed to be asleep and motionless except when a leaf or blossom floated slowly by.

Expectation Sunday, 17 May

We shall not have a more lovely Sunday than this has been. The hawthorn bushes were loaded with their sweet May snow, and in the glowing afternoon sun the sheets of buttercups stretched away under the bright elms like a sea of gold.

Whitsun Day, 24 May

After Church I visited and read to old John Hatherell and Hannah gave me a glass of their excellent parsnip wine.

Whitsun Monday, 25 May

At 9 o'clock I went through the mowing grass of the homefield (Cambridge's) to the John Knights' dairy and Fair Rosamund brought me a jug and glass and dipped me up some sweet warm whey as she used to do last summer. She and her mother were breaking curd and making cheese in the great tin tub.

I went down to Greenway Lane Farm by the quiet meadows fragrant with the incense of evening prayers. How sweet and still and pure after the noise and dust and crowd and racket of the town, the fine and smart dresses, the tawdry finery, the flaunting ribbons and the uproar of the cheese market where the band was thundering and the dancers whirling. Here the sweet flowers were blossoming and the only sound was the birds singing very quietly.

Whitsun Tuesday, 26 May

This afternoon the Rural Dean, Mr Gray Lawson, came to visit and inspect our Church. I met the Churchwardens there at 2.30, and while we were waiting for the Rural Dean Farmer John Bryant and I cut down with a penknife a young elm which was growing at the foot of the Chancel wall beneath the East window and thrust the tree hurriedly into the great laurel bush in the corner which is the receptacle for all rubbish and withered decorations. The dead ivy which has been lately cut has been falling from the Church walls in great dusty rubbishy flakes, but Churchwarden Jacob Knight went to the Church with Emma Halliday yesterday and tidied up a bit. Presently the Rural Dean came and asked many questions, examined the Church within and without narrowly, looked behind the doors and into the books and stamped upon the wooden flooring by the Langley House pew till I feared he might go down into the vaults beneath. He asked about the state of the Tower roof and I offered to go up the shaky old ladder with him but he wisely and hastily declined. As he was walking backwards looking up at the Tower he stumbled backwards among the graves and might have dashed out his brains against the great altar tombs had I not seized him by the arm and held him up. He said our Church was a singular instance of the morning congregation being larger than the afternoon one. Finally he said he had no fault to find and could not pick a hole in our coats.

Croquet, tea and supper at Langley Green.

Thursday, 28 May
This morning as Thersie was in bed in the spare room, the shutters being closed, all but the small square hole cut in the shutters of the N.W. window, at the moment the postman came to the door at 6.45 she saw the figures of two little men or a man and boy, very small, walking up the ceiling. When the postman left the door the shadows went down the ceiling again and disappeared. But when sufficient time had passed for the postman to reach the curve of the drive and the copper beech, the two little figures appeared on the ceiling for a moment again. We were not able to find out from the servant whether the postman had a boy with him this morning as she did not see him come. It was a curious optical effect and one difficult to account for as there was no light behind or below which could throw upon the ceiling of this room the shadow of any figure upon the drive.

At the dairy it was butter morning and Fair Rosamund was making up the sweet rolls of rich golden butter. Mrs Knight says the butter is so golden at this time of year because the cows eat the buttercups. The reason why the whey is so sweet and wholesome in May and June is because the grass is so full of flowers and young sweet herbs. When I go to the Common Farm to drink whey I think of my grandmother, my mother's mother Thermuthis Ashe, then a fair beautiful young girl, and how she used to come across the meadows from the Manor house to this very dairy and drink whey here every morning during the sweet May Month.

Thursday, 4 June
Went to Bristol with my Mother on a market ticket. She went to see Miss Evans at 6 Oakfield Place, and I to visit Janet Vaughan of Newchurch at the Clergy Daughters' School. On the way up to Great George St where the C.D.S. is I went into the market to buy a nosegay of roses for Janet. As I was sitting in a confectioner's shop between the Drawbridge and College Green eating a bun I saw lingering about the door a barefooted child, a little girl, with fair hair tossed and tangled wild, an arch espiègle eager little face and beautiful wild eyes, large and grey, which looked shyly into the shop and at me with a wistful beseeching smile. She wore a poor faded ragged frock and her shapely limbs and tiny delicate beautiful feet were bare and stained with mud and dust. Still she lingered about the place with her sad and wistful smile and her winning beseeching look, half hiding herself shyly behind the door. It was irresistable. Christ seemed to be looking at me through the beautiful wistful imploring eyes of the barefooted hungry child. I took her out a bun, and I shall never forget the quick happy grateful smile which flashed over her face as she took it and began to eat. She said she was very hungry. Poor lamb. I asked her name and she told me, but amidst the roar of the street and the bustle of the crowded pavement I could not catch the accents of the childish voice. Never mind. I shall know some day.

In Great George Street, leading out of Park St, I did not know at first where to find the Clergy Daughters' School, but the sound of two or three pianos guided me to the top of the street where stood a large old-fashioned red brick house in a pretty garden. 'Is Miss Vaughan at home?' 'Yes,' and I was shown upstairs into a room overlooking the basin and sweep of the vast smoky town and the dark grey battlements of the Cathedral Tower rising above the avenues of College Green.

Presently I heard a sweet voice singing along the passages and Janet Vaughan came in much grown and with her hair cut short over the forehead, but unchanged in other ways and as sweet and simple and affectionate as ever. She gave me a long loving kiss and we sat down by the open window to talk. Then some ladies came in to see another of the girls of the school and I sent Janet to ask if we might go out into the garden. Leave was given and we went out into a pretty garden at the back of the house with steep sloping lawns and shady winding walks under the trees. Janet took me down a steep path into a secluded walk, dark and shady, at the bottom of the garden, called in the school traditions the 'Poet's Retreat'. Here we walked up and down talking of Clyro and Gilfa and Newchurch and old times. Then girls came out into the garden with their books and work and soon all the shady nooks were full of light dresses and bright pretty faces and pleasant voices.

The walk called the 'Poet's Retreat' was fringed with young trees upon some of which the girls had carved their initials. Upon the stem of a young beech whose bark was grimy black with Bristol smuts I carved Janet's initials J.V. and reluctantly at her earnest request my own R.F.K. above.

Sunday, 7 June
I had only three from the village to-night. Cissy Bryant, Emma Halliday and Martha Plank, and I spoke to them about temptation and the Temptation of Christ.

Later the warm soft night was laden with perfume and the sweet scent of the syringa.

Tuesday, 9 June
Went with my mother and Dora and Lettice Hazel[1] to the Isle of Wight by Salisbury and Stokes Bay. The heat was intense. The Wiltshire downs and Salisbury Plain were white and glaring with drought and chalk and dust in the scorching blinding sun. Everything seemed parched and dried up by the 2 months' drought

---

1. A maidservant.

except some brilliant patches of crimson sainfoin which lighted up the white hot downs and burning Plain with the purple bloom and splendours of heather. At Heytesbury a young handsome intelligent gentlemanly farmer got into the carriage, a man with a ruddy face, light brown hair, merry blue eyes and a white puggery on his hat. We fell into talk about the strike and lock-out in the Eastern Counties and the much vexed labour and wages question. He was on his way to Salisbury Market.

At Shanklin Station there was Lizzie James on the platform smiling to receive Lettice, unchanged since the old Llowes and Clyro days. And there were Gussie and Commerell to meet me and Mrs Cowper Coles outside the Station Gate in her wheel chair given her by the Duchess of Norfolk. So we went up to their house Newstead together and it was very pleasant seeing them all. Mrs Coles has got Newstead on a lease of 999 years. It is a pleasant well-arranged roomy airy house, very light and cheerful, near the edge of the Cliff with glimpses of the bright blue sea between the houses in front.

Thursday, 11 June
From the top of the hill how lovely was the view over Brading Harbour, the distant headlands and the white houses along their sides sparkling as clear as crystal in the evening sunshine and the white winged boats moving slowly round the shores (their topsails showing over the green fields) or standing across the calm blue sea

Friday, 12 June
Bathing yesterday and to-day. Yesterday the sea was very calm, but the wind has changed to the East and this morning a rough and troublesome [sea] came tumbling into the bay and plunging in foam upon the shore. The bay was full of white horses. At Shanklin one has to adopt the detestable custom of bathing in drawers. If ladies don't like to see men naked why don't they keep away from the sight? To-day I had a pair of drawers given me which I could not keep on. The rough waves stripped them off and tore them down round my ancles. While thus fettered I was seized and flung down by a heavy sea which retreating suddenly left me lying naked on the sharp shingle from which I rose

streaming with blood. After this I took the wretched and dangerous rag off and of course there were some ladies looking on as I
came up out of the water.

Thursday, 25 June
Went to London by the 11.5 mail. I left my carpet-bag at the
Paddington Cloak Room and went straight to the Academy exhibition at Burlington House which I reached shortly before 4
o'clock. There was a great press of people, 100 or more, round
Miss Thompson's famous picture 'Calling the Roll after the battle
of Inkerman'. A policeman stands on duty all day by this picture
from 10 o'clock till 6 in the evening saying, 'Move on, ladies.
Ladies, please move on'.

I met Teddy in the Exhibition and we dined together at the
Criterion. Not a bed was to be got at the Great Western Hotel, so
I put up at the Norfolk.

Friday, 26 June
Breakfasted with the Venables at 62 Warwick Square.

At ten o'clock I went to Victoria to get a train for the Crystal
Palace and the Handel Festival. I found a special train going, but
it was so late in starting that we did not reach the Palace till 11.30
when the doors had been open and all the best seats filled for half
an hour. I was a long way from the Orchestra and on one side yet
I heard all the 28 Choruses admirably. Some of the solos were
almost inaudible and all sounded like faint voices coming out of a
vast empty distance. Yet the duet 'The Lord is my Strength'
between the two sopranos Madame Otto Alvsleben and Madame
Lemmens Sherrington was lovely and the duet between the two
basses Santley and Signor Foli 'The Lord is a Man of War' was
grand, and Sims Reeves sang 'The Enemy said' as splendidly as
ever. Madame Lemmens' voice pierced like lightning. To my mind
the most marvellous part of this marvellous oratorio is the Chorus
describing the plague of darkness. In the thick heavy muffled
music you could feel the waves of darkness coming on.

Dined with the Venables at 62 Warwick Square and met
Tomkyns Dew and Capt., Mrs, and Miss Hope Adam.

Saturday, 27 June

I regret to say that against good advice and wise warning I went to see Holman Hunt's picture of the Shadow of Death. It was a waste of a good shilling. I thought the picture theatrical and detestable and wished I had never seen it. Left London at 2 o'clock and by 7 was visiting the sick people in the village.

Thursday, July Morrow

As John Couzens was clipping the turf edges of the lawn and beds he told me how for months while he was at work in this place for us, some years ago now, the Devil had tempted him to destroy himself. It came on first quite suddenly in Parson's Ground by the side of the old lane while he was cutting some flower sticks with a bill hook. He threw himself down on the ground in his misery, got away from his bill hook and at last dozed off. His sleep and appetite went from him, and he had no heart nor comfort in his work. He dared not be alone nor within reach of a knife for fear he should cut his throat. He often brought Alice his wife down to be with him while he was at his work and could only rest quiet at night as long as he had his arm round her, for he feared the devil would come and carry him away. He was utterly miserable and one day he went down on his hands and knees behind the great Portugal laurel bush on the lawn by the copper beech (it is cut down since) and cried and prayed terribly and as if his heart would break. This trouble and temptation lasted some months. He did not know what made it come on suddenly then, for he was in good health and spirits. He believed God sent it. For he began to feel how wicked he had been, cursing and swearing and drinking as a young man. The Devil tempted him to destroy himself because he was so wicked. Once when he went up into the loft to throw down some straw he was tempted to make an end of himself by throwing himself down.

'Master told me not to do anything that he didn't tell me, and not to do anything to myself, but what good were it to tell me that? Mr Headley came here one day and he said to me "Shake it off, John. Shake it off", but what good were that? That were easier said than done. 'Twere easy to say it.' Gradually the trouble and temptation passed away. 'I'm another man now,' he said,

'I've been a different man ever since. But,' he said earnestly, striking his hand upon his shears, 'I wouldn't have any poor creature go through what I went through then, and I wouldn't go through a week of it again for all Squire Ashe's fortune.'

Oh, how little we know of the agonies that are being endured within a few yards of us.

Friday, 3 July

I think continually of Daisy. She is seldom out of my thoughts now. I remember her best and she comes to me most often as I saw her at home in March 1873 when I spent a night at her house. I see even now her beautiful white bosom heaving under the lace edging of her dress, and the loose open sleeve falling back from her round white arm as she leaned her flushed cheek upon her hand looking anxiously at me as I coughed. I see her lean forward and hear the low anxious tone in which she asked, 'Does your cough hurt you?' I see her start up and fetch a lamp shade to keep the light from hurting my eyes. Sweet loving Daisy, sweet loving patient faithful Daisy.

Saturday, 11 July

To-day after 23 years I went to Britford again.

The Vicar has in his house a fine collection of stuffed birds among which are a pair of peregrine falcons which were shot, of all places in the world, on the spire of Salisbury Cathedral. The workmen shot them out of the eight doors at the base of the spire when the steeple was being restored. The Cathedral is generally haunted by peregrines which come from the sea coast cliffs and sit upon the spire whence they can see all the country round and where they think themselves safe. Morris walked with me to the Station in the evening and before us rose the great marvellous spire ever in sight across the flat meadows and beyond the river.

In the town I bought at Decks' a pair of his ten shilling gutta-percha-soled elastic boots.

Tuesday, 28 July

This morning Teddy set up the net and poles in the field just opposite the dining room windows and we began to play 'sphairi-stike' or lawn tennis, a capital game, but rather too hot for a summer's day.

Wednesday, 29 July

Last night the rats most provokingly carried off into their hole the contents of two dishes of apricots which had been gathered yesterday for our croquet party to-day and left on a shelf in the dining-room closet.

When I went to the Farm to drink my whey this morning I told them of our loss. Mrs Knight said that the rats went about overhead at night like race horses, and Mary declared that the walls of their lower cheese-room were lined with rats.

The weather this afternoon was lovely, not too hot, a gentle air moving the silver birch, and bright gleams of sunshine threw beautiful shadows across the lawn and the meadows. The lawn tennis was a successful diversion and afforded a good deal of amusement. About 30 people came, and we were disappointed of some 15.

Wednesday, 5 August

A splendid romp with Polly Tavener.

Thursday, 6 August

I received this evening a wild strange unhappy note from Susan Strange begging me to come and see her as soon as possible. She was worse and in some trouble of mind about herself. She was also troubled about her daughter Fanny who grieves her sadly by frequently lying and stealing. I told her she must correct the girl in time. 'I do flog her,' she said. 'And the other morning she was a naughty girl and her brother Joseph brought her in to me in her shimmy while I was in bed. I held her hands while Joseph and Charlie whipped her on her naked bottom as hard as ever they were able to flog her.'

Friday, 7 August

The pastures are burnt to a whitish livid green very pale and ghastly, but the clouds looked stormy and the sky was bright and lurid and wildly tumbled.

Saturday, 8 August

In the afternoon there was a very good cricket match on the Common between Langley Burrell and the Chippenham 2nd eleven. We were beaten by 2 runs, and up to the last moment it was anybody's match. I scored. Just at the end of the match I got a message from Peckingell that little Fanny Strange had suddenly been taken ill and wanted to see me. I went immediately. The child was in bed upstairs. I sat down by the bed and took her little hot hand. She seemed very feverish but was quite sensible and appeared to be much softened and humbled. If so the severe chastisement she has undergone may have had a happy effect and have broken her self-will and cured her of her faults. Her parents very wisely have not spared her nor the rod.

Monday, 10 August
To-day I went to Worthing to be present at Addie Cholmeley's wedding at Findon to-morrow. I left Chippenham at 10.15. At Salisbury I got into the train with a party of people going to South Sea and on the Island. There was an excellent old-fashioned boy in a chocolate jacket with a shiny peaked cap and a white ruffled frill standing out all round his neck like Punch's dog, a very refreshing sight in these degenerate days.

As we journeyed along the fair Sussex shore between the plain and the sea the gleaners were busy in the golden stubbles, the windmills whirled their arms in the fresh sea breeze, the shocks of corn circling changed places swiftly like a dance of fairies, and Chichester steeple rose fair and white far over the meads.

I thought Worthing Station pretty, light and elegant, with its vandyked glass roofs over the platforms. I drove at once to 11 Church Terrace, Mrs Smallwood's, the lodgings which Adelaide has taken and which she gives up to John Cholmeley and myself while she is at Findon Rectory for 2 days for the wedding. After tea and mutton chops I went out to the beach to view the town and the sea. I walked westward to the end of the esplanade. A heavy wrack of dark cloud drove up from the west promising a stormy night and I turned my solitary steps homeward or lodging-ward. And all the while, sweet Kathleen Mavourneen, thou wert in Worthing and near to me and I knew it not. But then I knew not thee, nor what happiness was in store for me in God's Providence. But had I not been a stricken fool I should have gone to Vaynona and been rewarded by seeing thee there.

Tuesday, 11 August

Addie Cholmeley's wedding day. This may be one of the happiest and most important days in my life, for to-day I fell in love at first sight with sweet Kathleen Mavourneen.

At the time appointed Miss Cholmeley came to the door with her brother Waldo and drove me to Findon, John Cholmeley coming afterwards with his sister Clara (Mrs Heanley). After a pleasant drive of 4 miles the carriage put us down at the Church-yard gate. In the Church we found Robert Heanley, the best man. I took a fancy to him at once for his pleasant frank open face. After we had been waiting in Church for some time he advised me to go out into the porch to watch the bridesmaids arrive and to be made acquainted with the young lady who was to be my companion for the day, I being one of the five groomsmen. So I went, little thinking whom I was to meet, and what a difference it would make to me.

A pretty bevy of bridesmaids was seen coming up the path in white and green. 'There,' said Miss Sarah Cholmeley to me, 'there is your bridesmaid, the tall dark one behind on the right hand side.' They came up and we were introduced. She was a tall handsome girl with very dark hair, eyebrows and eyelashes, and beautiful bright grey eyes, a thin high aristocratic nose, a sweet firm rosy mouth, beautiful white teeth, a well developed chin, a clear complexion and fresh colour. That was Kathleen Mavourneen as I first saw her. I noticed afterwards that she wore pearl earrings.

[The wedding is described.]

In the afternoon almost all the wedding party went up to that fine clump and height of the Downs called Chanctonbury Ring. Part of the way we drove and we walked up the steepest part. Kathleen was still my sweet companion. Under the lee of the clump I spread my coat on the turf and we sat there together on the hillside apart from the rest and looked over the wide and glorious landscape, bright plain and green pasture, blue hill and golden corn and stubble fields, till she could see over rich and variegated plain the white line of the Grand Stand on Epsom Downs some 30 miles away. And there we sat and talked and looked into each other's eyes and there I fell in love and lost my heart to the sweetest noblest kindest bravest-hearted girl in England, Kathleen Mavourneen. Chanctonbury, sweet Chanctonbury, thou wilt always be a green and beautiful spot in my memory. How sweet she was, how simple, kind, unaffected and self-unconscious, how thoughtful for everyone but herself, and so careful lest Montie on his crutches should trip over the roots in the wood. She spoke of her favourite *In Memoriam* and told me some of her difficulties and how deeply she regretted the enforced apparent idleness of her life, and I loved her a hundred times better for her sweet troubled thoughts and honest regretful words.

'I feel,' she said, 'as if I had known you a long time through your letters to Adèle. She used to talk of you a great deal to me. She was very fond of you.' I felt as if our souls were drawing together on the hillside and I thanked God that in His love and mercy He had brought us face to face and made our paths to cross. In His great mercy may they unite and remain one for ever. Oh, that this companionship of a day may grow and ripen into a companionship for life. Several little things happened during the day which led me to hope that she did not dislike me. She asked me to gather her a bunch of purple heather from the hillside. As we were driving home down the steep green down the wind blew cold and fresh as it met her, and she looked so sweet and grateful when I wrapped my coat round her to keep her warm.

When I was talking to Adelaide in her hearing in the drawing room about the Herefordshire wedding to which I was going, Kathleen turned sharply round as if she were pained and did not want me to go. What conceit. As if she cared. But love can live on very slender nourishment.

We came back from Chanctonbury Ring to Findon Rectory to high tea, after which I had a happy hour with Kathleen in the drawing room. She and Jessie Russell asked me to become a member of their Mutual Improvement Society, and we arranged all the details.

When the party broke up and I was returning to Worthing with Mrs Heanley and Miss Penelope Cholmeley, Kathleen kissed her mother fondly at the door and said to me, 'If you are going in my mother's carriage please not to let her talk, it isn't good for her'. Then she took me back into the dining room to shew me one of the pretty ornaments of the wedding cake that I had not seen at breakfast. After which she gave me one of the silver-leaved white orange flowers off the cake, and what I prized more than all she gave me unasked one precious stephanotis flower out of one of the bridal bouquets, a flower that I will keep till we are married if that should be God's will for us, and in any case until I die. At breakfast she had said to me as we rose from table, 'Take care of that cracker, don't let it be lost'. And I have that too and a motto out of one of the crackers which we pulled together and which she gave me to read. We parted with a long close warm clasp of hands that I felt was friendly and hoped might be affectionate.

We had a dark silent drive back to Worthing. No one spoke. We were all full of our own thoughts.

Wednesday, 12 August
In the night there was a torrent of rain but the morning broke clear and beautiful. I went out early into the town before breakfast and walked along the beach. Sea and town and everything were sparkling bright and clean after the storm in the clear shining after the rain. The bathing machines were running down into the sea, the sailors were busy about their boats and nets, and the sailors' wives sat working in the sunshine by their husbands' boats. Children were trooping out on to the beach before breakfast and everything looked bright, cheerful, busy and happy.

After breakfast I parted with John Cholmeley and wrote a note to Adelaide telling her of my love for Kathleen.

I left Worthing at 9.27. How much has happened since I entered it a few short hours ago, and how entirely everything is changed for me. Since I have been in love with Kathleen everything seems bright and beautiful, and I feel that I can love God and man better than I ever could before.

Sunday, 16 August
This morning I had a kind loving letter from Adelaide giving me some hope and encouragement about Kathleen which made me very happy for the rest of the day. I wrote a long letter to her on the same subject.

Friday, 21 August

Went with Dora to Clifton to spend the day with Adelaide at 1 Carlton Place. After an early dinner we went out on to the Clifton down and while the rest of the party accompanied by Anna went down into the slush and mire and darkness of the Giant's Cave, Adelaide and I sat on one of the seats on the edge of the Cliff looking down upon the Suspension Bridge talking of Kathleen Mavourneen. I shall never now see the Suspension Bridge from the Cliff without thinking of Kathleen.

Saturday, 29 August

Dora and I drove into the town and to the station to meet Thersie[1] who came up this evening to stay with us while Monnington Rectory is being prepared for them.

Monday, 31 August

When I went out with Jock this morning to walk across the common before breakfast there as usual were the three white tiddling lambs lying round the white gate. Immediately the three bold white lambs began to play with the black dog, to hunt him about and butt him sportively, while the dog with his ears laid back pretended to be afraid of the lambs, ran away from them, bounded back, faced them and occasionally took one of them by the ear.

I love to wander on these soft gentle mournful autumn days, alone among the quiet peaceful solitary meadows, tracing out the ancient footpaths and mossy overgrown stiles between farm and hamlet, village and town, musing of the many feet that have trodden these ancient and now well nigh deserted and almost forgotten ways and walking in the footsteps of the generations that have gone before and passed away.

The monument to David Ricardo in Harnish Churchyard cost £2000. The design was brought by Mr Ricardo himself from a tomb in Rome. The four figures were supposed to be marble and the price of marble was paid for them, but Francis Hull declares that once when he was set to clean the figures the surface began to shale off, he found they were made of composition and was

---

1. Kilvert's sister Thersie (Thermuthis) was the wife of the Rev. W. R. Smith.

obliged to stop his work. After this discovery the figures were boarded up every winter lest they should be cracked by the frost. The canopy is grey granite. The sculptor, Mr Pitts, destroyed himself afterwards.

Monday, 7 September
Went to the Farm, drank whey in the dairy, paid Jacob Knight £2 2s. for the use of the cricket ground on the Common, and took a game fowl's egg to Elizabeth Knight. As I returned I heard in Greenway Lane the old familiar sound once so common, the sound of the flail on the barn floor. I had not heard it for years. I looked in at the barn door and found a man threshing out his barley.

[After a round of visits Kilvert arrives at Clyro.]

Sunday, 13 September
I asked leave of the Vicar to go to Bettws Chapel this afternoon to preach in the old Chapel once more that I might have an opportunity of seeing some of my dear old friends.

As I came down the deep hollow lane between the Bird's Nest Dingle and Court Evan Gwynne I heard voices of women on the high bank above me coming up the field path home from evening Church. Then my own name struck my ear. 'They do say Mr Gilvert was in Church this morning', said a familiar voice in the dusk. 'Here he is,' I called laughingly from below. It was pretty and touching to see the delight of the women. They stretched their hands down lovingly to clasp mine and seemed as if they would have broken through the hedge in their eagerness and enthusiasm. 'Well,' cried a tall handsome woman, 'well, I did never see such a thing. I was just speaking your name and here you are. I have thought of you,' she added lovingly, 'I have thought of you fresher this week than for a long time. And here you are come.'

Monday, 14 September
Villaging in the morning.

At noon I started with Morrell and the Vicar and Curate (Prickard and Trumper) to walk to Aberedw across the hills. It was one of the loveliest days I ever saw and the mountains were in all their beauty of light and tender blue. We sat to take our luncheon upon the turf of the Beacons beside a tinkling rivulet over against Llanbedr Church. A sweet fresh wind was moving upon the hills and brilliant gleams of green and purple cloud shadows were flying upon the great landscape. In the narrow green sunny lanes the nuts still hung from the hazel tree and a small farmer driving a herd of fat red oxen put us into the right way with the beautiful courtesy of Radnorshire. Below us Bychllyn Pool lay in its hollow like a silver shield and the heather was blooming purple upon the hills. Over the rolling moor rose the pointed cone of Penpicca Hill and we came down into the grand amphitheatre which embosoms the twin valleys and the meeting of the sweet waters of the Edw and the Wye. From Aberedw we walked by the river side and the Nith to Erwood where we took the train to Hay.

Wednesday, 16 September
Visited poor Amy Powell who is in deep grief for the recent loss of her daughter Lizzie. Went to see Gina Beaven, the Mintons, Catherine Williams, Naomi Williams, John, Mrs Thomas, Miss Morgan at the Post Office, Mrs John Powell, Mrs Jones and James Jones at the Infant School, Jones the shoemaker and Caroline Price. In the afternoon I went to see Miss Chaloner, Hannah Whitney, Ada Chaloner, Mrs Williams at the Lower House, old John Morgan the soldier at the Bronith, Mrs Watkeys, and then on to Upper Cabalva. Annie had come down from Llywn Gwillim. Mr Dyke, Willie and Johnnie came home from the sheep fair at Hay, with Mr Wall. Lucretia Wall came down from the Chapel, and we had a merry tea party.

Thursday, 17 September
Went to Llysdinam. I never had a lovelier journey up the lovely valley of the Wye. A tender beautiful haze veiled the distant hills and woods with a gauze of blue and silver and pearl. It was a dream of intoxicating beauty. I saw all the old familiar sights, the broad river reach at Boughrood flashing round the great curve in the sunlight over its hundred steps and rock ledges, the luxuriant woods which fringe the gleaming river lit up here and there by the golden flame of a solitary ash, the castled rock-towers and battlements and bastions of the Rocks of Aberedw, the famous

rocky wooded gorge through the depths of which the narrow mountain stream of the Edw rushed foaming to its Aber to meet the Wye, the house of Pant Shoni gleaming white through the apple-laden orchard trees, the green Castle Mount, Llanvareth Church half hidden by its great dark yew, the sudden bend of the river below Builth, the Yrfon mouth above the little ancient town, and last but not least the grey-towered house of Llysdinam sitting on its green sunny hill backed by dark woods, and looking towards the river and the mountains of the South.

[Kilvert returns to Langley Burrell.]

Thursday, 24 September
This afternoon I walked over to Kington St Michael by Langley Burrell Church and Morrell Lane and the old Mausoleum and Langley Ridge and the Plough Inn. It was a day of exceeding and almost unmatched beauty, one of those perfectly lovely afternoons that we seldom get but in September or October. A warm delicious calm and sweet peace brooded breathless over the mellow sunny autumn afternoon and the happy stillness was broken only by the voices of children blackberry gathering in an adjoining meadow and the sweet solitary singing of a robin.

As I drew near Kington I fell in with a team of red oxen, harnessed, coming home from plough with chains rattling and the old ploughman riding the fore ox, reminding me vividly of the time when I used to ride the oxen home from plough at Lanhill.

In spite of the warm afternoon sunshine the solitary cottages, low-lying on the brook, looked cold and damp, but the apples hung bright on the trees in the cottage gardens and a Virginia creeper burned like fire in crimson upon the wall, crimson among the green. When I returned home at night the good Vicar accompanied me as far as the Plough Inn. The moon was at the full. The night was sweet and quiet. Overhead was the vast fleecy sky in which the moon was riding silently and the stillness was broken only by the occasional pattering of an acorn or a chestnut through the leaves to the ground.

Monday, Michaelmas Eve

This morning I had a kind thoughtful letter from Adelaide from 1 Carlton Place, Clifton, saying she thought it selfish not to let me know that Kathleen Mavourneen is within an hour's journey of me, staying with her, and asking me if I could trust myself to go down and see her and spend a day with her. So I am going and I shall see her again.

Thursday, October Day

This morning I went to Bristol to spend the day with Adelaide and Kathleen Mavourneen at 1 Carlton Place, Clifton. I took Adelaide down a basket of flowers and fruit, plums and grapes, and soon Kathleen Mavourneen was busied arranging the flowers in vases. She was looking very pretty and was most sweet and kind in her manner.

After a heavy storm the weather cleared and we projected a visit to St Mary Redcliffe on my way to the Station. Adelaide, Kathleen, Ella and I went down in a cab, a merry laughing party. The Church is still under repair, the roof of the nave being now nearly restored. The verger said the Church had been under the workmen's hands for the last 45 years, a thousand pounds being spent every year. We struck the sounding pillars near the Confessional, but they do not ring as they did formerly. Kathleen, Ella and I ascended the spiral staircase to the Muniments Room and saw the old wormeaten remnants of the chests in which Chatterton 'the marvellous boy, the sleepless soul that perished in his pride' averred that he had discovered the poems of Rowley the monk.

And there in the great windy dusty room as we looked out through the mullions of the glassless windows over the murky smoky misty city there came a sweet reminiscence of the sunny hillside of Chanctonbury Ring on the afternoon of the Findon wedding day. It was a reminiscence of Sir Walter Raleigh's Cloak which on that day had done good and sweet service, in the carriage and on the turf of the hillside.

Friday, 2 October

Prostrate with neuralgia.

Our ginger plant is now in magnificent blossom, a curious

tendrilled flower like an orchis, and the scent so strong that we have been obliged to turn the plant from the dining into the drawing room and thence into the hall.

Sunday, 4 October
Much better, but still weak.

This morning I had a kind letter from Adelaide from Clifton and Kathleen enclosed some hymns she had copied out for me and some references to passages in our favourite *In Memoriam*.

Monday, 5 October
Hannah Hood uses a curious word for 'gulp'. She says, 'I took two or three "glutches" of port wine'.

This month there is in the *Cornhill Magazine* an article on Crabbe's poetry. My Father says he remembers staying with the Longmires at Wingfield about the year 1830. They took him one afternoon to a book sale at Trowbridge, of which parish the poet Crabbe was then Rector. In the evening the whole party adjourned to the Rectory, where they found Crabbe playing whist with three friends in a large drawing room. Crabbe's son (who was acting as his father's curate) was present, a keen-looking laughable man, an exaggerated likeness of Henry Dew. He came forward to receive the visitors while Crabbe continued his game. My Father describes the poet as being a small plain insignificant-looking old man, bald and with a whitish yellow complexion.

Wednesday, 7 October
For some time I have been trying to find the right word for the shimmering glancing twinkling movement of the poplar leaves in the sun and wind. This afternoon I saw the word written on the poplar leaves. It was 'dazzle'. The dazzle of the poplars.

Saturday, 17 October
This evening I had a kind note from Mrs Heanley enclosing some of Kathleen's Mutual Improvement Questions and Answers and better still a beautiful and thoughtful comparison in dear Kathleen's own words of the views from Clifton Downs and Chanctonbury Ring. Her sweet pure thoughts came to me at a time when I sorely needed them and they have done me much good. But they show me only still more clearly what I have often

felt before, how much nobler and holier her thoughts are than mine, and how much higher she has climbed up the hill than I have done. Yet I am trying to follow, and I thank God that I ever knew her and (I hope I may say) won her friendship. She has indeed been, unconsciously, a good and guardian angel to me. Sweet Kathleen Mavourneen, God bless thee.

Wednesday, 21 October

John Hatherell said he remembered playing football with the men on Sunday evenings when he was a big boy and the Revd Samuel Ashe, the Rector, trying to stop the Sunday football playing. He would get hold of the ball and whip his knife into the bladder, but there was another bladder blown the next minute. 'Well', said the Rector in despair, 'it must go on.'

Friday, 23 October

When the Squire came to see John Hatherell last Sunday he reminded the old man of the nights they patrolled the roads together 45 years ago during the machine-breaking riots. Robert Ashe led a patrol of six men one half the night, and Edward Ashe headed another patrol of equal strength the other half. One night when Robert Ashe was patrolling the village with his men and keeping watch and guard against the machine-breakers and rioters, who were expected from Christian Malford and other villages, he seized by mistake old Mr Eddels, taking him in the dark for a machine-breaker or incendiary. The old man had come out at night in the innocence of his heart to get some straw from his rickyard.

Wednesday, 28 October

This morning we held a family conclave and indignation meeting about the Church singing. At last we resolved that as Mr Ashe has practically dismissed George Jeffries from his post as leader of the singing and rendering it impossible for the singing to go on upon the old footing, we must rather than give up singing in the service have a harmonium or some instrument in the Church, whether he likes it or not. We are prepared to give up the living and leave the place should we be obliged to do so rather than submit any longer to this tyranny. I don't think it will come to this. No such luck as to leave Langley. We should all be better and happier elsewhere, more independent and what is most important of all we should have more self-respect. For my own part I should for many reasons be glad and thankful to go. I don't know how it will end. I suppose I shall stay here as long as my Father lives, no longer.

Thursday, 29 October

At 8.30 this morning we sent the harmonium to the Church on the trucks with John and George and soon after 10 o'clock Fanny and I followed to see where it ought to be placed and hear how it sounded. Though a small instrument it quite filled the Church with sound. We placed it in the Baptistery close by the Font. This morning was an epoch in the history of Langley Church and the first sound of an instrument within the old walls an event and sensation not soon to be forgotten. How this innovation, necessary though it has become, will be received by the Squire no one can tell. He has forced us to do it himself and opened the way for the change by dismissing George Jeffries, the chief singer, from his post of leader of the Church singing, but we expect some violence of language at least.

Carried Annie Savine a rice pudding and some old linen to bind up her face and Elizabeth Bourchier's leg.

Sunday, Allhallowmas Day 1874

All has gone off well. Fanny played the harmonium nicely and the singing was capital. The congregation were delighted and some of them could hardly believe their ears and the Squire said nothing for or against, but he came to Church twice.

Monday, 2 November

By the 12.40 train I went down to Keynsham with my Father on our way to pay a visit to Aunt Emma at Dr Fox's private lunatic asylum at Brislington. The morning was dull, thick and gloomy, threatening rain, but just before we got into Bath a sunbeam stole across the world and lighted the Queen of the West with the ethereal beauty of a fairy city, while all the land blazed gorgeous with the brilliant and many coloured trees. Almost in a moment the dull dark leaden sky was replaced by a sheet of brilliant blue and the lovely city shone dazzling and lustrous upon the hill sides, her palaces veiled with a tender mist and softened by delicate gleams of pearl and blue.

As we walked up from Keynsham to Brislington my Father told me he had heard his grandmother say that she remembered the time in the middle of the 18th century when the only public conveyances were stage waggons. She remembered the stage waggon that plied between Bath and Bristol and spent a whole day on the journey, stopping for dinner at Keynsham, and returning from Bristol to Bath the next day. This same old lady, my great-grandmother, I have heard my Father say, could remember the Royal troops passing through Bath on their way to meet the Young Pretender when he was out in 'the '45'.

Brislington Asylum is a fine palatial-looking building very beautifully situated on the high ground between Keynsham and Bristol, and the grounds are large and well kept. I was glad to see and renew my acquaintance with Mrs Hopton, the matron, who was once housekeeper at Sydney College. She told us that it was a bad day with Aunt Emma who was in unusually good health, therefore more violent and excitable than usual. She asked us to go out into the garden to see her where she was sitting quietly, rather than bring her into the house where she might make a great noise. Mrs Hopton accompanied us out on to a nice large lawn, in which stood a magnificent weeping willow. There was a high ivied wall running round three sides of this lawn and the house bounded it on the fourth.

Aunt Emma was sitting on a low seat in a sunny corner doing some work, with a cat or two cats on her lap. She appeared to me dingily dressed in black and she wore a hideous brown straw mushroom hat. She started up full of her grievances at once but stopping to say to me, 'There is a great friend of yours here. Mrs Hopton has quite lost her heart to you', while poor Mrs Hopton turned round and round and did not know which way to look. Aunt Emma said she had been placed and was kept at Brislington by a conspiracy and by the Government who must all have their heads cut off. She was in daily danger of her life and was cursed and sworn at for a 'damned bitch'. She had just been hunted out of the house like a wild beast. Mrs Bullock and Mrs Ford were in conspiracy against her life, and Dr Charles Fox's. Dr Charles dared

not sleep in his own house for fear of being murdered and he was
obliged to sleep in the asylum every night .

As we walked up and down the lawn, Aunt Emma in the
middle holding each of us by the arm, I heard a strange uproar
proceeding from the house. It sounded at first like a woman's
voice in voluble expostulation and argument, then loud im-
passioned entreaty rising swiftly into wild passionate despairing
cries, which rent the air for some time and then all was still.
When we went into Mrs Hopton's room to have a cup of tea
Aunt Emma accompanied us to the garden door of the house and
knocked loudly and imperiously till a maid servant came. 'I must
go back and collect my work', she said to us. 'I will follow you
directly. Let the door remain unlocked for a few minutes', she
said authoritatively to the servant. 'Very well, Miss', answered
the girl. Presently came a knock at the door of Mrs Hopton's room
where we were at tea. Mrs Hopton rose and went to the door,
then with an astonished look and an angry flush on her face she
threw the door wide open and announced Aunt Emma. 'But', she
muttered aside, 'how did you get in? This is against all rule.' She
went out to reprove the maid for leaving the door unlocked.

'Did you see another lady in the garden when we went out?'
Mrs Hopton asked me. 'No, I saw no one.' 'She saw you and
called you by your Christian name, "Frank Kilvert, Frank
Kilvert". I went to her and got her indoors immediately.' 'But
who is it?' 'Well, you must not let it go any further but her name
is —— ——.' I lifted up my hands in sorrow and amazement. Is it
possible? And were hers those piteous passionate despairing cries
that I heard? Poor child, poor child. If I had only known. Poor
beautiful unfortunate —— ——.

Tuesday, 3 November
This morning between breakfast and luncheon I walked up to
Bowood to see the beeches by way of the Cradle Bridge, Tytherton
Stanley and Studley Hill. I went into Bowood Park by the Studley
Gate and turned sharp to the left down a drive that brought me
soon into the very heart and splendour of the beeches. As the sun
shone through the roof of beech boughs overhead the very air
seemed gold and scarlet and green and crimson in the deep places

of the wood and the red leaves shone brilliant standing out against the splendid blue of the sky. A crowd of wood pigeons rose from the green and misty azure hollows of the plantation and flapped swiftly down the glades, the blue light glancing off their clapping wings. I went by the house down to the lakeside and crossed the water by the hatches above the cascade. From the other side of the water the lake shone as blue as the sky and beyond it rose from the water's edge the grand bank of sloping woods glowing with colours, scarlet, gold, orange and crimson and dark green. Two men were fishing on the further shore of an arm of the lake and across the water came the hoarse belling of a buck while a coot fluttered skimming along the surface of the lake with a loud cry and rippling splash.

To eye and ear it was a beautiful picture, the strange hoarse belling of the buck, the fluttering of the coot as she skimmed the water with her melancholy note, the cry of the swans across the lake, the clicking of the reels as the fishermen wound up or let out their lines, the soft murmur of the woods, the quiet rustle of the red and golden drifts of beech leaves, the rush of the waterfall, the light tread of the dappled herd of deer dark and dim glancing across the green glades from shadow into sunlight and rustling under the beeches, and the merry voices of the Marquis's children at play.

Why do I keep this voluminous journal? I can hardly tell. Partly because life appears to me such a curious and wonderful thing that it almost seems a pity that even such a humble and uneventful life as mine should pass altogether away without some such record as this, and partly too because I think the record may amuse and interest some who come after me.

Wednesday, 4 November
This evening I had my first Wednesday winter evening service and lecture at the school and reviewed the events of the last seven months, the funeral of Dr Livingstone, the visit of the Czar, the Spanish war, the Thorpe railway disaster, the explosion of benzaline and gunpowder on the Regent's Park Canal, the Bengal Famine, shipwrecks and collisions at sea, the *Cherson*, the *Candahar* and *Kingsbridge*, etc.

Sunday, 8 November

At Morning Church there was a pleasant sight. Vincent, the Langley Burrell policeman, who is not often able to attend service was there with all his sons and amongst them Frank the fine handsome young dragoon in his bright scarlet uniform home on furlough.

After morning service Dora went out to Mr Ashe in the churchyard and asked him to head the subscription list to buy a new harmonium. He said that neither he nor any of his household should give a farthing for he disapproved of any music in a church beside the human voice and he also apprehended a chronic difficulty in finding some one to play the instrument. I walked from church with dear Sarah Hicks to her house at the Pound. 'Oh', she said earnestly, with indignant tears swelling in her beautiful large dark eyes, 'oh, it's a comfort to know that there's a time coming when no one will be able to reign over us and when we shall be as good as those who are so high and proud over us now.' Patience, dear Sarah, patience a little while longer. And then ——

Monday, 9 November, Teddy's birthday

Dora went to the Woods and to the John Knights' this morning collecting subscriptions for the harmonium. Mr Wood was from home, but the Knights came forward most handsomely. Every member of the family at home put down his or her name and the sum of their contributions amounted to a guinea. I was greatly touched for I know it is quite as much as they can afford. This afternoon I went to the Barrow with the subscription paper and left it there. When I stated that the Squire had declined to give anything young John Bryant burst into a scornful laugh. The Churchwarden took his eldest son Tom aside to the window to look over the subscription list in the fading light and promised to return it to-morrow. Alice Couzens volunteered sixpence and said that other cottagers would like to help.

Tuesday, 10 October

The subscription list was returned from the Barrow at breakfast time this morning signed with the names of almost all the Bryant family, their subscriptions amounting in all to £1. This is very kind and liberal for they are not rich and they have had heavy losses this summer, three cows amongst the rest. Called on the Lawrences to ask for a subscription for the harmonium. They were very kind and readily gave me 12/6. Then Mrs Lawrence burst forth with a harangue and her views upon Church Music. 'I like the music in Church. I don't like everything to be so melancholy, melancholy. I had rather hear a good whistle in Church than nothing. I knew two young ladies who whistled beautifully a first and a second. No, they didn't whistle in Church.'

Wednesday, 11 November. Martinmas Day

We are in trouble at the school now because a few days ago Mr Ashe came angrily in to Miss Bland the schoolmistress and ordered her always to keep all three windows and the door of the schoolroom open during schooltime, except in very cold weather when one window might be shut. He said in a fierce determined way. 'This is my school and I will have my word attended to. If you don't do as I tell you, Miss Bland, instead of being your friend I'll be your enemy'. What a speech for an elderly clergyman. It is almost incredible. And there are the poor little children crying with the cold. Cruel. Barbarous. And of course the parents are indignant and the numbers of the children falling off.

Thursday, 12 November

Mrs Banks said the Squire had been very unkind to her. He had sent her some rough notes about the cream being bad and complained fiercely of the pigs straying into the woods.

This evening in reply to my letter to Llysdinam I got a most kind letter from Mrs Venables enclosing £2.2 for our harmonium, £1 from herself, 10/- from Mrs Henry Venables, 6/- from dear little Katie, and Mr Venables who got the P.O.O. made the money even. What a difference in the spirit and atmosphere of Llysdinam and Langley House.

Monday, 16 November

This afternoon I called at Rawlings for the Matthews' subscription to the harmonium, 10/- heartily given and more cordially offered if wanted. Alice Matthews said quaintly, 'How strange it is that the Squire is such a distant man about music'.

Thursday, 19 November

At last the new harmonium has come. Mr Rooke the maker
brought it up from Weymouth to-day. Our churchwarden Jacob
Knight, his uncle Thomas Knight, and his cousin Ralph Knight
and I assembled at the Church between one and two o'clock and
there we had to wait an hour and half before the harmonium
came up from the Station in a low cart under the care of Mr
Rooke, our John, and one of the Company's men.

At last the harmonium hove in sight and with a long pull and
strong pull and a pull all together we carried it from the road to
the porch and there unpacked it. The instrument was placed in a
little seat behind the pillar at the west end of the Church where
by taking out the back of the seat we made a little chamber for
it.

Sunday, 22 November

A raw cold foggy frosty morning and to-day we had the first
fire in Church. The Squire came in with Mrs Ashe and Syddie as
usual, but as soon as he saw or smelt the fire in the stove he
turned round and went hastily out again. This morning our new
harmonium was played in Church for the first time. It is a beautiful instrument with a soft sweet tone and Fanny managed it very
well. I think the people were pleased and Mrs Ashe and Syddie
whom we saw after the service said they liked the instrument
very much. The singing of the Choir and the congregation in the
Old Hundredth Psalm and the Trinity Hymn was especially good
and hearty.

Tuesday, 24 November

In the afternoon I walked over to Kington St Michael to see the
sick Vicar. He was better and downstairs in the drawing room.
He was as full of life and fun as ever and told me he had heard his
mother say that my great-great-grandmother, old Mrs Martyn of
Kennet, once sent to my great-grandmother, Mrs Ashe of Langley
Burrell, her daughter, a pair of earrings by broad-wheeled
waggon, the only public conveyance in those days.

Tuesday, December Day

My Mother writes from Monnington that William had just been at a clerical meeting at Mr Phillott's, the Rector of Stanton-on-Wye, and came back not very deeply impressed by the brilliancy of some of the Herefordshire Clergy.

She mentions too a story which seems almost incredible but which she states is well known to be true. Mr Ormerod, the Rector of Presteign, who has a living of £1000 a year but who is nevertheless always over head and ears in debt, has every Sunday two Celebrations of the Holy Communion at which he always puts upon the plate his pocket knife by way of alms, saying that he has no change. After service he returns his knife to his pocket, but (it is stated) invariably forgets to *redeem* it.

Friday, 4 December

As we went down to Lacock last evening we fell in with Mr Roach the Vicar standing at his gate. He walked into the village with us saying he was cold and sorrowful, for his daughter had just returned from Chippenham with the sad news that in the terrible gale of last Sunday morning the *La Plata* telegraph cable-laying ship foundered after springing a leak and went down off Ushant in the Bay of Biscay with sixty souls, amongst whom was the Captain of the ship, Captain Dudden, who married poor Georgia Spencer. The Spencers are in deep grief and they dare not tell the poor young widow of her loss as she is expecting her first child and very delicate. It is very remarkable that Captain Dudden sailed on this fatal voyage with a strong and sad reluctance, weighed down by a dark and sorrowful presentiment that he would never return. He made his poor young wife promise that she would not look at a newspaper till after her confinement and he told Lloyd's agent if and when the ship went down to telegraph, not to his wife, but to his father-in-law at Chippenham. Yet then there was no presage of a storm.

Thursday, 10 December

In consequence of an invitation from Adelaide Cholmeley I went to Bristol this morning and spent a happy merry day with her and Ella and Jessie Russell who is staying with them at 1 Carlton Place. Adelaide was very kind and encouraged me very much about matters in Lincolnshire. She said, 'Katie likes you very much'. Katie, dear Katie, wanted very much to write to me and could not understand why she should not. 'Why,' she said, remonstrating with her Mother, 'Jessie writes to him.' Dear Katie, she is as brave and true as steel. Well, patience, patience, hope and wait. The course of true love never did run smooth. But I do long and yearn to see her again. Adelaide has brought back from Lincolnshire a charming vignette of Katie. It is a grand, noble face, very handsome and something much better than handsome. Adelaide lent me her old photograph of Katie in her riding dress to go on a long visit to Langley.

Jessie Russell is a capital girl, nice, bright, lively and amusing and perfectly unaffected. After our early dinner she, Ella and I went for a walk over the Suspension Bridge along the edge of Nightingale Valley and through the Leigh Woods beautiful even in winter. Adelaide was obliged to stay at home with a cold. It was a bright frosty day and we had a merry happy walk, Jessie in fits of laughter at the story of my visit to the young ladies' school in Great George St when the Lady Principal was horrified to discover that I was not as she had thought 'quite an old gentleman'. Reached home at 7 o'clock in time for the night school, bringing our children a cocoa nut to their great delight.

Saturday, 12 December

There is a beauty in the trees peculiar to winter, when their fair delicate slender tracery unveiled by leaves and showing clearly against the sky rises bending with a lofty arch or sweeps gracefully drooping. The crossing and interlacing of the limbs, the smaller boughs and tender twigs make an exquisitely fine network which has something of the severe beauty of sculpture, while the tree in summer in its full pride and splendour and colour of foliage represents the loveliness of painting. The deciduous trees which seem to me most graceful and elegant in winter are the birches, limes, beeches.

Monday, 14 December

This evening at 5 o'clock I took 21 of our schoolchildren into Chippenham to the Temperance Hall to see a Panorama of the African travels of Dr Livingstone. One of the most favourite pictures with the children was the Funeral of Dr Livingstone in Westminster Abbey. The Abbey was first shown empty. Then by a slight dioramic effect or dissolving view the open space in the Nave gradually melted into the forms of the funeral party, Dean Stanley reading the service and the mourners grouped round the flower wreath-covered coffin.

Thursday, 17 December
This morning after long suspense and waiting we were thankful to receive the happy news that dear Thersie was safely confined of a fine boy at Monnington Rectory at 10 p.m. Tuesday, 15th December. Thank God for this and all His mercies.

Tuesday, 22 December
Mrs John Knight tells me that the Malmesbury people are commonly called 'Jackdaws', to their intense disgust. It is a common saying among folks going to Malmesbury, 'Let us go and see the Malmesbury Jackdaws'. I remember hearing many years ago, I think among the people of Kington St Michael, that jackdaws are often called in these parts 'The Parsons from Malmesbury Abbey'. Perhaps the grey polls of the birds may have suggested the shaven polls of the monks, or the thievish habits of the jackdaws may have called to remembrance some tradition of the rapacity of the Abbot of Malmesbury.

Thursday, Christmas Eve
Writing Christmas letters all the morning. In the afternoon I went to the Church with Dora and Teddy to put up the Christmas decorations. Dora has been very busy for some days past making the straw letters for the Christmas text. Fair Rosamund and good Elizabeth Knight came to the Church to help us and worked heartily and well. They had made some pretty ivy knots and bunches for the pulpit panels and the ivy blossoms cleverly whitened with flour looked just like white flowers.

The churchwarden Jacob Knight was sitting by his sister in front of the roaring fire. We were talking of the death of Major Torrens on the ice at Corsham pond yesterday. Speaking of people slipping and falling on ice the good churchwarden sagely remarked, 'Some do fall on their faces and some do fall on their rumps. And they as do hold their selves uncommon stiff do most in generally fall on their rumps.'

I took old John Bryant a Christmas packet of tea and sugar and raisins from my Mother. The old man had covered himself almost entirely over in his bed to keep himself warm, like a marmot in its nest. He said, 'If I live till New Year's Day I shall have seen ninety-six New Years.' He said also, 'I do often see things flying about me, thousands and thousands of them about half the size of a large pea, and they are red, white, blue and yellow and all colours. I asked Mr Morgan what they were and he said they were the spirits of just men made perfect.'

Saturday, S. Stephen's Day
This morning, soon after breakfast, Lucy Halliday came up to ask me to go and see Hannah Williams as she was worse. I went immediately and found her in a sad state of suffering. The proud haughty beautiful face was laid low at last and flushed with pain, the thick black hair contrasting vividly with the white pillow as the poor child tossed her shapely head, rolling wearily from side to side seeking, seeking rest, and finding none. Then for a minute she lay silent with closed eyes and flushed cheek buried in the pillows, and then once more began the bitter pain and the weary moaning. 'Oh, mother, oh, mother.' Her father knelt at the foot of the bed holding her feet tenderly, for the agony was in her legs and feet. Last Wednesday night while carrying a bucket of water from the well she slipped upon the icy path and fell heavily upon her back. We fear her spine was injured for though she suffers acute pain in her legs she cannot move them. The poor wild beautiful girl is stopped in her wildness at last, and perhaps by the finger of God.

I saw Hannah Williams again this afternoon and sat awhile by her bedside repeating the Evening Hymn 'Sun of my soul'.

This evening Teddy left us to return to London. A sharp frost, the stars brilliant and the roads glassed with ice. I went with him to the white gate where we parted and I turned off across the dark icy fields towards the village to try to read Hannah Williams to sleep. She had sunk to sleep two minutes before I got there, said her mother, coming noiselessly and gratefully to the head of the stairs. The light shone through the night from the sick girl's chamber window, the night was still, an owl hooted out of the South and the mighty hunter Orion with his glittering sword silently overstrode the earth.

Sunday, Childermas Eve

Before I went to Church this morning I went to see Hannah Williams. Before I reached the cottage I heard the poor girl's distressing moans. They were moving her in her bed and it was heartrending to hear her. After tea I went to see Hannah and try to read the poor child to sleep. I stayed there an hour or more turning her in bed every quarter of an hour. She says I turn her and lift her better than any one else.

Monday, Childermas Day

To-day we heard by a short telegram of the awful calamity of the burning of the emigrant ship *Caspatria* near the Cape of Good Hope bound for New Zealand. Four hundred and forty persons burnt in her. One boat reached St Helena with three survivors who had lived on the flesh of their companions.

I went to see Hannah Williams. The inflammatory rheumatism has gone partly out of her legs but her poor hands are now in fiery agonizing pain. She can bear them in almost boiling water. I talked to her very seriously about her past wild conduct since her Confirmation, and prayed with her. Then I read her the May Queen, New Year's Eve, the Conclusion, the Miller's Daughter, and St Agnes Eve, hoping to read her to sleep, but in vain.

I met the doctor (Mr Spencer) here this morning. He told me he had feared at first inflammation of the spinal cord which might have carried Hannah off in 48 hours.

Thursday, New Year's Eve

Edwin Law told me of an infallible receipt for warming cold and wet feet on a journey. Pour half a glass of brandy into each boot. Also he often carries a large pair of stockings with him to wear over boots and trousers. He has been a long time in Nova Scotia.

My mother and I sat up by the dining room fire to watch the Old Year out and the New Year in. Soon after eleven o'clock the Chippenham bells began pealing and continued to ring at intervals till after midnight. The wind had veered into the South and brought the sound of the bells to us very distinct and sweet across the river, so that we could plainly hear when they began and paused and all the change-ringing and the firing of the bells. At a quarter to twelve I began to think earnestly of dear Katie and to pray for her. I knew she would be watching, praying and thinking of me. I had laid before me on my desk the photograph of her in her riding habit and the New Year's card I had just received from her. She seemed to be very near me. I felt her love all round me and I was very happy. My last thoughts and prayers in the Old Year 1874 were for her.

1875

Friday, New Year's Day

I went across to Hannah Williams. I had not seen her for two days and there was a brilliant look of glad welcome on the proud beautiful face, as the wistful dark eyes seemed to say, 'Where have you been? I thought you had forgotten me.'

Sunday, 3 January

One New Year's Day Mr Rich, the Vicar of Chippenham, was administering the Holy Communion when a poor man taking the Chalice into his hand wished the Vicar 'A Happy New Year'.

Tuesday, 12 January

John Hatherell told me this evening that he recollects when a boy being one of the bearers at the burial of a gipsy girl 12 years of age. He had forgotten her name but we looked in the parish registers and found the entry of the funeral. The girl's name was 'Limpedy Buckland'. She was buried in Langley Burrell Church-yard in the year 1809 on the 29th of April. She died in the tents of her people in Sutton Lane opposite the gate of Sand Furlong. The road was then a green lane. When John and the other lads who were to be bearers reached the tents of the tribe they found a clean white cloth laid upon the green grass with bread, cheese, and beer, and an old woman, the mother or grandmother of the dead girl, put her hand into her pocket and gave each of the bearer lads a shilling. Then the lads carried the girl to her grave and a white sheet was thrown over the coffin. Limpedy Buckland the gipsy girl was buried in the south-eastern corner of the church-yard under the great yew.

Hannah Hatherell said she well remembered old Constant Smith the gipsy. Probably this was 'Constance Smith a gipsy', the mother of 'Muperella' whose burial appears in the registers of Langley Burrell. Hannah also remembers well old Ted Buckland the gipsy who murdered Judy Pearce at the lone house between Sutton and Seagry, since called Murder Cottage on that account.

This Ted Buckland used to go about wrapped in a white blanket girt about his waist with a girdle and pinned together over his chest with a skewer. My mother saw him brought to my grandfather's house at Langley Fitzurse after the murder in this same costume.

William Ferris told me to-day his reminiscences of the first train that ever came down the Great Western Railway. 'I was foddering', he said, 'near the line. It was a hot day in May some 34 or 35 years ago, and I heard a roaring in the air. I looked up and thought there was a storm coming down from Christian Malford roaring in the tops of the trees, only the day was so fine and hot. Well, the roaring came nigher and nigher, then the train shot along and the dust did flee up.'

Thursday, 14 January

I went to see――. She was sitting alone upstairs in her bedroom. She had finished her last book this morning and I brought her some more. I thought there was a softened and more affectionate look in her face and eyes, as she spoke to me. I was begging her earnestly to try to be more steady in her conduct when she got well and saying how deeply grieved I should be were she to become wild and wilful again. Taking her hand and looking earnestly and lovingly upon her I said, 'You do like me a little bit, don't you?' A loving light came into the girl's beautiful face and eyes. 'Yes,' she said impulsively, 'a great deal.'

'Dear child, and I do love you so much. I have loved you through it all. It has not been always with you quite as it should have been, has it, dear?' She dropped her eyes sadly and penitently. 'No,' she whispered in a low voice. 'But you will try to be good and steady now, dear, won't you? I do so want you to be a good girl.' 'I will try,' she said humbly but firmly.

Friday 15 January

Speaking to the children at the school about the Collect for the 2nd Sunday after the Epiphany and God's peace I asked them what beautiful image and picture of peace we have in the xxxiii Psalm. 'The Good Shepherd,' said I, 'leading His sheep to –?' 'To the slaughter,' said Frederick Herriman promptly. One day I asked the children to what animal our Saviour is compared in the Bible. Frank Matthews confidently held out his hand. 'To an ass,' he said.

Saturday, 16 January

In the Common Field in front of the cottages I found two little figures in the dusk. One tiny urchin was carefully binding a handkerchief round the face of an urchin even more tiny than himself. It was Fred and Jerry Savine. 'What are you doing to him?' I asked Fred. 'Please, Sir,' said the child solemnly. 'Please, Sir, we'm gwine to play at blindman's buff.' The two children were quite alone. The strip of dusky meadow was like a marsh and every footstep trod the water out of the soaked land, but the two little images went solemnly on with their game as if they were in a magnificent playground with a hundred children to play with. Oh, the wealth of a child's imagination and capacity for enjoyment of trifles.

Wednesday, 20 January

I went to luncheon to-day at Langley House to meet Mence who came there last Monday. I have not been inside the doors of Langley House since last July, and then I went there unasked to get the Squire's subscription for the cricket club.

Thursday, 21 January

I went round the premises late at night to see if the outhouses were locked up. All was still and the white pig lying in the moonlight at the door of his house, fast asleep, with the moon shining on his white face and round cheek.

Saturday, 23 January

When I went to bed last night I fancied that something ran in at my bedroom door after me from the gallery. It seemed to be a skeleton. It ran with a dancing step and I thought it aimed a blow at me from behind. This was shortly before midnight.

Septuagesima Sunday, 24 January

Last night I dreamt I saw a great whale caught in Weymouth Bay. I watched the huge dark bulk heave and tumble in the sea.

Then the boats put out with harpoons and lances. The battle raged and drifted out of sight of the dream, but the bay was crimson with blood.

Saturday, 30 January

I dined at Langley House. It is a long time since I dined there, more than a year I think. Syddie was looking lovely. Thersie dined with us and Syddie came in to dessert. The Squire appeared in the drawing room before dinner in a long grey dressing gown, took Mrs Money Kyrle down and dined at a little table by himself, joining however in the talk. Colonel Money Kyrle took the foot of the table. After the ladies had left us we sat before the fire over a bottle of '51 port discussing the Prayer Book Dissenters till nearly 10.30. I took Thersie down to dinner. We had a woodcock which had been shot in the Marsh by the Squire.

Tuesday, Candlemas Day

I went to see Benjamin Hawkins. 'The times were much harder for poor folk when I was a lad, let people say what they will,' said Benjamin. Sometimes when an outstanding field rick was threshed or brought into the barn the shepherd or carter had the privilege of planting a few potatoes there and he was so overjoyed with his good fortune that he thought he had got a small farm. There was no such thing known then as planting potatoes in the field, and this made every foot of the garden ground so precious that people could not spare room for flowerbeds. Some of the old women would have a flower border and raise a few pinks and roses and a little thyme and lad's love, make up the flowers into knots and nosegays, and sell them at a halfpenny apiece. The lads would buy them and stick them in their hats on Sundays. Nosegays were very much sought after. Benjamin thought the new law compelling boys to go to school till they are 12 years old a bad law, unjust and hard upon the parents.

Friday 5 February

My mother tells us that when she was a little child of three or four years old she was sent every morning with a nurse from her father's house at Langley Fitzurse to the village school kept by Dame Fairlamb at the Pound, Langley Burrell, in the cottages where old blind Thomas Jefferies lived and died. My mother was not allowed to play with the village children but when school was over she was taken home by the nurse. Dame Fairlamb was one of the real old fashioned dames, severe and respectable with rod and spectacles. Afterwards my Mother went to the Moravian school at East Tytherton daily on a donkey which she urged forward by rattling a bunch of keys in his ear.

Shrove Tuesday, 9 February

Dined at the Paddocks. People were talking about Mr Torrens' will (late of Corsham) which left £70,000 between his butler and housekeeper. Some remarks were passed too upon a set of verses that appeared in the *Devizes Gazette* upon the Chippenham Ball, author unknown and the tone of the verses low.

Friday, 12 February

I went to see old Sally Killing. She is very comfortable and contented now sitting in her cosy chimney corner, with Aileen for her lady's maid. Aileen told me of the sad uneven marriage at St Paul's Church, Chippenham, last week, the daughter of the clergyman of [—] married to her father's groom with whom, unknown to her parents, she had been keeping company for *five* years. But how without her parents' knowledge? The groom's sister made the young lady's dresses and the groom used to drive the young lady to see her dressmaker. A sad story.

Sunday, St Valentine's Day

Shortly after noon to-day, at the time the folk were coming out of morning Church, the village Patriarch old John Bryant quietly ended his long earthly pilgrimage and passed away from amongst us, we hope and trust to a better country. The old man died very calmly and peacefully like a little child falling asleep. He was baptized July 30th, 1780, but he was probably born in 1779.

Monday, St Valentine's Morrow

The Miss Mascalls were justly indignant and amazed that Mrs Prodgers and her children should have been introduced into the new painted east window in Kington St Michael's Church, 'Suffer little children to come unto me'. Mrs Prodgers and her children actually sat for their likenesses and she is introduced as one of the mothers, in the most prominent position. The whole thing is the laughing stock of the village and countryside.

Tuesday, 16 February

Miss Bryant told me that her grandmother, Miss Buy of Langley Brewery, asked her grandfather George Bryant to marry her, and bitterly repented it afterwards. George Bryant was a very fine handsome man and Miss Buy said to him, 'Why do you go courting a woollen apron when you might have a muslin apron?'

Thursday, 4 March

Old William Halliday told me he had heard from the old people of Allington and especially from the Taverners, when he was young, strange tales of ancient times and how the world was once full of 'witches, weasels (wizards) and wolves'. Old William also told the story of how old Squire Sadler Gale of Bulwich House at Allington made himself wings and flew off the garden wall. 'Watch I vlee!' he cried to the people. Then he dashed down into the horsepond.

Saturday, 6 March

A sudden and blessed change in the weather, a S.W. wind, pouring warm rain, and the birds in the garden and orchard singing like mad creatures, the whole air in a charm and tumult of joy and delight.

Thursday, 11 March

It was a fine clear starry night and the young moon was shining brightly. Near the school I overtook a lad of eighteen walking slowly and wearily, who asked me how far it was to Sutton. He said he had walked down to-day from Broad Hinton, 7 miles the other side of Swindon. He was seeking work and could find none. He was very tired, he said, and he seemed downcast and out of spirits. He had just asked the Sutton baker to give him a lift in his trap, promising to give him a pint of beer, but the baker surlily bade him keep his beer to himself and refused to pull up and take the lad in, giving him leave however to hang on behind the trap from Broad Somerford to Seagry. He had tried to get a bed at Somerford but the inn was full of navvies who are making the new railroad to Malmesbury from Dauntesey.

There was no room for him in the inn. I thought it might encourage and cheer the lad up if I kept company along the road to Sutton so we walked together and I showed him the short cut across the fields. As we went we fell into talk and the lad began to be confidential and to tell me something of his story. It was a simple touching tale. 'I was born', said the lad, 'at a little village near here called Corston, but I have been knocking about the country looking for work. I have some aunts in Corston.' 'But have you no father or mother?' I asked. The simple chance question touched a heart still tender and bruised with a great sorrow and opened the floodgates of his soul. The lad suddenly burst into tears. 'My Mother was buried to-day,' he sobbed. 'I walked up to Broad Hinton yesterday, to try to get work, for my stepfather would not keep me any longer and I could get no work in Corston. I would have stayed to follow my mother to the grave but I had no black clothes except a jacket and couldn't get any. She was the best friend I had in the world and the only one. I was with her when she died. She said I had better die too along with her for I should only be knocked about in a hard world and there would be no one to care for me. And I've found her words true and thought upon them often enough already,' added the poor boy bitterly with another burst of heart-broken tears.

'My name is Henry Estcourt Ferris,' the lad went on, in answer to some questions of mine. 'My father's name is Estcourt. He is a labouring man working in Wales as a boiler maker. He ran away from my Mother and forsook her six months before I was born. My Mother's maiden name', said the poor boy with some hesitation, 'was Ellen Ferris.' Alas, the old, old story. Trust misplaced, promises broken, temptation, sin and sorrow, and the sins of the parents visited upon the children. When we got to Sutton we went to three places, two inns and a private lodging house, to try to get the lad a bed. A villager in the street told us of the lodging house, but everywhere the lad was refused a bed and from each house in succession he turned wearily and hopelessly away with a faint protest and remonstrance and a lingering request that the good people would please to try if they could not put him up, but in vain, and we plodded on again towards Chippenham where he knew he could get a bed at the Little George. The poor fellow was very humble and grateful. 'I shouldn't have been near so far along the road as this, if it hadn't been for you, Sir,' he said gratefully. 'You've kind of livened and 'ticed me along.' I cheered him up as well as I could and gave him a bit of good advice. He hoped to get a place at Chippenham Great Market to-morrow. The lights of Langley Fitzurse shone brightly through the dark night. ''Tis a long road,' said the lad wearily. At the Hillocks stile we parted at length with a clasp of the hand and a kindly 'Goodbye' and I saw the last, for ever probably in this world, of the motherless boy.

Friday, 19 March

I was very much annoyed this evening by a note from Marion Vaughan saying that my last letter to Netta had been forwarded by Matilda to her at the C.D.S. at Bristol, that Miss Winter had opened the letter, read it, refused to give it to Netta, and then laid it before the Committee, and that the Honorary Secretary had written to Mr Vaughan saying that if Netta continued to receive letters from me he must withdraw her from the school.

Easter Tuesday, 30 March

As I walked up and down our drive within the white gate in the fresh mild evening shortly before 8 o'clock I saw through the trees a light from the Manor House nearly half a mile away. The light was obscured continually, apparently by the figures passing before it, and it seemed to come from the dining-room where the Squire was at dinner and probably the constant darkening of the light was produced by the maids writing at table and passing every moment almost between the window and the lights on the table.

Wednesday, April Eve

This evening Teddy left us and went back to London. I walked down with him to the station. He went up by a broad gauge train and in the smoking carriage, the atmosphere of which I could not have endured for a minute and could hardly bear to stand near the door even.

Monday, 5 April

Left Langley for Monnington-on-Wye with Dora. William met us at Moorhampton with the dog cart and chestnut horse Paddy, and drove us to Monnington. I like the look of the place very much. The house is large and comfortable and the situation pretty, roomy and pleasant. One great feature of the place is the famous 'Monnington Walk', a noble avenue of magnificent Scotch firs bordering a broad green ride, stretching from Brobury Scar (a red sandstone precipice beetling over the winds of Wye) to Monnington Court House, where the aunt of Owen Glendower lived.

Tuesday, 6 April

When I awoke a woodpigeon was crooning from the trees near the house and the early morning sunshine glinted upon the red boles of the gigantic Scotch firs in Monnington Walk. I rose early and went out. The morning was fresh and bright with a slight sunshiny shower flying. Hard by the Church porch and on the western side of it I saw what I knew must be the grave of Owen Glendower. It is a flat stone of whitish grey shaped like a rude obelisk figure, sunk deep into the ground in the middle of an oblong patch of earth from which the turf has been pared away, and, alas, smashed into several fragments. And here in the little Herefordshire churchyard within hearing of the rushing of the Wye and close under the shadow of the old grey church the strong wild heart, still now, has rested by the ancient home and roof tree of his kindred since he fell asleep there more than four hundred years ago. It is a quiet peaceful spot.

In the afternoon Thersie, Dora, Florence and I called at Monnington Court and were kindly received by the worthy Churchwarden farmer and his wife, Mr and Mrs James, who showed us the fine old oak carving and the banqueting room. In the garden of the Court House was dug up a few days ago a huge silver coin which Mr James showed us and which looked to me like a crown of Charles I. On one side of the coin was a king crowned, armed and mounted. Mr James went with us to the Church which is light and pleasant and cheerful within and seemed well cared for. He told us that in the great flood of February 6, 1852, he and the present Sir Gilbert Lewis of Harpton (then Rector of Monnington), had punted in a flat-bottomed boat across the Court garden, in at the Church door, up the Nave and into the Chancel.

Thursday, 8 April

A sad accident lately befell the poor strange Solitary, the Vicar of Llanbedr Painscastle. He was sitting by the fire in his little lone hut at Cwm Cello that lies in the bosom of Llanbedr Hill when he either dropped heavily asleep or had a fit and fell full upon the fire. Before he could recover himself his stomach, bowels and thighs were dreadfully burnt, and he has had to stay away from Church for three Sundays. Yet he will let neither doctor nor nurse come near him. The poor solitary. He used to visit Sarah Bryan kindly and assiduously when she lay a-dying and was a great and lasting comfort to her. She died very happy.

Tuesday, 13 April

I had not been in Builth since that memorable day to me, May 29th, 1865, the day never to be forgotten when I walked alone over the hills from Clyro to Builth and first saw the Rocks of Aberedw, the day I first saw Painscastle and the ruined Church of Llanbedr, and the morning sun shining like silver upon Llanbychllyn Pool, and descended from the great moor upon the vale of Edw and saw, in the orchard of the newly yellow-thatched cottage near the Court Mills, the two beautiful chestnut-haired girls at play with the children under the apple boughs. Then every step was through an enchanted land. I was discovering a new country and all the world was before me. How different it is now, just ten years afterwards. But then there was a glamour and enchantment about the first view of the shining slate roofs of Builth and the bridge and the winding reaches of the broad and shining river which even now cling about the place and have never quite been dispelled. A strange fascination, a beautiful enchantment hangs over Builth and the town is magically transfigured still.

Oh, Aberedw, Aberedw. Would God I might dwell and die by thee. Memory enters in and brings back the old time in a clear vision and waking dream, and again I descend from the high moor's half encircling sweep and listen to the distant murmur of the river as it foams down the ravine from its home in the Green Cwm and its cradle in the hills. Once more I stand by the riverside and look up at the cliff castle towers and mark the wild roses swinging from the crag and watch the green woods waving and shimmering with a twinkling dazzle as they rustle in the breeze and shining of the summer afternoon, while here and there a grey crag peeps from among the tufted trees. And once again I hear the merry voices and laughter of the children as they clamber down the cliff path among the bushes or along the rock ledges of the riverside or climb the Castle Mount, or saunter along the narrow green meadow tree-fringed and rock-bordered and pass in and out of Llewellyn's cave, or gather wood and light the fire amongst the rocks upon the moor, or loiter down the valley to Cavan Twm Bach and cross the shining ferry at sunset, when the evening shadows lie long and still across the broad reaches of the river. Oh, Aberedw, Aberedw.

Holy Thursday, 6 May

John Couzens says he is very fond of dry bread, as dry and hard as he can get it. 'When I was out mowing,' he said, 'I used to throw my wallet and my victuals on the swath and let the sun *bless it* from bait to bait. I wanted it all crust.'

Expectation Sunday, 9 May

I went out late last night to lock the white gate. The wind had dropped and all was still, save for the occasional slow dripping of the trees after the last heavy shower. Against the clean bright sky every leaf and twig stood out with marvellous distinctness, and as I approached the gate the moonlight streamed in up the avenue, dark with foliage, from the wide empty open Common, like moonlight streaming into a dark house through an open door. The ground was still wet and shining with the rain, and the gigantic shadow of the gate projected by the moonlight was cast far up the avenue in huge bars upon the shining ground.

Monday 24 May

This afternoon I walked over to Lanhill. As I came down from the hill into the valley across the golden meadows and along the flower-scented hedges a great wave of emotion and happiness stirred and rose up within me. I know not why I was so happy, nor what I was expecting, but I was in a delirium of joy, it was one of the supreme few moments of existence, a deep delicious draught from the strong sweet cup of life. It came unsought, unbidden, at the meadow stile, it was one of the flowers of happiness scattered for us and found unexpectedly by the wayside of life. It came silently, suddenly, and it went as it came, but it left a long lingering glow and glory behind as it faded slowly like a gorgeous sunset, and I shall ever remember the place and the time in which such great happiness fell upon me.

Thursday, 27 May
My bedroom is illuminated all day with a beautiful rosy light from the glorious blossom of the pink may on the lawn.

Wednesday, June Morrow
Austin told me that when his present farm boy, Robert Jefferies, worked at the Barrow the young Bryants held him down in the furrow and ploughed him into the ground. It reminded me of Uncle Francis trying to bury Uncle Richard when they were boys at Caroline Buildings in Bath. He had got him into the hole up to his waist when someone came by and interrupted him. In a fury he flung the spade at Richard to cut him in two and finish him at once, but the spade fell on his own foot and Francis swore like a trooper.

Friday, 4 June
Mrs Vincent told me that her husband had not suffered so much lately from the pressure of water upon his heart which had been sensibly relieved by the water running out at his heels.

Monday, 7 June
I walked to Langley Grove through the mowing grass. Dear little Katie opened the door to me and her father Farmer Lessiter was better and sitting downstairs at tea. When I went away and shook hands with him at parting he gave me a kind look out of his blue eyes and said, 'I wish I were as strong as you, Sir. I know you must be a very strong man. When I was in bed the other day and you shook hands with me I felt as if an electrifying machine had gone all through me and I feel the same now. I made the remark after you were gone that you must be a very strong man. There is something so stiff to lean against in your grasp.'

'Oh,' I said, 'you will be as strong as I am again in a few days.'

'No,' said the stout farmer, with a sad shake of the head and a sorrowful look in his blue eyes. 'No, I shall never be as strong as you are any more.'

Tuesday, 8 June

How delightful it is in these sweet summer evenings to wander from cottage to cottage and from farm to farm exchanging bright words and looks with the beautiful girls at their garden gates and talking to the kindly people sitting at their cottage doors or meeting in the lane when their work is done. How sweet it is to pass from house to house welcome and beloved everywhere by young and old, to meet the happy loving smiles of the dear children at their evening play in the lanes and fields and to meet with no harsher reproach than this, 'It is a longful while since you have been to see us. We do all love to see you coming and we do miss you sorely when you are away.'

Wednesday, 9 June

Foxham seems to be in a sad state ecclesiastically. Mrs Peglin told us that the Curate, Mr Rivett-Carnac, who walks about in a cassock, was attacked one day by their gander which tore a grievous rent in his 'petticoats'. He said he should tell his friends what a 'ferocious house guardian' Mrs Peglin kept. 'Perhaps, Sir,' suggested the old lady slyly, 'the gander was excited by some peculiarity in the dress.'

Saturday, 12 June

I went to see my dear little lover Mary Tavener, the deaf and half dumb child. When I opened the door of the poor old crazy cottage in the yard the girl uttered a passionate inarticulate cry of joy and running to me she flung her arms round my neck and covered me with kisses. Well, I have lived and I have been loved, and no one can take this from me.

Monday, 14 June

Villaging. Visited Mrs Lawrence who amused me by a description of how she fell down the cellar stairs from top to bottom by reason of her 'grasping on vacancy' instead of grasping a pound of candles which were hanging against the wall. When she revived herself and came up, 'Charles,' she said to her husband, 'I am almost dead. I have fallen from the top of the cellar stairs to the bottom.' 'You couldn't have done it,' said Charles incredulously from under the bedclothes. 'I *have* done it, Charles,' she shouted, infuriated at his unbelief.

Friday, 18 June

Battle of Waterloo. ' 'Tis sixty years since.' The veterans who meet at the yearly banquet must be growing very few and feeble. It must be a small sad gathering now, and soon there will be fewer and then there will be none.

I passed by the ruined sheds which sadly, regretfully, mark the site of the ancient small homestead of Watling Street. The dwelling house has entirely disappeared and the scene of so many joys and sorrows, hopes and fears, is now waste, silent and desolate, and overgrown with nettles and weeds. What a pity that these ancient humble farms should be destroyed and thrown into the great farms, thereby taking away all the poor man's prizes and the chance of his rising in the world.

Tuesday, 22 June

I have been working all the afternoon in our meadows with the haymakers, Farmer Jacob Knight, John Couzens, Hannah, Mary and Joseph Hatherell and Emma Halliday. We have got a lot of beautiful green fragment hay up in cock.

Wednesday, Midsummer Eve

Another beautiful haymaking day. We all worked hard and got the hay up in beautiful condition, I pitching the last four loads with Jacob Knight. We finished about nine o'clock of a lovely warm Midsummer's Eve.

Thursday, Midsummer Day

And a lovely day it has been, soft, warm and sunny. I took the young cuckoo out of his nest, put him in the great wicker cage, and hung the cage up in the hawthorn hedge close to the old nest that the hedge sparrows might feed their charge.

Gathering strawberries. As the day wore the weather became more and more beautiful till at last the evening grew the loveliest I think I ever saw. The rich golden light flooded the lawn and clean freshly cleared meadows, slanting through the western trees which fringe the Common's edge. Even the roan cows, and the Alderney especially, glowed with a golden tinge in the glorious evening sunlight. From the wide common over the thick waving fragrant grass came the sweet country music of the white-sleeved mowers whetting their scythes and the voices of their children at play among the fresh-cut flowery swaths. The sun went down red under a delicate fringe of gold laced cloud, the beautiful Midsummer evening passed through twilight and gloaming into the exquisite warm soft Midsummer night, with its long light in the north slowly, softly lingering as Jupiter came out glorious in the south and flashed glittering through the tresses of the silver birches softly waving, and the high poplars rustled whispering and the Church clock at Draycot struck ten and I longed to sleep out of doors and dream my 'Midsummer night's dream'.

Monday, 5 July

Left Chippenham for the Isle of Wight. Reached Shanklin between 4 and 5 o'clock, the heat all the way very great in the sun in spite of a fine breeze. It was most refreshing and delightful embarking in the steam boat with the salt air blowing cool, the sea dimpling, sparkling and shimmering, the Island smiling in the glorious afternoon sunlight and the tall white-sailed yachts standing stately up and down the Solent and flying over the bright blue water.

Wednesday, 7 July

At 5 o'clock we all went down to the beach leaving Mrs Cowper Coles in her Bath Chair on the top of the Cliff. Mrs Powles, Miss Deason, Gussie and Alice sat down by the bathing machine to sketch Sampson's Cottage at the mouth of the Chine. Minna, Sherard, Commerell, Cowper Todd and I set to work to dig sand castles and trenches. The tide was going out, a number of children were paddling in the shallow water left by the white retreating surges, and it was a fair sight to watch the merry girls with their pretty white feet and bare limbs wading through the little rippling waves or walking on the wet and shining sand. Oh, as I watched them there came over me such a longing, such a hungry yearning to have one of those children for my own. Oh that I too had a child to love and to love me, a daughter with such fair limbs and blue eyes archly dancing, and bright clustering curls blown wild and golden in the sunshine and sea air. It came over me like a storm and I turned away hungry at heart and half envying the parents as they sat upon the sand watching their children at play.

Tuesday, 13 July

This morning after breakfast I started to walk to Bembridge through Sandown and Yaverland. The morning was blue and lovely with a warm sun and fresh breeze blowing from the sea and the Culver Downs. As I walked from Shanklin to Sandown along the cliff edge I stopped to watch some children bathing from the beach directly below. One beautiful girl stood entirely naked on the sand, and there as she half sat, half reclined sideways, leaning upon her elbow with her knees bent and her legs and feet partly drawn back and up, she was a model for a sculptor, there was the supple slender waist, the gentle dawn and tender swell of the bosom and the budding breasts, the graceful rounding of the delicately beautiful limbs and above all the soft and exquisite curves of the rosy dimpled bottom and broad white thigh. Her dark hair fell in thick masses on her white shoulders as she threw her head back and looked out to sea. She seemed a Venus Anadyomene fresh risen from the waves.

I missed the road by the windmill on the height and went too far round to the right, but at last returning by the Cross Roads I came to Bembridge. Bosomed amongst green, pretty cottages peeped through the thick foliage and here and there a garden shone brilliant with flowers. A long beautiful road, dark, green and cool and completely overarched with trees, led towards the sea and in a high meadow the haymakers in their white shirt sleeves, the dark horses and the high loaded waggon stood out clear against the brilliant blue waters of the Channel. Farther on a broad and beautiful avenue led down to the water's edge. The trees were chiefly sycamore and ash, and high and thickly overarching they cast a twinkling chequering shadow upon the ground, a perpetual restless flicker of dancing leaves that in the sun and sea wind moved ceaselessly quivering. Only two or three children were moving up and down in the chequering sunlight and shadow. At the end of the avenue the bright blue sea was framed in a perfect round low arch of dark foliage, and passing under the arch I came out upon an open terrace from which a pretty winding path wandered amongst the woods which fringe the shore and sweep down to the water's edge. Spithead was full of great ships black and monstrous. The Channel Fleet had come in the day before and was lying off the opposite shore. The sun shone bright on the green slopes and woods and white houses of St Helens across the smooth blue harbour of Brading, a woman sat solitary under the trees looking across the sea to the Hampshire coast, and the only sound that broke the peaceful stillness were the rustling of the firs and poplars overhead and the clapping of the white sail of a pilot boat as it flapped idly from the yard in the soft sea breeze.

[Kilvert returns to Langley Burrell.]

Monday, 19 July
I called on Mrs Martin. She was busy picking pheasants' feathers to make a pillow. Talking of feather beds she said, 'Pheasants' feathers will do very well for a bed, but not pigeons' feathers. People don't like to sleep on pigeons' feathers.' 'Why not?' I asked. 'Well,' said Susan Martin mysteriously, 'folk do say that a person can't die on pigeons' feathers.'

At 7 o'clock came on another terrible storm of rain much worse than the one in the afternoon. I was in my room reading when I heard Fanny screaming to me from top of the house. Rushing up the back stairs I found that the cistern was overflowing and deluging the water closet, the tank room, and the bathroom and the kitchen. I was obliged to put on a mackintosh and stand in the water closet holding up the handle to relieve the cistern while the water ran down upon my head like a shower bath.

Saturday, 24 July
Going into the Churchyard I found they were beginning the restoration of Chippenham Church and digging the foundations for the new North aisle. Draper Wharry's assistant at the Chemist's shop told me that things were not managed nicely

when the tombstones and graves were necessarily interfered with. He said scalps with hair still on them were left lying about and that he himself had seen a hedgehog tearing at the arm of a body which still had flesh upon it.

Sunday, 8 August

As I went to Church in the sultry summer afternoon the hum and murmur of the multitudinous insects sounded like the music of innumerable bells. As I sat on the terrace reading Farrar's *Life of Christ*, the evening was soft, dark and cloudy and filled with sweet scents of earth and flowers. At the gloaming a robin suddenly flew into the trees overhead and began singing his latest evensong in the sycamore.

Tuesday, 10 August

At the Barrow Cottages I found Alice Couzens at home and Charlotte Knight told me the sad story of Mrs Sarten's confinement, how the doctors could not get the dead baby from her for two days and were obliged to cut the poor girl almost to pieces. They said she would die in two hours but she still lives and it is hoped will live, as she has survived a fortnight.

Thursday, 12 August

I walked across to Kington St Michael to be present at the school feast. As we were swinging the children under the elms that crown the Tor Hill a girl came up to me with a beseeching look in her eyes and an irresistible request for a swing. She was a perfect little beauty with a plump rosy face, dark hair, and lovely soft dark eyes melting with tenderness and a sweet little mouth as pretty as a rosebud. I lifted her into the swing and away she went. But about the sixth flight the girl suddenly slipped off the swing seat feet foremost and still keeping hold of the ropes she hung from the swing helpless. Unfortunately her clothes had got hitched upon the seat of the swing and were all pulled up round her waist and it instantly became apparent that she wore no drawers. A titter and then a shout of laughter ran through the crowd as the girl's plump person was seen naked hanging from the swing. O ye gods, the fall of Hebe was nothing to it. We hustled her out of the swing and her clothes into their proper place as soon as possible and perhaps she did not know what a spectacle she had presented. I believe it was partly my fault. When I lifted the girl into the swing there were many aspirants for the seat and in the struggle and confusion I suppose I set her down with her clothes rumpled up and her bare flesh (poor child) upon the board and as her flesh was plump and smooth and in excellent whipping condition and the board slippery, they managed to part company with this result. Poor child, when she begged so earnestly for a swing she scarcely contemplated the exhibition of herself for the amusement of the spectators. I shall never see the elms on the Tor Hill now without thinking of the fall of Hebe.

Thursday, 19 August

In the newspapers this morning we saw the account of the Royal yacht the *Alberta* with the Queen on board going from Osborne to Portsmouth running down, cutting in two and sinking Mr Heywood's yacht the *Mistletoe* in Stokes Bay with a loss of three lives, the master, the mate and Miss Annie Peel, the sister of Mrs Heywood. This is the first accident that has ever happened to the Queen in travelling and she is terribly distressed. It is an awkward thing for the Sovereign to destroy her own subjects. Of course it was no fault of hers but the Royal yacht was travelling too fast through the crowded waters of the Solent.

Wednesday, 25 August

I went to Britford Vicarage to stay with the Morrises till Saturday. Late in the evening we loitered down into the water meads. The sun was setting in stormy splendour behind Salisbury and the marvellous aerial spire rose against the yellow glare like Ithuriel's spear, while the last gleams of the sunset flamed down the long lines of the water carriages making them shine and glow like canals of molten gold.

Friday, 27 August

To-day I paid my first visit to Stonehenge. We had breakfast before Church and immediately after service Morris and I started to walk to Stonehenge, eleven miles. Passing through the beautiful Cathedral Close and the city of Salisbury we took the

Devizes road and after we had walked along that road for some six miles we saw in the dim distance the mysterious Stones standing upon the Plain. The sun was hot, but a sweet soft air moved over the Plain 'wafting' the scent of the purple heather tufts and the beds of thyme and making the delicate blue harebells tremble on their fragile stems. A beautiful little wheatear flitted before us from one stone heap to another along the side of the wheel track as we struck across the firm elastic turf. Around us the Plain heaved mournfully with great and solemn barrows, the 'grassy barrows of the happier dead'.

Soon after we left the Druid's Head and struck across the turf eastward we came in sight of the grey cluster of gigantic Stones. They stood in the midst of a green plain, and the first impression they left on my mind was that of a group of people standing about and talking together. It seemed to me as if they were ancient giants who suddenly became silent and stiffened into stone directly anyone approached, but who might at any moment become alive again, and at certain seasons, as at midnight and on Old Christmas and Midsummers Eve, might form a true 'Chorea Gigantum' and circle on the Plain in a solemn and stately dance. It is a solemn awful place. As I entered the charmed circle of the sombre Stones I instinctively uncovered my head. It was like entering a great Cathedral Church.

Crossing the river at Normanton Hatches we walked along the hillside through meadows and barley fields till we came to the hospitable Manor House of Great Durnford, the seat of Mr John Pinckney, where we found Mr and Mrs Pinckney, Mr Charles Everett and Major Fisher, the Champion archer of England, at luncheon. After luncheon the archers went out to shoot at a beautiful archery ground by the riverside. The ladies sat watching under the trees while the arrows flashed past with a whistling rush, and the glorious afternoon sunlight shone mellow upon the beeches, and the still soft air of the river valley was filled with the cooing of woodpigeons and the strange mournful crying of the moorhens and dabchicks, and three beautiful cows came down the glade from sunlight to shadow to their milking place, and the river flashed darkly past the boathouse and under the leaning trees, and a man rowed up the stream with his milkcans in a

boat from the meadows where he had milked a distant herd of
cows.

Saturday, 28 August
Left Britford, came home in pouring rain.

William Boscawen told us of a curious custom which is still kept
up in many parts of Wales. At the funerals offerings are made at
the graveside to the clergyman by the mourners and the offerings
are collected upon the grave shovel. This is a relic of the old
Catholic custom of offering money to the priest to say masses for
the soul of the departed.

He said that an old woman who had lately moved from her
parish into an adjoining one died there. Soon afterwards meeting
the husband Boscawen inquired about her last days, and received
the following account. 'Hun did send for the parson.' 'Well?'
'And hun did come and say that hun must repent of her sins.
'Yes.' 'And hun did sav as hun hadn't got any sins to repent of.'
'Well?' 'Then hun did say that as if hun hadn't got any sins
hun shouldn't come to see hun any more.' 'Well?' 'Hun didn't
come.' 'And then?' 'Hun died.'

Sunday, 29 August
John Hatherell told me that one night he had a sweet waking
dream. He thought one of his children was with him and sitting
on his bed. It was Ellen. And he said to her that he wanted to
kiss Some One. 'Kiss me, father', said Ellen. But he did not mean
that. There seemed to be Some One else there whom he was
feeling after. 'It was my sweet Jesus that I wanted to kiss,' said
the old man.

Saturday, 4 September
This beautiful autumn morning I went out to pray on the sunny
common. The luxuriant meadow grass shone green and silver
with the hoary webs and sheets of dew. The hills and woods
and distances were richly bloomed with azure misty veils, the
sweet sudden solitary song of the robin from the hornbeam broke
the morning calm. and here and there a yellow leaf, the herald
of Autumn, floated silently from the limes.

Dora and I drove to Seagry Vicarage to luncheon and to go

nutting with the Charles Awdrys' children in Seagry. We had a grand scramble and merry romp in the Seagry Woods racing up and down the green rides, clambering over the high gates gathering nuts, throwing burrs at each other and sticking them in the girls' hair amidst shouts and screams of laughter.

Monday, 6 September
All night the heavy drenching fog brooded over the land, clinging to the meadows long after the sun was risen, and it was not until after he had gained some height in the sky that he was able to break through and dispel the mists. Then the morning suddenly became glorious and we saw what had happened in the night. All night long millions of gossamer spiders had been spinning and the whole country was covered as if with one vast fairy web. They spread over lawn and meadow grass and gate and hawthorn hedge, and as the morning sun glinted upon their delicate threads drenched and beaded with the film of the mist the gossamer webs gleamed and twinkled into crimson and gold and green, like the most exquisite shot-silk dress in the finest texture of gauzy silver wire. I never saw anything like it or anything so exquisite as 'the Virgin's webs' glowed with changing opal lights and glanced with all the colours of the rainbow.

At 4 oclock Miss Meredith Brown and her beautiful sister Etty came over to afternoon tea with us and a game of croquet. Etty Meredith Brown is one of the most striking-looking and handsomest girls whom I have seen for a long time. She was admirably dressed in light grey with a close fitting crimson body which set off her exquisite figure and suited to perfection her black hair and eyes and her dark Spanish brunette complexion with its rich glow of health which gave her cheeks the dusky bloom and flush of a ripe pomegranate. But the greatest triumph was her hat, broad and picturesque, carelessly twined with flowers and set jauntily on one side of her pretty dark head, while round her shapely slender throat she wore a rich gold chain necklace with broad gold links. And from beneath the shadow of the picturesque hat the beautiful dark face and the dark wild fine eyes looked with a true gipsy beauty.

The sun shone golden on the lawn between the lengthening shadows and the evening sunlight dappled with bright green on the front of the Rectory with rick spots of light and shade. It lighted the broad gold links of the necklace and the graceful crimson figure of the dark handsome girl, and into the midst of the game came the tabby cat carrying in her mouth her tabby kitten which she dropped on the lawn and looked round proudly for applause.

Tuesday, 7 September
This morning I went to Bath. Having an hour to spare I went into the Catholic Cathedral. I knelt and prayed for charity, unity, and brotherly love, and the union of Christendom. Surely a Protestant may pray in a Catholic Church and be none the worse.

1876

Friday, 3 March

I went by the mahogany tree across the evening meadows to Peckingell. Farmer Austin was a little better. He told me that when his first child was born he was one day on business at Farmer Thomas Knight's at the Langley Burrell Manor Farm. The old farmer asked him if he did not want to have his wife downstairs again. Austin said he did, for it was very inconvenient her being upstairs so long and he missed her sorely. 'Then,' said Farmer Thomas Knight, 'I'll tell you what to do. You pinch the nurse on the stairs and make her holler out and that'll fetch the missis down fast enough.'

Saturday, 4 March

This morning I went to Bristol. I went to the bookbinder's, Williams, above the Drawbridge, and got dear Ettie's name stamped on the leather cover of an MS. book of my poems which I am copying out for her as an Easter offering.

Sunday, 5 March

Going to and returning from Church we met Meredith Brown and Arthur Coates walking. Meredith Brown looked very pleasant and friendly, but little did he suspect who made the beautiful sermon-case which I carried in my pocket.

Wednesday, 8 March

At noon I went to Ellen Matthew's cottage to see if she could give me a few garden violets to make up a little nosegay for Mrs Meredith Brown. In the afternoon I walked over to Langley Ridge with my violets to wish Mrs Meredith Brown 'Goodbye' as they break up their establishment for the season and move to London this week. Rain poured all the way but I was glad I went over to-day for I find they leave Langley on Friday. I found two ladies with Mrs Meredith Brown, one her cousin Miss Fitzroy and the other Lady Hobhouse of Monckton Farleigh. They had come over to lunch. I thought Miss Fitzroy very pretty. She was dark. Lady Hobhouse (the wife of Sir Charles Hobhouse) has golden hair. Their carriage was announced soon after I came in. I saw them to their carriage and returned to have a chat with my friend. She told me that after a fortnight in London they go to the Pines at Bournemouth where they spend Easter.

Saturday, 11 March

This fine drying March afternoon I walked over to Lanhill. How pleasant and familiar all the Lanhill faces did look.

It was getting dark as I wished my old friends 'Goodnight' and went up the familiar hill past the farm at its foot and the Church and Rectory, my own sweet birthplace on its brow, glimmering through the dusk. I felt like a spirit revisiting and wandering about the old haunts and scenes of its mortal existence. The lights at the Folly shone bright and cheerful across the park, the rooks and jackdaws rustled and flapped uneasily as they settled to rest in the tops of the trees in the wilderness, and one great lone star seemed to be watching as a guardian angel the old sweet home where I was born. Harden Ewyas, sweet Harden Ewyas. God be very gracious and merciful and lift up the light of His countenance upon thee my sweet birthplace and the dear house of my childhood. I have ever loved thee and ever shall until my heart die. If I forget thee let my right hand forget her cunning. Yea, let my tongue cleave unto the roof of my mouth if I prefer not Harden Ewyas in my mirth. Harden Ewyas, strangers dwell in thy houses and walk in thy gardens and the old familiar faces have passed away, but still I am there and thou art mine. The house remains the white house on the hill where I was born, there is the ivied Church across the lane to which I was first carried to be baptized, there are the meadows and gardens where I first played and gathered flowers. Each field and hill and bank has its own bright memories and its own sweet story.

Saturday, 18 March

Called with Dora at Pew Hill on our new neighbours. We found Mrs Adderley at home and liked her much. Her simple, unaffected, kind and gentle manner is very pleasing. It was a bright cold afternoon and the March sun shining on the distant chalk downs made them look green and very near, only as if two or three miles away. After I had seen Dora home the beautiful clear fresh bright evening and the clear dry hard roads tempted me to go for a brisk solitary walk. I went on to the Plough and up to the Ridge. It was the first time since last November that I have passed by the house without a feeling of great sadness. To-night I felt much happier as I thought of dear Ettie. But as I passed slowly by the house and looked up at the tall poplars swaying gently in the quiet evening air I could not help repeating to myself these lines from my little poem 'The Ridge', which I sent to Ettie.

> 'Along the ridge of this fair hill
> As day wanes hear its dying,
> I wander thinking of thee still
> Beneath the poplars' sighing
> That seems for thee in wordless grief
> To mourn so sadly swaying
> And seek a sorrowful relief
> Through inarticulate praying.'

How the sight of the double-gabled house and the tall poplars always bring that lovely face back to me with the remembrance of the happy days of last summer before all our trouble came and our separation. I went on past the head of the steep green lane in the site of the old Chapel and burying place where my great-grandfather was laid to rest, and thought of that sweet September evening when I walked up that green lane with dear Ettie and Ellie and wished them Goodbye. I lingered some time leaning over my favourite gate, the 'Poet's Gate', and looking at the lovely view. From time to time I looked back through the fringe of trees at the chimney stacks and double gables of the Ridge and half expected to see dear Ettie coming round the turn of the road. But, alas, she is far away beneath the pines that sigh beside the southern sea. At length twilight began to fall on the wide and lovely landscape. I turned away with a sigh and a heart full of sad sweet tender memories and passed over the village green among the pleasant friendly greetings of the kindly village people. I always seem to feel at home among these people in the village of my forefathers.

Sunday, 19 March

A cold dry day with a snowstorm in the evening. As we came in at the orchard door together after the morning service my dear Father said, 'As you were preaching there came back upon my ear an echo of the tones of the sweetest human voice I ever heard, the voice of John Henry Newman. No voice but yours ever reminded me of him.'

Monday, 20 March

To-day I actually mustered courage to go to dear Nonsuch again though there was a time and not so very long ago when I thought I could never go there any more. The day was brilliant and clear with a keen north wind and warm sun and the prospect from Derry Hill seemed boundless. The air was so clear that the Downs looked close and every little hollow and watercourse was visible. I reached Nonsuch in time for luncheon. Mr Gwatkin had an attack of gout. I did not go into the garden and left the house about four o'clock. As I crossed the first meadow the tower clock at Spye Park was striking four. At the end of the meadow I turned and looked back at the dear old picturesque Manor house, Ettie's sweet home. It stood bright and cheery in the brilliant afternoon sunshine, and the great twin larches on the lawn and the other trees were thickening so fast with swelling buds that they looked almost green. The teams were busy in the fallows, for it is almost the first day they have been able to get on the ground owing to the wet weather. As I drew near the Church a tall fair young lady with a blue dress and black jacket and luxuriant coils of very bright golden hair turned in at the Churchyard gate. She was accompanied by a little boy and went into the Church evidently to practise on the organ. I did not know who it was at the time but afterwards I learnt that it was Miss Ada Wyndham. I entered the Churchyard and walked round it till I heard the tones of the organ, when I stole softly into the Church that I might not disturb or annoy the fair organist. I saw the seats in the Chancel where dear Ettie and May used to sit and I seemed to feel them near me in their own dear Church. The organ ceased and I feared I should be discovered. The young lady, evidently unconscious of my presence, spoke kindly to the boy and asked if he was tired of blowing. He said 'No' and she began another tune. I stole quietly out of the Church and sat down on the steps of the porch listening to the organ and thinking of dear Ettie and May and the beloved feet which had so often come down that winding meadow path and trodden the steps of the porch where I was sitting. I thought of the last time I sat on those steps writing to dear Ettie on that happy evening the 6th of last October, of all the sweet strange sad story that has happened since. All the Bournemouth memories of last December came back upon me, and those wild sad sweet trysts in the snow and under the pine trees, among the sand hills on the East Cliffe and in Boscombe Chine.

Friday, 24 March

The family at the little farm of Gastons seems to me a very happy family. I think they have the true secret of happiness. When I entered they were all sitting at tea round the table. There was the patriarchal grandfather, Robert Crook, with his white smock-frock, rosy face, and the sweet kindly benevolent look in his eyes. The kindly people asked me to join them at their humble meal and I did not want a second invitation. The old man took up the sheet of music and looked at it. He is a musician and used to play the flute at Tytherton Church. Presently the old man rose with a courteous apology and went out to attend to the business of the little farm. 'Daddy! Daddy!' cried the children as their father passed the window and the strong comely pleasant-faced carpenter Palmer came in from his day's work, greeted me kindly, and sat down by the fire while his wife prepared his tea. I think he is a God-fearing man, and a fond husband and father. He told me how for ten years he had walked to and from Chippenham in the early morning and late night in wild weather, often in times of flood and in such darkness that he had sometimes to go down on his knees with his little lantern to see if he was in the path, but how he had always been cheered and brightened and helped by the thought of the beacon light of home and the wife and children and the love that awaited him there.

Wednesday, 29 March

Visited William Pinnock, the old blind man, and took him from my mother a basin of Mid-Lent frumenty. He said he had only tasted it once in his life. He used when he was a ploughboy on a farm in Melksham Forest to be sent every Mothering Sunday with a jug of frumenty from Melksham Forest to a house in Lacock Village.

Thursday, 30 March

A lovely warm sunny morning, the purple plumes of the silver birch fast thickening with buds waved and swayed gently in the soft spring air against the deep cloudless blue sky. The apricot blossoms were blowing and under the silver weeping birch the daffodils were dancing and nodding their golden heads in the morning wind and sunshine. This afternoon rain came on. I went down to Greenaway Lane and called on Mrs Morgan. Then I went to the James Knights'. Pretty Bessie came to the door with a bright smile of welcome and brought me into the warm cosy kitchen where her beautiful sister Mary was at tea with the younger girls who had just come in from school. Kitty is growing very pretty and was full of fun and romping spirits. It was a charming picture as the mother sat on the settle between her two fair blooming daughters with the other children grouped about them. Then Kitty ran out into the rain and puddles in the farmyard and came in so wet that her shoes and stockings had to be stripped off, her lovely limbs were unencumbered with drawers and Bessie tossed her in the air, and for my benefit turned up her legs, showing her beautiful bottom and thighs white and soft and warm and rosy and as pretty as a picture.

Monday, 3 April

This morning my Mother and Dora drove up to Studley Hill to see poor Betsy Penny and Mary Strange. They found Mary going mad, and Betsy quite distraught between this and her gathering cancer.

Wednesday, 12 April

The evening was sunny and brilliant as I went home across the bright evening meadows, the sun glinting upon the white smock-frocks of the work people as they crossed the meadows on their way home after their work was done.

This morning I walked into Chippenham and posted a long letter and a MS. book of my poems to dear Ettie.

This evening I had received from dear Ettie two such sad sweet little verses, beginning 'When shall we meet again'. I think she had composed them herself. I took the verses from my pocket and read them again in the gathering twilight. They were very sweet but very sad and made me feel strangely unhappy. I could not quite tell what they meant.

Thank God for a bright beautiful happy Easter Day.

I waited for the postman thinking that Easter morning might bring me a line from dear Ettie to explain the sweet sad verses of Easter Eve. Soon I saw the postman coming by a meadow path across the sunny Common. He held several letters and a paper parcel and my heart beat with hope and expectation as he put them into my hand. But there was nothing from Ettie and I went sorrowfully back to the house.

There was a large congregation this morning. There were 41 Communicants beside the parson and clerk, the largest number that I or any one else had ever seen in Langley Church at once. The alms were £1.3.10.

When all the people had left the Church and no one remained but the Clerk putting away the sacred vessels I walked alone round the silent sunny peaceful Churchyard and visited the graves of my sleeping friends Jane Hatherell, Mary Jefferies, Anne Hawkins, John Jefferies, George Bryant, Emily Banks, John Hatherell, Limpedy Buckland the gipsy girl, and many more. There they lay, the squire and the peasant, the landlord and the labourer, young men and maidens, old men and children, the infant of days beside the patriarch of nearly five score years, sister, brother, by the same mother, all in her breast their heads did lay and crumble to their common clay. And over all she lovingly threw her soft mantle of green and gold, the greensward and buttercups,

daisies and primroses. There they lay all sleeping well and peacefully after life's fitful fevers and waiting for the Great Spring
morning and the General Resurrection of the dead. John
Hatherell, the good old sawyer, now sleeps in the same God's
acre to which he helped to carry the gipsy girl Limpedy Buckland
to her burial more than sixty years ago.

Wednesday, 19 April
No letter from Ettie again. I cannot think why. I am afraid
something must have happened. To-day I went to Monnington,
leaving Chippenham by the up mail at 11 o'clock. Stormy weather.

Thursday, 20 April
This morning I received a long sad sweet loving letter from my
darling Ettie, a tender beautiful letter of farewell, the last she
will ever be able to write to me. With it came enclosed a kind
friendly little note from young Mrs Meredith Brown, so friendly
and so kind, saying she is afraid Ettie and I must hold no further
communication by letter or poetry or any other way. I know it.
I know it. She is right and I have been, alas, very very wrong.
She says she knows I care for Ettie too much to wish to cause
her needless unhappiness. It is true. She does me justice and yet
no more than justice. I will not make my darling sorrowful or
cause her to shed one unnecessary tear, or tempt her to do wrong.
The best and only way left me of showing my love for her now is
to be silent. But oh, I hope she will not quite forget me. She says
she never will. Yet perhaps it is selfish of me to wish this, and it
may be better for her that she should. I hope, I hope, I have not
done her any harm or wrong. She says, God bless her, that I never
have. How kind and gentle she has always been to me, how sweet
and good, how patient and forbearing, how noble and generous,
how self-sacrificing and devoted, how unselfish and loving. Ettie,
Ettie, my own only lost love, yet not lost, for we shall meet in
heaven. Ettie, oh Ettie, my own dear little girl.

As I walked round the Rectory garden at Monnington this morning thinking of Ettie's last letter and all the wild sweet sorrowful
past the great everlasting sigh of the majestic firs, as mournful
and soothing as the sighing of the sea, blended with my mood and

sympathized with the sadness of my heart. The beautiful weeping birch too wept with me and its graceful drooping tresses softly moving reminded me with a strange sweet thrill of Ettie's hair.

Saturday, 22 April

A lovely summer morning which I spent in sauntering round the lawn at Monnington Rectory watching the waving of the birch tresses, listening to the sighing of the firs in the great solemn avenue, that vast Cathedral, and reading Robert Browning's 'In a Gondola' and thinking of dear Ettie. To-day there was a luncheon party consisting of Andrew and Mary Pope from Blakemere, Mr and Mrs Phillott from Staunton-on-Wye, Houseman, and Mr Robinson from Norton Canon. After they had left William and I walked up to the top of Moccas Park, whence we had a glorious view of the Golden Valley shining in the evening sunlight with the white houses of Dorstone scattered about the green hillsides 'like a handful of pearls in a cup of emerald' and the noble spire of Peterchurch rising from out of the heart of the beautiful rich valley which was closed below by the Sugar Loaf and the Skyrrid blue above Abergavenny. We came tumbling and plunging down the steep hillside of Moccas Park, slipping, tearing and sliding through oak and birch and fallow wood of which there seemed to be underfoot an accumulation of several feet, the gathering ruin and decay probably of centuries. As we came down the lower slopes of the wooded hillside into the glades of the park the herds of deer were moving under the brown oaks and the brilliant green hawthorns, and we came upon the tallest largest stateliest ash I ever saw and what seemed at first in the dusk to be a great ruined grey tower, but which proved to be the vast ruin of the king oak of Moccas Park, hollow and broken but still alive and vigorous in parts and actually pushing out new shoots and branches. That tree may be 2000 years old. It measured roughly 33 feet round by arm stretching.

I fear those grey old men of Moccas, those grey, gnarled, low-browed, knock-kneed, bowed, bent, huge, strange, long-armed, deformed, hunchbacked misshapen oak men that stand waiting and watching century after century biding God's time with both feet in the grave and yet tiring down and seeing out generation after

326

generation, with such tales to tell, as when they whisper them to each other in the midsummer nights, make the silver birches weep and the poplars and aspens shiver and the long ears of the hares and rabbits stand on end. No human hand set those oaks. They are 'the trees which the Lord hath planted'. They look as if they had been at the beginning and making of the world, and they will probably see its end.

Sunday, 23 April

One of the quiet peaceful Monnington Sundays. I like a Sunday at Monnington, it is so calm and so serene. There is no hurry, no crowd, no confusion, no noise.

The silver birch droops and waves her long dusky tress as a maiden with delicate white limbs and slender arm and hands lets down her long hair and combs it to the curve of her beautiful knees shrinking from sight and hiding herself in the dusky cloud and twilight of her tresses rippling to her feet.

Then I love to walk up the great avenue, as up a vast and solemn Cathedral aisle, while the wind sighs through the branches of tall sombre Scotch firs overhead and makes mournful music as it breathes upon that natural Aeolian harp which is the organ in that Cathedral. The Choir is comprised of the wild birds and with their songs chimes in the flowing river as it rushes over the rocks and the voices of bells ringing for service from the hillsides around.

The three bells of Monnington begin to chime quickly from the Church Tower beyond the old grey mansion of the Glendowers. We stroll down the lane over the pitched pavement. Along the larches which line the old slanting mouldering lych-gate sit four or five boys. The bells stop, the clerk French appears standing bareheaded in the churchyard by the flat and broken gravestone of 'Owen Glendwrdwy divine', looking to see if any one is coming to church. An old man and two or three women heave in sight coming along the high walk by the side of the low osier bed now gay with the golden clumps of marsh marigolds. The Priest's bell strikes up, we enter the church and robe in the vestry, the chief farmer (James of Monnington Court) comes in in his grey coat, followed by his wife. Thersie plays the harmonium and the service begins. I read prayers in the morning and William preached, a slight but masterly and impressive sermon.

Wednesday, 26 April
This morning I bade farewell to sweet kind hospitable beautiful Monnington and came to Clyro.

Friday, 28 April
At Llan Thomas some of the girls were playing croquet on the bright sunny lawn with a Miss Ravenscroft who had come to spend the afternoon with them. Lady Hereford, who had brought her from Tregoyd, was out fishing with her eldest son Robert Devereux and Mary Thomas. In the drawing room I found Mrs Thomas looking well, bright and cheery. She has got through this winter better than usual. Daisy came into the drawing room, shy, confused and blushing painfully, but looking very nice and well.

After the game of croquet was over Charlotte and Edith Thomas took me to the Church by my request to see their Easter decorations. Then we came back to afternoon tea and found the fishing party returned with empty baskets. Edith showed me her beautiful drawings of wild flowers and fungi. No sooner had Lady Hereford and her party gone than I found she had taken my umbrella and left me a much better one, a fine silk umbrella in place of my zenilla. Edith and Daisy took me to the garden and were very kind to me, Daisy giving me a sprig of sweet verbena, and we had a nice long talk together. When I went away they sent me half a mile or more along the road and we had a merry laughing walk. It was so pleasant, just like the dear old times, and the girls were so nice and cordial and friendly. I do like those girls. They half expected to meet their sisters coming home from a walk or pretended to, but as Mary and Grace did not appear they were obliged to turn back with a pleasant affectionate 'Goodbye'. After we had parted Daisy turned and called back with a bright sweet loving look, 'Please give my best love to your sister'.

As I went back I called at the almshouses again and knocked at Mrs Michael's door. 'Come in, Sir,' she said, 'Florrie's¹ come. She

---

1. Florence Hill.

is in the other room.' 'Florrie, Florrie!' she called. The door of the inner room opened gently and Florrie entered. I never saw anything so lovely. A tall beautiful stately girl with an exquisite figure, a noble carriage, the most lovely delicate and aristocratic features, gentle loving blue eyes shaded by long silken lashes, eyebrows delicately arched and exquisitely pencilled, and beautiful silky tresses of golden brown hair falling in curling clusters upon her shoulders. And the loveliest part of it all was that the girl seemed perfectly unconscious of her own loveliness. Well, I thought, you will make some hearts ache some day.

She was indeed as Mrs Vaughan said 'beautiful and wild and stately, a true mountain child'. I was dazzled by her beauty and almost overcome with emotion. The girl dropped a pretty courtesy and smiled. I took her little slender hand. 'Do you remember me, Florence?' 'Oh yes, Sir,' she said, opening her blue eyes wide with a sweet surprised look peculiar to herself. She had a quick timid almost breathless way of speaking in a low undertone, half frightened, half confiding, which completed the charm. I asked after my old schoolgirl pupil, her sister Eleanor. 'Eleanor will be sure to be very sorry not to see you, Sir,' said Florence in her quick sweet timid voice and manner. 'I am going home to-morrow for a few days,' she added breathlessly. I resolved instantly to pay a visit to the Upper Noyadd and see her and Eleanor and the kindly people at her dear home, the mountain farm. I was obliged to tear myself away from her. I could scarcely part. One more look, one more clasp of the tiny slender hand. 'Good-bye, darling.' Good-bye, Florence, sweet lovely beautiful Florence, rightly named 'The Flower', the Flower of light and sweetness and loveliness. Good-bye, dear, dear mountain child. Until to-morrow. To-morrow we shall meet again. Meanwhile angels ever bright and fair watch over thee, and happy be thy dreams.

[Kilvert goes to Llysdinan.]

Thursday, 4 May

Breakfast at 8 with the Archdeacon, train at 9, he to Doldowlod and I look at St Harmon's. Soon after leaving Rhayader the railway leaves the valley of the Wye and enters the sweet vale of Marteg by a wild and narrow gorge which soon opens, broadens and settles down into a winding valley shut in by gentle hills about which are dotted lone white cottages and farms. The little by-station of St Harmon's is kept by a handsome, pleasant-faced woman, very stout, who lives in a cottage on the line. The Church stands close to the station on a little mount half veiled by a clump of trees. It was built in the Dark Ages of fifty years ago and was simply hideous. But ugly as it appeared externally the interior was worse and my heart sank within me like a stone as I entered the door. A bare cold squalid interior and high ugly square boxes for seats, a three-decker pulpit and desk, no stove, a flimsy altar rail, a ragged faded altar cloth, a singing gallery with a broken organ, a dark little box for a vestry and a roof in bad repair, admitting the rain. Such was St Harmon's Church as I first saw it.

[Kilvert returns to Langley Burrell.]

Sunday, 14 May
My Father and Mother being away at Norwood staying with Sam and Emmie I had the two services to myself. Preached in the morning from the day's Epistle, James i. 17, on Good Gifts. In the afternoon I preached from the Gospel for the day, xvi. 7. 'Nevertheless I tell you the truth. It is expedient for you that I go away.'
I walked on to Kington to help Edward Awdry and preached the same sermon, telling the people at Langley and Kington the sweet sad story of how those words came to me as a token in Salisbury Cathedral on that dark sorrowful winter's day, the 7th of last December, the day I parted from and saw the last of my darling Ettie. I told them how one dark cold snowy day in midwinter a man who had just parted perhaps for ever from his dearest friend came almost broken-hearted to a Cathedral city, and how being delayed there on his journey for some hours he wandered about the cold desolate snowy streets, sick at heart, broken-spirited, well nigh broken-hearted, with the tender loving despairing words of the last farewell ringing in his ears as he still seemed to feel the last long lingering pressure of the hand and the last long clinging embrace and passionate kiss and the latest sorrowful imploring look and beseeching word, 'Don't forget'. I told them how the broken-hearted man wandered at length into the Cathedral close

as the short winter twilight was fast passing into night, and saw
the leafless boughs of the elms bare against the sky and the great
spire towering dark amongst the murky snow clouds and the
snow on the Cathedral roof and the lighted windows of the great
Church shining through the dark and heard the roll of the distant
organ which reminded him that it was the hour of Evensong. I
told them how the sorrowful traveller went into the Cathedral
and how, as he entered, the second lesson for the day was being
read from the 16th Chapter of St John's Gospel and how the
first words that fell on his ear were those from the 7th verse,
'Nevertheless I tell you the truth. It is expedient for you that I
go away, for if I go not away the Comforter will not come unto
you, but if I depart I will send Him unto you.' I told them how the
broken-hearted man took the words as a sign and token from
heaven and how they comforted him greatly for he thought it
might be better for his friend that they had parted and that he
had gone away and he hoped that now his dear friend might be
comforted. All this I told them. But I did not say that I was the
broken-hearted traveller, that the story was my own, and that I
was speaking of one of the great sorrows of my life.

Monday, 22 May
To-day I went to Oxford by the 1 o'clock train to pay a visit to
my dear old College friend Anthony Lawson Mayhew at his new
home St Margaret's, Bradmore Road. I had not been to Oxford
for two years. The first sight of the old University from the
railway, and the noble cluster of famous towers and spires always
rouse in me an indescribable thrill of pride and love and
enthusiasm. There is nothing like Oxford.

Mayhew met me at the station at 3 o'clock. He came straight
from the Taylor Buildings where he had been attending a lecture
given by a Dane named Thomassen fresh from Copenhagen. The
lecture was on the Slavonic languages and as the lecturer had a
severe sold and a 'Slavonic cough' and spoke in a very low voice
Mayhew was not much wiser. We walked up into the dear old
streets. As a heavy shower came on we went into the Radcliffe
library where I became engrossed by a life of Heine. When the
shower had passed we wandered towards St Margaret's. In the

Parks we met Griffiths, the present Warden of Wadham, a kind pleasant courteous old gentleman, and Spurling whom I remember as a very junior scholar when I took my degree and went down. He is now Dean of Keble College. We also met a short stout gentleman with a double chin and large umbrella, a kindly face and a merry eye, who buttonholed Mayhew and began to inveigh in an aggrieved tone against the folly, perversity and bad taste of the University residents and visitors in rushing in crowds of 1200 to hear the Bishop of Derry (Alexander) give an ornamental rhetorical flourish by way of a Bampton Lecture in the morning and leaving himself (Professor Pritchard, Professor of Astronomy and Select Preacher) to hold forth to empty benches in the afternoon. He thought it was a sin and a shame. He declared the Bishop's Bampton Lectures to be growing worse week by week and to be an insult to the understanding of the University. 'Sir', he said, 'they are barren, there is nothing in them at all. They neither satisfy the intellect nor touch the heart. I have in my pocket', he continued, 'a letter from a Manchester gentleman who is steeped to the eyes in cotton. He says that he was spending Sunday in Oxford and he heard in the University Church what he will never forget as long as he lives.' At this point the Professor's merry eye twinkled and he smiled broadly. Thinking that the Manchester gentleman's remark applied to the balderdash which the Professor represented the Bishop's Bampton Lecture to have been and taking my cue from the Professor's smile I here laughed loud and long. The Professor eyed me oddly and went on with his story, from which I was horrified to learn that the remark in the Manchester gentleman's letter applied not to the Bishop of Derry's Bampton Lecture but to Professor Pritchard's own select sermon which had touched the cotton lord to the heart and done him much spiritual good. And I had received the recital of this interesting, touching and solemn episode with a loud and derisive laugh. Meantime my dear old absent-minded friend had become oblivious of dinner and we arrived an hour too late, to find that the ladies, his wife and mother, had waited half an hour and then had given us up for lost.

After dinner we went down to the river and saw the Boat races very well from the Queen's Barge. In Merton Meadows we overtook 'David' Laing, now Fellow of Corpus, and we came upon him again on board the Barge. David was in an odd excitable defiant mood and whilst walking backwards like a ' peacock in his pride' and declaring that he would rather be a drunkard than a teetotaller, because there would be some pleasure and satisfaction out of drink and drunkenness, he was very like to have got enough to drink and to have put his paradox to the test for he suddenly staggered as if he were really intoxicated, overbalanced himself, and nearly fell into the river. Then David suddenly became hospitable and invited us to breakfast on Saturday, but shortening his notice of invitation like a telescope he gradually brought us nearer to his view and heart and at last it was settled that we should breakfast with our old college friend in his rooms at Corpus to-morrow.

Tuesday, 23 May
Mayhew and I went this morning to Corpus to breakfast with Laing. David has luxurious double rooms, oak-panelled, in the Fellows' Buildings, one of his windows commands a prospect of the Cathedral, Merton Meadows and the Broad Walk, and from another there was what David called an *'ancient'* and very beautiful view of some of the old picturesque buildings and the tower of Merton and the pinnacles of Magdalen Tower rising grandly above the distant elms. We had a merry laughing breakfast spiced with many college stories and recollections of old days. David read us some of his own poetry describing the solitude of a mountain in the Highlands of Scotland, a pretty poem, and treated us also to a selection from the Jacobean poets and the beautiful noble lines to his dead wife by Richard King, Bishop of Chichester. These were quite new to me, and they impressed me deeply.

After breakfast we took leave of David and strolled into the College gardens where I had never been before and along the high terraced walk upon the old town wall overshadowed by the drooping feathering limes. As we walked upon this lime terrace we heard the bells beginning to chime for the ten o'clock service down at Magdalen and we resolved to go to Magdalen Chapel. Scarcely were we seated in the stalls than we heard the rustle of footsteps and white wings and the angel choir new-lighted on this earthly shore came in and took their places. Then followed the praying of the sweet solitary voice answered by the chorus of angels and the splendid storm of the anthem as we 'heard once more in college fanes the storm their high-built organs make and shake the prophets blazoned in the panes'.

After Chapel we passed through the cloisters and sauntered round Magdalen Walks where the milk-white hawthorns drooped over the Cherwell and the sun came dazzling and flickering through the glorious canopy of the young fresh green foliage and chequering the floor of Addison's Walk with moving light and shade.

In the afternoon I went with sweet Ruthie and Ethel and their father and mother to the Boat Race. As we went down I taught the children the names of the different Colleges and halls and they were very apt scholars. It was cold and gusty on the river. Mortie Rooke whom we met last night gave us a ticket for the Oriel barge and the children were delighted while the old scene passed before my eyes like a familiar dream, the moving crowd upon the banks, the barges loaded with ladies and their squires, the movement of small boats, canoes and skiffs darting about the river, punts crossing with their standing freights of men huddled together, then the first gun booming from Iffley, people looking at their watches, the minute gun five minutes later and last the report which started the boats and told us they were off. Then the suspense, the listening, the straining of the eyes, the first movement in the distant crowd now seen to be running, the crowd pouring over the Long Bridges, the far away shouting rising into a roar as the first boat came round the point with the light flashing upon the pinion-like motion of the rising and falling oars, the river now alive with boats, the strain and the final struggle, the plash of oars, the mad uproar, the frantic shouting as the boats pass the flag scatheless, then the slow procession following, the victors rowing proudly in amongst plaudits from the barges and the shore while the vanquished come humbly behind.

Wednesday, 24 May

To-day we went by train to Eynsham on our way to luncheon
with Dr Higgs at Handborough Rectory. His waggonette met
us at Eynsham and we arrived at Handborough in a drenching
thunder shower, but received a very kind warm welcome which
made up for everything. A stout elderly lady with fierce eyes
and teeth was in the drawing-room. She was a visitor staying
in the house. She was introduced to me as 'Mrs Stone'. Soon
I discovered that she was 'the great Mrs Stone' of Streatley, the
aunt of Emily Morrell, of whom I have heard Hopewell Morrell
speak so often, and we found many mutual friends to talk about.
At luncheon Mrs Stone amused us very much. It seemed that
Mrs Stone always jobbed her horses at £90 a year for the pair.
Mrs Higgs accused her of extravagance. Mrs Stone bridled and
fired up and turning to Mrs Higgs with the fiercest expression
of her fierce eyes and teeth said emphatically, 'The last words
that Mr Stone said to me before he died were, "Anne", he said,
"whatever you do be sure you always job your horses".' I was
deeply impressed by the sagacity, foresight and thoughtfulness
of the late Mr Stone and filled with admiration at the care which
he showed for the stable arrangements of Mrs Stone's establishment in the days of her approaching widowhood, but I was so
much surprised at his selection of a topic upon which to spend his
latest words and his last breath that I did not know which way
to look, and some other members of the company were in the same
condition. But we felt that we were in possession of the result
of the late Mr Stone's acute observation and long experience and
of the accumulated wisdom of his life. Mrs Higgs also amused
us by a naive description of her engagement and waiting for a
living. At length Handborough became vacant and the engagement terminated happily in a marriage. 'And then', she said, with
grand decision and personal emphasis, 'and then I came to Handborough.' The Doctor seemed to be a secondary personage, to
move dimly in the background and to follow humbly in the wake
of his better half.

After luncheon we were taken to see a beautiful Alderney calf,
one of the most beautiful little creatures I ever beheld, pure fawn
without a speck of white and with the eyes and limbs of a deer.

The Doctor proposed to guide us to the calf house but his wife and daughter gently smiled to scorn the idea of his being able to find the way to the calf and scarcely suspected him of knowing that there was one.

Then we visited the Church which has many fine and interesting points and amongst the rest of the fine remains of a Rood Screen and Rood Loft. Mrs Stone despised this screen and advised the Doctor to pull it down as so much lumber. 'Why', I said, 'it's worth its weight in gold.' 'Have it down then', said Mrs Stone promptly.

Holy Thursday, 25 May
Ascension Day. Mayhew and I made a rush for Magdalen Chapel this morning but were too late, Chapel having begun at 9.30 as is usual on Saints' Days. We loitered through the Botanical Gardens and up the Broad Walk. At length while wandering about Merton we heard the roll of the organ and went in to the Ante Chapel. Service was going on in the Chapel and the first words that struck upon our ears were the opening sentences of that fearful Athanasian Creed. We remained in the stalls in the Ante Chapel.

When service was over and the very small congregation had passed out we sauntered through the quadrangle till we came to the iron gate of the college gardens. It was open and we went in. I had never been in Merton Gardens before. They are very beautiful and the famous Terrace Walk upon the old city walls and the lime avenue are most delightful. The soft green sunny air was filled with the cooing of doves and the chiming of innumerable bells. It was a beautiful peaceful spot where abode an atmosphere of calm and happy security and the dewy garden was filled with a sweet green gloom as we loitered along the celebrated Terrace Walk, looking on one hand from the ancient City walls upon Merton Meadows and the Cathedral spire rising from the grey clustered buildings of Christ Church and the noble elms of the Broad Walk which hid from us the barges and the gay river, and delighting on the other side in the picturesque grey sharp gables of Merton College half veiled by the lime avenue rising from the green soft lawns and reposing in the silence and beauty and retirement of the shady happy garden. We suddenly became aware that the peace of this paradise was being disturbed by the voices and laughter and trampling of a company of people and immediately there came into sight a master and a bachelor of arts in caps and gowns carrying a ladder on their shoulders assisted by several men, and attended by a number of parish boys. Every member of the company bore in his hand a long white peeled willow wand with which they were noisily beating and thrashing the old City walls and the Terrace Walk. 'They are beating the bounds', exclaimed Mayhew. The master of arts was Knox, the Vicar of the Merton living and parish of St John the Baptist, the bachelor of arts was one of the Fellows of Merton and the men in attendance were Churchwardens, clerks, sidesmen and parish authorities. The ladder was let down over the city walls at two places where the walls were crossed by the parish bounds and at certain important points which it was desired that the boys should keep in mind they were made to scramble for sweetmeats We determined to follow the procession and see the end. We came down into Deadman's Walk and then passed up a flight of steps and through an iron gate into Corpus Gardens. Here we were stopped by a gate of which the key could not be found for some time. In this quarter the parish boundary ran through an outhouse where used to be an ancient wheel for raising water. In this outhouse a cross was scratched upon a particular stone to mark where the boundary passed through the wall. By this time the missing key had been found and we found ourselves in the private garden of the President of Corpus, Matthias Wilson. It seemed to be an ancient custom here that those who beat the bounds should be regaled with bread, cheese and ale from the private buttery of the President of Corpus. Accordingly we gathered under an old archway while the customary dole was handed out to us over the buttery hatch. Here Knox took occasion to remark in his merry laughing mischievous way with a sidelong look at Mayhew and myself that all those who beat the bounds were expected to contribute towards the expenses of the Church. The proposed offertory however produced nothing and when we had finished our bread, cheese and ale we passed on through a pretty conservatory where the President came out of his library to speak to Knox and Mayhew. The bounds now led us through an outer court where the parish boys were liberally splashed with cold water by undergraduates from the windows of the upper rooms. Eventually we emerged close by Canterbury Gate and went into Oriel. Here there was a grand uproar in the quadrangle, the men threw out to the boys old hats (which were immediately used as footballs), biscuits were also thrown out and hot coppers, and the quadrangle echoed with shouting and laughter and the whole place was filled with uproar, scramble, and general licence and confusion. Knox could scarcely get his boys under control again, but at length we went up the hall steps, down through the cloisters into the kitchen precincts where there was a Hogarthian scene and a laughable scrimmage with the young flat-white-capped cooks that might have furnished a picture for the Idle Apprentice. The procession passed next up Oriel Lane and here we left them.

This afternoon Mayhew and I attended the evensong of the Ascension at New College Chapel. Before the service began, finding the cloister gate open, we strolled round the grey peaceful green cloisters where high overhead the two great bells were chiming sweetly and deeply for evensong in the tall old turreted grey tower. There is something about the cloisters of New College which is more grey and hoary and venerable than anything about the cloisters of Magdalen. They have an air of higher antiquity and a more severely monastic look. Indeed one half expects still to meet grey monkish figures still pacing round the stone-flagged cloisters or crossing the square open greensward in the centre and looking up and listening to the bells chiming overhead in the great grey Tower.

The Chapel was filled with people. There were 'High Prayers', a magnificent tempest of an Anthem, and a superb voluntary after the service during which people stood about in picturesque groups in the light streaming from the great West window or sat listening in the Antechapel stalls.

We went to hear Father Stanton preach at St Barnabas. The service was at 8 o'clock and the evening light was setting behind the lofty Campanile as we entered. The large Church was almost full, the great congregation singing like one man. The clergy and choir entered with a procession, incense bearers and a great gilt cross, the thurifers and acolytes being in short white surplices over scarlet cassocks and the last priest in the procession wearing a biretta and a chasuble stiff with gold. The Magnificat seemed to be the central point in the service and at the words 'For behold from henceforth all generations shall call me blessed' the black biretta and golden chasuble (named Shuttleworth) advanced, was 'censed' by the thurifer, then took the censor from him and censed the cross, the banners, the lights and the altar, till the Church was all in a fume. At least so Mayhew said. I myself could not see exactly what was done though I knew some ceremony was going on. It appeared to me to be pure Mariolatry. Father Stanton took for his text 'He is altogether lovely', Canticles ii. The matter was not original or interesting, and the manner was theatrical and overdone. I should think every eye in that great congregation was quite dry. The text was repeated constantly in a very low die-away tone. The sermon came after the Third Collect. I was disappointed in it and so I think were many more. After the service there was an offertory and a processional hymn, and then round came the procession down the South aisle and up the nave in the following order. First the thurifer in short white surplice and scarlet cassock swinging a chained censer high in the air and bringing it back with a sudden check and violent jerk which brought the incense out in stifling cloud. Next an acolyte in a similar dress bearing aloft a great gilt cross. Then three banners waving and moving above the heads of the people in a weird strange ghostly march, as the banner-bearers steered them clear of the gaslights. After them came two wand-bearers preceding the clergy, Father Stanton walking in the midst and looking exhausted, the rear of the procession being brought up by the hideous figure of the emaciated ghost in the black biretta and golden chasuble.

As we came out of Church Mayhew said to me, 'Well, did you ever see such a function as that?' No, I never did and I don't care if I never do again. This was the grand function of the Ascension at St Barnabas, Oxford. The poor humble Roman Church hard by is quite plain, simple and Low Church in its ritual compared with St Barnabas in its festal dress on high days and holidays.

Friday, 26 May

This evening my host and hostess gave a pleasant dinner party. The guests were Mr and Mrs Spurling, Mr and Mrs Wallace and Mrs Wallace's sister, the Wallaces being all kindly Scots. Mrs Mayhew's music in the evening was a great treat. She plays exquisitely.

Before dinner the children took me upstairs to see their nursery and playroom and rocking horse upon which Ethel rode fearlessly. While I was in the day nursery dear lovely little Janet was brought up wrapped in a dressing gown sweet and fresh from her evening bath and was put to bed. Then the girls would have me go into the next room to see Janet in bed. So we went in and found her pretty and rosy with tumbled curly hair lying in her little soft white nest contentedly sucking chocolates. I sat down upon her bed and the rest gathered and so Queen Janet held her court as pleased as possible. But she was not satisfied to remain in bed and soon had her round plump limbs out from under the sheets with the innocent simplicity of childhood and her pretty little white feet in my lap, as she sat bolstered up by the pillows smiling, rosy and curly, and still contentedly sucking her chocolate. Dear Ruthie stood by her little sister kind, sweet and motherly. They share their little bed together, 'two dumplings' as Ruthie said. The children brought and showed me their little treasures, but Janet was still the centre of the Court group and reigned from her bed as from a throne. Then the father dressed for dinner came in to see his children and wish them 'Good night'. It was a lovely family group, a beautiful picture.

Monday, 29 May

Oak-apple day and the children all came to school with breast-knots of oak leaves.

Trinity Sunday, 11 June

This morning came a letter from the Bishop of St David's offering me the Vicarage of St Harmon's. I wrote and accepted it. Then it has come at last and I must leave my dear old home and parish and say goodbye to Langley and all my dear kind friends there. It will be a hard bitter wrench and a sorrowful, a very sorrowful parting. It seems dreadful to leave my Father alone at his age and with his infirmities to contend with the worries and anxieties of the parish and at the tender mercies of a curate. I hope I have not acted selfishly in leaving him. But at my age I feel that I cannot throw away a chance in life and our tenure of this living is a very precarious one. It is 'the warm nest on the rotten bough'. I have not sought this or any other preferment. Indeed I have rather shrunk from it. And as it has so come to me without my wish or seeking of my own it seems as if the Finger of God were in it and as if I were but following the calling of His Voice and the beckoning, guiding and leading of His Hand.

Monday, 19 June

Walked into Chippenham early, caught the Vicar in Church just after morning prayers, and got him and the Rector of Kelloways (Clarke) to sign my Letters Testimonial which I then forwarded to Gloucester by the early post for the countersignature of our own Bishop.

This afternoon I went down out of the heat and glare of the summer day into the cool green shades of the Happy Valley. Thence I went on up the opposite slope of the green hill through the beautiful meadows to Langley Fitzurse. As I mounted the slope there were lovely glimpses of the far blue hills and chalk downs seen through the tops of the luxuriant elms of the Happy Valley, which lay beneath me, a sea of rich bright green foliage. To me this was all enchanted ground for Ettie's dear sake. I came into a long narrow meadow sloping down from Langley Ridge at its head to the Happy Valley at its foot. In this meadow about half way down the slope, grew three beautiful elms all a-row and lower still a solitary tree the midst of the meadow. In a sweet day-dream I seemed to see the white frocks of three girls sitting on the grass and nestling under the shadow of the elms in the sultry midsummer afternoon. I knew them and amongst them shone like stars the one pair of dark eyes that once were all the world to me, and again I saw that rare sweet smile provoked by love's caresses and the glimmer of those white and pearly teeth as the sweet rosebud lips pouted and parted for an instant like a swift and sudden sunburst, quickly passing, for those rosy sister lips were so fond of kissing each other that they could not be kept asunder long.

At the top of the long green meadow near the double-roofed grey house with red chimney stacks which stands upon Langley Ridge between the dark cypresses and green poplar spires, there grew two large holly bushes and amongst the dark green glossy leaves of one holly thicket had twined a slender graceful trailing spray of wild briar rose spreading its arms abroad, over-arching, and swing to and fro in the soft summer air and bright sunshine. The spray was starred with blossoms, not the pale pink or white flowers, but roses of a deep rich red fit to twine round Ettie's lovely brow or wreathe in her dark clustering curls. But, alas, it would have been a crown of thorns.

[Kilvert visits London.]

Saturday, 24 June

Midsummer Day, and the cuckoo singing from Gipsy Hill. Walked to sweet green Dulwich and visited the picture gallery. Rembrandt's immortal servant girl still leaned on her round white arms a-smiling from the window as she leaned and smiled for three hundred years since that summer's day when her master drew her portrait and made her immortal, imperishable and ever young. St Sebastian still raised his eyes to heaven with the sublime pathetic look of tender submission and gentle resignation. The strange solitary white angel still hovered down through the gloom in Jacob's Dream. The Oriental-looking Spanish flower girl still offered her flowers for sale. The Spanish boys still laughed audibly and went on with their game, and Albert Cuyp's cows grouped on a knoll at sunset stood or lay about in the evening glow chewing the cud and looking placidly over the wide level pastures of Holland.

In the afternoon I went with Katie, Mary and Charlotte to the Crystal Palace and saw over the heads of the people Myers' Grand Hippodrome girls riding and jumping through hoops, performing horses, elephants, etc.

1877

Monday, 31 December

A fine mild spring morning, bright sunshine, the river full, swift and brown, but falling, the cedars and the bright green lawn terraces very lovely in the morning sunshine. As I crossed Bredwardine Bridge I went in to see the Jenkinses who have kept the bridge toll gate for 2 months. They seem nice old people. The old woman was full of strange stories of the countryside. She had felt beforehand and predicted the coming of the great rainstorm and waterspout which fell on the Epynt Hills in the summer of 1854 in July, and swept away the Lawrences' house on the Dihonn brook near Builth. She had lived for years at the Holly Bush on the northern slope of the Black Mountain and her husband had kept school in the Baptist Chapel at Capel y Ffin. 'There are strange things about the Black Mountain,' she said, 'but I have travelled the hills at all hours, night and day, and never saw anything bad. One time I had been working late at the Parc on the southern side of the Mountain down in the dingle and I was coming home pretty late in the dark. It was about February or March. As I came over the Bwlch y fingel I was singing to keep my courage up, and I was singing a hymn out of an old book for I thought I wouldn't sing anything but what was good then. It was a fine starlight night and just as I got down into the plain I heard beautiful singing overhead, like the singing of birds. They seemed to be some great birds travelling. I could not see them but they sang and whistled most beautiful, and they were just overhead. They seemed to be going away down the mountain towards Caedwgan. And I said to myself, "God bless me from here, there will be a funeral from that house", and sure enough within a month a dead person was carried out from Caedwgan.'

I sat up till after midnight to watch the Old Year out and the New Year in. The bells rang at intervals all the evening, tolled just before the turn of the night and the year and then rang a joy peal, and rang on till one o'clock. After I had gone to bed I saw from where I lay a bright blaze sprung up in the fields beyond the river and I knew at once that they were keeping up the old custom of Burning the Bush on New Year's Day in the morning. From the Knap, the hill above the village masked by the two clumps of trees, the whole valley can be seen early on New Year's Morning alight with fires. Burning the Bush, as it can be seen also from the hill at Bettws, Clyro, on which the old Chapel stands.

1878

New Year's Day

In the lane between Great and Little Fine Street I met James
Davies, my churchwarden. He took off his hat with a profound
and courteous bow and 'the compliments of the season' and turning conducted me to his house where I saw his wife and daughter
Jane and grandniece. They were all most kind and courteous. 'I
should not like to insult you, Sir, this morning,' said the handsome grey-haired grey-eyed churchwarden, 'but will you drink a
glass of my home-made cider?' So I did and drank the healths all
round, while he signed the paper declaring that I had read the 39
Articles and the Declaration of Assent thereunto.

Wednesday, 2 January

A thick dark mild morning with a Scotch mist. Showed my
father round the garden and over the Church. He was much
pleased with everything. The house and garden were much larger
and more beautiful than he had supposed. Both he and my mother
are delighted with the place. My father especially admired the
old Norman 12th or 13th century work in the Church and more
particularly the South doorway arch and the carving over the
Devil's Door (the North door).

Friday, 4 January

In the *Standard* yesterday there was a leading article on the election of John Henry Newman to an honorary fellowship at Trinity
College, Oxford, which interested my dear Father much. He
remembers Newman well at Oriel. He told me that some years
after he had left Oxford, Uncle Francis, who had letters of introduction to Newman, called upon him when he was Vicar of St
Mary's. He spoke to Newman about my Father. 'I remember him
well,' said Newman, 'he left a fragrant memory behind him in
Oriel.'

Saturday, 5 January

Speaking of the blowing of the Holy Thorn and the kneeling and weeping of the oxen on old Christmas Eve (to-night) Priscilla said, 'I have known old James Meredith 40 years and I have never known him far from the truth, and I said to him one day, "James, tell me the truth, did you ever see the oxen kneel on old Christmas Eve at the Weston?" And he said, "No, I never saw them kneel at the Weston but when I was at Hinton at Staunton-on-Wye I saw them. I was watching them on old Christmas Eve and at 12 o'clock the oxen that were standing knelt down upon their knees and those that were lying down rose up on their knees and there they stayed kneeling and moaning, the tears running down their faces." '

Monday, 7 January

I went to the little farmhouse of Dolfach on the hill to see the Holy Thorn there in blossom. The tree (a graft from the old Holy Thorn at Tibberton now cut down) bloomed on old Christmas Eve and there were 15 people watching round the tree to see it blow at midnight. I found old John Perry sitting at tea by the cheerful firelight in the chimney corner. His kind daughter gave me a bit of a spray of the Holy Thorn which was gathered from the tree at midnight, old Christmas Eve. She set great store by the spray and always gathered and kept a bit each year. The blossoms were not fully out and the leaves were scarcely unfolded but the daughter of the house assured me that the little white bud clusters would soon come out into full blow if put in soft water.

Saturday, 19 January

I am glad to hear that Ettie Meredith Brown is to be married in April to Mr Wright, the brother of her brother-in-law.

Tuesday, 29 January

Mary Matthews had just come from Dowlais. She said the distress there was terrible and pitiful, the people perishing of hunger and the distress in Merthyr worse than at Dowlais.

Tuesday, 5 February

To-day was the Tithe audit and tithe dinner to the farmers, both held at the Vicarage. About 50 tithe payers came, most of them very small holders, some paying as little as 9d. As soon as they had paid their tithe to Mr Heywood in the front hall they retired into the back hall and regaled themselves with bread, cheese and beer, some of them eating and drinking the value of the tithe they had paid. The tithe-paying began about 3 p.m. and the stream went on till six. At 7 I sat down to dinner with the farmers.

The Pen Pistyll turkey boiled looked very noble when it came to table. At the foot of the table there was roast beef, and at the sides jugged hare and beefsteak pie, preceded by pea soup, and in due course followed by plum pudding, apple tart, mince pies and blancmange, cheese and dessert. It was a very nice dinner, thanks to Dora, and I think they all liked it and enjoyed themselves.

Thursday, 14 February

To-day I went for the first time into the kitchen garden on the Brobury side of the river. There were some old Espalier pears and apples and some young peach, nectarine and apricot trees against the walls, and one fine fig tree. The garden frames were in a very ruinous state.

Friday, 15 February

A day indoors nursing a bad cold and troublesome cough. Read *The Marquis of Lossie*, the sequel of *Malcolm*, by George Macdonald, but inferior to it, I think.

Arthur went to Staunton in the evening to fetch a bottle of cough mixture for me from Mr Giles. It was a beautiful moonlit night and from my bedroom window I could see the moonbeams shining in the basin of the fountain on the lawn and broken shattering as the water was stirred into little waves by the night breeze. The white house was bathed in a flood of brilliant moonlight, a strange weird contrast to the black solemn cedars.

Saturday, 16 February

Another day indoors nursing against Sunday. A lovely spring day, bright and warm and joyous with birdsinging. The crocuses are beginning to appear in the garden and in the churchyard some of the graves are white and beautiful with snowdrops. Emily walked to Staunton to get another bottle of medicine for me from Mr Giles. It was a beautiful warm moonlit evening. Looking from my bedroom window I saw the moon shining in the river which was streaming as with flakes of fire under the black cedars.

Tuesday, 26 February

At 10 a.m. went on the box of Miss Newton's brougham to the reopening of Mansel Grange Church after a good restoration. More than 25 clergy in surplices. The Bishop preached in the morning, the Archdeacon, Lord Saye and Sele, in the afternoon. It was difficult to say which was the worse sermon. The former was a screed, the latter a rigmarole, but the rigmarole was more appropriate and more to the purpose than the screed. A nice luncheon at the Stanhopes' at Byford Rectory. I was with a small party at a table in the study at which Miss Stanhope presided. The large party was in the dining room. Good congregations and the offertories amounted to nearly £50 and cleared off the debt on the Church. The weather dry and the roads good, a satisfactory day. Many people laugh at the old Baron's sermons, but the cottagers like them for he is plain and homely and speaks of names and places that they know. When Moccas Church was restored and reopened Lord Saye and Sele preached in the afternoon and told the people that Moccas was so called from 'the badgers which came down to the river to eat the fish.' It is supposed he meant otters, and that he had in some strange confused way mixed up together otters, badgers and pigs, for Moccas is so called from the swine (Welsh *Moch*) which used to feed on the acorns in the great oak forest.

Saturday, 2 March

A bright lovely Spring day.

I went down the green lane between the orchards and through a gate which brought me under the gable of a small farmhouse picturesquely placed among orchards and crofts on the green hillside sheltered from the west winds, and looking towards the rising sun. A few steps brought me round to the front of the house. In the door stood a tall fair comely girl with a clear fresh open face, kind grey eyes, and golden brown hair, Annie Abberley.

She welcomed me in kindly and set a chair by the fire. She was expecting her father in to his dinner, she said. Annie said she had been house and parlourmaid at Pont Vaen when I was at Clyro. And now she keeps her father's at the Upper Cwm. 'It is a wonderful place for birds,' she said, 'the cuckoo sings here all night long. And only the other night I heard a blackbird keep on waking up and whistling through the night. Sometimes when I have [been] up and out early, starting father for Hereford at daylight, I have stood out in the orchards listening to the singing of the birds. On a clear day we can see the steeple of All Saints' Church in Hereford, there I can see it now through that apple bough against the far blue hill.' We were standing out in the fold. 'It is a very quiet place here', Annie went on, 'and we don't see many people passing, but it is very peaceful and a pleasant prospect, and I like to be amongst the fields and orchards and to hear the singing of the birds and we are content.' 'How wise,' I thought, and said, 'to be content and happy with the beauties and the blessings that lie around.' The father who had been looking after his lambs now came in to his dinner, a swarthy peculiar-looking man in a smock frock. As we stood at the door talking a voice floated up from the Lower Cwm through the evening air singing the Canadian Boat Song.

Quinquagesima Sunday, 3 March
As I walked in the Churchyard this morning the fresh sweet sunny air was full of the singing of the birds and the brightness and gladness of the Spring. Some of the graves were as white as snow with snowdrops. The southern side of the Churchyard was crowded with a multitude of tombstones. They stood thick together, some taller, some shorter, some looking over the shoulders of others, and as they stood up all looking one way and facing the morning sun they looked like a crowd of men, and it seemed as if the morning of the Resurrection had come and the sleepers had arisen from their graves and were standing upon their feet silent and solemn, all looking toward the East to meet the Rising of the Sun. The whole air was melodious with the distant indefinite sound of sweet bells that seemed to be ringing from every quarter by turns, now from the hill, now from

the valley, now from the deer forest, now from the river. The chimes rose and fell, swelled and grew faint again.

[Kilvert leaves for Langley Burrell.]

Tuesday, 5 March

Spencer came to see me and said I had congestion of the lungs. Indoors all day nursing myself. This evening I was worse than I have been at all and could hardly draw breath from the tightness of the chest.

Friday, 8 March

Letters from Bredwardine. My Father seems to have managed very well at Brobury Church on Ash Wednesday evening. Dora says she walked with him to Crafta Webb and they visited John William (Jack my Lord). When the old man saw my Father he turned up his eyes and ejaculated devoutly, 'My blessed God, is it his father?'

To-day we got back into the dining room to our great comfort. The room has been recarpeted with a square new handsome bordered Brussels. The old oilcloth has been taken up and the boards round the carpet stained and varnished.

Saturday, 9 March

I went out for a little while on the terrace this morning and walked up and down on the sunny side of the house. After how many illnesses such as this have I taken my first convalescent walk on the sunny terrace and always at this time of year when the honeysuckle leaves were shooting green and the apricot blossoms were dawning and the daffodils in blow. But some day will come the last illness from which there will be no convalescence and after which there will be no going out to enjoy the sweet sights and sounds of the earthly spring, the singing of the birds, the opening of the fruit blossoms, the budding dawn of green leaves, and the blowing of the March daffodils. May I then be prepared to enter into the everlasting Spring and to walk among the birds and flowers of Paradise.

First Sunday in Lent, 10 March

I went to Church in a fly with Mary who rode in great state and pride. The morning sun was shining fair and bright as we walked up the path to the Church. There was a sweet stillness and Sunday peace upon everything. Multitudes of daffodils grew about the Church, shining in the bright spring sunlight. I never saw daffodils in such numbers or so beautiful. They grew in forests, multitudes and multitudes, about the park and under the great elms, most of them in full blossom. As we went in we saw fresh groups of daffodils under the trees, golden gleam after golden gleam in the sweet sunshine. It was quite dazzling.

Monday, 11 March
To-day I wrote to Mr C. T. Longman, to whom I had received an introduction from Mrs Middleton Evans of Llwynbarried, to ask him if and on what terms he would publish a small book of poems for me.

Friday, 15 March
This morning came a letter from Mr Longman, very courteous but not encouraging the idea of my publishing a book of poems.

[Kilvert returns to Bredwardine.]

Tuesday, 26 March
Called at the Bridge Gate house on the Merediths, Mrs Meredith told me she had seen better days. She once kept the Monmouth Gap Hotel and a coaching establishment of 18 horses, 16 of which died of influenza at one time. Then her husband died and she moved with her 5 children to the shop opposite the hotel, and brought them up. Her second husband was a small timber merchant who was ruined by the failure of a man in the same business. Now they have come down to keep a turnpike gate.

This evening while we were at prayers and singing the hymn 'My God, my Father while I stray' Dora suddenly fell on the floor in a fainting fit. I thought she had only overbalanced herself, slipped and fallen against Florence who was looking over her hymn book, but Louisa rushed forward crying, 'She's fainting, Sir!' and helped me to raise her and lay her back in an easy chair while Arthur stood aghast. I called to Emily to run for cold water. Dora soon came round again and drank a glass of sherry. She said she had never quite lost consciousness. She had been singing a good deal and her dress was tight and the east wind made her feel ill and she caught her breath and could not get it again.

Saturday, 30 March
Indoors all day with a bad headache and fresh cold and greater tightness of chest. Charles and Tom Palmer walked over from Eardisley to see me. The day was bitterly cold with a cruel E. wind and whilst they were here a wild snowstorm came on.

Tuesday, April Morrow
I had long wished to pay a visit to Maurice Richards the woodman's cottage in the wood and as to-day was fine and drying I determined to go. After dinner I climbed up by the Clerk's house to Mary Jackson's and found her alone and ill with a bad cold and very poor and destitute and lonely. I filled up her application for relief to the next Jarvis Charity meeting, and she told me of the death of her young daughter by consumption and her husband's agonizing but happy death from internal cancer, the result of an old wound, a log of timber having fallen upon his back in the sawpit where he was under-sawyer when a young man.

Mary Jackson showed me my way over the wattled stiles and along the bankside, through the wood to the woodman's cottage. It was a beautiful afternoon, the larches in the sheltered hollows were thickening green and waving their first tender green feathers and the woods were full of the singing of birds. As I went through the wood I heard a sudden sharp rustling and struggling amongst the dry leaves and sticks and then some animal began to scream violently. A little chestnut-coloured creature was darting and struggling about upon the ground with such furious vehemence and extraordinary rapidity that I could not for some time make out what it was. The animal had evidently been caught in a trap by the hind leg. At first I thought from its bushy tail that it was a squirrel. Finding that it could not free its leg from the teeth of the powerful gin the little creature after darting about and struggling with the most inconceivable swiftness and furious violence, turned like a wild beast at bay and faced me like a lion with its eyes flaming with fury and its lips drawn savagely so as to bare its teeth. It was a beautiful and graceful little creature

with a bushy tail, a body arched like a greyhound, glossy chestnut
fur on the back and sides and underneath a pale delicate yellow.
I think it was a stoat. I could not help but admire the courage
of the little creature and the steadiness and fierceness with which
he gazed at me. Then he turned with pathetic curiosity and con-
cern to look at the trap and his imprisoned and wounded leg, and
fearing that the leg might be broken or that he might be left
there to die of hunger, with one blow on the back of the head I
put him out of his fear and pain.

I went on to Maurice Richards' cottage seated in a pleasant nook
in the wooded hillside looking towards the rising sun and 'towards
Lady Lift' as Mrs Richards said. Her kindly pleasant comely face
carried me back to Clyro and reminded me strongly of Mrs
Vaughan the shoemaker's wife and widow. The garden was in the
most exquisitely neat order and the house beautifully clean. I
took a great fancy to the place and the people.

Thursday, 4 April
Lady Cornewall called and kindly brought me another bottle of
the Syrup of Hypophosphate of lime.

Easter Day, 21 April
I took the 3 full services. There were 20 guests at the H.C., the
largest number I have yet seen in Bredwardine. Alms 18/9¼. Good
congregations at all 3 services. I was very thankful to be able to do
it all myself without troubling anyone. My voice was stronger and
clearer to-day than it has been at all since my illness.

Friday, 26 April
To St Harmon's by 9.10 train to marry David Powell and
Maggie Jones of Tylare. Mrs Jones of the Gates had made a triumphal arch of moss over the Churchyard gate and flowers were
strewn in the bride's path. Maggie was surprised and delighted
to see and be married by her old friend. Fog signals were laid on
the line and the wedding party issued from Church just as the
noon train came down with the banging of crackers and guns and
a great crowd at the station crossing gates. The wedding party
and guests went to the Sun where I joined them for a minute to
drink a glass of wine to the health of the bride and bridegroom

and then walked on to Cwm yr ychen. 'Is the bride in the family way?' asked her grandmother, old Mary Jones, with eager interest. 'I hope not,' I said.

' 'Tis a pity but what you had stayed here,' sighed the clerk deeply as I carved for him at dinner.

Saturday, 27 April
Neuralgia very troublesome all the week, no sleep at nights.

Friday, 3 May
After breakfast I went to Lyncam and engaged Morgan's house-keeper, Mrs Price, as our housekeeper at Bredwardine Vicarage. She is to have £14 a year to begin and to come to us Monday, May 13. Old May Day. She has been having £12 a year from Morgan, who gives her an excellent character.

Saturday, 4 May
Left Llysdinam by 12.30 train and returned to Bredwardine.

4th Sunday after Easter, 19 May
Yesterday a new wire bird door (the gift of Miss Newton) was hung at the main door. We have been much troubled by the birds in the Church lately, and have been obliged to close the painted East window to keep out the swallows who were darting in and out with mud and building a nest against the wall just over the altar. I was sorry to interfere with them, but it was necessary for they were scattering mud all over the place.

Tuesday, 21 May
Finer. Sir George Cornewall sent me £13.10 towards the repair of Bredwardine Church Tower, very handsome.

Monday, 27 May
Showery. Sent Shoolbred and Co. a cheque for £50 on account of a bill of £230.9.6 for furniture.

Monday, 3 June
A calm bright dewy heavenly morning, very peaceful soft and warm, with the sun veiled tenderly. I went out early and walked in the lower garden amongst the dewy roses by the river, James Meredith came down from Prospect between 7 and 8 with a nose-gay of sweet white stocks for the wedding. The people are very

kind, thoughtful and take much interest in the affair. At 10.45 we set off for Kinnersley Station. We had a comfortable journey and saw my Father, Mother and Fanny at Paddington. My Father and Mother went to St Barnabas Vicarage, Kensington, to stay with the Hesseys; Thersie and Dora to stay with Eunice at Dilston House, Upper Norwood; Fanny, Teddy and I to Norris' Hotel, Kensington.

Tuesday, 4 June
To-day Teddy was married to Nellie Pitcairn at St Barnabas Church, Kensington. Teddy and I (his groomsman) left Norris' Hotel at 9.30 and drove to 13 Colville Terrace where the brothers Pitcairn have rooms and where the breakfast was given. He dressed there and we drove down to St Barnabas Vicarage. Wedding at 11.15. My Father performed the ceremony, assisted by Dr F. Hessey. The fees were enormous, £3.3. After the wedding we drove to 13 Colville Terrace where there was a merry breakfast. At 2 the bride and bridegroom left for Ryde or Shanklin. A pretty happy wedding and for the first time for many years we were all together as a family again.

Thursday, 20 June
In the morning I weeded the raspberry bed in the lower garden. Afternoon walked to a garden party at Eardisley Vicarage. A very pleasant evening. Palmer took me aside as soon as I came in and offered me from Canon Walsham How the permanent Chaplaincy at Cannes. He thought it might perhaps be desirable to accept it on account of my health.

Friday, 21 June
The longest day. Wrote to my Father, Mr Venables, Spencer and Canon Walsham How about the Cannes Chaplaincy. The weather very sultry. The Royal Artillery were firing on the Black Mountain. I took it for thunder.

Saturday, 22 June
A fine summer's day. Very hot. Walked to Monnington to luncheon. On the way called on Miss Cornewall who has lately come back from Cannes to ask her information about the place.

She was very kind and told me much. She said she thought the Chaplaincy must be a very delightful position. Mr Giles came in to see one of the servants. I asked if I ought to go to Cannes on account of my health. He said, 'Go by all means. It is the very place. It may prolong your life for some years.'

Monday, 24 June, Midsummer Day
Weather fine and hot. Corresponding and thinking with some perplexity about the offer of the Cannes Chaplaincy.

Thursday, 27 June
Wrote to Palmer and Walsham How to decline the Cannes

Friday, 12 July
I called on Mrs Godsall to see her daughter (the wife of Lord Lyons' coachman or stud groom) and the 4 grandchildren, 2 girls and 2 boys, lately come from Paris on a visit to their grandparents. The coachman's wife told me that her husband drove Lord Lyons into Paris from Versailles on the last day of the Commune troubles. The firing was still going on in the streets and he could hardly drive the carriage for the dead bodies.

Chaplaincy, and wrote to my Father, the Venables, Miss Higginson and Miss Cornewall, announcing my decision.

Monday, 15 July
At 5.15 my Father and Mother arrived from Langley, driven by Barnes of Moorhampton in a waggonette drawn by a stout grey cob, a lovely evening and fine day for travelling, cloudy and cool in the morning. Reading *Ruth*[1] outside the library window, and watching for the travellers to cross the bridge with my opera glass, when I heard the carriage coming I jumped up and forgot my glass which fell upon the stones and broke. George Phillott came up from Moccas in his punt and gave a better account of his father who was taken very ill on Friday last. I went down with him in the boat to Moccas, a lovely voyage with glorious evening lights and shadows on the water, indescribably beautiful. Walked back by Dipple Wood. My Mother and Dora went to the Cottage after supper to hear Basil Harwood play the organ.

---

1. Presumably the novel by Mrs Gaskell.

Thursday 18 July

Hotter and hotter. My Father and I went to Talyllyn to fish in Llangorse Lake. About noon we got into a shoal of perch and killed 5 dozen or more in 2 hours, not large ones. We pulled them out as fast as we could put the lines in.

Thursday, 5 September

Paid Miss Newton 16/8 for 25 gallons of cider at 8d. a gallon.

Friday, 6 September

A lovely autumn day opening with a slight wind and tender mist on the river, then ripening into a splendid golden mellow afternoon. Visited Priscilla Price and was much interested by her account of her reminiscences of the days when George the Fourth was King.

'When George IV was crowned I was living in London at 31 Russell Square in service with Squire Atkinson. I remember seeing the procession but could not see much for the great crowds of people and when I got home safe I would not go out again. Queen Caroline went to the Abbey too in Alderman Wood's Carriage. She was staying at Alderman Wood's house at the time. The King would not let her be crowned with him. They told her at the Abbey door that she might come in if she liked to sit in a back seat, but she would not do that and drove away again. The soldiers were ordered not to touch their hats to her but they all saluted her. That night there was a great illumination. All those who took the King's part put lights in their windows and those who took the Queen's part put none. We did not know what to do but at last we put up lights. But when Squire Atkinson came up from Brighton that night he told us to take the lights down again, saying he wasn't going to light up his house for *him*. Two great crowds were going about all night. One was for the King and the other for the Queen. The King's crowd shouted "Lights up!" and the Queen's crowd shouted "Lights down!" One crowd smashed the dark windows and the other smashed the lighted windows and people did not know what to do. I saw Queen Caroline on a balcony. She came out and made her obeisance on every hand. She was nice-looking, to my mind, with a pleasant face. I saw the King too but not so plain as the Queen. He was riding by in a close carriage. He was a passable looking man, but not so well-looking as the Queen. I thought he was dressed very old-fashioned in breeches and waistcoat and a wig. The King was not very well liked upon. Nine days after the King was crowned the Queen died (?). I was washing and stoning the steps before the front door one morning when I heard a sound that shook the town. I was frightened and ran in thinking something dreadful had happened to London, but they told me it was the tolling of the great bell at St Paul's and that one of the Royal Family must be dead because the great bell only tolled for them. Then we heard that Queen Caroline was dead. There was a great deal of talk at that time in London about the quarrel between the King and the Queen. There was about six for one and half a dozen for the other. Some believed the Queen had done wrong and some didn't. We thought the King was too hard upon the Queen and I favoured the Queen.

'It was a terrible day when Queen Caroline was buried. They would not let the funeral go by the main streets. It was to go by the back streets. But the people blocked up the back streets with carriages, carts and coaches and forced the procession to go by the great streets. There was a great mob and the funeral could not go on. Then there was a disturbance and the soldiers fired upon the people. My sister who was living in service at No. 5 Montague Street was in the crowd that day and the second woman from her was shot.

'I saw the Princess Charlotte once but I don't remember where it was or what she looked like. She was a strip of a girl. The King would not let her see her mother. But once she escaped and ran out into the street and called a hackney coach. "Drive me to Buckingham House!" she cried. "Drive me to Buckingham House!", and I believe she was driven there.

'I saw the first steamboat that ever was in the Thames pass under London Bridge. There used to be a saying that no vessel could pass under the middle arch of London Bridge for there was something in the water that would suck the vessel in. However, the steamboat started from Westminster Bridge with a number of people on board and passed through the middle arch of London Bridge and was not sucked in.'

12th Sunday after Trinity, 8 September

The anniversary of the sudden death by apoplexy of the Rev. John Houseman, late Vicar of Bredwardine and Rectory of Brobury. I alluded to this in the morning sermon and also to the Sittingbourne railway disaster and the terrible calamity of Tuesday last on the Thames near Woolwich when the *Princess Alice*, excursion steamboat, was run down by the *Bywell Castle*, screw collier, and more than 700 people drowned.

Monday, 9 September

I had a serious talk with Ellen Lewis of the turnpike gate house. She is in great distress and very anxious about herself. She was much terrified by the heavy thunderstorm of Saturday night last. She thought the end of the world might be come and feared she was not fit to meet it.

Friday, 13 September

Visited Jack my Lord at Crafta Webb. John told me how he and his family got the nickname of 'Lords' or 'My Lords'. His father when a boy worked for old Mrs Higgins at Middlewood. She was displeased with him one day because he would not do something that she told him, and said scornfully that she supposed he was as great a person as 'My Lord North'. From this simple circumstance the nickname of 'Lords' or 'My Lords' has clung to this family for 3 generations.

Sunday, 15 September

Mrs Jenkins told me that as she was dressing at her window about 5 a.m. she saw a creature which she thought at first was a calf rush madly into the little stable in the fold and then dash out again, hop over the stone wall into the brook, and away. About half an hour after 2 couple of white hounds and a couple of bloodhounds came hunting down the lane with the keepers riding after them and she learnt from the keeper (Hicks) that the animal she had taken for a calf was a buck. They had rifles with them and they had followed the deer all night over part of the Black Mountain. The hounds lost the scent in the water but struck it again and ran into the buck at Upper Castleton. The deer was taken to Mr Medlicott's farmhouse to be cut up and a cart was sent for it from Moccas. Mrs Jenkins said she went into the stable after the buck had bolted from it and saw by the hoof marks and the mud which the deer had brought in with it that the poor hunted creature in its frantic terror and attempts to escape and hide itself had climbed up into the manger and tried to scramble into the rack.

Monday, 23 September
To-day I received a kind letter from Rosie Meredith Brown saying that Ettie would sail for India on October 5 to be married there. I wrote to both of the sisters.

[Kilvert goes to Langley Burrell.]

Friday, 25 October
Went to Bath. Bought 6 pairs of kid gloves at Hampers at 1/6 a pair.

Wednesday, 30 October
Left Langley. Fine morning. Afternoon wild and stormy with sheets of rain and hail and snow lying on the Black Mountain and Radnor Hills.

Monday, 11 November
School. Flood falling. So far the second greatest flood of this century. Before breakfast I went down to the bridge to see how the Jenkins family were. Soon after I passed last night the river came down with a sudden rush and wave and filled the road full of water and they had to escape to the trap, carrying their children on their backs, wading through water knee deep, and leaving 3 feet of water in the house, the house also being surrounded by water and the water running in at front and back. Mr Stokes kindly rode down from the Old Court to see if they were safe, the water was then up to his horse's girths. Many people were flooded out of their houses at Letton and Staunton and spent the night on the Bredwardine Bridge watching the flood. A number of cattle and colts were seen to pass under the bridge in the moonlight and it was feared they would be drowned. Some women saw a bullock swept down under the bridge at noon to-day. Mr W. Clarke told me that the Whitney iron railway bridge was

carried away last night by the flood and 2 miles of line seriously damaged. No trains can run for 3 months, during which time the gap will be filled by coaches.

Monday, 25 November

Went to stay at Rhayader Vicarage with the Langhames. The country all under ice and snow. Walked up to St Harmon's. Went down to the drill hall at 7.30 to see the Rhayader volunteers drill, but the hall was deserted and the volunteers had gone out to see or take part in the Rebecca riots,[1] a large party of Rebeccaites being out spearing salmon below Rhayader Bridge. We watched the spearing from the Bridge, a most picturesque sight.

Wednesday, 27 November

I had a letter from Mr Venables proposing that I should take Sam Cowper Coles as a pupil. Wrote to Dora on the subject. I think I shall take the boy, 13 years old at £80 a year.

Advent Sunday, December Day

Hoarse as a raven.

Saturday, 7 December

Indoors all day with a bad sore throat, very hoarse, deaf, stupefied and stunned. Expecting Mr Giles. He came at evening, and prescribed tannin and glycerine to paint the interior of the throat.

2nd Sunday in Advent, 8 December

Fine and cold in the morning, overcast in the afternoon, glass falling and snow threatening. Good congregations.

In the bright sunny morning the sheep were all dotted white about the green slopes across the river. They were all lying down almost at even distances from each other. It was a peaceful pastoral scene. There is a still green beauty peculiar to a fine winter's morning and afternoon which is not seen in summer.

---

1. The Rebecca Riots were caused by a secret society of Welshmen in 1843. Their object was to abolish turnpike gates, of which they destroyed many by night. The leader of these bands was always dressed as a woman and called Rebecca. See Genesis, xxiv. 60.

Monday, 16 December

The ground very slippery and dangerous. Children sliding on the Wye below Bredwardine Bridge where the river is frozen half-across. At Moccas Bridge the Wye is frozen entirely over. Snow began to fall at 9 a.m. and continued to fall till 2 p.m.

Tuesday, 17 December

Sharp frost again last night. The snow clouds cleared off and the day became cloudless and blue and brilliant. The bridge in the sunshine was most beautiful. We have cut down several of the shrubs, evergreen oak, Portugal laurel and larustinus under the cedar nearest the house and the laurel garden hedge so as to let in more light and a pretty view of the lawn, river and bridge.

As I went up the steep snowy hill to Bethell I pursued the fast retreating and ascending wan sunshine of the still winter afternoon. I overtook the sunshine just before I got to the lone house on the bleak windy hill top. All the valley and plain lay bathed in a frosty rosy, golden glow, and just as I got to Cae Perthan the sun was setting behind the lone level snowy blue-white line of the Black Mountain and the last rays were reddening the walls and chimney stack of the solitary cottage. As I came down into the sheltered hollow of the Lower Cwm in the twilight I heard rising from the cottage in the dingle across the brook a woman's voice addressing a naughty child and uttering that threatening promise which in this form is probably as old as the English language and in some form is perhaps as old as the world. 'I'll whip your bottom!' Were bottoms so formed that they might be whipped? or why since the foundation of the world has this part of the human body been universally chosen to suffer chastisement?

Wednesday, 18 December

Alice of England was buried at Hesse Darmstadt this afternoon. Had I known it in time the Bredwardine and Brobury Church bells should have been tolled. I regret much that this mark of respect to the memory of our dear Alice should have been inadvertently and unintentionally omitted.

Friday, 20 December

Hard frost. I reached the school with great difficulty owing to the icy state of the roads especially on the hillside. Called at the Cottage. Miss Newton has given a text to Bredwardine Church for Christmas and an I.H.S. banner to Brobury. Advent service in Bredwardine Church at 7 p.m. Sir George Cornewall walked over from Moccas to preach, coming through the field and supporting himself in the slippery places with a spud walking stick. Between 30 and 40 people in Church which we thought a fair congregation considering the weather and icy roads.

Saturday, 21 December

St Thomas' Day. Hard frost. Roads icy, many accidents to man and horse from slipping and falling. Called on Mrs Williams who said her children were out 'slithering'. Climbed up the steep icy bank to Godsalls with great difficulty. There I found a son come home from Canada with his wife. He seemed weak and ill, but very pleasant and intelligent. He had been in Hamilton, knew a good deal about Francis Edwin Kilvert, now Mayor and Member for Hamilton, and was interested to know that he was my first cousin. He had recognized the name. He had often seen Sir John Macdonald. I told him that Lady Macdonald was a playfellow of mine. He gave me much interesting information about the Indian tribes and free traders and political parties in the Dominion.

Monday, 23 December

Very hard frost. The Wye froze across below Bredwardine Bridge between the Vicarage garden and the Brobury Shore. It has been frozen over and the ice passable for some time at Moccas. Visited Priscilla Price and took her a pudding and some mincepies for Christmas. Snow deep on the hill.

Tuesday, 24 December, Christmas Eve

Very hard frost. Brilliant sunshine on sparkling snow. After breakfast I went to the Old Weston to see the poor Davieses and comfort them concerning their child. On the road I met David Davies the father, the shepherd at the Weston, on his way to the village to order the coffin and to the Churchyard to mark out the ground for the grave. He told me it was not Andrew as I had been informed and supposed, but little Davie who was dead. The father seemed greatly distressed and indignant because he thought the child's life had been thrown away by some mistake of the doctor. I went on to the house of mourning. Margaret Davies seemed very glad to see me and her-humble gratitude for my visit was most touching. She took me upstairs into the room where the dead child was lying on the bed and turned down the sheet from his face. I never saw death look so beautiful. There was no bandage round the chin. The pretty innocent child face looked as peaceful and natural as if the child were asleep and the dark curls lay upon the little pillow. I could hardly believe he was dead. Leaving the face still uncovered the poor mother knelt with me by the little bedside while I prayed for them all. She was deeply touched and most humbly grateful. Before I left the room I stooped and kissed the child's forehead, and the mother did the same. It was as cold and as hard as marble. This is always a fresh surprise. I had not touched death for more than 30 years, and it brought back the sudden shock that I felt when as a child I was taken into a room at Hardenhuish Rectory where our little sister lay dead and was told to touch her hand.

Margaret Davies told me that before Little Davies died he saw a number of people and some pretty children dancing in a beautiful garden and heard some sweet music. Then someone seems to have called him for he answered. 'What do you want with me?' He also saw beautiful birds, and the men of the Weston (who carried him to his funeral). He thought his little sister Margaret was throwing ice and snow on him. (The snow fell on the coffin at the burial). On the road I overtook Miss Stokes and went into the Old Court with her but before Kate could come and speak to me my nose began to bleed and I was obliged to fly.

Wednesday, Christmas Day
Very hard frost last night. At Presteign the thermometer fell to 2 degrees, showing 30 degrees of frost. At Monnington it fell to 4. Last night is said to have been the coldest night for 100 years. The windows of the house and Church were so thick with frost rime that we could not see out. We could not look through the Church windows all day. Snow lay on the ground and the day was dark

and gloomy with a murky sky. A fair morning congregation considering the weather. By Miss Newton's special desire Dora and I went to the Cottage to eat our Christmas dinner at 1.30 immediately after service.

Immediately after dinner I had to go back to the church for the funeral of little Davie of the Old Weston who died on Monday was fixed for 2.15. The weather was dreadful, the snow driving in blinding clouds and the walking tiresome. Yet the funeral was only 20 minutes late. The Welcome Home, as it chimed softly and slowly to greet the little pilgrim coming to his rest, sounded bleared and muffled through the thick snowy air. The snow fell thickly all through the funeral service and at the service by the grave a kind woman offered her umbrella which a kind young fellow came and held over my head. The woman and man were Mrs Richards and William Jackson. I asked the poor mourners to come in and rest and warm themselves but they would not and went into Church. The poor father, David Davies the shepherd, was crying bitterly for the loss of his little lamb. Owing to the funeral it was rather late before we began the afternoon service. There were very few people in Church beside the mourners. The afternoon was very dark. I was obliged to move close to the great south window to read the Lessons and could hardly see even then. I preached from Luke ii. 7. 'There was no room for them in the inn,' and connected the little bed in the churchyard in which we had laid Davie to rest with the manger cradle at Bethlehem.

In spite of the heavy and deep snow there was a fair congregation at Brobury Church. I walked there with Powell. The water was out in Brobury lane. As we came back a thaw had set in and rain fell. By Miss Newton's special wish I went to the Cottage and spent the evening with Dora. The Cottage servants had invited the Vicarage servants to tea and supper and they came into the drawing room after supper and sang some Christmas Carols.

Sunday, 29 December
Sudden thaw and break up of the frozen river. Huge masses and floes of ice have been coming down the river all day rearing, crushing, grinding against each other, and thundering against

the bridge. A crowd of people were on the bridge looking over the parapet and watching the ice pass through the arches. The ground very slippery and dangerous, people walking along the ditches and going on all fours up Bredwardine Hill and across the Lion Square. Emma Jones' mother came all the way from Dorstone to Bredwardine in the ditches. Price was obliged to go up the hill from the Cottage to his house on all fours and Jane Davies of Fine Street confessed to Dora that she had to crawl on the ice across the Lion Square on her hands and knees.

It was very slippery and dangerous as I went to Brobury. Coming back the water was out across the lane and giving Clara Powell my lantern to hold I carried her in my arms across the water.

1879

New Year's Day

I sat up last night to watch the old year out and the new year in. The Church bells rang at intervals all last night and all to-day. At 6 I went to Crafta Webb to begin my cottage lectures there. It was raining fast when I started, but when I got as far as the Common I noticed that the ground was white. At first I thought it was moonlight. Then I saw it was snow. At Crafta Webb the snowstorm was blinding and stifling, and I passed by Preece's cottage where I was going to hold the lecture without seeing it in the thickness of the driving snow. Before the lecture I went in to see old John Williams. On opening the door I was confronted by the motionless silent figure of a person veiled and wearing a conical cap which I presently discovered to be a dead pig hanging up by its snout. John Williams deplored my being out in such a night and said it was not fit for me. There were not many people at the service but the usual faithful few. When I came back the storm was worse and so thick and driving that I was glad I was between hedges and not out on the open hill. The young people at the servants' party seemed to be enjoying themselves with dancing and singing. After supper they came into the dining room to sing to me each with a comical cap out of a cracker on her head. Then there was a snapdragon and they went away about 10.30.

Friday, 10 January

I reached home at 5 o'clock just before my first pupil Sam Cowper Coles came in Baynham's trap from Kinnersley Station. He came from 98 Queen's Gate from the Evan Thomases to-day and slept there last night and came up from the Isle of Wight (Newstead, Shanklin) yesterday.

Saturday, 11 January

Took Sam for a walk up Bredwardine Hill in the afternoon. Carried Priscilla Price a pudding, etc. Went on to the Old House and saw

Thomas Davies. Speaking of the necessity of renting land according to his capital the old farmer said, 'I couldn't cut rumps of beef out of mouse's legs'.

We called at James Meredith's. Jane took a great fancy to Sam. 'You are a beauty,' she said. 'You are the prettiest young gentleman out. Don't you think so?' 'No,' said Sam. 'I do,' said Jane.

We found the snow very deep in places and almost impassable. The sky looked black, heavy and full of snow.

Tuesday, 14 January

Last night the river rose rapidly and at midnight the ice was rushing down in vast masses, roaring, cracking and thundering against the bridge like the rolling of a hundred waggons. By morning the river had sunk and left huge piles of ice stranded on the banks.

Friday, 17 January

I think Sam is getting on with his reading and writing which were very bad. His arithmetic is his strongest point. He is very backward and ignorant.

Saturday, 18 January

Fine afternoon. Walked with Sam to Crafta Webb. Visited Jack my Lord, Betty Matthews, Samuel and Anne Williams. All the people take a great fancy to Sam and his fair pink and white face and light hair. Betty Matthews made a great piece of work over him and his fair head. 'Dear little fellow!' and Jack my Lord asked if he was a parson and if he was my brother.

Tuesday, 21 January

Very cold with bitter E. wind and hard frost. Visited Carver and Davies of the Old House. William Davies of Llanafan came in. The father and son were telling me of the games and sports, the fights and merriments, that went on in old times upon Bredwardine Knap. 'What kind of games?' I asked. 'I wouldn't suggest,' said William Davies, 'that they were of any spiritual good.'

Tuesday, 4 February

At 7 p.m. the farmers came to dine at the Vicarage. I had ten guests, Haywood, Evans, Stokes, Preece, Price, Parry, Bates, James

Griffiths, James and Tom Davies. The dinner was very nice. White soup, roast beef, boiled chickens and ham, curried rabbit, stewed woodpigeons, beef-steak pie, potatoes and stewed celery, plum pudding, custard, plum tart, mince pies, apricot jam tart.

Friday, 7 February
The birds are beginning to sing again by the river after the hard frost and the long winter.

Septuagesima, 9 February
The first snowdrops appeared in the Churchyard.

Tuesday, 11 February
Hay Castle. Dinner at 6. At 7.45 the omnibus took us all to the Volunteer concert at the Drill Hall. News came to-day of the terrible disaster inflicted by the Zulus on the 24th Regiment at Rorke's Drift, S. Africa. Col. Thomas much affected by the news and obliged to leave the concert room. He knew the officers intimately when the 24th were quartered lately at Brecon.

Wednesday, 12 February
A lovely morning and a heavenly blue day. After lunch Bishop drove me home. A pleasant sunny drive but the roads very bad from the frost. The frost had cracked the parapet of Merbach Bridge from top to bottom. Stopped at Meredith's at Traveller's Rest and ordered a 27 lb. tub of salt butter.

Thursday, 28 February, March Eve
Walking in the garden in the evening I discovered that the intense frost of last month had caused a slip and settlement of the rail on the terrace walk and caused the wall supporting the terrace to bulge dangerously. A large slice of the Vicarage river bank just below the hydraulic ram has slipped into the river, the churchyard wall has bulged, Brobury Churchyard wall has been thrown down by the frost, the walls all over the place have been strained and shaken, the plaster is peeling and shelling off the house and conservatory, and the steps from the upper to the lower garden are in ruins. This is the work of the frost of 1878–1879.

Tuesday, 4 March

A large box came from Langley from my dear Mother full of all sorts of good things, something for everyone, even arrowroot for the poor people. Sam was much pleased to be remembered with some candied fruits.

Wednesday, 12 March

When I came home from Moccas last night Dora showed me a letter she received to-day from James Pitcairn asking her to marry him. This took me entirely by surprise, but I foresee that she will do so.

INDEX

MORE ABOUT PENGUINS, PELICANS, PEREGRINES AND PUFFINS

For further information about books available from Penguins please write to Dept EP, Penguin Books Ltd, Harmondsworth, Middlesex UB7 0DA.

In the U.S.A.: For a complete list of books available from Penguins in the United States write to Dept DG, Penguin Books, 299 Murray Hill Parkway, East Rutherford, New Jersey 07073.

In Canada: For a complete list of books available from Penguins in Canada write to Penguin Books Canada Ltd, 2801 John Street, Markham, Ontario L3R 1B4.

In Australia: For a complete list of books available from Penguins in Australia write to the Marketing Department, Penguin Books Australia Ltd, P.O. Box 257, Ringwood, Victoria 3134.

In New Zealand: For a complete list of books available from Penguins in New Zealand write to the Marketing Department, Penguin Books (N.Z.) Ltd, Private Bag, Takapuna, Auckland 9.

In India: For a complete list of books available from Penguins in India write to Penguin Overseas Ltd, 706 Eros Apartments, 56 Nehru Place, New Delhi 110019.

CHANGE IN THE VILLAGE
George Bourne

'The era of change in the village is by no means over; on the contrary, it is more likely that the greatest changes have yet to come.'

No one was more qualified to chart the passing of an era in rural life than George Sturt, who took his pen-name from The Bourne, the village in Surrey which was the subject of his study. Himself the son of a wheelwright, he was descended from the village community, without being strictly of its number, and thus well equipped as a disinterested but intuitive observer. *Change in the Village* is a detailed and careful examination of the nature of village life at the turn of the century; dispassionate, objective yet curiously moving. George Bourne clearly loved his village, but it was a love more in the tradition of Cobbett than Miss Mitford – he recognized the changes that were essential for the survival of the village and identified them with a sympathetic view of the inevitable completely lacking in sentimentality.

First published in 1912, this book provides a startlingly accurate forecast of the evolution of pastoral life, and stands both as a fascinating record of the English countryside as it was, and a sound prediction of what it was to become.

Penguin Country Library

THE GOSHAWK
T. H. White

Stories of close relationships between men and beasts – *Born Free* or *Ring of Bright Water* – possess peculiar fascination. To this T. H. White added an individuality of style and independence of philosophy which make *The Goshawk* a classic of its kind. As David Garnett has written:

'*The Goshawk* is the story of a concentrated duel between Mr White and a great beautiful hawk during the training of the latter – the record of an intense clash of wills in which the pride and endurance of the wild raptor are worn down and broken by the almost insane willpower of the schoolmaster falconer. It is comic; it is tragic; it is all absorbing. It is strangely like some of the eighteenth-century stories of seduction.'

'Mr White impregnates every sentence with the fire of passion and mellows it with the tenderness of affection. I rank *The Goshawk* as a masterpiece' – Guy Ramsey in the *Daily Telegraph*